THE PSYCHOLOGY OF STRENGTH AND CONDITIONING

An effective strength and conditioning programme underpins the training regime of every successful athlete or sportsperson, and it is now widely recognised that psychology plays a significant role in the application of strength and conditioning principles. This is the first book to examine the importance of psychological factors in strength and conditioning and to offer a comprehensive overview of current research, theory and best practice.

Written by a team of leading international researchers and practitioners, this book looks at how psychology influences training and performance and how training can influence an individual's psychological well-being. It explores a range of key topics in contemporary sport psychology and athletic training, including:

- mental skills training
- behaviour change
- psychology in professional practice
- psychological problems, including exercise dependence, eating disorders and steroid use.

Throughout, this book combines evidence-based research with discussion of the practical issues facing athletes, coaches and sport science professionals. By first developing our understanding of the latest psychological skills and techniques used by athletes and coaches to maximise strength and conditioning training and performance, and then the ways other psychological factors influence, and are influenced by, strength and conditioning training, this book represents invaluable reading for all advanced students, researchers, trainers and sport scientists with an interest in strength and conditioning or sport psychology.

David Tod is a Lecturer in Sport and Exercise Psychology at Aberystwyth University, UK, and has developed courses on the psychology of strength and conditioning for several other universities. He also sits on the British Association for Sport and Exercise Science Strength and Conditioning Special Interest Group Committee as the psychology expert.

David Lavallee is Professor and Head of the School of Sport at the University of Stirling, UK. He is an Associate Fellow and Chartered Psychologist of the British Psychological Society. Professor Lavallee has published over 100 scholarly publications, including four edited books and two authored books, and is an associate editor and on the editorial board for several journals in the field of Sport and Psychology.

THE PSYCHOLOGY OF STRENGTH AND CONDITIONING

Edited by David Tod and David Lavallee

Routledge
Taylor & Francis Group

LONDON AND NEW YORK

First published 2012
by Routledge
2 Park Square, Milton Park, Abingdon, Oxon OX14 4RN

Simultaneously published in the USA and Canada
by Routledge
711 Third Avenue, New York, NY 10017

Routledge is an imprint of the Taylor & Francis Group, an informa business

British Library Cataloguing in Publication Data
A catalogue record for this book is available from the British Library

Library of Congress Cataloging in Publication Data
The psychology of strength and conditioning / edited by David Tod and David Lavallee.
p. cm.
1. Physical education and training—Psychological aspects. 2. Physical
fitness—Psychological aspects. 3. Sports—Psychological aspects. 4. Muscle strength.
I. Tod, David. II. Lavallee, David, Ph. D.
GV342.22.P84 2011
613.71—dc23

ISBN 978-0-415-57408-2 (hbk)
ISBN 978-0-415-57409-9 (pbk)
ISBN 978-0-203-85518-8 (ebk)

Typeset in Bembo
by Book Now Ltd, London

CONTENTS

ILLUSTRATIONS

Figures

Table

CONTRIBUTORS

Shawn M. Arent – Rutgers University, New Jersey, USA
Susan H. Backhouse – Carnegie Research Institute, Leeds Metropolitan
    University, UK
Derwin King-Chung Chan – University of Nottingham, UK
Christian Edwards – University of Worcester, UK
Nick Galli – California State University, Northridge, USA
Devon L. Golem – Rutgers University, New Jersey, USA
Martin Hagger – Curtin University, Western Australia
Bruce D. Hale – Penn State Berks, Reading, PA, USA
Dave Keatley – University of Nottingham, UK
David Lavallee – University of Stirling, UK
Magnus Lindwall – University of Gothenburg, Sweden
Michael McGuigan – New Zealand Academy of Sport, AUT University,
    New Zealand
Sarah McLachlan – University of Nottingham, UK
Stephen D. Mellalieu – Swansea University, UK
Gyozo Molnar – University of Worcester, UK
Todd G. Morrison – University of Saskatchewan, Canada
Justine J. Reel – University of Utah, USA
David Shearer – University of Glamorgan, UK
Dave Smith – Manchester Metropolitan University, Crewe, UK
David Tod – Aberystwyth University, UK

INTRODUCTION

David Tod

ABERYSTWYTH UNIVERSITY, UK

David Lavallee

UNIVERSITY OF STIRLING, UK

Why write this book?

The idea for this book emerged when I (D.T.) attended a recent National Strength and Conditioning Association conference. In reviewing abstracts, about 30 per cent were either based in, or related to, psychology. Despite the good-natured banter from physiologist and biomechanist colleagues that psychology had no place in the sport and conditioning world, the amount of psychology-related material at the conference illustrated that psychological knowledge was given serious consideration by many strength and conditioning scientists. Also, we have been privileged to provide sport psychology services to many athletes from various strength and power-based sports. Generally, these athletes also believed psychological factors influence, and are shaped by, participation and performance in strength and conditioning-based sports and activities.

To date, however, the lion's share of the professional strength and conditioning literature seems directed towards physiology and biomechanics. Psychology, if acknowledged, is typically afforded a single chapter, and it is difficult to do the subject justice in 30 pages or less. Yet athletes and coaches tell us psychological factors are as important as other variables in the strength and conditioning realm. *The Psychology of Strength and Conditioning* attempts to bring together the latest thinking of several of the most influential scholars bridging the boundary between psychology and strength and conditioning.

Although not often recognised, many sport and exercise scientists, and others, have conducted high-quality research that has exposed the role of psychological factors in strength and conditioning. As students, and even today, we read and re-read works by Alan Klein, Lee Monaghan, Dave Collins, William Kraemer and Larry Tucker because they extend our knowledge of the area. Psychology of strength and conditioning research might be considered across three levels. For some topics (e.g. drive for muscularity), interactions between strength and conditioning and psychological variables are apparent with recognisable bodies of literature. For other topics (e.g. performance enhancement), the body of knowledge is not as readily apparent, but when shifting through the research, the existing literature begins to emerge. Some topics (e.g. models of behaviour change) are only beginning to be examined scientifically, but play an important role in strength and conditioning. We believe the topics presented in *The Psychology of Strength and Conditioning* address all three levels.

Bringing together the diverse topics from creative scientists provides opportunities to learn about the current state of scientific study on the psychological factors in strength and conditioning. The result is a volume we hope is indispensable for people interested in the area. As a minimum, this book provides a helpful resource for practitioners, students and researchers. Potentially, the text provides an impetus for the creation of more courses and the development of fascinating, high-quality and interdisciplinary research. Also, in keeping with our belief that both psychology and strength and conditioning are applied disciplines that can make positive contributions to individuals' lives, a section in each chapter is devoted to practical application where authors were confident they could offer such suggestions.

Human psychology is the study of people, examining what we do, think and feel, and why we behave, think and feel as we do in the contexts of our lives. The authors in the current book are interested in examining why we do what we do, from different perspectives, in the strength and conditioning realm. For example, who are the people most likely to use risky performance and physique enhancing drugs, and why do they engage in such behaviours? If we understand behaviour and the mechanisms underpinning those actions, then we may be in positions to help people avoid the negative, and obtain more of the positive, consequences associated with strength and conditioning. For example, knowing what types of exercise may enhance body image helps practitioners tailor exercise regimes towards individuals' goals. In developing their chapters, we asked authors to consider: What do we know? What do we not know? What do we need to know? And, based on what we know, how can we help others? We also gave authors scope to select the topics within their expertise they believed best illustrated current thinking and research.

How is this book organised?

We organised this book so that readers can delve into one or more specific topics as desired. It is not essential to read the text from the beginning. Each chapter can be read independently and is focused on a specific area. The chapters share four characteristics. They define the scope of the topic, review current knowledge, identify future research and provide practical applications (where possible). Discussion questions are also included to promote pedagogy.

The first three chapters focus on behaviour change. Chapter 1 deals with common applied sport psychology strategies designed to help individuals develop the mental attributes contributing to optimising strength and conditioning performance. Chapter 2 focuses on models of behaviour change, identifying ways of understanding and helping people initiate and maintain involvement in strength and conditioning activities. Chapter 3 examines the latest research on psychological monitoring of strength and conditioning. These three chapters provide strength and conditioning practitioners and other professionals with guidance on how to help individuals maximise the physical gains (performance and otherwise) from their strength and condition programmes.

The motif of Chapters 4 and 5 is the current understanding regarding the positive psychological effects of strength and conditioning. Chapter 4 deals with self-perceptions and Chapter 5 examines mental health. These two chapters reveal that strength training, aerobic training and other forms of conditioning each play a role in psychological health. They also provide practitioners with guidance on how to help individuals maximise the psychological gains from their training regimes.

The next four chapters focus on the potential dark side. Chapter 6 examines exercise dependence, Chapter 7 focuses on the drive for muscularity, Chapter 8 investigates eating disorders and disordered eating and Chapter 9 discusses drug use in the strength and conditioning environment. These four chapters provide guidance on the ways people who have debilitating perceptions about their global physique, who are obsessed with exercise, who engage in unsafe nutritional practices and who consume risky and illegal substances can be assisted towards a healthy lifestyle.

Chapter 10 focuses on strength and conditioning coaches' professional development. Although a new area of research, we believe that helping practitioners understand themselves, how they change with experience, and how they influence their interactions with athletes, will assist them to provide outstanding services to clients. Existing strength and conditioning literature focuses on the technical knowledge (e.g. exercise prescription and programme design). When interacting with practitioners, we often hear that individual strength and conditioning coaches have a great influence on service delivery outcomes. Good coaches, for example, can inspire, whereas lesser skilled practitioners may dampen client enthusiasm.

It is a delight for us to present *The Psychology of Strength and Conditioning*, an empirically based and practically oriented volume. This book has been written for practitioners, upper-undergraduate and postgraduate students and researchers interested in the psychology of strength and conditioning. We hope to hear from those of you who throw yourselves in *The Psychology of Strength and Conditioning* and then wish to share your thoughts with us.

1

MENTAL SKILLS TRAINING AND STRENGTH AND CONDITIONING

Stephen D. Mellalieu

SWANSEA UNIVERSITY, UK

David Shearer

UNIVERSITY OF GLAMORGAN, UK

Introduction

The importance of the mental aspect of performance has long been acknowledged by those involved within sport. Indeed, sport psychology as a subject of study possesses a significant history with over a century of scientific inquiry (cf. Feltz & Kontos, 2002). Despite this legacy, sport psychology provision for athletes and teams in high-performance sport is often overlooked in favour of other areas of sports science support (e.g. physiological and biomechanical). This lack of provision is largely due to the perceived objectivity of the natural sciences and their tangible measurement approaches; psychological services are often viewed as lacking the ability to demonstrate treatment efficacy (cf. Smith, 1989). Additionally, there has been very little integration of applied sport psychology with other disciplines in sports science (cf. Vealey, 1994; Wylleman, Harwood, Elbe, Reints, & de Caluwé, 2009). Since the emergence and acknowledgement of strength and conditioning (S&C) as both an applied field and research area in its own right, recent years have seen literature within the discipline discussing the contribution that psychological factors make to enhancing physiological performance (e.g. Tod, Iredale, & Gill, 2003). In a field where new training techniques and theories are constantly being generated, implemented and evaluated, the search for performance gains is paramount, be they psychological, biomechanical or otherwise. Fundamental elements within this search therefore are the questions: can psychological factors contribute to enhanced S&C performance? and, if so, how can these factors be implemented or developed (trained) in sports performers?

The aim of this chapter is to review the literature that has examined the use of psychological techniques in the form of mental skills training (MST) to enhance S&C performance. Specifically, our objectives are to summarise the prominent psychological techniques that have been purported to influence S&C performance in the sport psychology literature, and then discuss the proposed mechanisms by which these potential performance gains may manifest themselves. The structure of this chapter will comprise eight sections. First, we contextualise mental skills and define their related terms. Next, the main body of the chapter considers the literature examining the four main psychological methods used in MST, namely goal setting, mental imagery, self-talk and the techniques that fall under the label of activation management. Initially each strategy is defined, and then the literature examining its effect on S&C performance is discussed. We then consider the underlying mechanisms proposed to explain the effects of these techniques on performance. The third and fourth sections of the chapter consider the implications of the current knowledge in the area for future research and practice. Finally, we close the chapter with a brief summary and conclusion on the literature discussed.

Because of the focus of this text, our review will only consider the effects of psychological techniques on S&C performance. We note there is a body of literature examining other components such as physical coordination or the cognitive and perceptual elements of performance. We also note that it would be impossible to fully describe each psychological method and discuss its respective relationship with performance within the confines of a solitary chapter. For excellent comprehensive reviews of MST and its relationship with performance, the reader is directed to edited texts with one or more chapters devoted entirely to each of the respective psychological techniques (e.g. Horn, 2008; Mellalieu & Hanton, 2009; Singer, Hausenblas, & Janelle, 2001).

Contextualising MST

One of the most considered topics within sport psychology has been the identification of the psychological factors that characterise successful and/or peak performance (Krane & Williams, 2010). A wealth of literature adopting both quantitative and qualitative methods has explored the differences between the successful and unsuccessful performances of athletes and teams (e.g. Gould, Guinan, Greenleaf, Medbery, & Peterson, 1999; Gould, Weiss, & Weinberg, 1981; Krane & Williams, 2010) and those individuals who possess superior psychological abilities such as mental toughness (Connaughton & Hanton, 2009). While there have been few investigations in relation to specific S&C performance as such (researchers have chosen to examine sports rather than individual elements of performance), a wide range of professional and Olympic sports comprising significant S&C elements have been studied. Collectively, across the various studies, regardless of the type of sport or activity, a number of common psychological characteristics have emerged including: self-regulation of activation states, high self-confidence, better concentration, being in control, positive preoccupation with one's sport (images and thoughts) and determination and commitment (Krane & Williams, 2010).

When considering the psychological factors that potentially influence S&C performance, it is salient to distinguish between psychological skills or characteristics and psychological methods or strategies (Vealey, 1988). Psychological skills or characteristics are athlete qualities that directly influence performance, such as an individual's ability to maintain high levels of motivation when faced with a long period of rehabilitation from injury, their capacity to remain confident when experiencing a poor run of form or deselection or their ability to manage the effects of anxiety and maintain focus to conduct successful skill execution during performance. Psychological methods or strategies are techniques that help athletes enhance their psychological (and other) skills and/or enhance performance. In the discipline of sport psychology, there are four basic psychological strategies that are the most established and commonly cited: goal setting, mental imagery, self-talk and relaxation (Hanton, Wadey, & Mellalieu, 2008; Hardy, Jones, & Gould, 1996). While the majority of researchers tend to acknowledge these techniques as the 'big four', we will incorporate another method, that of 'psyching-up', with the skill of relaxation, to be labelled 'activation management'. Our reason for this is twofold; first, relaxation (commonly associated with psyching-down) and psyching-up represent the opposite ends of the continuum of techniques associated with the psychological skill of activation management (i.e. managing one's level of physical and mental readiness for competition; Hardy et al., 1996). Moreover, and second, the S&C literature has historically tended to pay considerable attention to psyching-up routines because of their anecdotal association with power and strength gains via 'getting psyched' (Tod et al., 2003). For the purposes of this chapter and ease of classification, we therefore consider the four methods of goal setting, mental imagery, self-talk and activation management and their effects upon S&C performance. We do note however that activation management is strictly a psychological skill in its own right (e.g. the ability of an athlete to achieve the desired level of mental and physical activation required to perform effectively) as opposed to a specific technique or strategy.

The process by which individuals systematically and consistently undertake practice of psychological techniques to enhance and refine psychological skills with a view to performance gains is commonly referred to as psychological or MST (Weinberg & Williams, 2010). MST has experienced a tremendous surge in popularity in sport psychology research and practice over the past two decades as it provides a positive approach to performance enhancement by helping athletes develop mental skills, perform well and enjoy sport (Holliday et al., 2008). Indeed, the proactive and systematic nature of MST appeals to both coaches and athletes, and solid empirical support documents its ability to enhance athletic performance (Greenspan & Feltz, 1989; Meyers, Whelan, & Murphy, 1996; Vealey, 1994; Weinberg & Comar, 1994). The remainder of the chapter now considers each of the four psychological methods, the evidence for their impact upon S&C performance and the mechanisms purported to explain these performance effects.

Goal setting

What is goal setting?

Goal setting has been a prominent topic in the applied sport psychology literature (Gould, 2006; Hardy et al., 1996). A goal is defined as 'What an individual is trying to accomplish, it is the object or aim of an action' (Locke, Shaw, Saari, & Latham, 1981, p. 126). Specifically, goals are cognitive mechanisms that can enter or recede from consciousness at different times depending on the demands of the situation. They are purported to possess both direction and amount/quality dimensions that focus behaviour and provide a minimal standard for performance to be attained (Burton, Naylor, & Holliday, 2001, p. 498). The basis of the research into goal effects in sport derives from the seminal work of Locke and Latham (1985) examining motivational techniques for enhancing motivation and task productivity in industry and work settings (see Kingston & Wilson, 2009, for a more detailed consideration). Locke and Latham (1985) argued that the effects of goal setting in industrial and organisational psychology could be transferred to sports and physical activity contexts because of the similarities between the achievement of end outcomes and the cognitive processes required to undertake the required actions.

Goal setting research in sport has been studied through two principal avenues (cf. Burton & Naylor, 2002). The first approach considers goals as a direct technique for enhancing motivation and subsequent performance behaviour through regulation of attention and effort, and is the focus of this section. The second is to consider goals as the context for the cognitive drivers for involvement in activities. Here, achievement goal theory suggests performers who engage in achievement contexts to demonstrate competence adopt goals that reflect their cognitive beliefs (in a task- or ego-oriented manner) of what is required to maximise achievement in that specific context (cf. Harwood, Hardy, & Swain, 2000). Individuals who feel successful/competent when they experience gains in mastery (i.e. improve their own performance, regardless of others) are said to be task involved. Individuals who feel successful/competent when they outperform others (i.e. norm referenced) are said to be ego involved (Kingston & Wilson, 2009). While a consideration of the literature on goal perspectives is beyond this chapter, investigation of the impact of achievement goals upon individual goal setting practices of performers in S&C contexts is a salient point for researchers to consider in future (cf. Kingston & Wilson, 2009).

Over 500 studies have been conducted into the goal–performance relationship in industrial and sports settings (see Burton, 1992, 1993; Locke & Latham, 1990; Weinberg, 1994). The consensus of reviews of these studies suggests that goals which are specific and difficult in nature lead to greater performances compared to when individuals set vague, do your best or no goals at all. In considering this relationship, a number of moderators (cf. Kingston & Wilson, 2009) have emerged that are proposed to influence goal commitment, including: (a) Difficulty – the degree of task difficulty set; (b) Specificity – the precision of the goal set as opposed to a general or do your best target; (c) Proximity – considering goals in a temporal context as short, medium or long term in nature; (d) Focus – whether targets set are performance, process or outcome in their nature; (e) Feedback – the provision of feedback towards goal progress/achievement; and (f) Commitment – the degree to which goals are assigned, cooperative/participative or self-set. We will subsequently discuss the literature that has specifically explored these goal moderators when examining goal setting effects in S&C activities and tasks.

Does goal setting enhance S&C performance?

Recent descriptive research has provided a wealth of insight into the goal setting practices of sports performers (e.g. Burton, Pickering, Weinberg, Yukelson, & Weigand, 2010; Burton, Weinberg, Yukelson, & Weigand, 1998; Munroe-Chandler, Hall, & Weinberg, 2004; Weinberg, Burton, Yukelson, & Weigand, 2000; Weinberg, Butt, Knight, & Perritt, 2001). Across all competitive levels (adolescent, collegiate, Olympic), the findings suggest that athletes use goals and know about their potential ability to enhance performance, but possess ambiguity regarding how best to employ them to maximise their effectiveness (Burton et al., 2001). Reviews into the experimental relationship between goals and sport performance (e.g. Burton & Naylor, 2002; Burton et al., 2001; Hall & Kerr, 2001) suggest two clear findings. First, setting goals enhances sporting performance and, second, effective goal setting is a more complex process than commonly acknowledged. For example, in Burton et al.'s (2001) review of 56 publications which experimentally examined the goal setting–performance relationship, 44 observed moderate or strong effects, for a 78.6 per cent effectiveness rate (p. 409). Within these effects the majority of studies provide support for goal setting in improving the performance of physical skills across a wide range of sports and activities (Burton & Weiss, 2008; Weinberg & Butt, 2005). However, the research investigating goal setting effects on specific S&C tasks/components is less prevalent. In the following section, we discuss these effects in relation to the overall effectiveness of goal setting, and then where studies exist, in relation to the relevant goal moderators proposed to influence the goal–performance relationship.

In relation to general goal effectiveness on performance (i.e. comparisons of goals vs. no goal conditions), the studies conducted suggest that setting goals improves the acute and chronic display of muscular strength. For example, Ford et al. (2005) identified the presence of a goal was found to enhance vertical jump performance in trained soccer players. In another study, Boyce and Wayda (1994) observed that goal setting led to a greater increase in leg press strength over a 9-week intervention period among novice female weight trainers compared with a control group who were told to do their best. In relation to conditioning performance, a number of studies have demonstrated that setting goals is associated with increased performance on muscular endurance tasks (e.g. Tenenbaum, Pinchas, Elbaz, Bar-Eli, & Weinberg, 1991). For example, Tenenbaum et al. found that groups of high-school students who were set various goals performed better than the no goal group on a 3-minute sit-up over the course of the 10-week experimental period.

The research examining the specific effects of goal moderators upon S&C performance has been less extensive than general investigations of goal effectiveness. Indeed not all goal types or moderators have been researched. In relation to goal difficulty, the sport literature suggests that moderately difficult goals are more effective than difficult goals (Weinberg, 1994). Support for these findings can be found in S&C studies (e.g. Bar-Eli, Tenenbaum, Pie, Btesh, & Almog, 1997; Lerner &

Locke, 1995). For example, Lerner and Locke (1995) found both medium and hard goal group conditions outperformed the do your best group on the performance of a sit-up task. Similarly, in relation to goal specificity, a number of studies observed that setting specific as opposed to general do your best targets led to increases in S&C performance on both muscular endurance (sit-up tests; Hall & Byrne, 1988; Bar-Eli et al., 1997; Tenenbaum et al., 1991; Weinberg, Bruya, Longino, & Jackson, 1988) and strength measures (e.g. hand dynamometer; Hall, Weinberg, & Jackson, 1987). To date, Bar-Eli, Levy-Kolker, Tenenbaum, and Weinberg's (1993) study is the most comprehensive examination of goal specificity in a range of aerobic, anaerobic and strength tasks. Specifically, support was found for the principles of goal specificity in a range of tasks such as a hill run, rope-climb, 3-kilometre distance run and dynamometer handgrip.

Of the remaining S&C studies into goal moderator effects, only goal proximity has been considered. Findings suggest that the setting of both short- and long-term (as opposed to in isolation) goals leads to improved performance on muscle endurance tasks such as sit-up tests (Bar-Eli, Hartman, & Levy-Kolker, 1994; Hall & Byrne, 1988; Tenenbaum et al., 1991). In addition, it is also important to note that intervention research has found that goal setting enhances the performance of tasks which are influenced by strength and power (e.g. rugby union, Mellalieu, Hanton, & O'Brien, 2006; speed skating, Wanlin, Hrycaiko, Martin, & Mahon, 1997; and ice-hockey, C. D. Anderson, Crowell, Doman, & Howard, 1988). For example, Mellalieu et al. demonstrated improvements in selected performance behaviours (tackles made, turnovers won at the contact area) using self-generated goals with five collegiate rugby players over an entire competitive season. Other studies have demonstrated improvements using goal setting as part of a MST package. For example, Mamassis and Doganis (2004) utilised a MST package improving conditioning on physical tasks related to various elements of tennis performance.

Taken together, the literature suggests that setting goals enhances performance on S&C-based tasks. There is strong support that moderately difficult and specific (as opposed to do your best) goals lead to greater performance gains. Some support also exists for setting short-, medium- and long-term goals together rather than in isolation. None of the other proposed goal moderators have received specific attention in respect of specific S&C contexts, although intervention studies have provided support for goal setting interventions in sports associated with S&C components.

How does goal setting influence S&C performance?

Locke and Latham (Latham & Locke, 2007; Locke & Latham, 2002) have highlighted four mechanisms that underpin the goal setting process (cf. Burton et al., 2001). Specifically, goals exert their influence upon performance by: (a) directing individuals' action by focusing attention on a specific task or activity, (b) enhancing the amount of effort and intensity invested in the task or activity, (c) facilitating persistence on the task/activity despite the likelihood of failure or adversity and

(d) allowing performers to engage in processes/problem-solving behaviours that work towards developing new strategies to achieve their goals. The powerful motivational properties of goals are apparent from the first three explanations for goal setting effects upon behaviour. Indeed, it is readily apparent as to how setting goals can enhance performance in specific S&C tasks in the short term (i.e. during a specific weightlifting or anaerobic conditioning session). However, the final mechanism can account for the longer term changes in behaviour across more complex tasks and processes. For example, consider a performer who wants to maximise the benefits of setting goals during each weightlifting or anaerobic conditioning session participated in. The individual will need to organise themselves a structured programme of targets with which to achieve strength and/or anaerobic gains to work towards their desired goals for the respective phase of conditioning (e.g. tapering into a competition or tournament). Thus, promoting the development of new strategies through such indirect mechanisms allows the athlete to maximise the benefits of the direct motivational goal mechanisms and train 'smarter' as well as longer and harder (Burton et al., 2001).

While the majority of studies provide support for the effects of setting goals in enhancing performance, it is important to note that some studies have reported equivocal effects upon changes in skill execution (cf. Burton et al., 2001). A number of possible methodological reasons have been offered for these mixed effects and the lack of goal–performance effects in comparison to those observed in the work and occupational psychology area in general. Indeed, these equivocal results have been the focus of discussion and debate in the sport psychology literature (see Hall & Kerr, 2001) and include: (a) problems with individuals in control groups spontaneously setting their own goals; (b) participants in goal setting groups confounding results by setting personal goals that conflict with those set by investigators; (c) participants in sport-specific studies operating close to their performance limits, such that there may not be sufficient room for improvement to allow goal setting effects to be demonstrated; and (d) researchers failing to use adequate goal implementation strategies to allow goal setting to be effective. Indeed, Burton et al. suggest that goal setting is a process that involves more than just identifying a target, requiring the performer to develop action plans, identify barriers, obtain feedback and evaluate progress towards goal achievement.

Imagery

What is imagery?

Imagery is an accepted and commonly used technique for enhancing sport performance among athletes and coaches and has arguably received the most scientific inquiry among the big four methods discussed in this chapter (Hall, Mack, Paivio, & Hausenblas, 1998; Martin, Moritz, & Hall, 1999). Imagery is a mental process involving multisensory experiences in the absence of actual perception (Murphy, Nordin, & Cumming, 2008). Imagery differs subtly from terms such as 'visualisation' and 'mental practice' (Murphy & Martin, 2002). For example, *visualisation* refers to a specific sensory modality, in this case vision, whereas imagery comprises a variety of 'quasi sensory/perceptual experiences' (Richardson, 1969, p. 2). Moreover, where imagery is a specific mental process that can be practised, *mental practice* can encompass other forms of mental processes such as self-talk or modelling (Murphy & Martin, 2002).

Contemporary thinking regarding the relationship between imagery and sporting performance, and the subsequent design of imagery interventions, has been significantly influenced by Martin et al.'s (1999) applied model of imagery use that describes the manner in which performers use imagery to obtain cognitive, affective and behavioural outcomes. Essentially, the model proposes that the content of an athlete's image should be based on the intended outcome desired (i.e. a performer wishing to improve their confidence on a power clean lift should imagine themselves performing a power clean lift confidently). The effectiveness of the outcomes of the imagery employed are proposed to be mediated by the sport situation (training, competition, recovery, rehabilitation, etc.), the imagery ability of the performer and the types of imagery used. In Martin et al.'s model, five types of imagery are recognised (although others have been acknowledged; see Cumming & Ramsey, 2009). These imagery types are based on Paivio's (1985) analytical framework that proposes imagery serves both cognitive and motivational functions that operate at general and specific levels: (a) Cognitive specific (CS): Imagery of sport skills or rehabilitation exercises (e.g. a dead lift, penalty kick in rugby union); (b) Cognitive general (CG): Imagery of strategies, game plans and routines (e.g. imaging performing a complex conditioning test, set move or team play); (c) Motivational specific (MS): Imagery of specific goals and goal-oriented behaviour (e.g. lifting a personal best 'clean and jerk', achieving a personal best on a 3-kilometre run); (d) Motivational general arousal (MGA): Imagery of somatic and emotional experiences (e.g. stress, anxiety and excitement about an upcoming lift); and (e) Motivational general mastery (MGM): Imagery of coping and mastering challenging situations (e.g. staying focused and positive after making a poor lift, being confident in an important match or competition).

Although the applied model has been the driving force for the majority of imagery research since its proposal over a decade ago, some qualifications have recently been discussed in the literature regarding the conceptual differences between the use of the terms imagery 'content', 'type' and 'function' (cf. Murphy et al., 2008; Short, Ross-Stewart, & Monsma, 2006). Specifically, the term 'imagery type' has been used interchangeably to refer to both content (imaging oneself perfectly executing a dead lift) and function (e.g. skill learning/refinement improving one's dead lift technique) of an athlete's imagery. Moreover, the terms 'type' and 'function' have often been employed synonymously (Short et al., 2006). To overcome the confusion, Murphy et al. (2008) have recently proposed that *imagery type* be used for describing the content of an image, *imagery function* the purpose or reason for employing the image, and *imagery outcome* the result of the imagery with respect to its impact on the performer's behaviour.

Does imagery enhance S&C performance?

Descriptive studies surveying imagery use in athletes suggest that elite, higher level or more experienced performers tend to report more use of imagery when compared to their lower level or less experienced counterparts (e.g. Cumming & Hall, 2002; Hall et al., 1998; Orlick & Partington, 1988). With respect to experimental-based studies, considerable attention has explored the impact of imagery upon the learning of motor skills and subsequent performance. The consensus of the numerous reviews conducted in the literature suggests that, overall, increases in the learning and successful execution of motor skills of both a cognitive and physical nature occur when performers engage in imagery (e.g. Cumming & Ramsey, 2009; Driskell, Copper, & Moran, 1994; Feltz & Landers, 1983).

Early research examining imagery–performance relationships tended to focus on the influence of imagery upon the learning and execution of motor skills in laboratory-based contexts with untrained individuals. However, more contemporary studies have sought to consider the influence of imagery intervention training programmes on performance, albeit with novice or collegiate populations (for an exception, see Shearer, Mellalieu, Shearer, & Roderique-Davies, 2009). Indeed, guided by Martin et al.'s model of imagery use, studies have focused upon the impact of employing imagery upon three broad categories: (a) the learning and performance of skills and strategies; (b) the modification of cognitions; and (c) the regulation of arousal and competitive anxiety (see Cumming & Ramsey, 2009, for a review). Research specifically focused on S&C has examined imagery as either a training modality to increase strength over time or as a psyching-up strategy designed to influence the immediate display of muscular force (we consider psyching-up as a technique in more detail later in the chapter).

With respect to S&C performance, imagery training has been found to lead to increases in strength measures such as finger, elbow and hip flexor strength (e.g. Ranganathan, Siemionow, Liu, Sahgal, & Yue, 2004; Shackell & Standing, 2007; Smith & Collins, 2004; Smith, Collins, & Holmes, 2003; Yue & Cole, 1992). Additional studies have examined the effects of imagery upon S&C performance in conjunction with the investigation of psychological outcomes. For example, Feltz and Riessinger (1990) investigated the effects of imagery in conjunction with performance feedback in enhancing self-efficacy beliefs and performance on a muscular endurance task. Their results indicated that the participants who engaged in imagery initially had significantly longer performance times and greater self-efficacy than the feedback alone or control individuals.

Although considerable focus has been paid to imagery effects upon strength tasks, little research has considered the potential impact on conditioning activities of a longer based duration. Where conditioning tasks have been considered, studies have tended to use imagery as part of an overall multimodal MST package (e.g. Patrick & Hrycaiko, 1998; Thelwell & Greenlees, 2001, 2003). For example, Thelwell and Greenlees examined the effects of a MST package on competitive gymnasium triathlon performance comprising a 2-kilometre row, a 5-kilometre cycle and a 3-kilometre run. Increases in performance and mental skill usage were observed across all participants, with follow-up qualitative data revealing imagery served motivational, coping (pain management) and tactical (decision making) functions to achieve these improvements. Finally, a number of studies have looked at imagery effects upon conditioning related variables, such as flexibility (cf. Guillot, Tolleron, & Collet, 2010). For example, Vergeer and Roberts (2006) studied the effects of movement and stretching imagery on increases in flexibility across a 4-week flexibility training programme using an active and passive range of motion around the hip assessment criteria. They noted a number of flexibility gains positively correlated with imagery that was similar to, or matched, the actual motor experience (imagery vividness). Interestingly, the use of imagery has also been associated with greater behavioural and clinical recovery outcomes for athletes undergoing physical rehabilitation programmes when injured (see Evans, Mitchell, & Jones, 2006, for a review). For example, Cupal and Brewer's (2001) examination of the effects of a relaxation and guided imagery intervention on knee strength, re-injury anxiety and pain following anterior cruciate ligament reconstruction showed greater knee strength and less re-injury anxiety and pain for the treatment compared to the placebo and control group participants. Knee strength was correlated with both a reduction in re-injury anxiety and pain reduction. Possible mechanisms underlying the intervention effects included participants' enhanced perception of control, greater engagement in the rehabilitation programme (because reductions in re-injury and anxiety and pain helped them to relax) and enhanced motivation.

In summary, while the literature overall suggests that imagery can be used as a technique to enhance the learning and execution of motor skills, there is little evidence to support the direct use of imagery as a replacement for physical training. The current data indicates that regular imagery can supplement physical training for novice individuals, although more studies are needed. Also, imagery may be useful for trained individuals when they are unable to work out, such as being injured. Imagery, however, may also play an indirect role in enhancing S&C performance through its indirect effects on modification of cognitions (e.g. enhanced self-efficacy, reduced competitive anxiety), regulation of activation states and behavioural change (i.e. increased motivation through changes in persistence and maintenance of effort).

How does imagery influence S&C performance?

As we have already discussed, Martin et al.'s (1999) applied model of imagery use has played a significant part in shaping how researchers have explored the relationship between imagery and sporting performance. However, while it has provided a guide for research and applied work, it does not purport to detail the mechanisms behind the imagery–performance relationship.

A number of theories have been proposed to explain imagery effects upon motor skill learning and performance. For example, bioinformational theory (Lang, 1977, 1979) describes both the information processing and psychophysiology of imagery use. Images stored in the brain are a functionally organised, finite set of propositions, activated in the long-term memory, and consist of stimulus, response and meaning propositions. The stimulus propositions describe the content of an image (e.g. the crowds watching in front of the lifting platform at an event or competition), whereas response propositions describe the individual's response to the stimulus proposition (e.g. feeling anxious at the sight of the crowd prior to commencing a pre-lift routine). Response propositions are thought to be doubly coded, with representations at both the conceptual and motor output level (Cuthbert, Vrana, & Bradley, 1991). The meaning component takes into account the meaning of the image generated to each individual. This meaning will depend on the individual's experiences, such that two individuals who use the same imagery script would generate very different images, emphasising the need for individualised imagery interventions. Consequently, changes in behaviour through imagery are explained through the interaction between the propositions of the image and the associated motor programme.

Although a detailed discussion of the mechanisms behind imagery's direct and indirect effects is beyond the scope of this chapter (for comprehensive reviews see Callow & Hardy, 2005; Murphy et al., 2008), we now consider a recent sport-specific application of imagery's effect upon performance, namely the PETTLEP model of motor imagery (Holmes & Collins, 2001, 2002). The PETTLEP model of motor imagery is grounded in the notion that a functional equivalence exists between imagery and motor performance. Essentially, similar brain areas that are responsible for coordinating overt physical movements are activated when individuals image the same actions. Subsequent engagement in imagery practice therefore results in neural activity which modulates subsequent motor and sports performance (cf. Cumming & Ramsey, 2009). Effective imagery is therefore indicative of the ability to activate these areas successfully. PETTLEP is an acronym representing the elements of the motor imagery model (i.e. **P**hysical, **E**nvironment, **T**ask, **T**iming, **L**earning, **E**motion and **P**erspective). To maximise the intervention's effectiveness, the individual needs to engage in imagery that resembles the actual performance as closely as possible. Physical refers to congruency between the physical nature of the imagery and the actual performance (e.g. a lifter imaging a power clean should wear clothing similar to that as if they were performing that task, assume the physical position of a power clean and ideally be holding the bar itself in the start position); environment refers to the physical environment in which the imagery is being performed. For example, an individual should be at the running track if they are imaging sprint work that is actually performed on the track. Task suggests the image should mimic the actual task as closely as possible. Consequently, the image of the completion of a successful personal best dead lift should replicate the exact components of that lift. The timing aspect suggests the image should be in 'real-time' matched to that of the task. Learning suggests that the image should correspond with the individual's specific stage of learning and develop as their actual skill level improves. Emotion represents the extent to which the image encapsulates all the emotions of the actual performance of the task. Last, perspective describes how the image should take the viewpoint of the athlete during the actual performance; that is to say, either from an internal (in your own body) or external (seeing yourself on film or DVD) perspective in relation to the performer. To further maximise functional equivalence to physical practice, the PETTLEP model is advocated to include stimulus, response and meaning propositions based on bioinformational theory.

Subsequent research investigating the PETTLEP has provided evidence supporting its principles in achieving successful sports imagery interventions. Specifically, more functionally equivalent imagery has more significant improvements on sports performance when compared to imagery of less functional equivalence (Callow, Roberts, & Fawkes, 2006; Smith & Collins, 2004; Smith & Holmes, 2004; see Shearer, Holmes, & Mellalieu, 2009, for a detailed review). It should be noted though that these studies have tended to measure individual or combined elements of the PETTLEP model (e.g. physical and environmental elements). A recent attempt to incorporate all the elements of the model has suggested that imagery can be as effective as physical practice on the performance of a gymnastics skill (cf. Smith, Wright, Allsopp, & Westhead, 2007).

Self-talk

What is self-talk?

Although self-talk is a technique commonly attested to by sport psychology practitioners to enhance athletes' performance, and performers themselves report frequently using self-talk in their training and competition, the scientific evidence supporting the self-talk and performance relationship is less pronounced. A significant contribution to this lack of evidence is the historical lack of attention into the topic when compared to others of the big four methods. However, self-talk has recently experienced an upsurge of research investigating its conceptualisation and various functions (Hardy, Gammage, & Hall, 2001; Hardy, Hall, & Hardy, 2004). Self-talk refers to those automatic statements reflective of, and deliberate techniques (e.g. thought stopping) athletes use to direct, sports-related thinking (Hardy, Oliver, & Tod, 2009, p. 38). Self-talk is proposed to be multidimensional in nature comprising five overlapping dimensions (Hardy et al., 2009). Specifically: (a) *frequency* – how often self-talk is used; (b) *overtness* – whether the self-talk is audible or inaudible to other individuals (e.g. spoken to oneself or out loud); (c) *valence* – the content of the self-talk in relation to whether it is positive or negative in nature; (d) *motivational orientation* – whether performers interpret their self-talk in a motivational or de-motivational context; and (e) *function* – the perceived purpose of the self-talk use, broadly separated into self-instruction or motivational outcomes. Hardy et al. (2009) have also recently proposed a framework to facilitate the study and understanding of self-talk in sport. Their framework describes the potential antecedents and consequences of self-talk and the proposed mechanisms that underpin its relationship with performance. Personal-level antecedents of self-talk include factors such as cognitive processing preferences, belief in self-talk and personality traits. Situational factors refer to the task difficulty, match or competition circumstances, coaching behaviours exhibited, and the competitive setting (practice vs. competition). Performance-oriented consequences include enhanced skill execution, strength, etc., while the potential mechanisms underlying self-talk effects upon sports performance are separated into cognitive, motivational, behavioural and affective outcomes.

Does self-talk enhance S&C performance?

Descriptive research undertaken using qualitative measures suggests that athletes and coaches believe self-talk use is associated with performance enhancement (e.g. Gould, Eklund, & Jackson, 1992; Hardy et al., 2004), while quantitative studies have found correlations between the various forms of self-talk and a range of performance criteria (e.g. Highlen & Bennett, 1983). With regards to experimental investigations, Hardy et al.'s (2009) review of the self-talk literature concludes that the majority of studies provide evidence to suggest that self-talk leads to improved skill execution and learning across a range of sport and exercise movements and participants, from novices to elite-level performers.

Within the experimental studies considering self-talk and performance, a number of studies have shown that self-talk enhances performance in S&C-based movements. These include activities such as throwing, distance running, sprinting, vertical jumping and leg extension (Edwards, Tod, & McGuigan, 2008; Hatzigeorgiadis, Theodorakis, & Zourbanos, 2004; Mallett & Hanrahan, 1997; Theodorakis, Weinberg, Natsis, Douma, & Kazakas, 2000; Tod, Thatcher, McGuigan, & Thatcher, 2009). Within this literature, support has also been provided for the principles of the matching hypothesis (i.e. certain types of self-talk might be better suited to different tasks). Specifically, instructional self-talk has been shown to enhance performance by stimulating correct actions through proper attentional focus and movement patterns (Theodorakis et al., 2000). Motivational self-talk on the other hand typically focuses athletes on performance outcome and improves skill execution by building confidence, enhancing effort, increasing energy expenditure and creating positive moods (via an internal focus of attention; Wulf & Prinz, 2001). Consequently, based on these distinctions, motivational self-talk appears to be better suited to strength and endurance-based movements. For example, Edwards et al. (2008) found that motivational self-talk led to higher vertical jump performance compared with instructional or no self-talk. Their results appear to parallel other research indicating that performers may benefit more from directing their attention to the effects of their movements (or an external focus of attention) than their actual movements (an internal focus of attention; Wulf & Prinz, 2001). An external focus may also allow automatic control processes to regulate movements, whereas an internal focus may interfere with natural control processes (Hardy et al., 2009).

With regards to conditioning performance of longer duration, fewer studies have been conducted. Weinberg, Smith, Jackson, and Gould (1984) compared associative, dissociative and positive self-talk strategies on the performance of a 30-minute endurance run. Results indicated no significant performance differences between groups on the endurance run. On the leg lift task, however, participants in the positive self-talk and dissociation conditions held their legs out significantly longer than those individuals in the association condition. More recently, R. A. Hamilton, Scott, and MacDougall (2007) assessed the effectiveness of three different self-talk interventions (regulated positive self-talk, assisted positive self-talk and assisted negative self-talk) on the 20-minute cycling ergometer endurance performance of cyclists who worked out twice a week for a 5-week period. Increases in performance in all groups were observed with the greatest increase being found in the assisted positive self-talk condition. Additional evidence for self-talk enhancing endurance performance comes from other studies that have used self-talk as a component of an overall MST package. For example, Thelwell and Greenlees' (2003) study of the effects of a MST package on gymnasium triathlon performance noted that both motivational and instructional self-talk were reported by participants as being utilised to strengthen motivation and overcome fatigue and enhancing focus on process and task relevant goals, respectively.

Overall the evidence to support the effects of self-talk on S&C performance is positive. The studies conducted suggest that self-talk can help performers learn and develop their movement skills quicker, and accelerated learning may enhance aspects that contribute to overall competitive performance. In addition, self-talk, particularly that of a motivational form, can help produce improvements in S&C (endurance-based activity) performance.

How does self-talk influence S&C performance?

A number of mechanisms have been proffered to explain how self-talk may exert its effects upon performance. Broadly, these can be classified into four categories: cognitive, motivational, behavioural and affective (see Hardy et al., 2009). *Cognitive* mechanisms refer to processes such as information processing, concentration and attention control/style. Specifically, athletes indicate that they use self-talk to increase focus and concentration and direct/redirect attention (Hardy et al., 2001). Some preliminary evidence exists suggesting self-talk may enhance athletes' levels of focus and concentration in the learning and execution of sports skills (Hardy et al., 2009) and reduce the number of inappropriate or interfering thoughts during skill performance (Hatzigeorgiadis, Zourbanos, & Theodorakis, 2007). With respect to attention control/style, performers have reported use of self-talk to direct appropriate attention during soccer (Johnson, Hrycaiko, Johnson, & Halas, 2004), water polo (Hatzigeorgiadis et al., 2007) and tennis tasks (Landin & Hebert, 1999). Recent thinking proposes that individuals can possess an internal focus of attention that involves concentration on body movements (e.g. the quadriceps muscles working eccentrically during the lowering phase of a squat) or an external focus attending to the effects of the body's action (e.g. maintaining eye contact with yourself in the mirror on the up phase of the squat in order to maintain correct lifting 'form'). Based on this distinction, the literature suggests that an external attention focus aids motor learning more than an internal focus (the reader is directed to the work of Wulf & Prinz, 2001, for more detailed explanations of these mechanisms). Despite the intuitive appeal, however, to date no conclusive evidence exists to support self-talk as a technique for shifting performers' attention focus using Wulf and Prinz's conceptualisation of attention (see J. J. Bell & Hardy, 2009).

Motivational mechanisms for performance enhancements through self-talk have been proposed using Bandura's (1997) self-efficacy theory. Self-efficacy, a situation-specific form of self-confidence, has been found to have a moderate influence on performance and factors such as effort, positive affect and behavioural persistence (see Short & Ross-Stewart, 2009). Of the antecedents to self-efficacy (i.e. mastery experience, vicarious experience, imaginal experience, emotional arousal and verbal persuasion), positive self-talk is purported to exert its influence as a type of 'self-delivered' verbal persuasion that influences effort, persistence and performance (cf. Hardy, 2006).

The third proposed explanation for self-talk effects on performance refers to *behavioural* mechanisms. Specifically, that changes in movement patterns may occur as a function of the type of self-talk engaged (e.g. instructional vs. motivational). Surprisingly, despite the obvious nature of this research question, little research has considered movement pattern changes. Some studies have supported improvements in technical skills in sports such as tennis using instructional self-talk (e.g. Landin & Hebert, 1999); however, movement patterns have been subjectively assessed (e.g. observer checklists). More recently, however, studies have adopted objective movement kinematics to demonstrate motivational self-talk leads to enhanced strength (vertical jump) and mechanical performance (e.g. Tod et al., 2009).

The last proposed mechanisms suggest that self-talk can change performers' *affective* responses which consequently influence performance. While considerable literature in other fields of psychology has demonstrated a strong link between self-talk and affective responses, the literature in sport psychology is sparse in comparison. The studies that have been conducted focus on self-talk as an effective technique for anxiety control, thereby managing the effects of anxiety upon sports performance (see Hardy et al., 2009). Although self-talk has been used in combination with other techniques (e.g. imagery) as part of a cognitive restructuring intervention (e.g. Hanton & Jones, 1999), some studies provide support for self-talk as an anxiolytic intervention technique. For example, Hatzigeorgiadis et al. (2007) reported reductions in both cognitive and somatic anxiety after the adoption of anxiety control versus instructional self-talk.

To date, a lack of evidence exists to support explanations as to how self-talk might enhance skill execution. Of the four explanations discussed, the literature would tend to support improved concentration and more efficient movement patterns. However, each of the mechanisms for why self-talk might enhance skill execution and performance really only provide a partial explanation (i.e. it is not clear why self-talk might lead to changes in movement patterns). It is most likely that the four explanations work in tandem to produce the desired changes. For example, as a result of improved concentration, performers are able to produce more efficient movement patterns. Improved concentration may also help individuals avoid negative mood states that disrupt efficient movement.

Activation management

What is activation management?

Before outlining the strategies that fall under the broad term of activation management, it is first important to distinguish between the terms 'activation' and 'arousal' (Hardy et al., 1996). This distinction (or lack of) has been a conceptual weakness in a large part of the literature to date as the terms have often been employed interchangeably (Hardy et al., 1996). Hardy et al. (p. 118) refer to the work of Pribram and McGuiness (1975) who distinguish the cognitive and physiological activity that results in response to a new/external input (stimuli) to the system (i.e. arousing agent), and the cognitive and physiological activity that is geared towards preparing a planned response appropriate to the current situation (activation responses). Hence, *activation* is viewed as the cognitive and physiological activity geared towards preparing a planned response to some anticipated situation. A performer engaging in relevant mental strategies as part of a pre-competition or pre-match routine would therefore be said to be engaging in actions to achieve the desired activation state to perform. Consequently, rather than discuss *levels* of activation for athletes, Hardy et al. suggest considering appropriate activation *states*, as some sports may require high or low levels of certain systems (i.e. cognitive activation). Activation states are also task specific, as different components of a sporting activity may utilise different cognitive and physiological subsystems (cf. Parfitt, Jones, & Hardy, 1990).

Arousal is discussed in terms of the physiological and cognitive activity which occurs in relation to a new input (stimuli) to the system, suggesting a lack of planned preparation on the part of the performer in a relatively short time frame. Arousing agents tend to be actions taken immediately prior to an activity. For example, weightlifters slapping their heads or shouting out loudly just before they proceed to set themselves for their lift on the platform would be utilising an arousal technique. Based on this distinction, activation management strategies are therefore viewed as those techniques performers actively engage in to facilitate a task-specific ideal performance state. Within the broad categorisation of activation management, we discuss the specific skills of relaxation (psyching-down) and psyching-up. It is important to note though that, if we take into consideration the distinction between arousal and activation, a number of techniques that fall under the label of psyching-up are those used directly prior to skill execution (e.g. slapping one's head directly prior to a lift) and are strictly arousing agents as opposed to specific activation management strategies (e.g. undertaking a systematic warm-up routine in the hour preceding competition). While we do not wish to take up any further space with conceptual debate, for the purposes of this section we will consider both under the umbrella term of activation management. However, it is important that researchers are aware of this subtle but important distinction when conducting future investigation into the relationship between activation management and performance outcomes.

It is also important to make the distinction that relaxation techniques have been deployed to not only lower activation states, but to also deal with the emotional symptoms associated with the demands of competition (i.e. competitive anxiety). In this respect, we differentiate between techniques that help athletes prepare their overall activation states in readiness for the task demands of the sport, and those that specifically target the reduction or restructuring of competitive anxiety symptoms associated with competition. Indeed, the final of the big four techniques, activation management, is often termed 'stress management' because of this overlap. For the purposes of this section, we focus predominantly on the techniques that increase or reduce activation states (i.e. relaxation and psyching-up). However, we will also consider within the discussion of relaxation techniques the anxiety or stress management strategies that have been used in S&C research to alter competitive anxiety symptoms (for a comprehensive review of stress management strategies in sport, see Thomas, Mellalieu, & Hanton, 2009).

What are relaxation techniques?

Relaxation techniques can be broadly categorised into physical and mental categories. Examples of common physical relaxation techniques utilised in sport include progressive muscular relaxation (PMR) which derives from Jacobson's (1938) text on the subject with a view to lowering muscle tension. PMR requires athletes to systematically focus their attention on muscle groups throughout the body and progressively tense and relax each group in turn. More recent adaptations include applied relaxation techniques (e.g. Ost, 1988) that enable the athlete to develop the ability to relax various muscle groups across varying time periods (e.g. 15, 5 and 2 minutes or 10 seconds). This speeding up of relaxation has the advantage of enabling the psychologist and athletes to develop relaxation strategies to specific situations prior to, during or following competition as desired (cf. Hardy et al., 1996). Cognitive or mental relaxation strategies such as transcendental meditation (cf. Benson & Proctor, 1984) generally entail a mode of meditation with individuals focusing on regulation of breathing and repetition of a form of key word or 'mantra' (Hardy et al., 1996). Similar to physical strategies, cognitive techniques can be practised and deployed across different timescales to suit the requirements of the athletes and their sports (see Jones, 1993).

Relaxation strategies to deal with undesirable or unwanted competitive anxiety symptoms have been based upon the premise that the technique should be 'compatible' with or 'matched' to the client's dominant anxiety response (Davidson & Schwartz, 1976). Specifically, Davidson and Schwartz's multi-process theory proposes the 'matching hypothesis' and the notion that relaxation interventions would be more effective if they were directed at the dominant symptoms experienced (i.e. cognitive or somatic). Hence, cognitive relaxation procedures would have a primary impact on reducing cognitive anxiety, while a somatic technique would have the greatest influence on reducing unwanted somatic anxiety. In contrast, other researchers have also noted cross-over effects in the application of the matching hypothesis, due to the fact that cognitive anxiety and somatic anxiety display a level of shared variance (i.e. any attempt to reduce one of the anxiety components is likely to influence the other). Consequently, it has been suggested that interventions should be designed to treat both cognitive and somatic anxiety simultaneously. Within this proposal, one school of thought purports that matched interventions will reduce both forms of anxiety due to cross-over effects (Davidson & Schwartz, 1976), whereas a second view proffers support for treatments that combine cognitive and somatic treatments through the use of multimodal treatment packages (Meichenbaum, 1975, 1985; Smith, 1980) including stress inoculation training (Meichenbaum, 1975, 1985) and stress management training (Smith, 1980) that combine the methods of imagery, self-talk and relaxation to develop a coping skills programme (see Burton, 1990; Hardy et al., 1996).

What are psyching-up strategies?

In contrast to specific relaxation methods, 'psyching-up' is an umbrella term that refers to the self-directed systematic (more or less) sequences of cognitive, emotional and physical actions performed just prior to, or even during, movement to enhance performance (Tod et al., 2003). Cognitive strategies involve active mental processes designed to change or influence existing thought patterns (Theodorakis et al., 2000) and are designed to increase physical and mental activation, narrow attention and build self-confidence (Brody, Hatfield, Spalding, Frazer, & Caherty, 2000), which athletes perceive will lead to performance gains (cf. Tod et al., 2003).

Do relaxation strategies enhance S&C performance?

With respect to the effect of relaxation techniques on S&C actions, the evidence suggests the use of somatic relaxation techniques (i.e. those that reduce muscle tension throughout the body) leads to reduced strength performance (Murphy, Woolfolk, & Budney, 1988; Pierce, McGowan, Eastman, Aaron, & Lynn, 1993). Contemporary anxiety researchers (e.g. Hanton and colleagues) have also identified that the application of anxiety reduction strategies may be detrimental to performance. Specifically, attempts to reduce mental or physical anxiety symptoms in sports where high activation task demands are required (such as those involving gross muscular activity) may have concomitant effects upon activation state, thereby reducing overall readiness to deal with the task demands (cf. Mellalieu, Hanton, & O'Brien, 2004). In such cases, it has been advocated that performers attempt to restructure their cognitions from negative and debilitating to positive and facilitating to forthcoming performance (i.e. 'hearts in the fire, heads in the fridge'; see Mellalieu, Hanton, & Shearer, 2008). A subsequent line of research inquiry has therefore adopted a 'restructure' approach to stress management with sports performers, as opposed to the traditional 'reduction' approach (see Thomas et al., 2009).

In contrast to the negative effects on performance via reduction in activation states, relaxation techniques can lead to indirect performance improvements by helping to remove distracting, worrisome or negative thoughts from athletes' minds, and allow them to think about the relevant cues for their upcoming performance or action. For example, Maynard, Smith, and Warwick-Evans (1995) used a somatic intervention in the form of an applied relaxation technique with semi-professional football players. Following an 8-week period of applied relaxation, when compared with the control group, the intervention group showed significant decreases in cognitive and somatic anxiety intensity, and significantly more facilitative interpretations of somatic anxiety symptoms.

In addition to specific relaxation strategies (i.e. cognitive versus somatic), there is also a body of literature that supports multimodal stress management packages as an effective means of reducing anxiety and enhancing performance on complex sports movements and skills. Specifically, Smith's (1980) stress management training technique has been found to be successful in reducing anxiety-related symptoms across the sports of football (Smith & Smoll, 1978), figure skating (Smith, 1980), running (Kenney, Rejeski, & Messier, 1987; Ziegler, Klinzing, & Williamson, 1982) and volleyball (Crocker, 1989; Crocker, Alderman, & Smith, 1988). Similarly, adaptations of Meichenbaum's (1975, 1985) stress inoculation training have been successfully applied across the sporting populations of basketball (DeWitt, 1980; S. A. Hamilton & Fremouw, 1985; Meyers & Schleser, 1980; Meyers, Schleser, & Okwumabua, 1982), abseiling (Mace & Carroll, 1985; Mace, Carroll, & Eastman, 1986), running (Ziegler et al., 1982) and gymnastics (Mace & Carroll, 1989; Mace, Eastman, & Carroll, 1987).

Although these studies point to the obvious benefits of stress management training and stress inoculation training in relation to lowering levels of anxiety symptom intensity, limited information can be gleaned from the studies in relation to the performance-enhancing effects of the techniques. Further, the multimodal nature of the interventions applied renders it difficult to ascertain which specific component parts (versus the total programme used) provide the beneficial reducing influence over anxiety-related symptoms (cf. Burton, 1990). More recently, a limited number of studies have empirically tested the effectiveness of interventions formulated under the umbrella of the restructuring approach to anxiety management with the sports of swimming (Hanton & Jones, 1999), tennis (Mamassis & Doganis, 2004), field hockey (Thomas, Maynard, & Hanton, 2007) and rugby union (Mellalieu, Hanton, & Thomas, 2008). All of these studies have used derivatives of single-subject multiple-baseline designs together with some form of multimodal intervention as the stress management programme associated with their work. Here, changes in symptom interpretation (both cognitive and somatic) from debilitative to facilitative, and improvements in performance, have been observed. For example, Hanton and Jones (1999) examined the effects of a multi-modal intervention containing the skills of goal setting, imagery and self-talk on swimmers debilitated by anxiety symptoms. In addition to changes in symptom intervention from debilitative to facilitative, Hanton and Jones observed 3 per cent improvement in performance, which equated to 2–3 seconds' reduction in race times.

Does psyching-up enhance S&C performance?

Overall the research that has considered the effects of psyching-up on muscular force production suggests that such routines can enhance maximal strength, muscular endurance and power (Tod et al., 2003). Of these supporting findings, the majority of the research has considered how psyching-up influences dynamic maximal strength (Elko & Ostrow, 1992; Gould, Weinberg, & Jackson, 1980; Theodorakis et al., 2000; Tynes & McFatter, 1987; Weinberg, Gould, Yukelson, & Jackson, 1980, 1981; Whelan, Epkins, & Meyers, 1990) on tasks such as a handgrip dynamometer (Shelton & Mahoney, 1978), leg extension (Weinberg et al., 1980) and bench press (Tod, Iredale, McGuigan, Strange, & Gill, 2005). Overall, in this situation, the psyching-up effect appears to be robust (Tod & McGuigan, 2006). In contrast, fewer studies have studied the effects upon muscle endurance (Caudill & Weinberg, 1983; Lee, 1988; Weinberg, Jackson, & Seaborne, 1985), and none have considered the effects upon conditioning tasks or activities of an endurance-based nature. For example, in relation to muscle endurance, Caudill and Weinberg compared the psych-up strategies of preparatory arousal, focused attention, imagery and quiet rest on a bench press exercise in a weight training class. All three psych-up strategies were found to lead to greater performance than the quiet rest condition.

One area of caution with these findings, and those examining the effects of psyching-up on performance in general, is that the majority of studies have been undertaken with novice lifters performing simple strength tasks (cf. Tod et al., 2005). More recent studies have compared trained individuals using a greater variety of muscular force measures with equivocal findings. For example, Tod et al. (2005) found that psyching-up increased force production during the five bench press repetitions on a modified Biodex isokinetic dynamometer in male and female participants with at least 1 year strength-training experience. In contrast, however, McGuigan, Ghiagiarelli, and Tod (2005) found that psyching-up did not increase one repetition maximum (RM) performance during the squat exercise in strength-trained individuals with over 4 years, mean training experience.

In summary, the literature indicates robust effects for psyching-up on muscular force production such that psyching-up routines enhance maximal strength and local muscular endurance. However, caution should be applied as these findings have been undertaken with untrained participants on simple tasks. The evidence is more ambivalent with regards to trained individuals on more complex compound tasks and activities. In contrast, relaxation techniques, particularly somatic ones, appear to be an inappropriate technique for enhancing S&C performance as they reduce the individual's task-specific activation states. However, such strategies may indirectly lead to performance gains as they serve to remove distracting, worrisome or negative thoughts from athletes' minds, and allow them to think about the relevant cues for their upcoming performance. In respect of more complex tasks, stress management strategies that allow performers to restructure thoughts and perceptions of their symptoms experienced from negative to positive appear to be effective, allowing performers to maintain or improve performance without reducing or altering their desired activation states for task execution (cf. Mellalieu, Hanton, & Fletcher, 2006).

How do relaxation strategies influence S&C performance?

Relaxation strategies may exert their influence upon performance through the management of the effects of demands or stressors imposed upon athletes when trying to maintain successful skill execution. Specifically, those strategies that have traditionally attempted to use relaxation techniques to reduce competitive anxiety symptoms, thereby leading to enhanced performance. Contemporary thinking on the anxiety performance relationship suggests however that merely attempting to 'reduce' either cognitive or somatic anxiety symptoms alone will not guarantee performance increments and, in S&C contexts, can actually inhibit performance (cf. Thomas et al., 2009). For example, under the tenets of the catastrophe model, cognitive anxiety determines whether the effect of physiological arousal (from which somatic anxiety symptoms derive) on performance will be smooth and small, large and catastrophic, or somewhere in between these two extremes (Woodman & Hardy, 2001). Consequently, elevations in cognitive anxiety can have positive performance consequences dependent upon the levels of physiological arousal experienced. Moreover, these effects are moderated by the influence of other variables such as the self-confidence of the performer and the complexity of the task (cf. Hardy, Parfitt, & Pates, 1994; Woodman & Hardy, 2001).

Mechanistic explanations provide further support for the effects of high cognitive anxiety upon performance and the tenets of the 'restructuring' approach to stress management. For example, processing efficiency theory (Eysenck & Calvo, 1992) suggests that a proportion of attentional capacity for the task is consumed by task irrelevant cognitive activity or worry, effectively reducing working memory capacity, thereby impairing processing efficiency and, possibly, performance (Eysenck, 1992). Alternatively, however, cognitive anxiety or worry may also signal the importance of the task to the individual and lead to an increased investment in the task if a below par performance is perceived (cf. Mellalieu et al., 2006). The experience of high levels of cognitive anxiety can therefore motivate a performer to increase his or her effort in preventing this anxious state from impairing performance, but at the expense of utilising a greater proportion of the available attentional resources (Nieuwenhuys, Pijpers, Oudejans, & Bakker, 2008). Consequently, while anxiety affects efficiency (the relationship between effective task performance and the use of attentional resources), it does not affect effectiveness (outcome in terms of performance accuracy; cf. Nieuwenhuys et al., 2008).

How does psyching-up influence S&C performance?

To date, there has been a lack of substantial support for why psyching-up routines might be effective in enhancing strength during closed-skill tasks (cf. Tod et al., 2003). Recently, however, Tod and Lavallee (in press) have attempted to provide a theoretical basis to the literature by offering three explanations. First, schema theory (Schmidt, 1975) suggests that the instructions for a task, such as the power clean, are represented in the nervous system of the body by a generalised motor programme. There is also a motor response schema that allows an individual to adjust their generalised motor programme to allow them to produce the desired action (e.g. generate sufficient force to squat a particular weight). Under the premise of schema theory, psyching-up routines assist athletes to select and adjust the suitable generalised motor programme so that they can achieve the desired outcome. For example, allowing performers to recruit more motor units when lifting heavier weights. The second explanation is based upon attention-control theory. Here it is suggested that psyching-up routines help performers organise their attention resources so they can focus on the relevant cues and avoid distractions (Boutcher, 1990). Finally, the activation set hypothesis (Schmidt & Lee, 1999) refers to an internal state associated with optimal task execution (e.g. level of activation, attentional focus, confidence, etc.). Under this approach, psyching-up routines facilitate performance by enabling performers to adjust their activation state to one that is desirable and appropriate for the upcoming task (see Hardy et al., 1996, for a detailed discussion).

Future research directions in MST and S&C performance

As with any emerging area or topic of research, a review of the extant literature tends to throw up more questions than answers. Here, we attempt to integrate some of the pertinent issues that have arisen from our review and synthesise them with some of the key developments/questions being currently raised in the study of MST and performance in the wider sport psychology literature.

Advanced versus basic MST

Although the findings discussed in the current chapter have conceptual and practical significance in terms of our knowledge regarding the effects of MST on S&C performance, it should be noted that the majority have only explored the independent as opposed to combined effects of each psychological method. Indeed, Hardy et al. (1996) have illustrated that athletes, coaches and applied sport psychologists often combine basic psychological techniques with other component parts (i.e.

other mental and/or physical skills) to create more advanced psychological strategies. Here, it is worth noting that Hardy et al. do not make the distinction between psychological skills and techniques/methods as they view them as skills in their own right. Specifically, they distinguish *basic* from *advanced* psychological skills, something that has often gone unacknowledged in the literature (cf. Hanton et al., 2008; Hardy et al., 1996). Put simply, psychological skills can be used in a single (i.e. basic psychological skills, such as imagery *or* self-talk) or combined fashion (i.e. advanced psychological skills, such as pre-competition routines that often combine imagery *and* self-talk). Other examples of advanced strategies include: simulation training, cognitive restructuring and overlearning of skills (Hanton et al., 2008; Hardy et al., 1996). While a number of advanced psychological strategies have been reported throughout the sport psychology literature (e.g. Hanton & Jones, 1999; Hays, Maynard, Thomas, & Bawden, 2007; Jones, 1993; Lonsdale & Tam, 2008; Thomas et al., 2007), there has been no investigation in the S&C field other than the broader consideration of psyching-up strategies. Intuitively, advanced psychological skills by their very (advanced) nature yield the potential (if used correctly) for greater performance gains due to their increased complexity and influence over behaviour and physical performance and are a salient area for exploration.

It is also important to note that there are other techniques in the literature that have been utilised to influence psychological skills and performance; however, due to space constraints, we were not able to fully consider them. For example, music is used by many individuals to assist with their S&C training. In comparison with the big four methods, fewer studies have examined the influence of music on S&C tasks and activities. However, in line with anecdotal evidence regarding the positive effects of upbeat music, motivational or simulative music may be associated with strength (Crust & Clough, 2006; Karageorghis & Terry, 2009). Future research is therefore needed to assess the salience of techniques such as music and other psychological methods, such as modelling (see Dowrick, 2000) or hypnosis (cf. Barker, Jones, & Greenlees, 2010), to compare with the big four not only in terms of effectiveness, but also their conceptual underpinning and subsequent basis for recommendation to S&C professionals for implementation into applied practice.

MST used across larger time phases

To date, the majority of MST studies have centred on exploring their effects at the micro level of competition (i.e. directly prior to or during performance or skill execution). There has been little or no consideration of the use of MST across larger time contexts at the 'macro' level of preparation. For example, in a recent study Mellalieu, Hanton, Shearer (2008) explored how international rugby union players prepared for performance in the week leading up to matches. A number of different psychological techniques were employed by the players at salient time periods to manage and manipulate their mental and physical activation and assist them in their mental and physical preparation for competition. The powerful influence of the team upon individual psychological constructs such as confidence, focus and attention was also noted across this time phase. While some studies have looked at how specific MST techniques may be used in practice or the off-season in sport (e.g. imagery; Munroe, Hall, Simms, & Weinberg, 1998), others have received little attention (e.g. self-talk; cf. Hardy et al., 2009) and none have looked at the direct influence upon specific S&C performance. The use and effects of MST across wider temporal periods in relation to S&C would therefore appear to be a fruitful avenue to consider.

In a similar vein, there has also been very little attention to the use of MST for post-competition recovery and training contexts. Specifically, no studies have considered how psychological methods may be used to facilitate recovery from competition and promote mental and physical readiness for future performances. The literature examining the science of recovery and training suggests that psychological markers (e.g. mood, perceived stress) can prove quick and effective indices of an individual's recovery state and readiness to train (see e.g. Kellmann, 2002; Main & Grove, 2009). Although there is a wealth of literature looking at MST use in injury rehabilitation (see Evans et al., 2006), and numerous studies have monitored training status and recovery, none have looked at specific use of MST interventions to manage the recovery and training process. For example, immediately post-competition the use of relaxation techniques may assist in reducing post-match activation and facilitate physiological recovery and growth. Intuitively, ensuring athletes are back to a refreshed state to commence training while minimising potential staleness and burnout is an area of great importance and relevance for S&C professionals, psychologists and coaches alike.

Adherence to MST and training interventions

Although scientific inquiry in sports science has been able to demonstrate the effectiveness of numerous performance-enhancing techniques, the success of translating these strategies in actual performance gains lies in the ability of the practitioner to ensure that the athlete undertakes the training regime as prescribed (Palmer, Burwitz, Smith, & Collins, 1999; Weinberg & Williams, 2010). Athletes' ability to adhere to the prescribed intervention therefore becomes a key and often overlooked aspect of the training process, particularly within the S&C field (A. G. Anderson & Lavallee, 2008). While a number of studies have examined potential personal and situational influences on mental skills practice and general adherence to MST (e.g. Bull, 1991), recent research has considered multi-disciplinary approaches to programme adherence. For example, Palmer and colleagues (Palmer, Burwitz, Dyer, & Spray, 2005; Palmer, Burwitz, Smith, & Borrie, 2000; Palmer et al., 1999; Palmer, Moore, & Herberle, 2004) have conducted a line of research inquiry utilising Maddux's (1993) revised theory of planned behaviour (TPB) to explore and predict training intentions and enhance actual adherence to endurance training of elite netball players. In addition, A. G. Anderson and Lavallee (2008) have found that the TPB and the theory of reasoned action (TRA) predict adherence to training in athletes recently introduced to a new S&C training regimen. Collectively, these results indicate that both the TPB and TRA potentially offer theoretical frameworks to examine adherence to new training regimens, and that they may be used to direct interventions to increase training adherence (see also Chapter 2). Future research should therefore not only look at the most effective ways of implementing MST and maximise programme adherence in S&C tasks and activities but also explore how knowledge of theories of motivation and adherence behaviour can be utilised in general S&C practice in relation to the successful delivery of physical programmes.

Periodisation of mental skills

In addition to promoting adherence, a number of other concerns have been raised with the ability to effectively implement MST with athletes (Weinberg & Williams, 2010). These include factors such as the ability of the practitioner to integrate mental and physical training to promote better mental practice and a more consistent transfer to competitive situations; building in variety and challenge to overcome boredom, ensuring that each workout systematically contributes to athletes' long-term development; minimising performance plateaus and slumps; and ensuring athletes are ready to play their best in major competitions. Future research development and understanding in the effectiveness of MST interventions seem to be tied to whether these concerns can be addressed effectively through creative and systematic programme development (Weinberg & Williams, 2010). One development strategy that has been largely ignored in MST programme design is *periodisation* – the cycling of the structure and delivery of training. While periodisation has been acknowledged in terms of physical and technical preparation of performers, little or no research has been undertaken in relation to MST. Recent steps to address this have been taken by Holliday et al. (2008) who have outlined processes by which the principles of periodisation may be integrated into MST use. As periodisation of MST is in its relative infancy, this would appear to be an area of research that will provide significant knowledge gains for S&C professionals in their attempt to maximise performance improvements.

Mechanisms by which MST influences performance – direct versus indirect

The ability to demonstrate objective performance improvements through behavioural change as a direct consequence of MST or psychological intervention is an essential facet of sport psychology research that has in the past not always been effectively demonstrated (cf. Smith, 1989). Indeed, the ability to determine causality in sport psychology has often been fraught with problems due to studies employing designs that lack either internal or external validity (or both), a failure to assess practical or clinical as opposed to statistical significance, and the utilisation of performance measures that have been too global or sensitive in nature (Hrycaiko

& Martin, 1996; Martin, Vause, & Schwartzman, 2005). The past decade however has seen a proliferation of applied intervention studies that have not only demonstrated the ability to influence psychological constructs directly, but also objective performance improvements (e.g. R. J. Bell, Skinner, & Fisher, 2009; Johnson et al., 2004; Rogerson & Hrycaiko, 2002; Thelwell, Greenlees, & Weston, 2006). Accompanying this maturity in the study of performance enhancement has been a more comprehensive exploration of the mechanisms that underlie MST's direct and indirect effects on performance, as highlighted in the main sections of this chapter. More recent approaches have therefore begun to emerge that have adopted an interdisciplinary stance to exploring MST effects on performance. For example, Tod and colleagues' (Edwards et al., 2008; Tod et al., 2009) investigations of the effects of self-talk upon strength are excellent examples demonstrating the value of MST in physical skills training. Elsewhere, Collins and colleagues (Collins, Jones, Fairweather, Doolan, & Priestley, 2001) have used movement kinematics to evaluate changes in movement patterns associated with concurrent changes in anxiety levels. Combining these and other interdisciplinary methods provides an interesting avenue and challenge for researchers to assess the apparent complex explanations for the mechanisms by which psychological techniques and MST manifest their performance effects.

Method considerations

Our final proposal for future research in MST in S&C centres on some of the methodological issues that have arisen from the existing research highlighted in our chapter. Indeed, the method issues that have arisen are characteristic of many areas of human science investigation. Specifically, we draw attention to characteristics of the samples utilised, the tasks undertaken and the overall experimental designs employed. With regard to the sample characteristics, often MST performance studies have not sampled populations with whom MST is actually utilised (i.e. elite or junior elite individuals). A large number of the studies reviewed in this chapter have used high-school, collegiate or non-elite populations, something akin to studies that use non-trained or sedentary subjects in physiological experiments. It is also worthy of note that female populations in the main have been under-investigated. Any potential effects of MST are therefore not only likely to be magnified and unrepresentative of the target population for which MST is typically used, but will yield findings that have little or no application to S&C practitioners and alike. To further enhance the efficacy regarding the preliminary evidence for the utility of MST for S&C performance improvements, future studies need to sample both male and female experienced/skilled performers.

In terms of application of knowledge and findings from these existing studies, we also note that many of the dependent variables or performance tasks undertaken have lacked ecological validity. For example, studies have assessed maximal strength using grip dynamometers or local muscular endurance via simple indices such as a 'sit-up' test, as opposed to more compound full body exercises (cf. McGuigan et al.,

2005; Tod & McGuigan, 2006). Indeed, of the more ecologically valid studies that have explored the effects of psychological methods, few have even considered muscle endurance or conditioning activities of longer duration, that are more indicative of the anaerobic and aerobic demands of many strength and power-based sports. Recent studies have however attempted to incorporate complex and compound exercises and actions akin to more real-world practical assessment of performance criteria (cf. Mellalieu, Hanton, & O'Brien, 2006). The challenge for future MST and S&C research therefore is to select tasks and performance criteria to allow conclusions that are as directly applicable to professional practice as possible. In this respect, a final limitation of a large number of the MST studies has been their undertaking in laboratory settings. While the use of such experimental designs allows the researcher to exert and maintain a large degree of control and internal validity over their findings, their utility in terms of practical implications is limited (Hrycaiko & Martin, 1996). In keeping with recent MST studies, we therefore encourage more applied research adopting greater ecologically valid methods. One example of such methods is single-subject designs, that allow for practical assessment and analysis of elite athletes with tailored and performance-enhancing interventions (cf. Martin et al., 2005).

Practical implications

This section will focus upon the practical implications that emanate from the literature that has examined the use of psychological techniques in the form of MST to enhance S&C performance. Although the knowledge base is less conclusive in comparison to the general MST and performance literature, there are a number of specific suggestions that can be offered to S&C practitioners:

1. Setting moderately difficult and specific (as opposed to do your best) goals will increase performance on S&C-based tasks.
2. Performers should be encouraged to set short-, medium- and long-term goals together rather than in isolation.
3. In addition to direct short-term benefits on performance via changes in motivation, promoting effective goal setting practices with athletes can lead to indirect performance improvements via 'smarter' as well as longer and harder training.
4. Imagery should be recommended as a complementary technique to enhance the learning and execution of new S&C tasks and skills alongside physical practice, or when physical practice is not possible.
5. Athletes should be encouraged to use imagery for indirect performance gains, such as enhancing confidence and motivation, reducing anxiety and achieving desirable pre-performance activation states.
6. Using motivational self-talk leads to improvements in S&C (endurance-based activity) performance.
7. Self-talk (instructional) can also be used to help performers learn and develop their movement skills quicker.

8.   Relaxation strategies (physical techniques) are inappropriate for S&C activities as they lower a performer's task activation state (physical and mental readiness).
9.   Anxiety (stress) management strategies that restructure perceptions of symptoms from negative to positive allow performers to maintain performance without reducing their desired activation states for task execution.
10. Psyching-up routines can be used to enhance maximal strength and local muscular endurance, particularly on single or basic tasks/exercises. Large performance gains especially occur for novice or untrained individuals.

Summary and conclusions

In this chapter, we have attempted to provide an overview of the literature that has examined the effects of MST upon S&C performance. In doing so, we have discussed the four prominent methods utilised and the varying levels of support observed for their effects upon S&C performance. As with the study of MST in sport psychology in general, there are clearly many unanswered questions as to how these effects are manifested and the extent to which direct implications for professional S&C practice can be drawn. However, what is clear is that the current literature suggests MST can enhance S&C performance. In addition, the existing body of research offers a number of fruitful areas for future investigation into the effects of MST upon S&C performance, many of which also apply to the broader area of research on MST and performance. Given the tangible and practical outcomes that can be delivered from S&C research, MST therefore represents an exciting avenue for sports psychology researchers and practitioners to pursue with their S&C counterparts.

Discussion questions

1.   Outline the differences between psychological skills or characteristics and psychological methods or strategies.
2.   Define MST.
3.   Discuss the mechanisms by which goals are proposed to exert their influence upon performance.
4.   Using Martin et al.'s (1999) applied model of imagery, describe the five types of imagery in relation to practical S&C examples.
5.   Briefly describe the dimensions that comprise self-talk using S&C examples.
6.   Explain the four mechanisms that underpin self-talk's influence on performance.
7.   With reference to S&C examples, outline the strategies that fall under the broad term of 'activation management'.
8.   Distinguish between the terms 'activation' and 'arousal'.
9.   Consider the reasons why some relaxation techniques may lead to reduced S&C performance.

10. Discuss some of the current method issues in the study of the effects of MST upon S&C performance.

References

Anderson, A. G., & Lavallee, D. (2008). Applying the theories of reasoned action and planned behavior to athlete training adherence behavior. *Applied Psychology, 57,* 304–312.

Anderson, C. D., Crowell, C. R., Doman, M., & Howard, G. S. (1988). Performance posting, goal setting, and activity-contingent praise as applied to a university hockey team. *Journal of Applied Psychology, 73,* 87–96.

Bandura, A. (1997). *Self-efficacy: The exercise of control.* New York: Freeman.

Bar-Eli, M., Hartman, I., & Levy-Kolker, N. (1994). Using goal setting to improve physical performance of adolescents with behaviour disorders: The effect of goal proximity. *Adapted Physical Activity Quarterly, 11,* 86–97.

Bar-Eli, M., Levy-Kolker, N., Tenenbaum, G., & Weinberg, R. S. (1993). Effect of goal difficulty on performance of aerobic, anaerobic and power tasks in laboratory and field settings. *Journal of Sport Behaviour, 16,* 17–32.

Bar-Eli, M., Tenenbaum, G., Pie, J., Btesh, Y., & Almog, A. (1997). Effect of goal difficulty, goal specificity and duration of practice time intervals on muscular endurance performance. *Journal of Sports Sciences, 15,* 125–135.

Barker, J., Jones, M. V., & Greenlees, I. (2010). Assessing the immediate and maintained effects of hypnosis on self-efficacy and soccer wall-volley performance. *Journal of Sport and Exercise Psychology, 32,* 243–252.

Bell, J. J., & Hardy, J. (2009). Effects of attentional focus on skilled performance in golf. *Journal of Applied Sport Psychology, 21,* 163–177.

Bell, R. J., Skinner, C. H., & Fisher, L. A. (2009). Decreasing putting yips in accomplished golfers via solution-focused guided imagery: A single-subject research design. *Journal of Applied Sport Psychology, 21,* 1–14.

Benson, H., & Proctor, W. (1984). *Beyond the relaxation response.* New York: Berkley.

Boutcher, S. H. (1990). The role of performance routines in sport. In J. G. Jones, & L. Hardy (Eds.), *Stress and performance in sport* (pp. 231–245). Chichester: Wiley.

Boyce, B. A., & Wayda, V. K. (1994). The effects of assigned and self-set goals on task performance. *Journal of Sport Exercise Psychology, 16,* 258–269.

Brody, E. B., Hatfield, B. D., Spalding, T. W., Frazer, M. B., & Caherty, F. J. (2000). The effects of a psyching strategy on neuromuscular activation and force production in strength trained men. *Research Quarterly for Exercise and Sport, 71,* 162–170.

Bull, S. (1991). Personal and situation influences on adherence to mental skills training. *Journal of Sport and Exercise Psychology, 13,* 121–132.

Burton, D. (1990). Multimodal stress management in sport: Current status and future directions. In G. Jones, & L. Hardy (Eds.), *Stress and performance in sport* (pp. 171–201). Chichester, UK: Wiley.

Burton, D. (1992). The Jekyll/Hyde nature of goals: Reconceptualising goal setting in sport. In T. Horn (Ed.), *Advances in sport psychology* (pp. 267–297). Champaign, IL: Human Kinetics.

Burton, D. (1993). Goal setting in sport. In R. N. Singer, M. Murphy, & L. K. Tennant (Eds.), *Handbook of research on sport psychology* (pp. 467–491). New York: Macmillan.

Burton, D., & Naylor, S. (2002). The Jekyll/Hyde nature of goals: Revisiting and updating goal setting research. In T. Horn (Ed.), *Advances in sport psychology* (pp. 459–499). Champaign, IL: Human Kinetics.

Burton, D., Naylor, S., & Holliday, B. (2001). Goal setting in sport: Investigating the goal effectiveness paradox. In R. N. Singer, H. A. Hausenblas, & C. M. Janelle (Eds.), *Handbook of sport psychology* (2nd ed., pp. 497–528). New York: Wiley.

Burton, D., Pickering, M., Weinberg, R. S., Yukelson, D., & Weigand, D. A. (2010). The competitive goal effectiveness paradox revisited: Examining the goal practices of prospective Olympic athletes. *Journal of Applied Sport Psychology, 22*, 72–86.

Burton, D., Weinberg, R. S., Yukelson, D., & Weigand, D. A. (1998). The goal effectiveness paradox in sport: Examining the goal practices of collegiate athletes. *The Sport Psychologist, 12*, 404–418.

Burton, D., & Weiss, C. L. (2008). The fundamental goal concept: The path to process and performance success. In T. Horn (Ed.), *Advances in sport psychology* (3rd ed., pp. 339–375). Champaign, IL: Human Kinetics.

Callow, N., & Hardy, L. (2005). A critical analysis of applied imagery research. In D. Hackfort, J. L. Duda, & R. Lidor (Eds.), *Handbook of research in applied sport and exercise psychology: International perspectives* (pp. 21–42). Morgantown, WV: Fitness Information Technology.

Callow, N., Roberts, R., & Fawkes, J. Z. (2006). Effects of dynamic and static imagery on vividness of imagery, skiing performance, and confidence. *Journal of Imagery Research in Sport and Physical Activity, 1.* Retrieved from www.bepress.com/jirspa/vol1/iss1/art2

Caudill, D., & Weinberg, R. (1983). The effects of varying the length of the psych-up interval on motor performance. *Journal of Sport Behaviour, 6*, 86–91.

Collins, D., Jones, B., Fairweather, M., Doolan, S., & Priestley, N. (2001). Examining anxiety associated changes in movement patterns. *International Journal of Sport Psychology, 31*, 223–242.

Connaughton, D., & Hanton, S. (2009). Mental toughness in sport: Conceptual and practical issues. In S. D. Mellalieu, & S. Hanton (Eds.), *Advances in applied sport psychology: A review* (pp. 317–346). London: Routledge.

Crocker, P. R. E. (1989). A follow-up of cognitive-affective stress management training. *Journal of Sport and Exercise Psychology, 11*, 236–242.

Crocker, P. R. E., Alderman, R. B., & Smith, F. M. R. (1988). Cognitive affective stress management training with high performance youth volleyball players: Effects on affect, cognition and performance. *Journal of Sport and Exercise Psychology, 10*, 448–460.

Crust, L., & Clough, P. J. (2006). The influence of rhythm and personality in the endurance response to motivational asynchronous music. *Journal of Sports Sciences, 24*, 187–195.

Cumming, J., & Hall, C. (2002). Deliberate imagery practice: The development of imagery skills in competitive athletes. *Journal of Sports Sciences, 20*, 137–145.

Cumming, J., & Ramsey, R. (2009). Sport imagery interventions. In S. D. Mellalieu, & S. Hanton (Eds.), *Advances in applied sport psychology: A review* (pp. 5–36). London: Routledge.

Cupal, D. D., & Brewer, B. W. (2001). Effects of relaxation and guided imagery on knee strength, re-injury anxiety, and pain following anterior cruciate ligament reconstruction. *Rehabilitation Psychology, 46*, 28–43.

Cuthbert, B. N., Vrana, S. R., & Bradley, M. M. (1991). Imagery: Function and physiology. In P. Ackles, J. Jennings, & M. Coles (Eds.), *Advances in psychophysiology (Vol. 4*, pp. 1–42). London: Jessica Kingsley.

Davidson, R. J., & Schwartz, G. E. (1976). The psychobiology of relaxation and related stress: A multiprocess theory. In D. I. Mostofsky (Ed.), *Behavioural control and modification of physiological activity* (pp. 399–442). Englewood Cliffs, NJ: Prentice Hall.

DeWitt, D. J. (1980). Cognitive and biofeedback training for stress reduction with university athletes. *Journal of Sport Psychology, 2*, 288–294.

Dowrick, P. W. (2000). A review of self-modelling and related interventions. *Applied and Preventive Psychology, 8*, 23–39.

Driskell, J. E., Copper, C., & Moran, A. (1994). Does mental practice enhance performance? *Journal of Applied Psychology, 79*, 481–491.

Edwards, C., Tod, D., & McGuigan, M. (2008). Self-talk influences vertical jump performance and kinematics in male rugby union players. *Journal of Sports Sciences, 26*, 1459–1465.

Elko, K., & Ostrow, A. C. (1992). The effects of three mental preparation strategies on strength performance of young and older athletes. *Journal of Sport Behaviour, 15*, 34–41.

Evans, L., Mitchell, I., & Jones, S. (2006). Psychological responses to sport injury: A review of current research. In S. Hanton, & S. D. Mellalieu (Eds.), *Literature reviews in sport psychology* (pp. 289–319). Hauppauge, NY: Nova Science.

Eysenck, M. W. (1992). *Anxiety: The cognitive perspective*. London: Lawrence Erlbaum.

Eysenck, M. W., & Calvo, M. G. (1992). Anxiety and performance: The processing efficiency theory. *Cognition and Emotion, 6*, 409–434.

Feltz, D., & Kontos, A. (2002). The nature of sport psychology. In T. Horn (Ed.), *Advances in sport psychology* (2nd ed., pp. 3–19). Champaign, IL: Human Kinetics.

Feltz, D., & Landers, D. M. (1983). The effects of mental practice on motor skill learning and performance: A meta-analysis. *Journal of Sport Psychology, 5*, 25–57.

Feltz, D., & Riessinger, C. A. (1990). Effects of in vivo imagery and performance feedback on self-efficacy and muscular endurance. *Journal of Sport and Exercise Psychology, 12*, 132–143.

Ford, K. R., Myer, G. D., Smith, R., Byrnes, R. N., Dopirak, S. E., & Hewett, T. E. (2005). Use of an overhead goal alters vertical jump performance and biomechanics. *Journal of Strength and Conditioning Research, 19*, 394–399.

Gould, D. (2006). Goal setting for peak performance. In J. Williams (Ed.), *Applied sport psychology: Personal growth to peak performance* (5th ed., pp. 240–259). New York: McGraw-Hill.

Gould, D., Eklund, R. C., & Jackson, S. A. (1992). 1988 U.S. Olympic wrestling excellence: II. Thoughts and affect occurring during competition. *The Sport Psychologist, 6*, 383–402.

Gould, D., Guinan, D., Greenleaf, C., Medbery, R., & Peterson, K. (1999). Factors affecting Olympic performance: Perceptions of athletes and coaches from more and less successful teams. *The Sport Psychologist, 13*, 371–394.

Gould, D., Weinberg, R., & Jackson, A. (1980). Mental preparation strategies, cognitions, and strength performance. *Journal of Sport Psychology, 2*, 329–339.

Gould, D., Weiss, M., & Weinberg, R. (1981). Psychological characteristics of successful and non-successful Big Ten wrestlers. *Journal of Sport Psychology, 3*, 69–81.

Greenspan, M. J., & Feltz, D. M. (1989). Psychological interventions with athletes in competitive situations: A review. *The Sport Psychologist, 3*, 219–236.

Guillot, A., Tolleron, C., & Collet, C. (2010). Does motor imagery enhance stretching and flexibility? *Journal of Sports Sciences, 28*, 291–298.

Hall, C., Mack, D., Paivio, A., & Hausenblas, H. (1998). Imagery use by athletes: Development of the sport imagery questionnaire. *International Journal of Sport Psychology, 29*, 73–89.

Hall, H. K., & Byrne, T. J. (1988). Goal setting in sport: Clarifying recent anomalies. *Journal of Sport and Exercise Psychology, 10*, 184–198.

Hall, H. K., & Kerr, A. W. (2001). Goal-setting in sport and physical activity: Tracing empirical developments and establishing conceptual direction. In G. C. Roberts (Ed.), *Advances in motivation in sport and exercise* (pp. 183–233). Champaign, IL: Human Kinetics.

Hall, H. K., Weinberg, R. S., & Jackson, A. W. (1987). Effects of goal specificity, goal difficulty, and information feedback on endurance performance. *Journal of Sport Psychology, 9*, 43–54.

Hamilton, R. A., Scott, D., & MacDougall, M. P. (2007). Assessing the effectiveness of self-talk interventions in endurance performance. *Journal of Applied Sport Psychology, 19*, 226–239.

Hamilton, S. A., & Fremouw, W. J. (1985). Cognitive-behavioural training for college basketball free-throw performance. *Cognitive Therapy and Research, 9*, 479–483.

Hanton, S., & Jones, G. (1999). The effects of a multimodal intervention programme on performers: II. Training the butterflies to fly in formation. *The Sport Psychologist, 13*, 22–41.

Hanton, S., Wadey, R., & Mellalieu, S. D. (2008). Advanced psychological strategies and competitive anxiety responses in sport. *The Sport Psychologist, 22*, 472–490.

Hardy, J. (2006). Speaking clearly: A critical review of the self-talk literature. *Psychology of Sport and Exercise, 7*, 81–97.

Hardy, J., Gammage, K., & Hall, C. (2001). A descriptive study of athlete self-talk. *The Sport Psychologist, 15*, 306–318.

Hardy, J., Hall, C. R., & Hardy, L. (2004). A note on athletes' use of self-talk. *Journal of Applied Sport Psychology, 16*, 251–257.

Hardy, J., Oliver, E., & Tod, D. (2009). A framework for the study and application of self-talk in sport. In S. D. Mellalieu, & S. Hanton (Eds.), *Advances in applied sport psychology: A review* (pp. 37–74). London: Routledge.

Hardy, L., Jones, G., & Gould, D. (1996). *Understanding psychological preparation for sport: Theory and practice of elite performers.* Chichester: Wiley.

Hardy, L., Parfitt, G., & Pates, J. (1994). Performance catastrophes in sport: A test of the hysteresis hypothesis. *Journal of Sports Sciences, 12*, 327–334.

Harwood, C., Hardy, L., & Swain, A. (2000). Achievement goals in sport: A critique of conceptual and measurement issues. *Journal of Sport and Exercise Psychology, 22*, 235–255.

Hatzigeorgiadis, A., Theodorakis, Y., & Zourbanos, N. (2004). Self-talk in the swimming pool: The effects of self-talk on thought content and performance on water-polo tasks. *Journal of Applied Sport Psychology, 16*, 138–150.

Hatzigeorgiadis, A., Zourbanos, N., & Theodorakis, Y. (2007). The moderating effects of self-talk content on self-talk functions. *Journal of Applied Sport Psychology, 19*, 240–251.

Hays, K., Maynard, I., Thomas, O., & Bawden, M. (2007). Sources and types of confidence identified by world-class performers. *Journal of Applied Sport Psychology, 19*, 434–456.

Highlen, P. S., & Bennett, B. B. (1983). Elite divers and wrestlers: A comparison between open- and closed-skill athletes. *Journal of Sport Psychology, 5*, 390–409.

Holliday, B., Burton, D., Sun, G., Hammermeister, J., Naylor, S., & Freigang, D. (2008). Building the better mental training mousetrap: Is periodization a more systematic approach to promoting performance excellence? *Journal of Applied Sport Psychology, 20*, 199–219.

Holmes, P. S., & Collins, D. J. (2001). The PETTLEP approach to motor imagery: A functional equivalence model for sport psychologists. *Journal of Applied Sport Psychology, 13*, 60–83.

Holmes, P. S., & Collins, D. J. (2002). Functional equivalence solutions for problems with motor imagery. In I. Cockerill (Ed.), *Solutions in sport psychology* (pp. 120–140). London: Thomson.

Horn, T. (2008). *Advances in sport psychology.* Champaign, IL: Human Kinetics.

Hrycaiko, D. W., & Martin, G. L. (1996). Applied research studies with single subject designs: Why so few? *Journal of Applied Sport Psychology, 8*, 183–199.

Jacobson, E. (1938). *Progressive relaxation* (2nd ed.). Chicago: University of Chicago Press.

Johnson, J. J. M., Hrycaiko, D. W., Johnson, G. V., & Halas, J. M. (2004). Self-talk and female youth soccer performance. *The Sport Psychologist, 18*, 44–59.

Jones, G. (1993). The role of performance profiling in cognitive behavioural interventions in sport. *The Sport Psychologist, 7*, 160–172.

Karageorghis, C. I., & Terry, P. C. (2009). The psychological, psychophysical and ergogenic effects of music in sport: A review and synthesis. In A. J. Bateman, & J. R. Bale (Eds.), *Sporting sounds: Relationships between sport and music* (pp. 13–36). London: Routledge.

Kellmann, M. (2002). Psychological assessment of underrecovery. In M. Kellmann (Ed.), *Enhancing recovery: Preventing underperformance in athletes* (pp. 37–55). Champaign, IL: Human Kinetics.

Kenney, E. A., Rejeski, W. J., & Messier, S. P. (1987). Managing exercise distress: The effect of broad spectrum intervention on affect, R.P.E. and running efficiency. *Canadian Journal of Sports Sciences, 2*, 97–105.

Kingston, K., & Wilson, K. (2009). The application of goal setting in sport. In S. D. Mellalieu, & S. Hanton (Eds.), *Advances in applied sport psychology: A review* (pp. 75–123). New York: Routledge.

Krane, V. M., & Williams, J. M. (2010). Psychological characteristics of peak performance. In J. M. Williams (Ed.), *Applied sport psychology: Personal growth to peak performance* (pp. 169–188). Boston: McGraw-Hill.

Landin, D., & Hebert, E. P. (1999). The influence of self-talk on the performance of skilled female tennis players. *Journal of Applied Sport Psychology, 11*, 263–282.

Lang, P. J. (1977). Imagery in therapy: An information-processing analysis of fear. *Behaviour Therapy, 8*, 862–886.

Lang, P. J. (1979). A bio-informational theory of emotional imagery. *Psychophysiology, 16*, 495–512.

Latham, G. P., & Locke, E. A. (2007). New developments in and directions for goal-setting research. *European Psychologist, 12*, 290–300.

Lee, C. (1988). The relationship between goal setting, self-efficacy, and female field hockey team performance. *International Journal of Sport Psychology, 20*, 147–161.

Lerner, B., & Locke, E. A. (1995). The effects of goal setting, self-efficacy, competition and personal traits on the performance of an endurance task. *Journal of Sport and Exercise Psychology, 17*, 138–152.

Locke, E. A., & Latham, G. P. (1985). The application of goal setting to sports. *Journal of Sports Psychology, 7*, 205–222.

Locke, E. A., & Latham, G. P. (1990). *A theory of goal setting and task motivation*. Englewood Cliffs, NJ: Prentice Hall.

Locke, E. A., & Latham, G. P. (2002). Building a practically useful theory of goal setting and task motivation: A 35-year odyssey. *American Psychologist, 57*, 705–717.

Locke, E. A., Shaw, K. N., Saari, L. M., & Latham, G. P. (1981). Goal setting and task performance: 1969–1980. *Psychological Bulletin, 90*, 125–152.

Lonsdale, C., & Tam, J. T. M. (2008). On the temporal and behavioural consistency of pre-performance routines: An intra-individual analysis of elite basketball players' free throw shooting accuracy. *Journal of Sports Sciences, 26*, 259–266.

Mace, R. D., & Carroll, D. (1985). The control of anxiety in sport: Stress inoculation training prior to abseiling. *International Journal of Sport Psychology, 16*, 165–175.

Mace, R. D., & Carroll, D. (1989). The effect of stress inoculation training on self-reported stress, observer's rating of stress, heart rate and gymnastic performance. *Journal of Sports Sciences, 7*, 257–266.

Mace, R. D., Carroll, D., & Eastman, C. (1986). Effects of stress inoculation training on self-report, behavioural and psycho-physiological reactions to abseiling. *Journal of Sports Sciences, 4*, 229–236.

Mace, R. D., Eastman, C., & Carroll, D. (1987). The effects of stress inoculation training on gymnastics performance on the pommel horse: A case study. *Behavioural Psychotherapy, 15*, 272–279.

Maddux, J. E. (1993). Social cognitive models of health and exercise behaviour: An introduction and review of conceptual issues. *Journal of Applied Sport Psychology, 5*, 116–140.

Main, L., & Grove, J. R. (2009). A multi-component assessment model for monitoring training distress among athletes. *European Journal of Sport Science, 9*, 195–202.

Mallett, C. J., & Hanrahan, S. J. (1997). Race modelling: An effective cognitive strategy for the 100 m sprinter? *The Sport Psychologist, 11*, 72–85.

Mamassis, G., & Doganis, G. (2004). The effects of a mental training programme on juniors' pre-competitive anxiety, self-confidence, and tennis performance. *Journal of Applied Sport Psychology, 16*, 118–137.

Martin, G. L., Vause, T., & Schwartzman, L. (2005). Experimental studies of psychological interventions with athletes in competitions: Why so few? *Behaviour Modification, 29*, 616–641.

Martin, K. A., Moritz, S. E., & Hall, C. R. (1999). Imagery use in sport: A literature review and applied model. *The Sport Psychologist, 13*, 245–268.

Maynard, I. W., Smith, M. J., & Warwick-Evans, L. (1995). The effects of a cognitive intervention strategy on competitive state anxiety and performance in semi-professional soccer players. *Journal of Sport and Exercise Psychology, 17*, 428–446.

McGuigan, M., Ghiagiarelli, J., & Tod, D. (2005). Maximal strength and cortisol responses to psyching-up during the squat exercise. *Journal of Sports Sciences, 23*, 687–692.

Meichenbaum, D. (1975). A self-instructional approach to stress management: A proposal for stress inoculation training. In C. D. Spielberger, & I. G. Sarason (Eds.), *Stress and anxiety (Vol. 1*, pp. 65–78). Washington, DC: Hemisphere.

Meichenbaum, D. (1985). *Stress inoculation training.* New York: Pergamon.

Mellalieu, S. D., & Hanton, S. (Eds.). (2009). *Advances in applied sport psychology: A review.* London: Routledge.

Mellalieu, S. D., Hanton, S., & Fletcher, D. (2006). A competitive anxiety review: Recent directions in sport psychology. In S. Hanton, & S. D. Mellalieu (Eds.), *Literature reviews in sport psychology* (pp. 1–45). Hauppauge, NY: Nova Science.

Mellalieu, S. D., Hanton, S., & O'Brien, M. (2004). Intensity and direction dimensions of competitive anxiety as a function of sport type and experience. *Scandinavian Journal of Science and Medicine in Sport, 14*, 326–334.

Mellalieu, S. D., Hanton, S., & O'Brien, M. (2006). Effects of goal setting on rugby performance. *Journal of Applied Behaviour Analysis, 39*, 257–261.

Mellalieu, S. D., Hanton, S., & Shearer, D. A. (2008). Hearts in the fire, heads in the fridge: A qualitative investigation into the temporal patterning of precompetitive psychological response in elite performers. *Journal of Sports Sciences, 26*, 854–867.

Mellalieu, S. D., Hanton, S., & Thomas, O. (2008). The effects of a motivational general-arousal imagery intervention upon preperformance symptoms in male rugby union players. *Psychology of Sport and Exercise, 10*, 175–185.

Meyers, A. W., & Schleser, R. (1980). A cognitive behavioural intervention for improving basketball performance. *Journal of Sport Psychology, 2*, 69–73.

Meyers, A. W., Schleser, R., & Okwumabua, T. M. (1982). A cognitive behavioural intervention for improving basketball performance. *Research Quarterly for Exercise and Sport, 53*, 344–347.

Meyers, A. W., Whelan, J. P., & Murphy, S. M. (1996). Cognitive-behavioural strategies in athletic performance enhancement. In M. Hersen, R. M. Eider, & P. M. Miller (Eds.), *Progress in behaviour modification (Vol. 30*, pp. 137–164). Pacific Grove, CA: Brooks/Cole.

Munroe, K., Hall, C., Simms, S., & Weinberg, R. (1998). The influence of type of sport and time of season on athletes' use of imagery. *The Sport Psychologist, 12*, 440–449.

Munroe-Chandler, K. J., Hall, C. R., & Weinberg, R. S. (2004). A qualitative analysis of the types of goals athletes set in training and competition. *Journal of Sport Behaviour, 27*, 58–74.

Murphy, S. M., & Martin, K. A. (2002). The use of imagery in sport. In T. Horn (Ed.), *Advances in sport psychology* (2nd ed., pp. 405–439). Champaign, IL: Human Kinetics.

Murphy, S. M., Nordin, S. M., & Cumming, J. (2008). Imagery in sport, exercise and dance. In T. Horn (Ed.), *Advances in sport psychology* (3rd ed., pp. 297–324). Champaign, IL: Human Kinetics.

Murphy, S. M., Woolfolk, R. L., & Budney, A. J. (1988). The effects of emotive imagery on strength performance. *International Journal of Sport Psychology, 10*, 334–345.

Nieuwenhuys, A., Pijpers, J. R., Oudejans, R. R. D., & Bakker, F. C. (2008). The influence of anxiety on visual attention in climbing. *Journal of Sport and Exercise Psychology, 30*, 171–185.

Orlick, T., & Partington, J. (1988). Mental links to excellence. *The Sport Psychologist, 2*, 105–130.

Ost, L. G. (1988). Applied relaxation: Description of an effective coping technique. *Scandinavian Journal of Behaviour Therapy, 17*, 83–96.

Paivio, A. (1985). Cognitive and motivational functions of imagery in human performance. *Canadian Journal of Applied Sport Science, 10*, 22S–28S.

Palmer, C. L., Burwitz, L., Dyer, A. N., & Spray, C. M. (2005). Endurance training adherence in elite junior netball athletes: A test of the theory of planned behaviour and a revised theory of planned behaviour. *Journal of Sports Sciences, 23*, 277–288.

Palmer, C. L., Burwitz, L., Smith, N. C., & Borrie, A. (2000). Enhancing fitness training adherence of elite netball players: An evaluation of Maddux's revised theory of planned behaviour. *Journal of Sports Sciences, 18*, 627–641.

Palmer, C. L., Burwitz, L., Smith, N. C., & Collins, D. (1999). Adherence to fitness training of elite netball players: A naturalistic inquiry. *The Sport Psychologist, 13*, 313–334.

Palmer, C. L., Moore, P., & Heberle, C. (2004). Fitness training beliefs, intentions and adherence of elite women hockey athletes. *Journal of Sports Sciences, 22*, 311–312.

Parfitt, G., Jones, G., & Hardy, L. (1990). Multidimensional anxiety and performance. In G. Jones, & L. Hardy (Eds.), *Stress and performance in sport* (pp. 43–80). Chichester, UK: Wiley.

Patrick, T. D., & Hrycaiko, D. W. (1998). Effects of a mental training package on endurance performance. *Sport Psychologist, 12*, 283–299.

Pierce, E., McGowan, R. W., Eastman, N. W., Aaron, J. G., & Lynn, T. D. (1993). Effects of progressive relaxation on maximal muscle strength and power. *Journal of Strength and Conditioning Research, 7*, 216–218.

Pribram, K. H., & McGuiness, D. (1975). Arousal, activation and effort in the control of attention. *Psychological Review, 82*, 116–149.

Ranganathan, V. K., Siemionow, V., Liu, J. Z., Sahgal, V., & Yue, G. (2004). From mental power to muscular power: Gaining strength by using the mind. *Neuropsychologia, 42*, 944–956.

Richardson, A. (1969). *Mental imagery.* New York: Springer.

Rogerson, J. L., & Hrycaiko, W. D. (2002). Enhancing competitive performance of ice-hockey goaltenders using centering and self-talk. *Journal of Applied Sport Psychology, 14*, 14–26.

Schmidt, R. A. (1975). A schema theory of discrete motor skill learning. *Psychological Review, 82*, 225–260.

Schmidt, R. A., & Lee, T. D. (1999). *Motor control and learning: A behavioural emphasis.* Champaign, IL: Human Kinetics.

Shackell, E. M., & Standing, L. G. (2007). Mind over matter: Mental training increases physical strength. *North American Journal of Psychology, 9*, 189–200.

Shearer, D., Holmes, P., & Mellalieu, S. D. (2009). Collective efficacy in sport: The future from a social neuroscience perspective. *International Review of Sport and Exercise Psychology, 2*, 38–53.

Shearer, D. A., Mellalieu, S., Shearer, C., & Roderique-Davies, G. (2009). The effects of a video-aided imagery intervention upon collective efficacy in an international paralympic wheelchair basketball team. *Journal of Imagery Research in Sport and Physical Activity*, Vol. 4: Iss. 1, Article 1.

Shelton, T. O., & Mahoney, M. J. (1978). The content and effect of 'psyching-up' strategies in weight lifters. *Cognitive Therapy and Research, 2*, 275–284.

Short, S. E., & Ross-Stewart, L. (2009). A review of self-efficacy based interventions. In S. D. Mellalieu, & S. Hanton (Eds.), *Advances in applied sport psychology: A review* (pp. 221–280). Oxon, UK: Routledge.

Short, S. E., Ross-Stewart, L., & Monsma, E. V. (2006). Onwards with the evolution of imagery research in sport psychology. *Athletic Insight: The Online Journal of Sport Psychology, 8*(3). Retrieved from www.athleticinsight.com/Vol8Iss3/ImageryResearch.htm

Singer, R. N., Hausenblas, H. A., & Janelle, C. (Eds.). (2001). *Handbook of research on sport psychology.* New York: Wiley.

Smith, D., & Collins, D. (2004). Mental practice, motor performance, and the late CNV. *Journal of Sport and Exercise Psychology, 26*, 412–426.

Smith, D., Collins, D., & Holmes, P. (2003). Impact and mechanism of mental practice effects on strength. *International Journal of Sport and Exercise Psychology, 1*, 293–306.

Smith, D., & Holmes, P. (2004). The effect of imagery modality on golf putting performance. *Journal of Sport and Exercise Psychology, 26*, 385–395.

Smith, D., Wright, C., Allsopp, A., & Westhead, H. (2007). It's all in the mind: PETTLEP-based imagery and sports performance. *Journal of Applied Sport Psychology, 19*, 80–92.

Smith, R. E. (1980). Development of an integrated coping response through cognitive affective stress management training. In I. G. Sarason, and C. D. Spielberger (Eds.), *Stress and anxiety* (*Vol.* 7, pp. 265–280). Washington, DC: Hemisphere.

Smith, R. E. (1989). Applied sport psychology in an age of accountability. *Journal of Applied Sport Psychology, 1,* 166–180.

Smith, R. E., & Smoll, F. L. (1978). Psychological intervention and sports medicine: Stress management training and coach effectiveness training. *University of Washington Medicine, 5,* 20–24.

Tenenbaum, G., Pinchas, S., Elbaz, G., Bar-Eli, M., & Weinberg, R. (1991). Effect of goal proximity and goal specificity on muscular endurance performance: A replication and extension. *Journal of Sport and Exercise Psychology, 13,* 160–173.

Thelwell, R. C., & Greenlees, I. A. (2001). The effects of a mental skills training package on gymnasium triathlon performance. *The Sport Psychologist, 15,* 127–141.

Thelwell, R. C., & Greenlees, I. A. (2003). Developing competitive endurance performance using mental skills training. *The Sport Psychologist, 17,* 318–337.

Thelwell, R. C., Greenlees, I. A., & Weston, N. J. V. (2006). Using psychological skills training to develop soccer performance. *Journal of Applied Sport Psychology, 18,* 254–270.

Theodorakis, Y., Weinberg, R. S., Natsis, P., Douma, I., & Kazakas, P. (2000). The effects of motivational versus instructional self-talk on improving motor performance. *The Sport Psychologist, 14,* 253–272.

Thomas, O., Maynard, I., & Hanton, S. (2007). Intervening with athletes during the time leading up to competition: Theory to practice II. *Journal of Applied Sport Psychology, 19,* 398–418.

Thomas, O., Mellalieu, S. D., & Hanton, S. (2009). Stress management in sport: A critical review and synthesis. In S. D. Mellalieu & S. Hanton (Eds.), *Advances in applied sport psychology: A review* (pp. 124, 161). London: Routledge.

Tod, D., Iredale, F., & Gill, N. (2003). 'Psyching-up' and muscular force production. *Sports Medicine, 33,* 47–58.

Tod, D., Iredale, F., McGuigan, M., Strange, D., & Gill, N. (2005). 'Psyching-up' enhances force production during the bench press exercise. *Journal of Strength and Conditioning Research, 19,* 599–603.

Tod, D., & Lavallee, D. (in press). *Psychology of strength and conditioning.* Champaign, IL: Human Kinetics.

Tod, D., & McGuigan, M. (2006). The efficacy of psyching-up on strength performance. In T. B. Selkirk (Ed.), *Focus on exercise and health research* (pp. 163–179). Hauppauge, NY: Nova Science.

Tod, D., Thatcher, R., McGuigan, M., & Thatcher, J. (2009). Effects of instructional and motivational self-talk on the vertical jump. *Journal of Strength and Conditioning Research, 23,* 196–202.

Tynes, L. L., & McFatter, R. M. (1987). The efficacy of 'psyching' strategies on a weight-lifting task. *Cognitive Therapy and Research, 11,* 327–336.

Vealey, R. S. (1988). Future directions in psychological skills training. *The Sport Psychologist, 2,* 318–337.

Vealey, R. S. (1994). Current status and prominent issues in sport psychology interventions. *Medicine and Science in Sports and Exercise, 26,* 495–502.

Vergeer, I., & Roberts, J. (2006). Movement and stretching imagery during flexibility training. *Journal of Sports Sciences, 24,* 197–208.

Wanlin, C., Hrycaiko, D. W., Martin, G. L., & Mahon, M. (1997). The effects of a goal setting package on the performance of speed skaters. *Journal of Applied Sport Psychology, 9,* 212–228.

Weinberg, R. S. (1994). Goal setting and performance in sport and exercise settings: A synthesis and critique. *Medicine and Science in Sports and Exercise, 26,* 469–477.

Weinberg, R. S., Bruya, L. D., Longino, J., & Jackson, A. (1988). Effect of goal proximity and specificity on endurance performance of primary-grade children. *Journal of Sport and Exercise Psychology, 10,* 81–91.

Weinberg, R. S., Burton, D., Yukelson, D., & Weigand, D. A. (2000). Perceived goal setting practices of Olympic athletes: An exploratory investigation. *The Sport Psychologist, 14,* 279–295.

Weinberg, R. S., & Butt, J. (2005). Goal setting in sport and exercise domains: The theory and practice of effective goal setting. In D. Hackfort, J. Duda, & R. Lidor (Eds.), *Handbook of research in applied sport and exercise psychology: International perspectives* (pp. 129–144). Morgantown, WV: Fitness Information Technology.

Weinberg, R. S., Butt, J., Knight, B., & Perritt, N. (2001). Collegiate perceptions of their goal setting practices: A qualitative investigation. *Journal of Applied Sport Psychology, 13,* 374–398.

Weinberg, R. S., & Comar, W. (1994). The effectiveness of psychological interventions in competitive sports. *Sports Medicine, 18,* 406–418.

Weinberg, R. S., Gould, D., & Jackson, A. (1980). Cognition and motor performance: Effect of psyching-up strategies on three motor tasks. *Cognitive Therapy and Research, 4,* 239–245.

Weinberg, R. S., Gould, D., Yukelson, D., & Jackson, A. (1981). The effect of pre-existing and manipulated self-efficacy on competitive muscular endurance task. *Journal of Sport Psychology, 4,* 345–354.

Weinberg, R. S., Jackson, A., & Seaborne, T. (1985). The effects of specific vs. nonspecific mental preparation strategies on strength and endurance performance. *Journal of Sport Behaviour, 8,* 175–180.

Weinberg, R. S., Smith, J., Jackson, A., & Gould, D. (1984). Effect of association, dissociation and positive self-talk strategies on endurance performance. *Canadian Journal of Applied Sport Sciences, 12,* 25–32.

Weinberg, R. S., & Williams, J. M. (2010). Integrating and implementing a psychological skills training program. In J. M. Williams (Ed.), *Applied sport psychology: Personal growth to peak performance* (6th ed., pp. 361–391). Boston: McGraw-Hill.

Whelan, J. P., Epkins, C. C., & Meyers, A. W. (1990). Arousal interventions for athletic performance: Influence of mental preparation and competitive experience. *Anxiety Research, 2,* 293–307.

Woodman, T., & Hardy, L. (2001). Stress and anxiety. In R. Singer, H. A. Hausenblas, & C. M. Janelle (Eds.), *Handbook of research on sport psychology* (pp. 290–318). New York: Wiley.

Wulf, G., & Prinz, W. (2001). Directing attention to movement effects enhances learning: A review. *Psychonomic Bulletin and Review, 8,* 648–660.

Wylleman, P., Harwood, C., Elbe, A. M., Reints, A., & de Caluwé, D. (2009). A perspective on education and professional development in applied sport psychology. *Psychology of Sport and Exercise, 10,* 435–446.

Yue, G., & Cole, K. J. (1992). Strength increases from the motor program: Comparison of training with maximal voluntary and imagined muscle contractions. *Journal of Neurophysiology, 67,* 1114–1123.

Ziegler, S. G., Klinzing, J., & Williamson, K. (1982). The effects of two stress management training programmes on cardio respiratory efficiency. *Journal of Sport Psychology, 4,* 280–289.

2

SOCIAL PSYCHOLOGICAL THEORIES AND MODELS

Sarah McLachlan, Derwin King-Chung Chan*,
Dave Keatley* and Martin Hagger***

*UNIVERSITY OF NOTTINGHAM, UK
**CURTIN UNIVERSITY, WESTERN AUSTRALIA

Social psychological theories and models are often adopted to identify and understand the factors that influence behaviour and behaviour change. Such theories and models are therefore of great potential use in understanding and increasing athletes' participation in strength and conditioning training. These theories and models provide a framework for predicting behaviour, describing the mechanisms underlying behaviour and identifying the causal determinants of behaviour as targets for intervention (Michie, Johnston, Francis, Hardeman, & Eccles, 2008). Within the field of sport and exercise, social cognitive theory (SCT; Bandura, 1977), the theory of planned behaviour (TPB; Ajzen, 1991) and self-determination theory (SDT; Deci & Ryan, 1985, 2000) have been identified as particularly useful in predicting behaviour. For example, the TPB has been applied directly to understanding strength and conditioning training behaviour (e.g. Mummery & Wankel, 1999). These theories have also been effective in informing behaviour change interventions in the sport and exercise domain (Chatzisarantis & Hagger, 2009; Hardeman et al., 2002) and could be applied to inform the development of interventions in strength and conditioning training with the aim of increasing athletes' participation in training regimens outside regular practice. The theories can be used to explain and modify important behaviours, such as sprint drills and weight training, as well as promoting other important adaptive outcomes such as athletes' psychological well-being. This chapter will provide an overview of each of the theories, empirical evidence of their effectiveness in understanding and changing behaviour, with examples from strength and conditioning training where literature is available, details of their augmentation and integration, and research directions for their further application to strength and conditioning training.

Self-determination theory

SDT (Deci & Ryan, 1985, 2000) is a theory of human motivation that can be applied to strength and conditioning training to understand factors determining an athletes' behavioural persistence or desistence in training. Within SDT, humans are viewed as innately predisposed towards psychological growth, mastery of challenges and the integration of intrapersonal and interpersonal experiences into a coherent sense of self (Deci & Ryan, 2000). SDT proposes that interactions between individuals and their environment determine the quality of their motivation, through the satisfaction of three fundamental needs for autonomy, competence and relatedness. The satisfaction of these needs is hypothesised to determine not only the quality of an individual's motivation, but also their behavioural performance, persistence and psychological well-being.

Autonomy refers to the need to experience oneself as the initiator and regulator of behaviour, competence shares some similarities with self-efficacy and describes the need to function as an effective agent in one's environment, and relatedness delineates the need for a sense of belonging among other individuals and more broadly within the community (Ryan & Deci, 2002). The theory also makes a broad distinction between intrinsic and extrinsic motivation. Intrinsic motivation is characterised by behavioural engagement for reasons of personal interest, satisfaction and enjoyment, while extrinsic motivation is defined as participation in behaviour to meet external contingencies, for example deadlines and tangible rewards. With regard to strength and conditioning training, intrinsically motivated behaviour would be evident if an athlete participated in weight training for the sheer enjoyment and satisfaction gained, while extrinsically motivated behaviour would be characterised by engaging in weight training to avoid being reprimanded by a coach or solely for obtaining a tangible reward like a trophy or money.[1] Intrinsic motivation has consistently been associated with a number of desirable outcomes, including behavioural persistence (e.g. Pelletier, Fortier, Vallerand, & Briere, 2001), performance (e.g. Black & Deci, 2000), positive affect (Standage, Duda, & Ntoumanis, 2005) and effort (e.g. Ferrer-Caja & Weiss, 2000) across a variety of domains, including sport and exercise.

In addition to making a broad distinction between intrinsic and extrinsic motivation, organismic integration theory (OIT; Deci & Ryan, 1985), a sub-theory of SDT, presents a continuum of qualitatively different forms of behavioural regulation situated between these two polar extremes (see Figure 2.1). Three types of extrinsic motivation are located on the continuum at intermediate points between intrinsic motivation and external regulation (the prototypical form of extrinsic motivation) and vary in the degree to which the motivation has been internalised by the individual such that it becomes consistent with their values, beliefs and aspirations (Deci & Ryan, 2000).

Integrated regulation is situated adjacent to intrinsic motivation and represents the most fully internalised form of external regulation, in which a behaviour has been fully assimilated with the self and comes to emanate from the individual. In strength and conditioning training, this may involve moving from a state in which endurance training is driven by external contingencies, such as rewards from the coach, to fully endorsing the behaviour and feeling that it has become an integral part of one's identity. Identified regulation falls next to integrated regulation and

Intrinsic motivation	Integrated regulation	Identified regulation	Introjected regulation	External regulation	Amotivation
Behaviour originates with and emanates entirely from the self.	Regulation for behaviour has been fully assimilated and is consistent with one's values, beliefs and aspirations.	Behavioural engagement for valued outcomes associated with behaviour. Partial internalisation of regulation and some endorsement from the self.	Behavioural engagement to avoid shame and guilt or to gain conditional self-worth.	Behaviour driven entirely by external contingencies, for example tangible rewards and externally imposed deadlines. No sense of ownership over the behaviour.	The absence of intention or clear motives to engage in the behaviour.

FIGURE 2.1 The SDT continuum of behavioural regulation, based on Deci and Ryan (2000)

describes behavioural participation arising from recognition of valued outcomes of the behaviour. This regulatory style is characterised by accepting actions and behaviours such that they are partially endorsed by the self. For example, badminton players motivated by identified reasons are likely to attend their conditioning (sprint drills, plyometric drills, weight training) sessions outside of normal practice, not because they necessarily enjoy or have intrinsic interest in the kinds of exercises and activities that they do in those sessions (particularly if they are repetitive and boring), but because they value the strength and power it gives them when it comes to their badminton practice and competition. Such outcomes are important to them and they will derive a sense of satisfaction from achieving them. Although they are not motivated to perform the behaviour itself, they are motivated to engage in the behaviour because it services a value or need that they feel is personally important.

Introjected regulation describes a form of behavioural regulation that is less autonomous or self-determined than identified regulation. Introjected regulation is situated between identified and external regulations on the continuum, and represents behavioural engagement to avoid aversive outcomes such as shame and guilt, or to obtain conditional self-worth. A rugby player whose conditioning is regulated by introjected regulation will experience self-imposed pressure relating to the maintenance of sprint drills, plyometric drills and weight training, and continue only to avoid threats to self-worth rather than through enjoyment, interest or truly valuing the increase in strength and power that are likely to result. Although this form of regulation has been partially internalised, behaviour arises from a sense of internal pressure and the regulation is not consistent with the integrated set of beliefs, desires and aspirations that form the coherent self-concept. External regulation represents behavioural engagement for entirely external contingencies. Engaging in additional endurance training for rugby solely to increase one's chances of winning a prestigious award in a subsequent competition is an example of an externally regulated reason or motive for acting. Finally, OIT also defines amotivation as a state in which individuals lack any intention to engage in a particular behaviour. Amotivation would be evident if a basketball player, for instance, had no plans to engage in strength training outside regular practice.

Participating in activities for integrated reasons is more likely to lead to sustained participation over time than activities arising from less autonomous forms of regulation, as they are more consistent with the self and are therefore accompanied by a greater sense of commitment and ownership (Deci & Ryan, 2000). Deci and Ryan (2000) proposed that the transformation of external regulation into personally endorsed and valued autonomous forms of regulation is part of an individual's normal development pattern. For the integration of external forms of behavioural regulation and the development of autonomous motivation to take place, it is essential that the social environment provides support for the three psychological needs. Support for autonomy has been defined as the provision of choice, a meaningful rationale and the acknowledgement of an individual's perspectives and feelings, while minimising the use of pressuring interpersonal communication styles (Chatzisarantis, Hagger, & Smith, 2007; Deci, Eghrari, Patrick, & Leone, 1994). In a strength and conditioning training context, this may involve providing choice regarding training exercises, acknowledging that the athlete may find particular aspects of the training difficult and avoiding the use of controlling language (e.g. avoiding 'commanding' or 'autocratic' terms like 'you must …' and 'you should …'). Importantly, the provision of autonomy support for athletes' strength and conditioning training will promote athletes' persistence outside regular practice and in the absence of coaches' or trainers' instructions or other external contingencies. Competence support refers to the presence of clear structure and facilitation to experience oneself as an effective agent in one's environment. In this respect, support for competence serves a similar purpose as support for self-efficacy. Within strength and conditioning training, coaches can help to foster a sense of competence in their athletes by assisting in the setting of appropriate goals for training and providing positive feedback that signifies athletes' progress towards personally endorsed goals. Support for relatedness is fostered through interaction with others in the social environment and the development of rewarding interpersonal relationships, for instance through active encouragement to work with others (Standage et al., 2005). Athletes' sense of relatedness can be enhanced through the use of training partners or mentors and through the provision of a supportive and nurturing environment for training.

Empirical evidence has attested to the role of these contextual supports in satisfying the three basic needs, and consequently yielding a range of adaptive outcomes, including engagement and well-being (e.g. Deci et al., 2001; Edmunds, Ntoumanis, & Duda, 2006; Gagne, Ryan, & Bargmann, 2003). The satisfaction of the needs for autonomy and competence has been shown to be critical in the development of intrinsic motivation, while fostering the satisfaction of all three needs has been linked with identified regulation (Markland & Tobin, 2010). These authors reported that autonomy occupies a unique position among the three needs in that its satisfaction is essential in the reduction of amotivation and the facilitation of self-determined forms of motivation. This is consistent with Deci and Ryan's (2000) contention that, although support for competence and relatedness may aid the integration process, it is essential that the individual experiences freedom to endorse and process values and regulations. Further, the process of internalisation can be halted by the mere absence of autonomy support, without the direct undermining of autonomy. The importance of autonomy support in fostering adaptive forms of motivation and well-being has also shown universality across cultures (e.g. Chirkov & Ryan, 2001).

Applying SDT to strength and conditioning

SDT has not yet been explicitly applied to explain motivation and behaviour in strength and conditioning training contexts. This is an important route to pursue, given the immense scope for the development of SDT-based interventions to promote self-determined motivation. The process of integration is particularly pertinent to strength and conditioning training, given the necessity of persistence for goal attainment. The transformation of behavioural regulation for training routines, for instance exercises in lifting, speed, agility and core stability, from externally regulated to autonomous, is important in ensuring effort, performance, behavioural persistence and the prevention of injury. Autonomous regulation is also likely to facilitate psychological well-being and prevent exhaustion and burnout (Gagne et al., 2003; Lonsdale, Hodge, & Rose, 2009).

SDT has, however, been applied widely in the sport and exercise domain and has been demonstrated to be important in the understanding of behaviour and in developing means to change behaviour (Chatzisarantis & Hagger, 2009; Chatzisarantis, Hagger, Biddle, Smith, & Wang, 2003; Ntoumanis, 2001). Although sport and exercise is distinct from strength and conditioning training, a framework could be usefully extrapolated for application to strength and conditioning behaviour. Consistent with findings in other domains, autonomous motivation in sport and exercise has been associated with greater participation in exercise, superior performance, increased effort and well-being (Edmunds et al., 2006; Gagne et al., 2003; Pelletier et al., 2001; Thøgersen-Ntoumani & Ntoumanis, 2006). Support for the continuum of behavioural regulation has also been established, for instance Lonsdale et al. (2009) showed that relationships between forms of behavioural regulation and athlete burnout varied systematically according to the type of behavioural regulation endorsed by the athlete, with athletes endorsing more self-determined forms of behavioural regulation less likely to experience burnout. Behaviour change interventions for exercise and health grounded in SDT have been successful in facilitating the integration process and associated adaptive outcomes (Chatzisarantis & Hagger, 2009; Fortier, Sweet, O'Sullivan, & Williams,

2007), and their application to strength and conditioning could be as effective. Combined interventions including autonomy support alongside other manipulations have also achieved success in increasing persistence and enhancing performance in sport and exercise. For example, Vansteenkiste, Simons, Lens, Sheldon, and Deci (2004) showed that framing an exercise-learning task in terms of intrinsic goals and providing autonomy support for this activity acted synergistically to improve processing, performance and persistence. Fortier et al. (2007) developed an exercise behaviour change intervention based on SDT, incorporating intensive support for both autonomy and competence (Williams et al., 2006). In comparison to a brief autonomy-supportive intervention condition, the intensive intervention resulted in greater perceived autonomy support, increased autonomous motivation through integration and higher physical activity levels at follow-up.

Particularly pertinent to strength and conditioning training is the association of integration with the state of flow that has been determined in a physical activity context (McLachlan & Hagger, in press). Flow describes a subjective state of optimal functioning, in which an athlete becomes totally immersed in, and 'at one with', their activity (Csikszentmihalyi, 1975, 1990), and has been strongly linked with autonomous motivation (Kowal & Fortier, 2000). In addition to the association between flow and optimal athletic performance (Jackson, Thomas, Marsh, & Smethurst, 2001), evidence has also suggested that cumulative experiences of flow may lead to the development of autonomous forms of motivation (Csikszentmihalyi, Rathunde, & Whalen, 1993). The facilitation of integration in a strength and conditioning context would therefore be beneficial not only in terms of increasing autonomous motivation and the endurance required in strength and conditioning programmes, but also in promoting flow, which is conducive to optimal performance. Achieving a state of flow in strength and conditioning would be characterised by total immersion in one's training regimen and reaching one's full potential in activities such as weight training, sprint drills and endurance running.

The process model postulated in SDT, referring to the proposed sequence between autonomy support, need satisfaction, behavioural regulation and behavioural outcomes (Williams et al., 2006), has been supported by empirical research in sport and exercise. An illustration of the SDT process model applied to strength and conditioning training is given in Figure 2.2. In keeping with the recent emphasis on the importance of identifying mechanisms and processes underlying behaviour change (e.g. Michie & Abraham, 2004), much research applying SDT to sport and exercise has focused on determining mediating variables through which contextual supports incur effects on motivation and behaviour. Contextual support for the three fundamental needs, for instance through the provision of opportunities for (a) choice, (b) a meaningful rationale, (c) structure and (d) facilitating the development of rewarding interpersonal relationships, has been associated with perceptions of autonomy, competence and relatedness (Gagne et al., 2003; Hollombeak & Amorose, 2005; Standage et al., 2005). Further, this need satisfaction has mediated the effect of need support on autonomous motivation (e.g. Amorose & Anderson-Butcher, 2007; Edmunds et al., 2006). This means that need support enhances

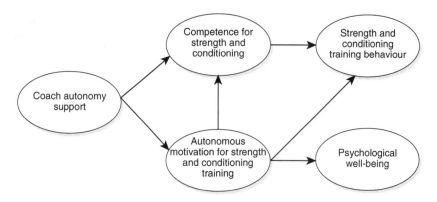

FIGURE 2.2 A modified SDT process model of health-related behaviour (Williams et al., 2006) applied to strength and conditioning training

autonomous motivation through the satisfaction of the three fundamental needs. Autonomous motivation has, in turn, predicted adaptive outcomes such as engagement in leisure-time exercise, exercise following cardiac rehabilitation and concentration and preference for challenge in physical education (PE; Chatzisarantis & Hagger, 2009; Edmunds et al., 2006; Russell & Bray, 2009; Standage et al., 2005). Need satisfaction has also been associated with indices of physical and psychological well-being, both directly (Reinboth, Duda, & Ntoumanis, 2004) and indirectly through autonomous motivation (Lonsdale et al., 2009).

Further research directions for the application of SDT to behaviour change in strength and conditioning training

Head and assistant coaches and trainers are advised to foster the process of integration in athletes when it comes to strength and conditioning training through the provision of basic need support, following the techniques developed in the sport and exercise domains (e.g. Chatzisarantis & Hagger, 2009; Fortier et al., 2007). This is important because fostering autonomous forms of motivation, integration and need satisfaction with respect to strength and conditioning training will lead to athletes being more likely to adhere to their programmes in the absence of any external contingency or influence from the coach. This is essential with respect to strength and conditioning training which, more often than not, is likely to be conducted by the athletes in their own time outside 'regular training'. In the absence of the coach and influence of teammates, the temptation to shirk this kind of training may be elevated unless the coach can foster autonomous reasons for engaging in the behaviour. Priority should be given to the implementation of autonomy support (Markland & Tobin, 2010), through the provision of choice regarding training schedules, a meaningful rationale for behavioural engagement and acknowledgement of the athlete's perspective and feelings. This will help to promote athletes' engagement in strength and conditioning

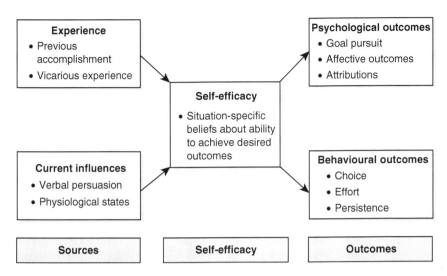

FIGURE 2.3 The relationships between sources of information, self-efficacy and outcomes in Bandura's (1977) SCT

be difficult for you' and 'You have clearly progressed towards your personal goals', foster better performance, increased enjoyment and persistence, while controlling statements, for instance 'You *must* improve your performance before the next training session', are likely to impede behavioural performance, persistence and enjoyment through the reduction of autonomous motivation (see above). Physiological states (e.g. autonomic arousal, anxiety, stress or self-confidence etc.) also affect a person's belief in their ability to successfully perform particular behaviours (Bandura, 1997). For example, a stressed or anxious individual will underperform (achieve fewer repetitions) or fail (drop the weights). These factors form sources of information in SCT.

Self-efficacy has a profound influence on self-regulation, which is the initiation and maintenance of self-control that is integrated and internalised by the individual (see Moller, Deci, & Ryan, 2006). Self-efficacy also affects perceived motivation, intentions to perform or continue a behaviour, affect (e.g. satisfaction) and performance (Biddle, Hanrahan, & Sellars, 2001). Individuals with high self-efficacy are more likely to persevere in the face of difficulty or failure, invest more time and commitment into the task and be more interested in the task and more willing to spend time solving problems (Bandura, 2001; Moores & Chang, 2009). Therefore, an individual with high self-efficacy will continue training, even when outcomes fall short of expectations or desires, attend training sessions regularly, be more focused on achieving good form and be willing to practise to attain better technique to avoid injury and get the most out of their training.

Finally, outcomes are proposed to affect behaviour in SCT. Outcomes may be divided into *psychological outcomes* and *behavioural outcomes*. Psychological outcomes are related to *goal pursuit* (e.g. the extent to which an individual strives to attain a particular goal, such as better technique, more repetitions), *affective outcomes* (e.g. emotional outcomes caused by performance of behaviour) and *attributions*. Attributions relate to whether a training task is seen as within the individuals' control, is affected by external (e.g. task difficulty or luck) or internal factors (e.g. ability or effort) or whether performance at the training task can be changed (see Weiner, Heckhausen, Meyer, & Cook, 1972). Behavioural outcomes can be split into *choice, effort* and *persistence*. Choice relates to an individual's decision to approach or avoid a behaviour, and supporting choice is therefore an important behaviour for coaches to adopt. Some individuals may feel apprehensive or averse to undertake a new regimen, so supporting the individual through this stage and helping them overcome these initial reactions is necessary and conducive to their overall performance (see also above). Effort relates to how much energy and focus a person puts into a task; quite simply, how much they are willing to invest (e.g. time, money, endurance) to attain a better technique, faster times or stronger muscles. Persistence indicates how long individuals continue the behaviour, for example whether they maintain training in their own time, over an extended period of time. All of these outcomes are important in maintaining individuals' overall performance and persistence and therefore need to be taken into account in training regimens to enhance strength and conditioning performance.

Applying SCT to strength and conditioning

As noted, a number of different experiential and current influences can affect an individual's self-efficacy, meaning self-efficacy can be modified or manipulated. Successful previous experience and mastery of behaviour are viewed as the most important factors influencing self-efficacy (Bandura, 1977). Therefore, highlighting previous accomplishments may serve to increase self-confidence and belief in current success (Feltz & Chase, 1998). If an athlete is reminded of previous accomplishments in terms of their strength and conditioning training regimen, this may prime self-competence in the current setting and increase chances of successful performance when carrying out future exercises in training. Vicarious encounters are an additional influence on current beliefs of ability. SCT assumes that the observation of a behaviour being performed reinforces correct execution of behaviour (Anderson, 2000; Hagen et al., 1998). For instance, watching a training partner successfully perform a weightlifting exercise is conducive to better lifts by the observer. An important extension to this has been the effect of mental imagery. Gould, Petlichkoff, Hodge, and Simons (1990) found that athletes rated imagery as an effective strategy for increasing self-efficacy. In addition, Feltz and Chase (1998) have shown that imagery positively affected performance on a laboratory muscular endurance task. Therefore, if training partners are not available, mental imagery may serve as an effective alternative. Interventions aiming to increase strength and conditioning could augment training by incorporating mental imagery into the regimen.

Social agents (e.g. coaches, trainers, training partners) have an important role in providing support to facilitate successful performances (Jackson & Beauchamp,

2010; Lent & Lopez, 2002). Social agents are therefore well positioned to promote athletes' self-efficacy through motivational encouragement or 'pep talks'. Effective verbal persuasion should incorporate references to other sources of information highlighted in SCT, for example previous performances, vicarious experiences and allusion to imagery of successfully conducting the behaviour, in addition to drawing on other theories such as SDT (see above).

Many of the effects of strength and conditioning training are not readily noticeable or obvious, particularly in the short term, such as stronger bones, improved body composition, muscle size increase and reduced risk of degenerative diseases (Chambliss & Murray, 1979; De Backer et al., 2008; Ott et al., 2004; Shirazi et al., 2007; Taaffe & Galvao, 2003). Bandura (1977, 1997) outlined the influence of outcome beliefs on behavioural responses, such that high levels of self-efficacy towards engaging in a particular behaviour to produce a desirable outcome will predict behaviour when the person also believes that performance of the behaviour will result in the desired outcome. To clarify this with an example, a person may have a high level of self-confidence to perform dumbbell curls to gain increased muscle mass. However, performance will be further improved if the individual also believes that performing the curls will actually result in increased muscle mass. Making noticeable changes to muscle mass takes a number of weeks; therefore the individual may begin to question whether the behaviour (e.g. dumbbell curls) is effectively producing the desired outcome (e.g. increased strength and size of biceps). It is at this stage that the athlete may be likely to desist from training. Coaches and trainers should, therefore, be aware of individuals' conflicting beliefs (Jackson & Beauchamp, 2010; Poag-DuCharme & Brawley, 1993) and offer support and encouragement to maintain commitment to performing a particular behaviour.

Furthermore, consideration of self-efficacy is important when athletes have taken a break from training or their sport, or are starting a new training regimen. During the first week of return from a period away from training, microtrauma (muscle tearing) and fatigue may occur, which are experiential and physiological sources of influence on self-efficacy that could diminish self-efficacy, leading to decreased performance and commitment. Coaches and trainers providing supportive encouragement, conducive to promoting self-efficacy, will be vital during this period.

Further research directions for the application of SCT to behaviour change in strength and conditioning training

SCT, and especially self-efficacy, has been adopted in a large body of research (e.g. Anderson, 2000; Feltz & Chase, 1998; Moores & Chang, 2009). The diversity of contexts and behaviours to which self-efficacy has been applied indicates its robust effects and influences on performance. The aim of this section has been to demonstrate that self-efficacy plays an important role in strength and conditioning performance. However, to date, there is a relative dearth of research in this area. Given the application of self-efficacy to other, related contexts (e.g. sports and exercise) as well as other fields (e.g. teaching), it seems likely that similar patterns will emerge when self-efficacy is applied to strength and conditioning contexts. Preliminary evidence suggests that self-efficacy is associated with baseline strength performance and can be manipulated, for instance through performance feedback and expressions of confidence in the individual's ability, to enhance future performance (Wells, Collins, & Hale, 1993; Wise, Posner, & Walker, 2004). Research has also indicated that expectations arising from environmental cues may have a pervasive effect on strength performance, perhaps through the desire to maintain self-efficacy (e.g. Ness & Patton, 1979). However, research still needs to be conducted to fully investigate the role of self-efficacy in strength and conditioning training. An effective means of conducting this research would be to first examine the performance (e.g. in terms of improvements in technique, endurance or strength) of athletes engaged in strength and conditioning training high or low in self-efficacy. Based on previous research, it is expected that those with higher self-efficacy will persist with training for longer and with better form. Individuals high in self-efficacy are more likely to complete more good quality (i.e. good form and speed) repetitions at higher weight intervals, than those lower in self-efficacy. Interventions should be adopted to facilitate those individuals with low self-efficacy. As coach–athlete interactions have been shown to facilitate or impede performance (Jackson & Beauchamp, 2010), this is an important recommendation for practice to improve athletes' performance. However, augmenting this with the other sources of influence on self-efficacy outlined in SCT should also be considered. Research should also investigate the relative effect of each of these sources in strength and conditioning training. Based on previous research (e.g. Anderson, 2000; Hagen et al., 1998), vicarious experience is assumed to provide a large influence on a number of sport performances (e.g. running, swimming, weightlifting). It would, however, be unwise to make this the sole focus of interventions and interventions should employ multiple techniques.

A comprehensive review, or meta-analysis, of self-efficacy is also needed to synthesise research on the effect of self-efficacy and its relevant antecedent factors on salient sport and exercise behaviours, including strength and conditioning training. This would provide insight into the sizes and robustness of the effect of self-efficacy on salient behavioural outcomes across a variety of related behaviours. Feltz and Chase (1998) provide a narrative review of 11 studies and found that 25 out of 29 tests conducted showed a significant explicit relationship between individuals' self-efficacy and sport performance. Therefore, while there appears to be a clear trend in the literature indicating the importance of self-efficacy to physical activity performance, a meta-analysis would provide more robust support for this.

Section summary: SCT and self-efficacy

- SCT identifies a number of experiential and situational influences on athletes' self-efficacy when performing various physical activities, exercise or sport.

- Self-efficacy describes athletes' feelings of competence and beliefs about their ability to perform an exercise in order to reach a desired outcome (e.g. faster sprint times, greater endurance, more repetitions and lifting heavier weights).
- Future research should investigate the role of self-efficacy in strength and conditioning training.
- Social agents (e.g. coaches, trainers) should adopt approaches that support individuals' self-efficacy and provide opportunity to promote self-efficacy for those with low levels of this construct.
- Integration of self-efficacy with other motivational constructs may provide more effective interventions for strength and conditioning training.

The theory of planned behaviour

The TPB (Ajzen, 1991), and its predecessor the theory of reasoned action (TRA; Ajzen, 1985), are prominent and well-researched theories in psychology for predicting human behaviours, particularly in the areas of health, exercise and sport (Armitage, 2005; Armitage & Conner, 2001; Hagger, Chatzisarantis, & Biddle, 2002). In a similar vein to SCT (Bandura, 1977), the TPB and TRA posit that behaviours are shaped by individuals' subjective experience (i.e. attitude) and normative influences (i.e. subjective norm). However, according to Ajzen (1985, 1991), the execution of behaviour is preceded by the formation of behavioural intentions.

Intention is an indicator of the willingness, effort and motivation people plan to exert towards a given target behaviour in the foreseeable future. It is regarded as the most proximal predictor of behaviour. In strength and conditioning settings, intentions may therefore serve as one of the most important indicators of one's orientation and level of motivation regarding future exercise training participation.

Ajzen (1985) initially proposed that intentions were a function of two psychological variables within the TRA: attitude and subjective norm. *Attitude* is a representation of one's beliefs regarding the propensity for a behaviour to lead to specific outcomes and an evaluation of whether those outcomes are desirable. Overall, attitude summarises how favourable or unfavourable the beliefs or attributes associated with the behaviour with respect to their corresponding importance (i.e. strength of the belief salience) are to an individual based on their judgement on several attribute dimensions (Ajzen, 1991, 2001). For instance, individuals who think that fitness training may lead to favourable consequences such as improvements in health, body shape and sport performance, in comparison to those who feel that it may result in unfavourable consequences such as wasting money and time, and fatigue, hold a much more positive attitude towards strength and conditioning exercises. *Subjective norm* refers to the social pressure or influence that individuals perceive from their significant others with respect to engaging in the behaviour. In particular, individuals evaluate the strength of subjective norm on the basis of both the normative beliefs (i.e. the appropriateness or acceptability of the behaviour under their perceived social environment) as well as their motivation to comply with the beliefs (Ajzen, 1991; Ajzen & Madden, 1986). For example, bodybuilding might give some people an impression of masculinity, so the subjective norm of female bodybuilders may reflect this perception.

However, having realised that the linkage between intention and behaviour is contingent on individuals' perceived control and volition over the behaviour, Ajzen (1991) revised the TRA by adding a further antecedent variable in the theory, perceived behavioural control (PBC), and renamed the modified theory the TPB. Ajzen (1991) proposed that PBC was conceptually similar to self-efficacy from SCT (see above), as it was also influenced by experience, skill level and perceived ability regarding individuals' past behaviours. In contrast, some researchers have argued that PBC represents perceived control over external barriers, while self-efficacy focuses more on the perception of personal ability, performance or capacity (Armitage & Conner, 1999; Terry & Oleary, 1995). These arguments reflect the definition of PBC provided by Ajzen (1991), that the product of both perceived control (i.e. resources, opportunity and difficulty of the behaviour) and perceived power (i.e. ability) determine the magnitude of PBC regarding the action. In other words, one's PBC regarding a conditioning exercise is not only influenced by factors associated with perceived power (e.g. past experience and level of mastery), but may also be based on factors associated with perception of control (e.g. external barriers and support). PBC is an important predictor of behaviour as not only does it exert influence on the behaviour directly, but also indirectly through its impact on intention (see Figure 2.4).

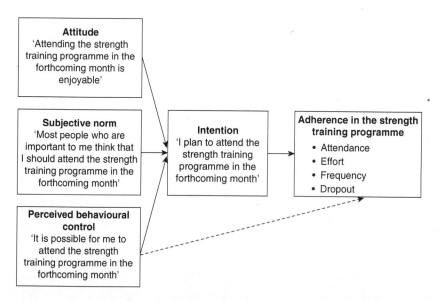

FIGURE 2.4 The TPB (Ajzen, 1991) and examples for strength and conditioning settings

Applying the TPB to strength and conditioning

There is a large amount of evidence supporting the validity of the TPB in the prediction of individuals' adherence to exercise and health programmes where the objectives of the programmes were to enhance fitness, body mass composition and endurance (e.g. Hagger et al., 2002; Hardeman et al., 2002; Hausenblas, Carron, & Mack, 1997). Only a few studies, however, have explicitly applied the theory to predict behaviour in strength and conditioning contexts (e.g. Ott et al., 2004; Shirazi et al., 2007; Taaffe & Galvao, 2003).

Nevertheless, applications of the TPB to strength and conditioning training contexts have indicated the utility of the theory in this field. For instance, netball players' adherence to endurance training (Palmer, Burwitz, Dyer, & Spray, 2005; Palmer, Burwitz, Smith, & Borrie, 2000), elite swimmers' adherence to intensive physical training (Mummery & Wankel, 1999) and students' adherence to aerobic exercise and weight training (Bryan & Rocheleau, 2002) were found to be directly related to intention and PBC. Consistent with the TPB framework, attitude, subjective norm and PBC also had positive associations with intention. Gardner and Hausenblas (2004) used the TPB variables to predict female adherence in a weight loss programme that involved both supervised cardiovascular activity and a low-calorie diet. It was found that participants' intention was positively related to dietary adherence but not to exercise adherence. Although these studies applied the TPB to predict individuals' adherence to training that incorporated strength and conditioning components, the focus was mainly on enhancing either physical performance or body shape rather than developing strength and physical conditioning for the purposes of sport performance. However, a recent study by Anderson and Lavallee (2008) explicitly applied the TPB to predict elite athletes' adherence in strength and conditioning training for sport performance. In the study, elite players from different sports took part in a strength and conditioning programme using free weights. It was found that participants' attendance at the programme was positively correlated with intention and PBC, but PBC appeared to be a stronger predictor of attendance. Attitude, subjective norm and PBC were positive predictors of the players' intention (Anderson & Lavallee, 2008), which was consistent with the proposed network of relationships within the TPB.

Accordingly, on the basis of the TPB, it is speculated that athletes will be more likely to follow a strength and conditioning programme if they are (a) motivated to do so in the future (intention) by the fact that they believe that the programme is (b) good/beneficial/enjoyable (attitude), (c) endorsed by the people they value (subjective norm) and (d) is believed to be achievable and that they have the capacity and resources to successfully perform the exercises stipulated in the programme (PBC). As such, by assessing individuals' evaluations on these TPB variables, the degree to which individuals would adhere to a conditioning programme could be estimated (cf. Anderson & Lavallee, 2008; Courneya & McAuley, 1995; Palmer et al., 2005). In contrast, if individuals obtain low scores on attitude, PBC or subjective norm towards the strength and conditioning programme, they are likely to have impaired intention and attenuated participation in the programme. Given that the TPB has been effective in predicting behaviour, the question remains as to whether physical trainers can foster individuals' involvement in strength and conditioning programmes by intervening to modify TPB constructs.

Interventions have been developed using the TPB as a framework to facilitate individuals' behaviour change in physical exercise. One of the earliest examples was given by Rodgers and Brawley (1993), who used videotapes with personalised persuasive messages and information which tapped the cognitive determinants of physical activity according to TPB. In addition, to facilitate participants' PBC or self-efficacy, the difficulty of the exercise programme increased progressively over time (Rodgers & Brawley, 1993). Although there was no control group against which to evaluate the effects of the intervention, a discriminant function analysis indicated that constructs from the TPB and SCT for exercise and eating behaviour reliably distinguished between those who adhered to and those who dropped out of the programme.

Chatzisarantis and Hagger (2005) successfully modified individuals' attitudes and intentions for leisure-time physical activity by addressing some modal salient exercise beliefs in an exercise promotion message. Modal salient exercise beliefs consist of behavioural beliefs (e.g. 'exercise is pleasurable to me'), normative beliefs (e.g. 'my friends believe that conditioning training makes people feel hot and sweaty') and control beliefs (e.g. 'free weight training is difficult for me as my muscle strength is poor'), which respectively serve as the foundation of individuals' attitude, subjective norm and PBC regarding the behaviour (Ajzen & Fishbein, 1980). Thus by emphasising positive beliefs and resolving negative beliefs in an exercise promotion message, we may enhance the credibility of arguments in favour of exercise participation, which may in turn lead to changes in beliefs and the TPB variables regarding the target behaviour (Ajzen & Fishbein, 1980). Jones, Courneya, Fairey, and Mackey (2005) obtained similar findings in an exercise promotion intervention using a message targeted at modal salient beliefs among cancer survivors. Recently, an intervention by Darker, French, Eves, and Sniehotta (2010) focused on enhancing individuals' PBC to promote regular walking. The intervention involved recall of successful experiences, goal setting, action planning and coping planning associated with the behaviour change towards walking, and was shown to be effective not only for enhancing individuals' attitude and PBC, but also for increasing the average time spent walking.

Recent studies have also reported alternative, non-TPB-based intervention techniques such as implementation intentions (i.e. planning *when, where, how* and *what* exercise or physical training will be done), decisional balance sheets (Milne, Orbell, & Sheeran, 2002; Prestwich, Lawton, & Conner, 2003) and positive message framing (Jones, Sinclair, & Courneya, 2003). These intervention techniques were not explicitly based on the TPB constructs, but adopted the TPB as a framework for understanding their effects. Similarly, a growing amount of research in the PE context has suggested that providing students with autonomy support (i.e. provision of choice, acknowledgement of perspective and a meaningful rationale for behaviour; see above) not only facilitates their intrinsic motivation for participating in PE classes, but also indirectly enhances their intention and other TPB variables for physical activity (Hagger & Chatzisarantis, 2009; Hagger, Chatzisarantis, Barkoukis, Wang, & Baranowski, 2005; Hagger et al., 2002; Hagger, Chatzisarantis, Culverhouse, & Biddle, 2003; Hagger et al., 2009). However, these techniques were not based on the TPB, but rather on complementary theories and models. TPB variables such as intention were therefore used only to measure the processes or outcomes of the interventions (Hardeman et al., 2002). The application of both TPB-based and non-TPB-based techniques may be useful for physical trainers to foster individuals' adherence to physical training, but further research is needed to test this directly in strength and conditioning settings. In summary, the TPB is a robust social cognitive model that displays substantial predictive power for behavioural engagement in strength and conditioning. Nevertheless, some methodological issues may limit the effectiveness of the TPB in providing a comprehensive understanding of the psychological factors that influence behaviour in this domain. These will be reviewed in the next section.

Further research directions for the application of the TPB to behaviour change in strength and conditioning training

One major debate in the field of social cognitive and motivational models applied to health behaviour is why the intention–behaviour relationship is often inconsistent across different studies. This discrepancy between intention and behaviour has been referred to as the intention–behaviour 'gap' (Hagger et al., 2002; Sniehotta, Scholz, & Schwarzer, 2005). Researchers have argued that intention might not necessarily predict variance in future behaviour beyond that predicted by past behaviour (Armitage, 2005; Hagger, Chatzisarantis, Biddle, & Orbell, 2001; Rhodes & Courneya, 2003; Sheeran & Orbell, 1999), and began to introduce alternative theories and methodological strategies to address the inconsistency between intentions and behaviour. The intention–behaviour gap has been attributed to the processes following intention formation because intenders might not always act according to their intentions (Orbell & Sheeran, 1998; Sheeran, 2002; Sniehotta et al., 2005). Thus, it is important to address the processes of goal pursuit during the time between formation of intentions and initiation of action. A plausible explanation for the intention–behaviour gap is that psychological processes associated with behaviours in the motivational phase (e.g. formation of intention) are likely to be different from those involved in the volitional or implemental phase (e.g. planning, behavioural maintenance and relapse control), thereby reducing the predictive validity of intentions for behavioural enactment (Gollwitzer & Brandstatter, 1997; Sniehotta et al., 2005). A growing body of literature proposes that bridging the intention–behaviour gap in the exercise domain could be achieved by maximising the self-control resources available to the individual (Hagger, Wood, Stiff, & Chatzisarantis, 2010) and investing self-regulatory effort in action planning (e.g.

implementation intentions; Milne et al., 2002; Prestwich et al., 2003). It is therefore important for future research to investigate these theoretical integrations.

Furthermore, the time interval between the assessment of intention and measurement of behaviour (Armitage, 2005), on-going progress towards goals (Chatzisarantis, Hagger, Smith, & Phoenix, 2004), maintenance of self-efficacy, action control (Sniehotta et al., 2005) and emotion (Mohiyeddini, Pauli, & Bauer, 2009) are all potential factors that may influence the relationship between intention and exercise behaviours. It would also be useful to look at whether different types of training with various purposes (e.g. endurance, bodybuilding, strength enhancement) may result in stronger or weaker intention–behaviour associations.

Further, very little is known about the personal and situational antecedents of TPB variables. For instance, personality characteristics may contribute towards determining individuals' engagement in particular types of strength and conditioning training through effects on the TPB variables. Bryan and Rocheleau (2002), for instance, found that extraverted individuals were more likely to endorse higher PBC for resistance training relative to introverts but this was not replicated for aerobic training. Further studies should therefore examine how personality may interact with situational factors such as the type of conditioning training. Moreover, it is important to investigate the effects of social environmental factors, including autonomy support (e.g. Hagger et al., 2009; see also earlier) and positive communication style (e.g. Jones et al., 2003; see also earlier) on the TPB variables, and how these factors can enhance individuals' attitude, subjective norm and PBC regarding a training programme.

Finally, it is important to note that the majority of studies have applied the TPB to predict behaviour rather than to foster behaviour change (e.g. Hagger et al., 2002; Hardeman et al., 2002). Future research should place more focus on adapting TPB-based research from theory into practice, for instance using the TPB to design behavioural modification interventions in strength and conditioning training (cf. Chatzisarantis & Hagger, 2005; Darker et al., 2010).

Section summary: the TPB

- The TPB is a social cognitive theory that aims to explain the decision-making processes of human behaviours.
- The TPB consists of four key psychological variables, namely attitude, subjective norm, PBC and intention.
- According to the TPB, attitude, subjective norm and PBC exhibit positive relationships with intention. Intention and PBC are expected to exert positive direct effects on strength and conditioning behaviours.
- Evidence supports the predictive validity of TPB in strength and conditioning settings; thus estimating adherence to a strength and conditioning programme could possibly be achieved by assessing the TPB variables of the individual in relation to the training.

- A number of techniques that were developed from the TPB and other theories appear to be useful in modifying attitude, intention, PBC and behaviour with regard to physical exercise. Further research is required to test these techniques in strength and conditioning settings.
- Research adopting the TPB still presents some challenges that require further research, including the imperfect prediction of behaviour from intention, lack of evidence about the antecedents of TPB variables and the shortage of behaviour change interventions in strength and conditioning contexts.

Overall conclusions, summary and avenues for further research

Social psychological theories and models provide frameworks for predicting and understanding strength and conditioning training behaviour. The TPB has already been employed successfully in explaining strength and conditioning behaviour, and future application of SCT and SDT in this context is recommended. SCT and SDT also offer a wealth of techniques for initiating behaviour change that could be applied by coaches and trainers to assist athletes to establish regular training routines. The implementation of support for self-efficacy would serve to improve performance and increase persistence in strength and conditioning training. Similarly, the provision of support for athletes' psychological needs for competence, relatedness and, in particular, autonomy would serve to enhance autonomous motivation through promoting the integration of strength and conditioning training into their repertoire of behaviours that are seen as need satisfying, and incur positive effects on performance, persistence and well-being. Practitioners may also benefit from focusing on the discrepancy between athletes' intentions and behaviour and teaching their athletes strategies such as implementation and continuation intentions to facilitate the successful translation of intentions to behaviour. These planning-based strategies prompt the automatic enactment of behaviour upon encountering either success or failure in goal striving or particular situational cues that have been linked with behaviour in conditional plans. Coaches and trainers should be aware of the fundamental importance of their role in affecting both the behaviour and well-being of their athletes and are advised to make use of the wealth of behaviour change strategies that have emerged from the SCT, TPB and SDT literatures. It is also recommended that practitioners consider the complementary nature of these theories when employing behaviour change strategies, for instance the importance of presenting verbal persuasion (a strategy based on SCT) in an autonomy-supportive manner (a strategy based on SDT), rather than focusing on any single theory in isolation.

Discussion questions

1. Identify the three SDT needs and strategies by which each may be promoted in the strength and conditioning context.
2. Give examples of each type of behavioural regulation as related to your sport.

3.   Discuss ways strength and conditioning coaches can enhance self-efficacy.
4.   What research is needed to help understand self-efficacy in strength and conditioning contexts?
5.   How might the four key psychological variables in TPB help strength and conditioning coaches predict client behaviour?
6.   Why does an intention–behaviour gap often exist and how might it be closed?

Note

1   It is important to note that tangible rewards such as trophies and money can be used effectively as motivating factors in strength and conditioning training if they are presented as informational regarding competence and achievement of personally referenced goals rather than as controlling and the only reason for engaging in the training. For instance, a trophy could be used to signify that an athlete has surpassed their previous personal best within a particular training exercise.

References

Abraham, C., & Michie, S. (2008). A taxonomy of behaviour change techniques used in interventions. *Health Psychology, 27*, 379–387.

Ajzen, I. (1985). From intentions to actions: A theory of planned behavior. In J. Kuhl, & J. Beckmann (Eds.), *From intentions to actions: A theory of planned behavior* (pp. 11–39). Berlin: Springer.

Ajzen, I. (1991). The theory of planned behavior. *Organizational Behavior and Human Decision Processes, 50*, 179–211.

Ajzen, I. (2001). Nature and operation of attitudes. *Annual Review of Psychology, 52*, 27–58.

Ajzen, I., & Fishbein, M. (1980). *Understanding attitudes and predicting social behavior.* Englewood Cliffs, NJ: Prentice Hall.

Ajzen, I., & Madden, T. J. (1986). Prediction of goal-directed behavior – Attitudes, intentions, and perceived behavioral control. *Journal of Experimental Social Psychology, 22*, 453–474.

Amorose, A. J., & Anderson-Butcher, D. (2007). Autonomy-supportive coaching and self-determined motivation in high school and college athletes: A test of self-determination theory. *Psychology of Sport and Exercise, 8*, 654–670.

Anderson, A. G., & Lavallee, D. (2008). Applying the theories of reasoned action and planned behavior to athlete training adherence behavior. *Applied Psychology, 57*, 304–312.

Anderson, R. B. (2000). Vicarious and persuasive influences on efficacy expectations and intentions to perform breast self-examination. *Public Relations Review, 26*, 97–114.

Armitage, C. J. (2005). Can the theory of planned behavior predict the maintenance of physical activity? *Health Psychology, 24*, 235–245.

Armitage, C. J., & Conner, M. (1999). The theory of planned behaviour: Assessment of predictive validity and 'perceived control'. *British Journal of Social Psychology, 38*, 35–54.

Armitage, C. J., & Conner, M. (2001). Efficacy of the theory of planned behaviour: A meta-analytic review. *British Journal of Social Psychology, 40*, 471–499.

Bandura, A. (1977). Self-efficacy: Toward a unifying theory of behavioural change. *Psychological Review, 84*, 191–215.

Bandura, A. (1997). *Self-efficacy: The exercise of control.* New York: Freeman.

Bandura, A. (2001). Social cognitive theory: An agentic perspective. *Annual Review of Psychology, 52*, 1–26.

Biddle, S. J. H., Hanrahan, S. J., & Sellars, C. N. (2001). Attributions: Past, present and future. In R. N. Singer, H. A. Hausenblas, & C. M. Janelle (Eds.), *Handbook of sport psychology* (pp. 444–471). New York: Wiley.

Black, A. E., & Deci, E. L. (2000). The effects of student self-regulation and instructor autonomy support on learning in a college-level natural science course: A self-determination theory perspective. *Science Education, 84*, 740–756.

Bryan, A. D., & Rocheleau, C. A. (2002). Predicting aerobic versus resistance exercise using the theory of planned behavior. *American Journal of Health Behavior, 26*, 83–94.

Chambliss, C. A., & Murray, E. J. (1979). Efficacy attribution, locus of control, and weight loss. *Cognitive Therapy and Research, 3*, 349–353.

Chatzisarantis, N. L. D., & Hagger, M. S. (2005). Effects of a brief intervention based on the theory of planned behavior on leisure-time physical activity participation. *Journal of Sport & Exercise Psychology, 27*, 470–487.

Chatzisarantis, N. L. D., & Hagger, M. S. (2009). Effects of an intervention based on self-determination theory on self-reported leisure-time physical activity participation. *Psychology and Health, 24*, 29–48.

Chatzisarantis, N. L. D., Hagger, M. S., Biddle, S. J. H., Smith, B., & Wang, J. C. K. (2003). A meta-analysis of perceived locus of causality in exercise, sport, and physical education contexts. *Journal of Sport & Exercise Psychology, 25*, 284–306.

Chatzisarantis, N. L. D., Hagger, M. S., & Smith, B. (2007). Influences of perceived autonomy support on physical activity within the theory of planned behaviour. *European Journal of Social Psychology, 37*, 934–954.

Chatzisarantis, N. L. D., Hagger, M. S., Smith, B., & Phoenix, C. (2004). The influences of continuation intentions on execution of social behaviour within the theory of planned behaviour. *British Journal of Social Psychology, 43*, 551–583.

Chirkov, V. I., & Ryan, R. M. (2001). Parent and teacher autonomy-support in Russian and U.S. adolescents: Common effects on well-being and academic motivation. *Journal of Cross-Cultural Psychology, 32*, 618–635.

Courneya, K. S., & McAuley, E. (1995). Cognitive mediators of the social influence–exercise adherence relationship: A test of the theory of planned behavior. *Journal of Behavioral Medicine, 18*, 499–515.

Csikszentmihalyi, M. (1975). *Beyond boredom and anxiety.* San Francisco: Jossey-Bass.

Csikszentmihalyi, M. (1990). *Flow: The psychology of optimal experience.* New York: Harper & Row.

Csikszentmihalyi, M., Rathunde, K., & Whalen, S. (1993). *Talented teenagers.* Cambridge, England: Cambridge University Press.

Darker, C. D., French, D. P., Eves, F. F., & Sniehotta, F. F. (2010). An intervention to promote walking amongst the general population based on an 'extended' theory of planned behaviour: A waiting list randomised controlled trial. *Psychology & Health, 25*, 71–88.

De Backer, I. C., Vreugdenhil, G., Nijziel, M. R., Kester, A. D., van Breda, E., & Schep, E. (2008). Long-term follow-up after cancer rehabilitation using high-intensity resistance training: Persistent improvement of physical performance and quality of life. *British Journal of Cancer, 99*, 30–36.

Deci, E. L., Eghrari, H., Patrick, B. C., & Leone, D. R. (1994). Facilitating internalization: The self-determination theory perspective. *Journal of Personality, 62*, 119–142.

Deci, E. L., & Ryan, R. M. (1985). *Intrinsic motivation and self-determination in human behavior.* New York: Plenum Press.

Deci, E. L., & Ryan, R. M. (2000). The 'what' and 'why' of goal pursuits: Human needs and the self-determination of behavior. *Psychological Inquiry, 11*, 227–268.

Deci, E. L., Ryan, R. M., Gagne, M., Leone, D. R., Usunov, J., & Kornazheva, B. P. (2001). Need satisfaction, motivation, and well-being in the work organizations of a former Eastern Bloc country: A cross-cultural study of self-determination. *Personality and Social Psychology Bulletin, 27*, 930–942.

Edmunds, J., Ntoumanis, N., & Duda, J. L. (2006). A test of self-determination theory in the exercise domain. *Journal of Applied Social Psychology, 36*, 2240–2265.

60 Sarah McLachlan *et al.*

Feltz, D. L., & Chase, M. A. (1998). The measurement of self-efficacy and confidence in sport. In J. L. Duda (ed.), *Advances in sport and exercise psychology measurement* (pp. 65–80). Morgantown, WV: Fitness Information Technology.

Ferrer-Caja, E., & Weiss, M. R. (2000). Predictors of intrinsic motivation among adolescent students in physical education. *Research Quarterly for Exercise and Sport, 71*, 267–279.

Fortier, M. S., Sweet, S., O'Sullivan, T. L., & Williams, G. C. (2007). A self-determination process model of physical activity adoption in the context of a randomized controlled trial. *Psychology of Sport and Exercise, 8*, 741–757.

Gagne, M., Ryan, R. M., & Bargmann, K. (2003). Autonomy support and need satisfaction in the motivation and well-being of gymnasts. *Journal of Applied Sport Psychology, 15*, 372–390.

Gardner, R. E., & Hausenblas, H. A. (2004). Understanding exercise and diet motivation in overweight women enrolled in a weight-loss program: A prospective study using the theory of planned behavior. *Journal of Applied Social Psychology, 34*, 1353–1370.

Gollwitzer, P. M., & Brandstatter, V. (1997). Implementation intentions and effective goal pursuit. *Journal of Personality and Social Psychology, 73*, 186–199.

Gould, D., Petlichkoff, L., Hodge, K., & Simons, J. (1990). Evaluating effectiveness of a psychological skills educational workshop. *The Sport Psychologist, 6*, 289–304.

Hagen, K. M., Gutkin, T. B., Wilson, C. P., & Oats, R. G. (1998). Using vicarious experience and verbal persuasion to enhance self-efficacy in pre-service teachers: 'Priming the pump' for consultation. *School Psychology Quarterly, 13*, 169–178.

Hagger, M. S., & Chatzisarantis, N. L. D. (2009). Integrating the theory of planned behaviour and self-determination theory in health behaviour: A meta-analysis. *British Journal of Health Psychology, 14*, 275–302.

Hagger, M. S., Chatzisarantis, N. L. D., Barkoukis, V., Wang, C. K. J., & Baranowski, J. (2005). Perceived autonomy support in physical education and leisure-time physical activity: A cross-cultural evaluation of the trans-contextual model. *Journal of Educational Psychology, 97*, 376–390.

Hagger, M. S., Chatzisarantis, N. L. D., & Biddle, S. J. H. (2002). A meta-analytic review of the theories of reasoned action and planned behavior in physical activity: Predictive validity and the contribution of additional variables. *Journal of Sport & Exercise Psychology, 24*, 3–32.

Hagger, M. S., Chatzisarantis, N. L. D., Biddle, S. J. H., & Orbell, S. (2001). Antecedents of children's physical activity intentions and behaviour: Predictive validity and longitudinal effects. *Psychology & Health, 16*, 391–407.

Hagger, M. S., Chatzisarantis, N. L. D., Culverhouse, T., & Biddle, S. J. H. (2003). The processes by which perceived autonomy support in physical education promotes leisure-time physical activity intentions and behavior: A trans-contextual model. *Journal of Educational Psychology, 95*, 784–795.

Hagger, M. S., Chatzisarantis, N. L. D., Hein, V., Pihu, M., Soós, I., Karsai, I., & Leemans, S. (2009). Teacher, peer, and parent autonomy support in physical education and leisure-time physical activity: A trans-contextual model of motivation in four nations. *Psychology and Health, 24*, 689–711.

Hagger, M. S., Wood, C. W., Stiff, C., & Chatzisarantis, N. L. D. (2010). Self-regulation and self-control in exercise: The strength-energy model. *International Review of Sport and Exercise Psychology, 3*, 62–86.

Hardeman, W., Johnston, M., Johnston, D. W., Bonetti, D., Wareham, N. J., & Kinmonth, A. L. (2002). Application of the theory of planned behaviour in behaviour change interventions: A systematic review. *Psychology & Health, 17*, 123–158.

Hausenblas, H. A., Carron, A. V., & Mack, D. E. (1997). Application of the theories of reasoned action and planned behavior to exercise behavior: A meta-analysis. *Journal of Sport & Exercise Psychology, 19*, 36–51.

Hollombeak, J., & Amorose, A. J. (2005). Perceived coaching behaviours and college athletes' intrinsic motivation: A test of self-determination theory. *Journal of Applied Sport Psychology, 17*, 20–36.

Jackson, B., & Beauchamp, M. R. (2010). Self-efficacy as a metaperception within coach–athlete and athlete–athlete relationships. *Psychology of Sport and Exercise, 11*, 188–196.

Jackson, S. A., Thomas, P. R., Marsh, H. W., & Smethurst, C. J. (2001). Relationships between flow, self-concept, psychological skills, and performance. *Journal of Applied Sport Psychology, 13*, 129–153.

Jones, L. W., Courneya, K. S., Fairey, A. S., & Mackey, J. R. (2005). Does the theory of planned behavior mediate the effects of an oncologist's recommendation to exercise in newly diagnosed breast cancer survivors? Results from a randomized controlled trial. *Health Psychology, 24*, 189–197.

Jones, L. W., Sinclair, R. C., & Courneya, K. S. (2003). The effects of source credibility and message framing on exercise intentions, behaviors, and attitudes: An integration of the elaboration likelihood model and prospect theory. *Journal of Applied Social Psychology, 33*, 179–196.

Kowal, J., & Fortier, M. S. (2000). Testing relationships from the hierarchical model of intrinsic and extrinsic motivation using flow as a motivational consequence. *Research Quarterly for Exercise and Sport, 71*, 171–181.

Lent, R. W., & Lopez, F. G. (2002). Cognitive ties that bind: A tripartite view of efficacy beliefs in growth-promoting relationships. *Journal of Social and Clinical Psychology, 21*, 256–286.

Lonsdale, C., Hodge, K., & Rose, E. (2009). Athlete burnout in elite sport: A self-determination perspective. *Journal of Sports Sciences, 27*, 785–795.

Markland, D., & Tobin, V. J. (2010). Need support and behavioural regulations for exercise among exercise referral scheme clients: The mediating role of psychological need satisfaction. *Psychology of Sport and Exercise, 11*, 91–99.

McLachlan, S., & Hagger, M. S. (in press). The development of a scale measuring integrated regulation in physical activity. *British Journal of Health Psychology.*

Michie, S., & Abraham, C. (2004). Interventions to change health behaviors: Evidence-based or evidence inspired? *Psychology & Health, 19*, 29–49.

Michie, S., Johnston, M., Francis, J., Hardeman, W., & Eccles, M. (2008). From theory to intervention: Mapping theoretically derived behavioural determinants to behaviour change techniques. *Applied Psychology, 57*, 660–680.

Milne, S., Orbell, S., & Sheeran, P. (2002). Combining motivational and volitional interventions to promote exercise participation: Protection motivation theory and implementation intentions. *British Journal of Health Psychology, 7*, 163–184.

Mohiyeddini, C., Pauli, R., & Bauer, S. (2009). The role of emotion in bridging the intention–behaviour gap: The case of sports participation. *Psychology of Sport and Exercise, 10*, 226–234.

Moller, A. C., Deci, E. L., & Ryan, R. M. (2006). Choice and ego-depletion: The moderating role of autonomy. *Personality and Social Psychology Bulletin, 32*, 1024–1036.

Moores, T. T., & Chang, J. C. (2009). Self-efficacy, overconfidence, and the negative effect on subsequent performance: A field study. *Information and Management, 46*, 69–76.

Mummery, W. K., & Wankel, L. M. (1999). Training adherence in adolescent competitive swimmers: An application of the theory of planned behavior. *Journal of Sport & Exercise Psychology, 21*, 313–328.

Ness, R. G., & Patton, R. W. (1979). The effects of beliefs on maximum weight-lifting performance. *Cognitive Therapy and Research, 3*, 205–211.

Ntoumanis, N. (2001). A self-determination approach to the understanding of motivation in physical education. *British Journal of Educational Psychology, 71*, 225–242.

Orbell, S., & Sheeran, P. (1998). 'Inclined abstainers': A problem for predicting health-related behaviour. *British Journal of Social Psychology, 37*, 151–165.

Ott, C. D., Lindsey, A. M., Waltman, N. L., Gross, G. J., Twiss, J. L., Berg, K., & Henricksen, S. (2004). Facilitative strategies, psychological factors, and strength-weight training behaviours in breast cancer survivors who are at risk for osteoporosis. *Orthopaedic Nursing*, *23*, 45–52.

Palmer, C. L., Burwitz, L., Dyer, A. N., & Spray, C. M. (2005). Endurance training adherence in elite junior netball athletes: A test of the theory of planned behaviour and a revised theory of planned behaviour. *Journal of Sports Sciences*, *23*, 277–288.

Palmer, C. L., Burwitz, L., Smith, N. C., & Borrie, A. (2000). Enhancing fitness training adherence of elite netball players: An evaluation of Maddux's revised theory of planned behaviour. *Journal of Sports Sciences*, *18*, 627–641.

Pelletier, L. G., Fortier, M. S., Vallerand, R. J., & Briere, N. M. (2001). Associations among autonomy support, forms of self-regulation, and persistence: A prospective study. *Motivation and Emotion*, *25*, 279–306.

Perreault, S., Gaudreau, P., Lapointe, M. C., & Lacroix, C. (2007). Does it take three to tango? Psychological need satisfaction and athlete burnout. *International Journal of Sport Psychology*, *38*, 437–450.

Poag-DuCharme, K. A., & Brawley, L. R. (1993). Self-efficacy theory: Use in the prediction of exercise behavior in the community setting. *Journal of Applied Sport Psychology*, *5*, 178–194.

Prestwich, A., Lawton, R., & Conner, M. (2003). The use of implementation intentions and the decision balance sheet in promoting exercise behaviour. *Psychology & Health*, *18*, 707–721.

Reinboth, M., Duda, J. L., & Ntoumanis, N. (2004). Dimensions of coaching behavior, need satisfaction, and the psychological and physical welfare of young athletes. *Motivation and Emotion*, *28*, 297–313.

Rhodes, R. E., & Courneya, K. S. (2003). Investigating multiple components of attitude, subjective norm, and perceived control: An examination of the theory of planned behaviour in the exercise domain. *British Journal of Social Psychology*, *42*, 129–146.

Rodgers, W. M., & Brawley, L. R. (1993). Using both self-efficacy theory and the theory of planned behavior to discriminate adherers and dropouts from structured programs. *Journal of Applied Sport Psychology*, *5*, 195–206.

Russell, K. L., & Bray, S. R. (2009). Self-determined motivation predicts independent, home-based exercise following cardiac rehabilitation. *Rehabilitation Psychology*, *54*, 150–156.

Ryan, R. M., & Deci, E. L. (2002). An overview of self-determination theory: An organismic-dialectical perspective. In E. L. Deci, & R. M. Ryan (Eds.), *Handbook of self-determination research* (pp. 3–33). Rochester, NY: University of Rochester Press.

Sheeran, P. (2002). Intention–behaviour relations: A conceptual and empirical review. In M. Hewstone, & W. Stroebe (Eds.), *European review of social psychology* (Vol. 12, pp. 1–36). Chichester, England: Wiley.

Sheeran, P., & Orbell, S. (1999). Implementation intentions and repeated behaviour: Augmenting the predictive validity of the theory of planned behaviour. *European Journal of Social Psychology*, *29*, 349–369.

Shirazi, K. K., Wallace, L. M., Niknami, S., Hidarnia, A., Torkaman, G., Gilchrist, M., & Faghihzadeh, S. (2007). A home-based, transtheoretical change model designed strength training intervention to increase exercise to prevent osteoporosis in Iranian women aged 40–65 years: A randomised controlled trial. *Health Education Research*, *22*, 305–317.

Sniehotta, F. F., Scholz, U., & Schwarzer, R. (2005). Bridging the intention–behaviour gap: Planning, self-efficacy, and action control in the adoption and maintenance of physical exercise. *Psychology & Health*, *20*, 143–160.

Standage, M., Duda, J. L., & Ntoumanis, N. (2005). A test of self-determination theory in school physical education. *British Journal of Educational Psychology*, *75*, 411–433.

Taaffe, D., & Galvao, D. (2003). Muscle strength but not functional performance is associated with falls self-efficacy in older men and women. *Journal of Science and Medicine in Sport*, *6*, 31.

Terry, D. J., & Oleary, J. E. (1995). The theory of planned behavior – The effects of perceived behavioral control and self-efficacy. *British Journal of Social Psychology, 34*, 199–220.

Thøgersen-Ntoumani, C., & Ntoumanis, N. (2006). The role of self-determined motivation in the understanding of exercise-related behaviours, cognitions and physical self-evaluations. *Journal of Sports Sciences, 24*, 393–404.

Vansteenkiste, M., Simons, J., Lens, W., Sheldon, K. M., & Deci, E. L. (2004). Motivated learning, performance, and persistence: The synergistic effects of intrinsic goal contents and autonomy-supportive contexts. *Journal of Personality and Social Psychology, 87*, 246–260.

Weiner, B., Heckhausen, H., Meyer, W. U., & Cook, R. E. (1972). Causal ascriptions and achievement motivation: A conceptual analysis and reanalysis of locus of control. *Journal of Personality and Social Psychology, 21*, 239–248.

Wells, C. M., Collins, D., & Hale, B. D. (1993). The self-efficacy–performance link in maximum strength performance. *Journal of Sports Sciences, 11*, 167–175.

Williams, G. C., McGregor, H. A., Sharp, D., Levesque, C., Kouides, R. W., Ryan, R. M., & Deci, E. L. (2006). Testing a self-determination theory intervention for motivating tobacco cessation: Supporting autonomy and competence in a clinical trial. *Health Psychology, 25*, 91–101.

Wise, J. B., Posner, A. E., & Walker, G. L. (2004). Verbal messages strengthen bench press efficacy. *Journal of Strength and Conditioning Research, 18*, 26–29.

3

PERCEPTUAL MONITORING IN STRENGTH AND POWER

Michael McGuigan

NEW ZEALAND ACADEMY OF SPORT, AUT UNIVERSITY, NEW ZEALAND

A commonly accepted training principle is that a period of loading followed by adequate rest results in improved performance (Lambert & Borresen, 2006). Due to this, monitoring the various psychological and fatigue responses to a training stimulus has become an important area of focus for many practitioners and researchers (Cormack, Newton, & McGuigan, 2008; Coutts, Slattery, & Wallace, 2007). The general purpose of this work has been to develop tools to assist in optimizing training programs and minimizing negative outcomes such as injury, illness, and/or excessive fatigue that limits the ability to train. A number of methods have been proposed to assist in this process. These include a variety of self-reporting questionnaires and perceptual measures such as the rating of perceived exertion (RPE; Foster, Heimann, Esten, Brice, & Porcari, 2001). Other objective markers such as neuromuscular and hormonal measures have also been proposed (Cormack et al., 2008). The challenge for the practitioner is the implementation and interpretation of data from valid and reliable measurement devices.

One problem facing strength and conditioning professionals and researchers is how to monitor the intensity of different modes and phases of resistance training. The session RPE method is a commonly used monitoring tool during exercise. The session RPE allows the subject to provide a global rating of the overall intensity of the exercise session, rather than reporting a series of RPE measures throughout the session, and is typically taken 30 minutes following a training session (Figure 3.1). The session RPE has been proposed as a valid and reliable method for monitoring the intensity of the global exertion of exercise (Foster, Florhaug, et al., 2001), including resistance training (Day, McGuigan, Brice, & Foster, 2004; McGuigan, Egan, & Foster, 2004; Sweet, Foster, McGuigan, & Brice, 2004). The session RPE is now commonly used in many exercise and sporting environments, as it also allows for calculation of measures such as training load, monotony, and strain. This chapter will provide a general introduction to RPE,

Rating	Descriptor
0	Rest
1	Very, Very Easy
2	Easy
3	Moderate
4	Somewhat Hard
5	Hard
6	-
7	Very Hard
8	-
9	-
10	Maximal

FIGURE 3.1 Modification of the category ratio RPE scale. The athlete is shown the scale approximately 30 minutes following the conclusion of the training bout and asked "How hard was your workout?"

discuss the session RPE method and the research that has been conducted in this area, and work through practical application of the method.

Various questionnaires and diaries can potentially be used to monitor strength training (Hopkins, 1991). In sport settings, athletes are often required to complete questionnaires to assess their perception of measures such as sleep quality, fatigue, muscle soreness, and mood. Psychological questionnaires such as Daily Analyses of Life Demands for Athletes (DALDA) and Recovery–Stress Questionnaire for athletes (RESTQ-Sport) can provide a simple and cost-effective monitoring tool for coaches and can be implemented on a regular basis (Coutts & Reaburn, 2008). This chapter will also discuss the limited research conducted on the use of questionnaires and diaries for monitoring strength training and outline some practical applications. In addition, future research directions will be discussed for these topics.

Resistance training is a mode of exercise that presents significant challenges in terms of monitoring and cannot be easily quantified using objective measurements (McGuigan & Foster, 2004). There has been no single accepted method to monitor the intensity that trainees are working at during a resistance training session. For athletes training for strength and/or power, for example, the use of training volume is an inadequate tool because of the overriding importance of training intensity (McGuigan & Foster, 2004). The importance of monitoring training load during resistance training is a critical part of successful programs since manipulation of volume, intensity, and recovery is imperative for optimizing results (Foster, 1998). The effects of resistance training are related to a number of different variables such as the type of exercise used, intensity, and volume (McGuigan & Foster, 2004). This relationship between training parameter and outcome supports the need for a valid and reliable method of monitoring training intensity, and methods such as session RPE have shown promise (Day et al., 2004). Resistance training represents a complex combination of perceptual signals including muscle mass recruited, type of exercise used, metabolic load, training status of the individual, and amount of load, all of which interact with the type of resistance exercise protocol employed. This complexity provides significant challenges to researchers aiming to develop well-designed training studies to investigate the issue of monitoring resistance training.

Rating of perceived exertion

The RPE scale has been studied extensively by exercise scientists and it is widely used in various exercise settings (Borg, 1982a; Kraemer, Noble, Clark, & Culver, 1987). Borg based the RPE scale on the notion that a measure of perceived exertion is the level of strain experienced during physical effort and that it can be estimated by a specific rating method. Borg developed a model known as the effort continua which suggests that subjective responses to exercise rely on physiological, perceptual, and performance signals (each is represented by an independent continuum; Borg, 1982a). This model also suggests that there is a functional link between these three continua (Borg, 1982a). Therefore, the perceptual response to exercise should provide relatively similar information as physiological responses during exercise performance (Borg, 1982b; Noble, Borg, Jacobs, Ceci, & Kaiser, 1983). Although RPE represents an individual's perceived effort, it has been shown to have significant correlations with objective measures of training stress such as heart rate (Alexiou & Coutts, 2008), blood lactate (Kraemer et al., 1987; Noble et al., 1983), and swim distance (Wallace, Slattery, & Coutts, 2009).

It has been proposed that RPE may be a practical way of monitoring the intensity of resistance training (McGuigan & Foster, 2004). The most commonly used formats of the Borg scale are the 6–20 (15-Category) and 0–10 (CR-10). The Borg 15-Category scale has been widely used to measure exercise intensity in clinical and sporting settings (Noble et al., 1983). A lot of early research was with aerobic exercise, but there is a growing body of literature investigating its use with resistance training (Gearhart et al., 2001; Gearhart, Lagally, Riechman, Andrews, & Robertson, 2009; Kraemer et al., 1987; Lagally & Amorose, 2007; Robertson et al., 2005). A number of studies have demonstrated the Borg scale to be an effective method of quantifying resistance training (Lagally et al., 2002; Robertson et al., 2005). The results of these studies show that performing fewer repetitions with a heavier resistance is perceived as being more difficult than lifting lighter resistance for more repetitions and that RPE is related to the %1RM. However, very few of these studies have used well-trained subjects or elite athletes. One study

(Kraemer et al., 1987) used the Borg CR-10 scale to monitor the perceptual responses of trained powerlifters and bodybuilders during high-intensity exercise with RPE being significantly correlated with lactate levels ($r = 0.84$).

A study examined RPE in active muscle during high-intensity and low-intensity training protocols (Gearhart et al., 2001). Each protocol consisted of performing one set of each of seven exercises. The high-intensity protocol involved lifting 90 percent 1RM for five repetitions with RPE values obtained following each repetition. The low-intensity protocol involved lifting 30 percent 1RM for 15 repetitions. The RPE values were obtained following every third repetition. The work done in each protocol was held constant, and the results showed that performing fewer repetitions using heavier resistance was perceived as more difficult than performing more repetitions of a lighter resistance. One study examined RPE during resistance training in women with participants performing three sets of the biceps curl exercise (Lagally et al., 2002). Each participant was randomly assigned to the intensity she or he would complete first, with the conditions being 30 percent (12 repetitions), 60 percent (6 repetitions), or 90 percent (4 repetitions) of 1RM. In this study, total work was also held constant. Data for the RPE of the active muscle and overall RPE were measured upon the completion of each set. The results of this study indicated increases in RPE of the active muscle and overall RPE with increases in exercise intensity.

Pictorial RPE scales have also been developed for use with resistance training. The OMNI Perceived Exertion Scale for Resistance Exercise was developed to be more reflective of exercise intensity and to be easier to understand, particularly for children (Robertson et al., 2003, 2005). Three descriptors are used in this scale: six verbal phrases (extremely easy, easy, somewhat easy, somewhat hard, hard, and extremely hard), four pictorials, and numerical figures from 0 to 10. One study examined the concurrent validity of the OMNI-Resistance Exercise Scale (OMNI-RES) to measure RPE in women and men performing leg extensions and bicep curls at 65 percent of 1RM (Robertson et al., 2003). RPE for the active muscles and the overall body were directly related to the total weight lifted (0.79–0.91). There were no gender differences in perceived exertion responses. The scale has previously been validated in children (Robertson et al., 2005). Faigenbaum, Milliken, Cloutier, and Westcott (2004) have established the validity and reliability of an 11-point numerical scale with five pictures for children engaging in resistance training. Clearly, RPE is a valid measure with resistance exercise (Robertson et al., 2003).

Session RPE

There is now a significant body of research that has investigated the use of session RPE with resistance training. Session RPE is different from the conventional RPE approach that asks subjects to rate with standardized verbal instructions how difficult they perceive the exercise to be for the entire session. The research to date has suggested that session RPE provides a valid (Sweet et al., 2004) and reliable (Day

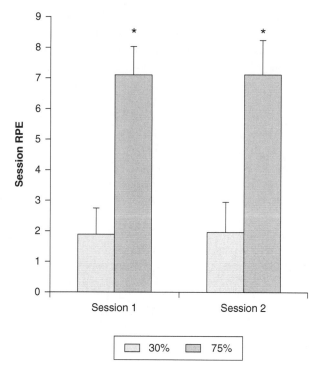

FIGURE 3.2 Session RPE data for the low-intensity and high-intensity sessions (mean ± SD). The symbol "*" denotes significant differences between 30 and 75 percent exercise bouts

et al., 2004; McGuigan et al., 2004) indicator of resistance training intensity. Similar to the research with RPE, higher intensity protocols produce higher session RPE values despite a decrease in the number of repetitions performed. Session RPE has also been shown to be reliable at quantifying resistance training at different intensities (r = 0.88–0.95; Day et al., 2004; McGuigan et al., 2004, 2008). Figure 3.2 shows an example of how session RPE can differentiate between high- and low-intensity resistance training (McGuigan et al., 2004). The method's effectiveness across a variety of resistance training intensities and modes of training has been demonstrated (Egan, Winchester, Foster, & McGuigan, 2006; Singh, Foster, Tod, & McGuigan, 2007). Using session RPE to quantify training load has the potential to be a mode- and intensity-independent method that can be used for intermittent, high-intensity exercise such as resistance training or plyometric training. Session RPE during easy, moderate, and high-intensity resistance training were compared to session RPE during comparable intensities of steady-state cycle ergometer exercise (Sweet et al., 2004). The study reported a high agreement between session RPE and 1RM during a range of resistance training sessions (Sweet et al., 2004). The rated intensity of exercise increased with %VO2peak and the %1RM. The results of this investigation also showed that session RPE was a valid method for quantifying the intensity of resistance training, and was generally comparable to aerobic training. Subjects were also asked to provide an RPE for the lifting portion only to help avoid any bias with large rest periods between sets. The lifting only value asked the subjects to provide an RPE that described the difficulty of the actual weight that they had to lift during the session. Session RPE and session RPE (lifting only) all increased as the percentage of 1RM increased despite a decrease in repetitions and total workload (Sweet et al., 2004).

The session RPE appears to be influenced more by resistance load than by volume, so performing more repetitions with a lighter load was perceived as being easier than performing fewer repetitions with a heavier load (Day et al., 2004). Sweet et al. (2004) also found that the RPE varies significantly among different muscle groups used because of differences in muscle mass (and therefore metabolic demand), range of motion, and the number of joints involved in a movement. The order in which the exercises are performed, the physiological characteristics of the muscle used, the mode of exercise for which the athlete is trained (i.e. the level of experience the athlete has in resistance training), and the time at which RPE is reported may also affect the result.

Session RPE has also been used to examine perceptual responses in competitive athletic settings (Borresen & Lambert, 2008; Coutts & Reaburn, 2008; Coutts et al., 2007; Serrano, Salvador, Gonzalez-Bono, Sanchis, & Suay, 2001). Researchers, for example, measured the intensity of judo competition using RPE (Serrano et al., 2001). The standard RPE and Borg category ratio 10 scale values were collected 10 and 30 minutes after fighting, with each athlete completing 2–3 fights during the competition. The 10-minute RPE value was used to describe the intensity of the last fight, while the 30-minute RPE value was used to describe the intensity of the entire competition. The 30-minute RPE values for the entire competition correlated to maximal blood lactate levels 1 and 3 minutes after fighting. Judo is a very high-intensity exercise which is similar to resistance training. The correlation between RPE 30-minute postcompetition and maximal blood lactate levels supports the use of session RPE to represent global intensity of exercise.

Previous studies have shown that RPE is mostly influenced by exercise intensity and not by the volume of exercise being performed (Day et al., 2004; Gearhart et al., 2001; McGuigan et al., 2004; Singh et al., 2007). Despite the complex nature of resistance exercise which involves a range of physiological cues, there does appear to be a fundamental similarity to the use of session RPE with monitoring other forms of exercise. Whether this method can be used effectively in other populations such as children and the elderly has yet to be confirmed. As children are psychologically less mature than adults, they may have difficulty using any type of RPE scale to provide a global rating of the exercise session. One study has shown the OMNI-RES to be reliable when used as a session RPE measure with children who are overweight or obese (McGuigan et al., 2008). However, the findings of this study indicate that the RPE values are higher when OMNI-RES measures are obtained following the whole training session than when expressed as an average for all exercise sets (McGuigan et al., 2008). This difference suggests that in children the session RPE provides different information than the average RPE across the entire session. However, there was a very high correlation between the session and average RPE ($r = 0.88$), and the session RPE method was highly reliable. Another investigation compared the effect of different resistance training protocols on metabolic and perceptual responses in ten healthy men with 6 months of weight training experience (Charro, Aoki, Coutts, Araujo, & Bacurau, 2010). Their results showed no difference in perceptual responses when the different protocols were matched for training load.

The timing of the rating is also important to standardize to minimize influence of the last part of the training on the subject's RPE of the whole training session. For this reason, session RPE is typically measured about 30 minutes after each training session to ensure that the perceived effort was referred to the whole session rather than the most recent exercise intensity (Foster, Florhaug, et al., 2001). One study by Singh et al. (2007) measured session RPE 5 minutes following completion of a workout and then every 5 minutes up until 30 minutes postexercise. There was no significant difference between values obtained 15 and 30 minutes postexercise suggesting that 15 minutes may be sufficient time to obtain a true global RPE.

Results of a number of studies have shown that the session RPE is a useful tool for measuring different types of resistance training sessions. One study compared three different resistance training techniques (traditional, super slow, and power) in the squat exercise (Egan et al., 2006). The study found that the super slow and traditional resistance training methods were perceived as being significantly more difficult than the maximal power method (Figure 3.3). There was no significant difference between the mean RPE measures taken following each set and the session RPE for each training method. RPE in its various manifestations seems to provide an accurate and simple window into the metabolic disturbances associated with different modes of exercise.

While the calculation of individual session load (RPE × duration) is common, other indices of total training stress for a given period (e.g. week, month) can also be determined (Foster, 1998; Foster, Heimann, et al., 2001). However, the most appropriate method of calculating these variables is debatable. Monotony, representing the variation in training load, and strain, representing the combined influences of load and monotony, are potentially important monitoring measures (Brink, Visscher, et al., 2010; Foster, Heimann, et al., 2001). Despite this, these indices are seldom reported in the literature (Brink, Visscher, et al., 2010; Foster, Heimann, et al., 2001; Putlur et al., 2004) as most studies focus on training load. This method (training load) has been used to highlight athletes who are negatively adapting to training and are at risk of developing overtraining (Foster, 1998).

The monitoring of measures of training load is important for coaches to determine if they are implementing the appropriately planned training stimulus. It has been reported that athletes trained harder than intended on an easy training session as prescribed by the coach (Foster, Heimann, et al., 2001). The opposite was found when hard training sessions were prescribed. There were moderate relationships

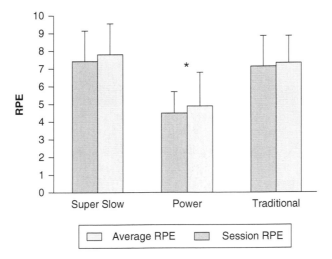

FIGURE 3.3 Average and session RPE values (mean ± SD) for traditional, maximal power, and super slow training sessions. The symbol "*" indicates that the maximal power RPE was significantly less than the traditional and super slow

between the training the coaches prescribed and what the athletes actually did in terms of training load ($r = 0.72$) and exercise intensity ($r = 0.75$; Foster, Heimann, et al., 2001). A small relationship was found for training duration ($r = 0.65$), which was somewhat surprising, particularly as duration is a relatively easy component of training to quantify. These findings suggest that either many coaches are not implementing their training programs according to intention or that athletes are unable to control their training intensity according to coaches' instructions. Regardless of the cause, this disparity in perception of training between athletes and their coaches may result in reduced performance. For this reason, it seems that it is necessary to develop a training monitoring system that allows coaches to plan and monitor the workloads undertaken by their athletes.

Questionnaires and training diaries

Various questionnaires and diaries can potentially be used to monitor resistance training and training in general (Hopkins, 1991). Somewhat surprisingly there is very little research in this area. The use of questionnaires to assess exercise levels, especially in large populations, is popular because their administration is cost-effective, easy, and does not interfere with training. However, their limitation is the fact that the athletes' responses are subjective (Hopkins, 1991). There are relatively few studies that have reported questionnaire or diary data specifically for resistance training.

Athletes are often required to complete questionnaires to record the perception of measures such as sleep quality, fatigue, muscle soreness, mood, and/or training quality. Psychological questionnaires such as DALDA, Profile of Mood States (POMS), and RESTQ-Sport have been used as a monitoring tool for sport coaches and can be implemented on a regular basis (Coutts & Reaburn, 2008; Coutts et al., 2007; Jones, Matthews, Murray, Van Raalte, & Jensen, 2010). The POMS can be used as a relatively immediate state measure of workload impact (Jones et al., 2010), whereas questionnaires such as the Athlete Burnout Questionnaire (ABQ) are designed to assess more long-term chronic impacts of workload (Cresswell & Eklund, 2005). Again these questionnaires are used within the scope of an entire training program and there is little research where they have been applied directly to resistance training.

Training diaries are commonly used to provide quantitative estimates of training volume. The diaries represent an effective method of assessing training longitudinally, despite limitations (Hopkins, 1991). One study studied the relationship between what athletes say they do in training and what they actually do (Borresen & Lambert, 2006). In the study, 15 men and 19 women who trained regularly self-reported their average weekly training duration for 3 weeks of training. During the following 2 weeks, training duration was recorded. There was a significant relationship ($r = 0.87$) between self-reported and recorded duration. Twenty-four percent of the participants overestimated the duration of training they were doing, and 17 percent underestimated their training duration. This amount of error in self-reported data has the potential to significantly affect the training prescription. Therefore, the authors recommended that the error be accounted for or some attempt is made to use physiological measurements to confirm self-reported data.

The RESTQ-Sport consists of 77 items that assess the frequency of stress- and recovery-related activities experienced in the previous 3 days and nights (Kellmann, Altenburg, Lormes, & Steinacker, 2001). The questionnaire has a total of 19 scales, including 12 general stress and recovery scales and seven sport-specific scales. There are seven scales that assess subjective strain, including general stress, emotional stress, social stress, conflicts/pressure, fatigue, lack of energy, and physical complaints. The recovery scales include success, social recovery, physical recovery, general well-being, and sleep quality. The seven sport-specific scales include stress scales (fitness/injury, burnout/emotional exhaustion, and disturbed breaks) and recovery scales (fitness/being in shape, burnout/personal accomplishment, self-regulation, and self-efficacy; Kellmann et al., 2001). The RESTQ-Sport is a practical tool for monitoring responses to training in team-sport athletes. Coutts and Reaburn (2008) evaluated whether the RESTQ-Sport could be used to measure changes in stress and recovery during intensified training in 20 semiprofessional rugby league players (which included resistance training). Throughout the study, all participants kept a logbook in which they were required to record their training time and training intensity for each session. The RESTQ-Sport scores with training were positively related to stress subscale scores and recovery subscale measures decreasing in the intensified training group and then normalizing following a 1-week taper.

The DALDA questionnaire (Rushall, 1990) has been used in several studies during periods of intensified training (Halson et al., 2002; Robson-Ansley, Blannin, &

Gleeson, 2007). The DALDA is divided into two parts: Part A represents the sources of life stress and Part B symptoms of stress. The questionnaire is normally completed by the athlete on a daily basis, and the athlete or coach can plot the daily responses to the questionnaire. Research suggests that its completion on a weekly basis does not reduce its sensitivity to changes in training load (Robson-Ansley et al., 2007). Peaks in the sum of the worse-than-normal responses that remain elevated for several days may indicate an athlete who has overreached and is at risk of developing overtraining syndrome (Robson-Ansley et al., 2007). The DALDA appears to be a sensitive indicator that is responsive to changes in training load, with researchers reporting significant increases in the symptoms of stress inventory in line with a decrease in immune function during a 2-week period of intensified training (Robson-Ansley et al., 2007). When training resumed to normal levels, the worse-than-normal scores in the symptoms of stress inventory returned to baseline (Robson-Ansley et al., 2007).

Training diaries have been used to study the training patterns of 36 athletes from a junior national rowing squad (Guellich, Seiler, & Emrich, 2009). All squad members were asked to record their daily training in a standardized training diary and to submit it to the national coach. Reliability of the athletes' training diaries was determined by using information reported to the national coach being compared with data reported directly to the researchers, group by 29 athletes participating in postal survey after the completion of the season. The data from the training diary and from the postal survey correlated with training frequency ($r = 0.88$) and training time ($r = 0.84$).

In another study, phone interviews were found to give better measures of training for validating a questionnaire (Liow & Hopkins, 1996). Validation of training over an extended period of time is difficult, because it is unrealistic to monitor and observe athletes for more than a few training sessions. One approach that has been suggested is to use a retrospective questionnaire and to validate the questionnaire against measures from a diary (Hopkins, 1991). Another approach has been to validate a short period of data from diaries against concurrent objective measures (Hewson & Hopkins, 1995).

Researchers investigated training loads and psychological data in 106 adolescent rugby union players (Hartwig, Naughton, & Searl, 2009). Measures of psychological stress and recovery were determined using the RESTQ-Sport. Training loads were estimated using weekly training diaries. At the end of the last training session for the week, players completed a 7-day training diary and were instructed to record all physical activities in the past week that had lasted 15 minutes or more. Team coaches and coaching staff confirmed that reported weekly training volumes approximated expected values. The RESTQ-Sport was administered before training sessions 2–3 days after weekend rugby matches, and the results showed that players with the highest training volumes during the season demonstrated more favorable recovery–stress states than moderate- and low-volume groups.

One study had 13 female basketball players (mean age 16 years) complete pre- and postseason interviews and maintain audio diaries during their season

(Tamminen & Holt, 2010). Each participant was issued with an audio recording device and was instructed to make recordings much in the same way that she would use a diary. A prompt sheet was provided to the athletes and they were asked to make an audio diary recording after at least one game or one practice per week. The use of audio diaries appeared to be effective in gathering information and could be a useful tool in terms of providing detailed information about athletes' responses to training sessions.

To monitor recovery, researchers have proposed the use of a recovery score to quantify the total quality of recovery (TQR; Kentta & Hassmen, 1998). One study investigated the relationship between training load, recovery, and monthly field test performance in young elite soccer players (Brink, Nederhof, Visscher, Schmikli, & Lemmink, 2010). Before each training session or match, they recorded their recovery score on a scale from 6 to 20. They also recorded session RPE following each training session. Modeling showed that every extra hour training or game play resulted in enhanced field test performance. However, session RPE and TQR scores did not contribute to the prediction of performance. In another study, researchers tracked an elite Japanese sprinter for 1 year, during which time session RPE and recovery scores were monitored on a daily basis (Suzuki, Sato, Maeda, & Takahashi, 2006). A mathematical model was used and the researchers were able to predict performance with a high degree of accuracy. Although there is a lack of published research data on the use of measures such as TQR, the method has excellent practical value as it is easy to administer, can be done on a daily basis, and educates the athletes about the nuances of recovery. The greatest value of these various questionnaires appears to be when they are integrated with other measures of a monitoring system (Brink, Visscher, et al., 2010; Cormack et al., 2008).

Online training diaries could provide an alternative to pen-and-paper methods in the regular assessment and monitoring of athletes. One study used online diaries to monitor incidences of illness in team-sport athletes (Cunniffe et al., 2009). Monitoring occurred over a 48-week rugby season in 30 rugby union players. Players were asked to record weekly illness symptoms with medical staff and also use an online training diary. Submitted self-reported diary illness data were compared with illness data recorded by medical staff. The results showed that the athletes reported just 19 percent of upper respiratory illness episodes to the medical staff.

Practical application of the session RPE method

The simplicity of the session RPE method makes it a useful tool for coaches and sport scientists. Its low cost and lack of reliance on technical expertise or equipment make it a user-friendly and practical method for monitoring resistance training and training in general. One of the benefits of using the session RPE scale is its measure of both psychological and physiological factors, therefore giving a more holistic indication of the global internal stress.

The existing literature would appear to provide support for the use of the session RPE method as a subjective estimate of training load during resistance training.

TABLE 3.1 Training diary demonstrating the calculation of training load, monotony, and strain

Day	Training activity	Session RPE	Duration (minutes or repetitions)	Load
Monday	Practice	6	120	720
	Weights	6	64	384
Tuesday	Practice	5	120	600
Wednesday	Match	7	180	1,260
Thursday	Practice	3	60	180
	Run	3	40	120
Friday	Practice	5	120	600
	Weights	7	72	504
Saturday	Practice	6	120	720
Sunday	Run	4	25	100
	Weekly load			5,188
	Monotony (mean daily load/SD)			1.45
	Strain (load × monotony)			7,541

It appears that this very simple method may be a useful technique for quantifying training load in a wide variety of athletic populations. The research that has been conducted would suggest that the session RPE method may provide a method for quantifying the exercise intensity component and allow calculation of a single number representative of the combined intensity and duration of training sessions.

The session RPE technique is easy to use, highly reliable, and consistent with objective physiological indices of the intensity of resistance training. By simply asking the athlete to rate the global intensity of the exercise bout and then multiplying by the duration of the training bout, a training load can be created (Foster, 1998). By using a training diary or spreadsheet, one can show the weekly pattern of exercise (Table 3.1). Accessory indices of training, such as load, monotony, and strain, can be calculated, potentially providing in index of the likelihood of negative training outcomes. Daily and weekly training loads calculated using this technique can be presented graphically, allowing the coach to have a visual representation of the periodization plan as experienced by the athlete. For example, an increased RPE to a standard work bout during each training cycle or over a week may be used as a guide for coaches to monitor for either increases in fatigue or reductions in fitness levels within individual athletes. Conversely, a reduction in RPE to these standard work bouts may indicate training adaptation. However, further research is required to validate the effectiveness of this method for monitoring changes in performance, fitness, and fatigue during exercise.

Ideally, the RPE should be obtained 30 minutes after the workout. Obviously this is not practical in all situations, and it could be obtained after the cool-down, which could be approximately 10–15 minutes after the last exercise bout (Singh et al., 2007). Practitioners should also be aware that the RPE does not always directly relate to the relative intensity used during resistance training and appears to depend on the mode of resistance exercise that is used (Egan et al., 2006; Singh et al., 2007). The practical usefulness of the session RPE method in quantifying training load is ideal when monitoring training needs to be quick and easy.

Another potential application of RPE is that it can be used as a method of tracking training progress. However, there is not a lot of research in this area. In terms of resistance exercise, tracking can occur by using RPE as a measure to monitor changes in strength as a function of the resistance training program (Gearhart et al., 2009). A session RPE value provided after each resistance training session would allow coaches to see changes in the perception of intensity when compared to previous session RPE values at a given intensity. The session RPE method can be considered a valid technique to prescribe work intensities and provide for progressive increases in resistance. Through the use of a session RPE scale, one could choose intensities at which to work (e.g. RPE 5) prior to the start of a workout and be highly confident that work intensities will stay within the "hard" range. This is much easier than having to use multiple measures of RPE throughout an exercise session. The session RPE scale appears to have potential as a method to prescribe work intensities for resistance training sessions and possibly providing information on progressive increases in intensity.

Practical application of questionnaires and diaries

Questionnaires have great potential for measuring and monitoring training. They can be simple and inexpensive to administer and they can provide data on most aspects of training. Unfortunately, there is limited data on the different forms of athlete questionnaires that have been used specifically for resistance training. In addition, very few studies provide useful detail about the questionnaire wording and few studies report validity and reliability of their questionnaires. Researchers therefore have to spend a considerable amount of time designing and trialing a questionnaire before using it for a study or for practice. When designing a training questionnaire, it would seem to be important to get the input of coaches and athletes who know how resistance training programs are put together, how training sessions are organized, and what terminology is used.

Practical application of these measures is also impacted by the length of the questionnaires. For example, the RESTQ consists of 76 items, POMS 65 items, and ABQ 15 items. There is the potential for regular or too frequent measurement resulting in poor data quality. Abbreviated versions of these questionnaires would appear to have some merit and more research is needed to determine the validity of such an approach and whether these correlate with existing physiological measures of training load.

Another limitation with questionnaires is errors in the individual's responses due to factors such as misinterpretation of the questions, being unable to remember specific training details, and/or under- or overestimating aspects of training. Measures of training derived from questionnaires are therefore usually less precise than those derived from observation or physiological monitoring (Hopkins, 1991). Lack of precision could possibly result in misinterpretation of relationships between training and outcomes such as performance or injury. Therefore, it is important to estimate the precision of measures derived from questionnaires and also determine the reliability of these tools.

Information on training from diaries has the advantage of being recorded following the training sessions rather than measured via a questionnaire that is generally completed at the end of a week or training period. In other respects, diaries present more problems than questionnaires. One of the limitations with training diaries is the issue of compliance where athletes can be somewhat haphazard with recording the required information. Strategies for increasing compliance include regular collection of diaries, reminding athletes regularly to complete their diaries, and keeping the format of the diaries simple and short. There can also be problems with analysis with large amounts of data being generated. This data overload can be minimized by using methods such as electronic recording sheets (e.g. Microsoft Excel or sheets where athletes record information that can be scanned and analyzed using custom software).

Future research directions

Additional research is needed to confirm the efficacy of the session RPE in different populations across a range of exercise modes. The majority of studies have been conducted using untrained or recreational athletes, with one study on children. Studies on elite athletes and older adults are needed to confirm previous findings on the use of session RPE in resistance training.

While training diaries are widely used by weight trainers, there needs to be more systematic research on their use in practical settings. Online training diaries are becoming more popular and could be used more extensively by researchers. While researchers have investigated the use of questionnaires over relatively short periods of training (weeks and months), there is limited information on the regular daily use of questionnaires over years of training. Maintaining a high compliance to the regular completion of questionnaires would depend on factors such as the length and nature of the questionnaire, type of responses required, and incidence of feedback to the athlete. Data on the long-term use and adherence to completing regular questionnaires and diaries by athletes would provide valuable information on the sensitivity and reliability of these methods.

Integration of perceptual and questionnaire data to make decisions about athlete preparation is a common approach in sports. However, there is a dearth of published research on the efficacy of these methods. Although there is reported evidence that subjective intensity scores are important in relation to overtraining and injury, further research is needed to investigate whether this also leads to better prediction of performance. Studies on the use of perceptual, questionnaire, and various physiological and performance tests and their use in resistance training monitoring would be extremely informative for practitioners.

While there is some research on athlete versus coach ratings of sessions, this is a relatively new area of research and more data are needed. Current monitoring practices typically provide retrospective quantification of a resistance training session. The information collected typically summarizes a completed session and is used to modify a subsequent session. It would be of great value to practitioners to have methods that can be used within a session to provide instantaneous feedback that can be used to make modifications to programming and to optimize training adaptations. For example, if an athlete rates an exercise or portion of a training session as being excessively difficult (when compared to a known baseline), this information could be used to make alterations to that part of the training. Alternatively, perceptual information could be used to provide targets for portions of a training session, for example performing an exercise at an intensity of "7" or "very hard."

Summary

Resistance training consists of a complex milieu of variables including sets, repetitions, rest periods, lifting velocity, and type of exercise performed. Therefore, resistance exercise represents a unique mode to study perceived exertion. Although the session RPE seems a relatively simple concept, it does appear that this method can be used to monitor intensity of resistance exercise. However, resistance training provides a complex model of exercise where these factors have the potential to affect the perceptual signal.

There are a number of different methods that can be used to monitor resistance training sessions. It appears that RPE provides a valid and reliable method of monitoring resistance training intensity and session RPE can delineate different training intensities. However, further research is required to determine its effectiveness across different methods of resistance exercise. Unlike aerobic exercise, there is no universally accepted method of monitoring resistance training. RPE has also been investigated by researchers and has been shown to correlate well with the intensity of effort. Recent studies have demonstrated that the session RPE can delineate intensities and provides a global rating of session intensity. This method is easy to use and requires a single measure of the workout intensity. This suggests that the session RPE approach is a valid method for evaluating resistance exercise and could be used to provide a quantitative basis for describing the periodization of training plans. A worked example showing how session RPE can be used to calculate various training indices was provided.

Training diaries and questionnaires also have tremendous potential for monitoring resistance training. They can be used to provide important information about all aspects of training. However, further research is needed to develop reliable and valid diaries and questionnaires that can be used for resistance training.

Discussion questions

1. What is the rationale for obtaining the session RPE 30 minutes following a training session? What are the practical implications of waiting this long before getting the measure?
2. What are some factors that need to be considered when designing a question-naire that can be used for monitoring resistance training?
3. Discuss some of the ways that the session RPE can be used by a strength and conditioning coach to assist with their training program design.
4. Identify some areas of future research in perceptual monitoring that would be of practical value to strength and conditioning coaches.
5. What type of information can training diaries provide for researchers and prac-titioners? How can diaries be made more effective for monitoring resistance exercise?

References

Alexiou, H., & Coutts, A. J. (2008). A comparison of methods used for quantifying internal training load in women soccer players. *International Journal of Sports Physiology and Performance, 3*, 320–330.

Borg, G. (1982a). Psychophysical bases of perceived exertion. *Medicine and Science in Sports and Exercise, 14*, 377–381.

Borg, G. (1982b). Ratings of perceived exertion and heart rates during short-term cycle exercise and their use in a new cycling strength test. *International Journal of Sports Medicine, 3*, 153–158.

Borresen, J., & Lambert, M. I. (2006). Validity of self-reported training duration. *International Journal of Sports Science and Coaching, 1*, 353–359.

Borresen, J., & Lambert, M. I. (2008). Quantifying training load: A comparison of subjective and objective methods. *Journal of Sports Physiology and Performance, 3*, 16–30.

Brink, M. S., Nederhof, E., Visscher, C., Schmikli, S. L., & Lemmink, K. A. (2010). Monitoring load, recovery, and performance in young elite soccer players. *Journal of Strength and Conditioning Research, 24*, 597–603.

Brink, M. S., Visscher, C., Arends, S., Zwerver, J., Post, W. J., & Lemmink, K. A. (2010). Monitoring stress and recovery: New insights for the prevention of injuries and illnesses in elite youth soccer players. *British Journal of Sports Medicine, 44*, 809–815.

Charro, M. A., Aoki, M. S., Coutts, A. J., Araujo, R. C., & Bacurau, R. F. (2010). Hormonal, metabolic and perceptual responses to different resistance training systems. *Journal of Sports Medicine and Physical Fitness, 50*, 229–234.

Cormack, S. J., Newton, R. U., & McGuigan, M. R. (2008). Neuromuscular and endocrine responses of elite players to an Australian rules football match. *International Journal of Sports Physiology and Performance, 3*, 359–374.

Coutts, A. J., & Reaburn, P. (2008). Monitoring changes in rugby league players' perceived stress and recovery during intensified training. *Perceptual and Motor Skills, 106*, 904–916.

Coutts, A. J., Slattery, K. M., & Wallace, L. K. (2007). Practical tests for monitoring perfor-mance, fatigue and recovery in triathletes. *Journal of Science Medicine in Sport, 10*, 372–381.

Cresswell, S. L., & Eklund, R. C. (2005). Changes in athlete burnout and motivation over a 12-week league tournament. *Medicine and Science in Sports and Exercise, 37*, 1957–1966.

Cunniffe, B., Griffiths, H., Proctor, W., Jones, K. P., Baker, J. S., & Davies, B. (2009). Illness monitoring in team sports using a web-based training diary. *Clinical Journal of Sport Medicine, 19*, 476–481.

Day, M. L., McGuigan, M. R., Brice, G., & Foster, C. (2004). Monitoring exercise intensity during resistance training using the session RPE scale. *Journal of Strength and Conditioning Research, 18,* 353–358.

Egan, A. D., Winchester, J. B., Foster, C., & McGuigan, M. R. (2006). Using session RPE to monitor different methods of resistance exercise. *Journal of Sports Science and Medicine, 5,* 289–295.

Faigenbaum, A. D., Milliken, L. A., Cloutier, G., & Westcott, W. L. (2004). Perceived exertion during resistance training by children. *Perceptual and Motor Skills, 98,* 627–637.

Foster, C. (1998). Monitoring training in athletes with reference to overtraining syndrome. *Medicine and Science in Sports and Exercise, 30,* 1164–1168.

Foster, C., Florhaug, J. A., Franklin, J., Gottschall, L., Hrovatin, L. A., Parker, S., ... Dodge, C. (2001). A new approach to monitoring exercise training. *Journal of Strength and Conditioning Research, 15,* 109–115.

Foster, C., Heimann, K., Esten, P., Brice, G., & Porcari, J. (2001). Differences in perceptions of training by coaches and athletes. *South African Journal of Sports Medicine, 8,* 3–7.

Gearhart, R. F., Goss, F. L., Lagally, K. M., Jakicic, J. M., Gallagher, J., Gallagher, K. I., & Robertson, R. J. (2001). Ratings of perceived exertion in active muscle during high-intensity and low-intensity resistance exercise. *Journal of Strength and Conditioning Research, 16,* 87–91.

Gearhart, R. F., Lagally, K. M., Riechman, S. E., Andrews, R. D., & Robertson, R. J. (2009). Strength tracking using the OMNI resistance exercise scale in older men and women. *Journal of Strength and Conditioning Research, 23,* 1011–1015.

Guellich, A., Seiler, S., & Emrich, E. (2009). Training methods and intensity distribution of young world-class rowers. *International Journal of Sports Physiology and Performance, 4,* 448–460.

Halson, S. L., Bridge, M. W., Meeusen, R., Busschaert, B., Gleeson, M., Jones, D. A., & Jeukendrup, A. E. (2002). Time course of performance changes and fatigue markers during intensified training in trained cyclists. *Journal of Applied Physiology, 93,* 947–956.

Hartwig, T. B., Naughton, G., & Searl, J. (2009). Load, stress, and recovery in adolescent rugby union players during a competitive season. *Journal of Sports Sciences, 27,* 1087–1094.

Hewson, D. J., & Hopkins, W. G. (1995). Prescribed and self-reported seasonal training of distance runners. *Journal of Sports Sciences, 13,* 463–470.

Hopkins, W. (1991). Quantification of training in competitive sports: Methods and applications. *Sports Medicine, 12,* 161–183.

Jones, M. T., Matthews, T. D., Murray, M., Van Raalte, J., & Jensen, B. E. (2010). Psychological correlates of performance in female athletes during a 12-week off-season strength and conditioning program. *Journal of Strength and Conditioning Research, 24,* 619–628.

Kellmann, M., Altenburg, D., Lormes, W., & Steinacker, J. M. (2001). Assessing stress and recovery during preparation for the world championships in rowing. *The Sport Psychology, 15,* 151–167.

Kentta, G., & Hassmen, P. (1998). Overtraining and recovery: A conceptual model. *Sports Medicine, 26,* 1–16.

Kraemer, W., Noble, B. J., Clark, M. J., & Culver, B. W. (1987). Physiologic responses to heavy-resistance exercise with very short rest periods. *International Journal of Sports Medicine, 8,* 247–252.

Lagally, K. M., & Amorose, A. J. (2007). The validity of using prior ratings of perceived exertion to regulate resistance exercise intensity. *Perceptual and Motor Skills, 104,* 534–542.

Lagally, K. M., Robertson, R. J., Gallagher, K. I., Goss, F. L., Jakicic, J. M., Lephart, S. M., ... Goodpaster, B. (2002). Perceived exertion, electromyography, and blood lactate during acute bouts of resistance exercise. *Medicine and Science in Sports and Exercise, 34,* 552–559; discussion 560.

Lambert, M., & Borresen, J. (2006). A theoretical basis of monitoring fatigue: A practical approach for coaches. *International Journal of Sports Science and Coaching, 1,* 371–388.

Liow, D. K., & Hopkins, W. G. (1996). Training practices of athletes with disabilities. *Adapted Physical Activity Quarterly, 13*, 372–381.

McGuigan, M. R., Al Dayel, A., Tod, D., Foster, C., Newton, R. U., & Pettigrew, S. (2008). Use of session rating of perceived exertion for monitoring resistance exercise in children who are overweight or obese. *Pediatric Exercise Science, 20*, 333–341.

McGuigan, M. R., Egan, A. D., & Foster, C. (2004). Salivary cortisol responses and perceived exertion during high intensity and low intensity bouts of resistance exercise. *Journal of Sports Science and Medicine, 3*, 8–15.

McGuigan, M. R., & Foster, C. (2004). A new approach to monitoring resistance training. *Strength and Conditioning Journal, 26*, 42–47.

Noble, B. J., Borg, G. A., Jacobs, I., Ceci, R., & Kaiser, P. (1983). A category-ratio perceived exertion scale: Relationship to blood and muscle lactates and heart rate. *Medicine and Science in Sports and Exercise, 15*, 523–528.

Putlur, P., Foster, C., Miskowski, J. A., Kane, M. K., Burton, S. E., Scheett, T. P., & McGuigan, M. R. (2004). Alteration of immune function in women collegiate soccer players and college students. *Journal of Sports Science and Medicine, 3*, 234–243.

Robertson, R. J., Goss, F. L., Andreacci, J. L., Dube, J. J., Rutkowski, J. J., Frazee, K. M., … Snee, B. M. (2005). Validation of the children's OMNI-resistance exercise scale of perceived exertion. *Medicine and Science in Sports and Exercise, 37*, 819–826.

Robertson, R. J., Goss, F. L., Rutkowski, J., Lenz, B., Dixon, C., Timmer, J., … Andreacci, J. (2003). Concurrent validation of the OMNI perceived exertion scale for resistance exercise. *Medicine and Science in Sports and Exercise, 35*, 333–341.

Robson-Ansley, P. J., Blannin, A., & Gleeson, M. (2007). Elevated plasma interleukin-6 levels in trained male triathletes following an acute period of intense interval training. *European Journal of Applied Physiology, 99*, 353–360.

Rushall, B. S. (1990). A tool for measuring stress tolerance in elite athletes. *Journal of Applied Sports Psychology, 2*, 51–66.

Serrano, M. A., Salvador, A., Gonzalez-Bono, E. G., Sanchis, C., & Suay, F. (2001). Relationships between recall of perceived exertion and blood lactate concentration in a judo competition. *Perceptual and Motor Skills, 92*, 1139–1148.

Singh, F., Foster, C., Tod, D., & McGuigan, M. R. (2007). Monitoring different types of resistance training using session rating of perceived exertion. *International Journal of Sports Physiology and Performance, 2*, 34–45.

Suzuki, S., Sato, T., Maeda, A., & Takahashi, Y. (2006). Program design based on a mathematical model using rating of perceived exertion for an elite Japanese sprinter: A case study. *Journal of Strength and Conditioning Research, 20*, 36–42.

Sweet, T. W., Foster, C., McGuigan, M. R., & Brice, G. (2004). Quantitation of resistance training using the session rating of perceived exertion method. *Journal of Strength and Conditioning Research, 18*, 796–802.

Tamminen, K. A., & Holt, N. L. (2010). Female adolescent athletes' coping: A season-long investigation. *Journal of Sports and Science, 28*, 101–114.

Wallace, L. K., Slattery, K. M., & Coutts, A. J. (2009). The ecological validity and application of the session-RPE method for quantifying training loads in swimming. *Journal of Strength and Conditioning Research, 23*, 33–38.

4

EXERCISE, SELF-ESTEEM AND SELF-PERCEPTIONS

Magnus Lindwall

UNIVERSITY OF GOTHENBURG, SWEDEN

'The self begins with the body, and people everywhere have bodies, but beyond that basic fact selves begin to vary' (Baumeister, 1995, p. 55). In a chapter on the link between exercise and self-perceptions related to the body, or physical self-perceptions (PSP), the quotation by Baumeister seems a very suitable point of departure. In the modern world, our body and self have to relate to everything around us, and, more importantly, our self has to relate to our own body, physique and physique-related competence. In this intimate and inevitable relationship, physical activity and regular exercise play important roles. Negative self-perception and low self-esteem are widely established markers of negative health and health-damaging behaviour, whereas positive self-perceptions and high self-esteem seem to accompany a wide array of positive factors linked to health, achievement and behaviour. Given the robust association of both self-perception/self-image and exercise with mental and physical health, a fundamental question is: What role does regular exercise play in the shaping of, and evaluation of, individuals' self-perceptions? This question constitutes the core of this chapter. I start by defining relevant terms, such as self-concept and self-esteem, and then examine the importance of PSP for the body. I then review the relationship between self-perceptions and exercise, and also propose a model that explains why exercise may be associated with enhanced self-perceptions. I then present research avenues that may increase current knowledge and present applied implications. Most studies in the area have focused on aerobic or general exercise modalities. As few previous studies have examined the specific role of strength training on self-perceptions, the base of the chapter is the relationship of general exercise with self-perceptions. Where possible, the examples from strength and conditioning will be provided. Given that modern strength and conditioning practitioners and researchers focus on various exercise modalities, strength and conditioning will be considered from an inclusive and broad perspective.

The self-concept, self-esteem and the physical self

The *self-concept* may be viewed as 'the individual as known by the individual' (Murphy, 1947, p. 996). The self-concept is broad and includes cognitive, affective and behavioural aspects. It is often used as an umbrella term that includes more specific concepts such as self-esteem and self-efficacy. *Self-esteem*, on the other hand, is viewed as a narrower, evaluative component of the self (Byrne, 1996; Harter, 1996). R. N. Campbell (1984) defined self-esteem as: 'the awareness of good possessed by self' (p. 9). The distinction between self-concept and self-esteem is vital, as they refer to different processes of the self that may have different effects on the general well-being and behaviour of the individual. In this context, self-concept may, at the individual level, be viewed as a descriptive or cognitive component (i.e. 'who am I?'), whereas self-esteem is the evaluative or affective component, answering the question: 'how do I feel about who I am?' (J. N. Campbell et al., 1996). However, the self-descriptive and self-evaluative processes of the self are inexorably intertwined and are often used interchangeably in research because it is difficult to describe the self without linking it to affect and evaluation (Byrne, 1996; Sonstroem, 1997a).

The self-concept may further be divided into different domains, that is, the way individuals perceive themselves in various areas in life. One such area, that seems relevant for exercise, is the *physical self*, defined as an individual's perceptions of himself/herself in the physical domain. According to the dominant multidimensional hierarchical model of the self (Shavelson, Hubner, & Stanton, 1976), the physical self may further be divided into several components, or subdomains, of physical competencies and appearance, such as perceptions of strength, endurance, sport ability and body attractiveness (Fox & Corbin, 1989). *Body image* today plays an important role in the development and maintenance of the self (Davis, 1997). For females especially (but also for males), a negative body image has been identified as a central component of major health problems such as eating disorders (Levine & Piran, 2004), obesity (Schwartz & Brownell, 2004) and depression (Cash & Pruzinsky, 2002). Modern definitions of body image focus on the internal representation of our outer appearance (Thompson, Heinberg, Altabe, & Tantleff-Dunn, 1999), or one's body-related self-perceptions and self-attitudes, including thoughts, beliefs, feelings and behaviour (Cash, 2004).

Another concept closely related to body image and the physical self is *social physique anxiety* (SPA; Hart, Leary, & Rejeski, 1989). The concept stems from the general construct of social anxiety, which reflects the anxiety people feel when they perceive themselves as being unable to behave, or present themselves, in ways that they think that others expect (Schlenker & Leary, 1982). Linked to the physical self, bodily flaws become social liabilities and potential sources for rejection and humiliation, at least in the subject's eyes. SPA is defined as: 'a subtype of social anxiety that occurs as a result of the prospect or interpersonal evaluation involving one's physique' (Hart et al., 1989, p. 96). It is posited that individuals with high SPA will be more likely than people with low SPA to avoid situations in which they are forced to reveal their physique (e.g. at the gym, on beaches or in swimming facilities) to others and thereby face a potential evaluation of others. Although this concept represents a fairly new area within sport and exercise psychology research, it has received substantial interest and attention during the last 10 years (Martin Ginis, Lindwall, & Prapavessis, 2007).

An important distinction has been drawn between global and domain-specific evaluations of the self. Global self-evaluations have been referred to as 'self-esteem' (Rosenberg, 1979), 'self-worth' (Crocker & Wolfe, 2001; Harter, 1993) or 'general self-concept' (Marsh, 1986a). The relation between the global and domain-specific facets in the self has been presented in several frameworks and models. One such model (see Figure 4.1), illustrating how self-perceptions (of the physical self) at varying levels of specificity are linked to self-esteem on a global level, has been outlined by Fox (1998).

In line with the theory of the hierarchical structure of the self (Fox, 1990, 1998; Shavelson et al., 1976), the model holds that there exist several measurable levels of PSP and that the link between these different levels and global self-esteem depends on where they are situated in the tree-like, or root-like, hierarchy of the model. For example, physical self-worth at the domain level should be more closely related to global self-esteem than should being able to complete a specific exercise in the gym or finishing a bout of running in a specific time.

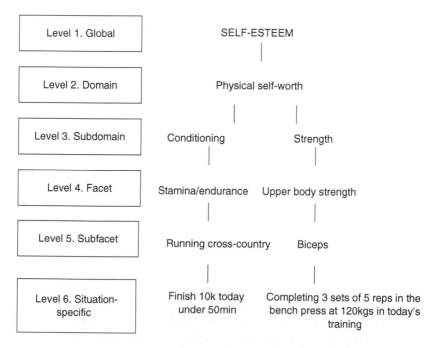

FIGURE 4.1 The link between self-esteem and self-perceptions in the context of the body. Adapted from Fox (1998)

Importance of the physical self and the body

From an exercise perspective, a relevant question seems to be how PSP are related to general self-concept or global self-esteem. That is, if individuals perceive themselves to be strong, be fit, and have an attractive body, does this also mean they will be more likely to have a high self-esteem and be content in general? The physical self, and PSP, have been demonstrated to have the closest relation to global self-esteem of the various domains in the self-concept models (e.g. Harter, 1993, 1999), thereby being the most predictive component of general self-regard. Looking into what specific domains of the physical self that are most strongly related to how individuals generally perceive their physical self and body (i.e. physical self-worth), bodily attractiveness has been reported to be the factor related most closely to general physical self-worth, with typical correlations of around $r = 0.7$ in most studies (Fox, 1997). The relationships between domains of perceived physical competence (e.g. sport ability, endurance/condition, strength) and self-esteem have on the other hand generally been found to be low to moderate in strength ($r = 0.15–0.40$). Supporting this notion, results from a recent cross-national study on the relation between self-esteem, PSP and importance of PSP, including over 1,800 university students from England, Sweden, Turkey and Portugal (Lindwall, Aşçi, Palmeira, Fox, & Hagger, 2011), again showed that body attractiveness was the PSP domain most strongly related to global self-esteem. This mirrors the findings that the average correlations between appearance and global self-esteem have typically been as high as between 0.7 and 0.8 (Harter, 1993). This relationship between physical appearance and self-esteem seems to be particularly strong in children, adolescents and young adults. Further supporting the link between physical appearance and global self-esteem, meta-analyses have shown self-esteem to be the strongest personality correlate of self-rated physical attractiveness (Feingold, 1992), and that attractive adults possess more favourable self-perceptions and perceive themselves to be more competent than unattractive adults (Langlois et al., 2000).

How should these strong links between self-esteem, physical self-worth and body attractiveness be interpreted and explained? According to Sonstroem (1997a) they can be interpreted from at least three different viewpoints: (a) an attractive body is, in the eyes of many people, synonymous with physical self-worth and self-esteem; (b) an attractive body is perceived as being synonymous with health and health is perceived as closely related to self-esteem and self-worth; and (c) the scales overlap due to the use of similar phrases in the item construction.

Another way of understanding why PSP and body image may be so clearly related to self-esteem is that being fit and having an attractive body is deemed to be important for many people. A theory proposed by James (1890) more than 100 years ago, which, although debated, has received support in modern research (Lindwall et al., 2011), states that, in domains deemed highly important by the individual, the general self-concept, such as self-esteem, will be affected by perceptions of competence, whereas the self-rating in domains interpreted as unimportant will have little impact on the general self-concept. Following this line of reasoning, the perceptions individuals holds of their competence linked to the physical self will be most strongly related to general self-esteem if they also feel these areas are important. If having well-developed muscles or a toned or slim body is important to a person, as it often is in the commercialised Western world for at least most young adults (for a review on the muscular ideal, see Cafri et al., 2005, and Chapter 7), the perceptions of failure to achieve this will most probably have a negative impact on general self-esteem. However, if the person does not feel body appearance or fitness is important, negative perceptions of one's competence linked to the body will probably have a negligible effect on self-esteem.

Importance of the physical self and the body in modern society

As stated by Fredrickson and Roberts (1997): 'bodies exist within social and cultural contexts' (p. 174). Hence, it may be useful to consider sociocultural perspectives when understanding the link between exercise, PSP and self-esteem. Indeed, the PSP and self-esteem of the individual are closely linked to social and cultural ideals, which through early socialisation are adopted and integrated in the self-system and hence influence its function. It has been suggested that the focus on exercise and the maintenance of the body, at least from an individualistic perspective, reflects the development of modern society, culture and, more specifically, the central values and attitudes of present-day Western lifestyles (e.g. Featherstone, 1991; Turner, 1992). In the pursuit of the highly valued fit and attractive body (the athletic ideal), the three areas of diet/nutrition, exercise and plastic surgery provide the most commonly used tools (Brownell, 1991a). Two assumptions are made in the search for the 'better' body: (a) the body is malleable (i.e. with the right training or programme everybody can succeed) and (b) the effort will be worthwhile in the end, that is, substantial rewards await. The latter notion receives empirical support from the fact that physical attractiveness and outer appearance are, in the eyes of many people, naturally associated with highly prized personality traits and characteristics, such as social competence, potency and adjustment (Eagly, Ashmore, Makhijani, & Longo, 1991; Feingold, 1992; Langlois et al., 2000). The perfect, or fit, body stands as a symbol for control and discipline, which are two highly esteemed virtues in modern society (Brownell, 1991a, 1991b). Through incorporating these ancient virtues into the lifestyle, individuals may control, discipline and hence sculpt their body to conform to the overarching body ideals of the modern era, ensuring substantial internal, as well as external, rewards (Leary, 1992; Martin Ginis et al., 2007). Moreover, information regarding people's exercise habits has been shown to affect the impressions that others form of them (Hodgins, 1992). More specifically, targets described as fit and regular exercisers were rated more favourably on a variety of personality variables than people described as not regular exercisers or fit, resulting in a form of positive exercise stereotype (Lindwall & Martin Ginis, 2006, 2008; Martin Ginis et al., 2007).

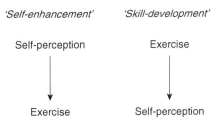

FIGURE 4.2 The relationship between exercise and self-perception from two different perspectives

The self and exercise: two perspectives

When considering possible explanations for the effects of any intervention on a specific factor, it is relevant to examine how that factor interacts with the environment. It has been suggested that self-esteem interacts with the environment in a two-way bi-directional process; that is, individuals are influenced, for good or bad, by the environment, but also operate on it, consequently affecting its influence on them. From this reasoning, two different hypotheses have been derived: the skill-development hypothesis (SDH) and the self-enhancement hypothesis (SEH; Marsh, 1986b; Sonstroem, 1997b, 1998; see Figure 4.2).

The SDH suggests that, by experiencing success and receiving rewards, people feel better about themselves and strengthen their perceived competence. Related to exercise and physical activity, the SDH holds that improvements in physical fitness or skills, which result, for example, from following a strength training programme, will lead to an enhanced sense of the self. Conversely, in accordance with the SEH, a high self-esteem may operate on the environment to maintain its status, that is, people with a high self-esteem tend to behave in accordance with their self-image to confirm it. For example, people with positive PSP linked to the subdomains of strength, will be more likely to further engage in regular strength training to gain positive appraisal from the self and others. Furthermore, it has been suggested that the development and evaluation of the self are affected by social and cultural factors. In this process, external standards, such as referred appraisal and social comparison, are important (Sonstroem, 1998). Referred appraisal describes how individuals think that significant others perceive them and how this, in turn, affects their self-image. Social comparison is the tendency for individuals to observe others and compare themselves with others. Hence, the social context has a significant impact on how people perceive and evaluate themselves.

Self-enhancement: effect of the self on exercise

People actively engage in a number of different strategies to improve, or maintain, self-esteem. For example, it is widely recognised that most people exhibit a modest bias towards self-enhancement (Taylor & Brown, 1988; Tesser, 1988). Self-enhancement strategies frequently used include the following: guiding the self towards domains in life that may result in success and positive affect (Harter, 1990; White, 1959), withdrawing or staying away from domains that may result in failure and negative affect and/or discounting the importance of these domains (Harter, 1993), constructing attributions that enable one to take pride in one's success and view failure as a learning experience (hoping for the best, being prepared for the worst; Blaine & Crocker, 1993), self-affirmation and self-verification at times when the self is under threat (Tice, 1993) and maximising social support and approval (Harter, 1996). Regular exercise may be viewed as an activity that incorporates several of the above-mentioned self-enhancement strategies. For example, being engaged in regular exercise is often related to improvement in areas that are highly deemed by the individual (being more fit, gaining muscle strength or improving sport-specific ability) and thereby to enhanced positive feelings of general competence and esteem. Moreover, if people feel they are competent in the domain ('I am fit and capable of successfully completing most exercises in the gym'), the chance of returning to that activity is quite high, whereas lack of competence in an area ('I am quite weak and not very fit') is linked to less chance of future engagement. Also, in the modern fitness and health-focused society, regular exercise is also related to achieving positive praise and social approval. Therefore, taking part in an exercise activity that one feels competent in is probably one of the most effective ways to improve self-esteem or maintain a positive self-image.

Harter's competence motivation theory

According to the theory (Harter, 1978), individuals will experience positive emotion and low anxiety if they are able to successfully master a task in conditions under which an internal locus of control is perceived. Therefore, the theory predicts that individuals whose self-perceptions of their physical ability are high will be more likely to take part in exercise and physical activity, because this affords the possibility of demonstrating competence. Hence, individuals with positive PSP and an internal locus of control should be more motivated to participate in exercise and physical activity and more likely to actually participate. Supporting this theory, several studies have demonstrated that more positive PSP are related to increased exercise participation for adults (Fox & Corbin, 1989; Lindwall & Hassmén, 2004; Sonstroem, Speliotis, & Fava 1992).

Self-presentation

Leary (1992) linked the concept of self-presentation to sport and exercise and argued that people express two motives in particular for exercising that reflect self-presentational motives: (a) improving or maintaining a highly valued physical appearance and (b) maintaining their social identities as athletic types, thereby gaining continued social praise for being fit and athletic. Furthermore, Leary proposed that self-presentational factors may influence several physical activity and exercise parameters, such as choice of physical activity, exercise and sport context, expressed and/or real degree of effort and exertion, and specific psychological phenomena linked to performance, such as choking under pressure and self-handicapping. In general, later studies have provided preliminary support for the notion that self-presentation is related to exercise cognitions, attitudes and behaviour (Hausenblas, Brewer, & Van Raalte, 2004; Martin Ginis et al., 2007).

Self-efficacy

Self-efficacy is one of the most investigated concepts within sport, exercise and health psychology (Bandura, 1997). Bandura (1986) defined it as: 'people's judgements of their capabilities to organise and execute a course of action required to attain designated types of performances' (p. 391). Extended research has consistently shown that exercise-related self-efficacy is linked to choice, effort, persistence and emotional dimensions of exercise behaviour, which makes it an important determinant of physical activity and exercise (Bandura, 1997; McAuley & Mihalko, 1998). More specifically, both long-term exercise participation and acute bouts of exercise seem to enhance self-efficacy (McAuley, Courneya, & Lettunich, 1991).

Self-determination theory

Self-determination theory (Deci & Ryan, 1985; Ryan & Deci, 2000; see Chapter 2) emphasises the role of three basic needs: competence, autonomy and relatedness to intrinsic motivation. The theory also posits that self-determination ranges from amotivation (lack of motivation), through four types of extrinsic motivation, to intrinsic motivation. This means that a person's motivation towards exercise behaviour changes gradually, rather than directly, from primarily external contingencies in the initiation process towards intrinsic motivation in later stages. Empirical support for the validity of the self-determination continuum has been documented in studies and in a meta-analysis (Hagger & Chatzisarantis, 2008). Linked to PSP, it has been suggested that self-determination theory may provide a vital missing link between self-esteem and behaviour (Biddle, 1997). In particular, in situations where direct rewards and paybacks to the invested behaviour are lacking, which makes the self-enhancement theory invalid as a source of explanation, the self-determination theory may be helpful. In the initiation process, for instance, people who start exercising primarily for expected future psychological and social benefits (e.g. appearance or health reasons), rather than for a direct physiological payback, may, through internalising the prior external motives to intrinsic regulations, justify their investment and maintain motivation for their behaviour long enough for them to reap other highly valued benefits, such as more positive perceptions of their physique and, eventually, a heightened sense of self-esteem.

Skill development: the effect of exercise on the self
Theoretical approaches to exercise, self-esteem and PSP

While there is a significant amount of anecdotal evidence for the positive effects of sport, exercise and physical activity on the self, less robust scientific evidence from

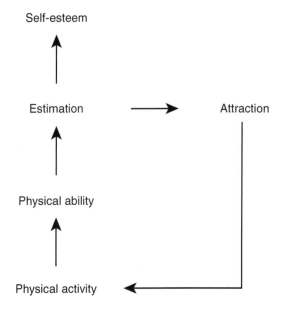

FIGURE 4.3 A psychological model for physical activity participation. Adapted from Sonstroem (1978)

well-designed and well-controlled studies exists (Fox, 2000a). Self-esteem is a frequently mentioned concept, both in the context of being a key mechanism in the general positive effect of exercise on depression and anxiety, and also for being a highly valued outcome of exercise in itself (Fox, 2000a). One of the first models to link PSP and self-esteem to exercise was presented by Sonstroem (1978, 1997a). The search for a variable mediating the association between fitness and self-esteem, thus functioning as a bridge between the physical world of activity and the psychological state of self-esteem, resulted in the psychological model for physical activity participation (see Figure 4.3). The model claims that participation in physical activity produces increased physical ability/fitness, which in turn brings about psychological benefits as reflected in positive changes in self-esteem. This alleged change in self-esteem is mediated by the factor estimation; that is, perceived physical competence and attraction. Consequently, increased fitness/physical ability would result in the enhancement of self-esteem in conjunction with increased perceived physical competence and attraction, which would lead to increased physical activity. Moreover, the model holds that people tend to engage in modes of behaviour that will maintain their positive self-esteem and that the drives towards self-enhancement and self-development are powerful motivational human forces that constantly affect our lives. Hence, the model may be viewed as based both on the skill-development and the self-enhancement hypotheses. The validity of the model has been tested with mixed outcomes. On the one hand, studies have demonstrated that estimation is related to physical fitness (Sonstroem, 1974, 1978), but on the other hand few studies have attempted, or managed, to show that increases in physical fitness cause increases in estimation. Relations between estimation scores and self-reports of exercise have been found (Fox, Corbin, & Couldry, 1985, Sonstroem, 1978), although the model in general has not been effective at predicting exercise adherence.

Based on the theory of Shavelson et al. (1976), Sonstroem and Morgan (1989) presented a model for examining the mechanisms of self-esteem change through exercise (adopting a skill-development perspective). The model, called the 'Exercise and Self-Esteem Model', explains how specific bouts of sport and exercise are translated into increased global self-esteem. The key constructs of this model are physical self-efficacy, physical competence, physical acceptance and general self-esteem. Physical self-efficacy plays a special role in this model, because it is viewed as the first cognitive link between higher-order psychological self-constructs (such as the four PSP subdomains, physical self-worth and global self-esteem) and actual behaviour (Sonstroem & Morgan, 1989). The notion of physical self-efficacy stems from the work of Bandura (1977, 1997) on his more general self-efficacy construct. It therefore denotes the strength and level of belief that one can perform a given physical task successfully. Physical competence refers to the broader perceptions and evaluations of one's body and its capacity; that is, a sort of overall, more stable summation of various physical self-efficacies. Physical acceptance refers to the perceived satisfaction individuals feel about different parts of their bodies. The rationale for implementing physical acceptance and competence into a self-esteem/ exercise model is that self-perceptions of one's body often tend to be closely related to general self-regard (Feingold, 1992; cf. Harter, 1993). Starting at the base of the model, objective evaluations of physical performance, enhanced through training, lead to an increased sense of physical self-efficacy (which is the first self-perception concept in the model and thus represents the bridge between the physical world and the perceptions of the physical self in the human psyche). Moving up in the model, increased physical self-efficacy influences the closely related physical competence and physical acceptance that are believed to affect global self-esteem. Later on Sonstroem, Harlow, and Josephs (1994) expanded the Exercise and Self-Esteem Model through the implementation of the four PSP subdomain variables of sport competence, condition, strength and body attractiveness and a fifth, general domain called physical self-worth (see Figure 4.4), naming it 'EXSEM' to separate it from the old model. Hence, the previous unidimensional concept of physical competence in the old model was replaced with a multidimensional concept of physical competence, which gives the model enhanced strength and potential for detecting mechanisms that underlie links between exercise and self-esteem and provides greater opportunities to test the discriminant validity of the model and to link it to external criteria (Sonstroem, 1997a). The validity of both the old model and, in particular, the new one has received support or partial support in several studies (Alfermann & Stoll, 2000; Sonstroem et al., 1994). With regard to the link between physical self-efficacy, the PSP subdomain variables, physical self-worth and self-esteem, it seems that physical self-efficacy is most closely related to the

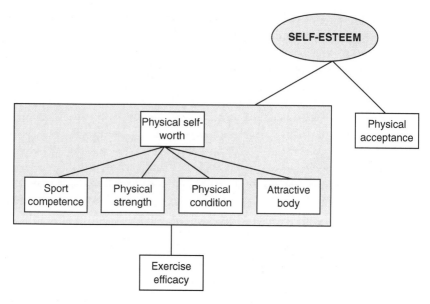

FIGURE 4.4 The expanded EXSEM model. Adapted from Sonstroem et al. (1994)

physical condition variable, whereas body attraction relates most strongly to physical self-worth, and thus indirectly to global self-esteem (Aşçi, Aşçi, & Zorba, 1999; Sonstroem et al., 1994). Consequently, viewed from an applied perspective, these trends imply that the physical self-perception subdomains that are most related to physical self-efficacy, and thereby easiest to change (physical condition), are not the same ones that are most highly related to the higher levels of general physical self-worth and self-esteem (body attractiveness).

Research examining exercise and self-esteem

Mirroring the above-mentioned positive relation between sport/exercise and body image, Sonstroem (1984) found in a narrative review of 16 studies that participation in exercise programmes was linked to increased self-esteem scores. However, as only ten studies included control groups, four had a randomised design and half contained 20 or fewer participants in the experiment group, the result of this review should be interpreted with caution.

Later on Fox (2000b) conducted an extensive meta-analysis of studies on exercise and self-esteem since 1970. Fox, compared to Sonstroem (1984), focused specifically on randomised controlled trials (RCTs). The reason for choosing RCTs was principally to recognise and overcome the previous difficulties in research on self-esteem of separating main effects from social desirability, expectancy, self-presentational strategy, pleasing the research leader and temporary versus lasting effects. In the meta-analyses, 36 RCTs were found. In addition to this, 44 non-randomised studies were identified for further consideration. The major conclusions drawn from this study were: (a) exercise is a valuable tool for increasing and maintaining physical self-worth and other PSP, as 78 per cent of the RCTs demonstrated a significant positive change in physical self-esteem; (b) half the studies showed no change in global self-esteem, although there were improvements shown – hence, changes in self-esteem do not seem to be automatic consequences of exercise; (c) positive effects were demonstrated for all age groups, but the effects seem to be greatest and clearest for children and middle-aged adults; (d) positive effects were shown both for women and men (however, as females constantly rate themselves lower on self-esteem, body image and physical self-worth, the facilitating effects may be greater for females); (e) weight training and aerobic training had the greatest impact in the short term, although a variety of other types of exercise also seem to have this beneficial effect on self-esteem; and (f) the effects of exercise are greatest for individuals with previously low self-esteem.

A more recent meta-analysis by Spence, McGannon, and Poon (2005) further examined the effect of exercise on self-esteem and included 113 studies. Based on the EXSEM model and its assumptions, they hypothesised that: (a) exercise participants who experience changes in physical fitness should also experience larger changes in self-esteem; (b) less physically fit individuals should experience larger changes in self-esteem compared to more fit individuals; (c) individuals with lower initial self-esteem should experience most change due to exercise; and (d) a larger dose of exercise (e.g. exercise with higher frequency, intensity and duration) should be related to larger changes in self-esteem. Overall, they found that participation in exercise led to a small, but significant, improvement in self-esteem. Significant changes in physical fitness were related to greater changes in self-esteem, supporting their first hypothesis. Moreover, although not statistically significant, individuals with lower initial self-esteem and physical fitness demonstrated larger changes in self-esteem compared with individuals starting off higher in terms of self-esteem and physical fitness. Similarly, a non-significant trend that exercising more frequently resulted in larger self-esteem gains compared with less frequent exercise was found.

A. Campbell and Hausenblas (2009) included 57 studies in their meta-analysis of exercise and body image. They also found a small but significant positive overall effect. This effect increased with more frequent exercise, but intensity, duration and length of exercise programme in terms of weeks did not influence the effect. Neither did gains in physical fitness result in a larger body image effect of exercise. The effect was roughly the same size for aerobic as well as for resistance exercise. Overweight individuals benefit somewhat more in terms of body image compared with non-overweight individuals.

To summarise the three meta-analyses on the effect of exercise on self-esteem, PSP and body image described above, it seems that engaging in regular exercise does increase the chances of improving one's self-concept, self-esteem and body image, although this effect in general is likely to be small. However, if one starts off being overweight and having lower levels of fitness and self-esteem, chances are higher that the exercise programme will result in larger improvements. In terms of gains in physical fitness, the pattern seems less clear. One meta-analysis found increased fitness to be related to more self-esteem improvement, whereas the other two found that physiological changes are not necessary for self-concept changes to occur due to exercise. Engaging in more frequent exercise (2–3 times per week or more) also appears to increase the chances of experiencing positive self-concept change. Another important notion is that exercise seems to have a stronger effect on more specific physical self-concepts (e.g. self-efficacy and PSP domains such as condition and strength) that are 'closer' to the activity, compared with more general measures such as global self-esteem. Hence, although exercise may have a small effect on broad psychological constructs such as self-esteem, it probably more often results in specific effects that are larger. For example, physically unfit and weak individuals with moderate self-esteem, but low perceived strength competence, may reap quite quick positive PSP changes and perceive themselves as much more competent in terms of strength after just a few weeks of strength training (depending on the adequacy of the programme and what support they have), whereas their self-esteem, that is influenced by so many more variables, may take a longer time to be affected by the training.

A relevant question linked to the focus of the book is, does strength and resistance training have the same potential for positive effects on self-concept and body image as aerobic training? The results from all three meta-analyses show that positive effects are possible to achieve with a range of different exercise activities and types, both aerobic activity as well as resistance and strength training. However, although the number of studies that have targeted strength training is much fewer in number compared with those using aerobic exercise, the effect sizes (a measure of the total effect of the included studies) in the meta-analyses are actually somewhat larger (non-statistically though) for strength training. This indicates that strength and resistance training may be at least as effective, if not somewhat more effective, for improving physical self-esteem and body image, particularly for overweight individuals who are probably physically stronger and thereby more able to experience mastery and competence even at the start of the programme.

Research examining the effect of exercise on PSP

Some studies specifically investigating the change of PSP (rather than self-esteem as described above) through exercise and aerobic programmes have failed to find significant changes on any PSP subdomain over 8–10 weeks of exercising (Aşçi, Kin, & Kosar, 1998; Caruso & Gill, 1992). Other studies have found significant increases in perceived strength, condition and physical self-worth (Page, Fox, McManus, & Armstrong, 1993) over an 8-week exercise programme undertaken by females, and improvements in physical self-concepts and self-esteem after a 6-month exercise programme, both for the experimental group and for the control group (Alfermann & Stoll, 2000). Aşçi (2003) found that participants in a physical training programme improved significantly over 10 weeks in only 4 of 11 measured PSP subdomains (physical activity, coordination, sport competence and flexibility) in addition to having a significant reduction on trait anxiety compared to the control group. A 6-month exercise intervention programme, investigating the effect of engagement in sport and exercise activities for previously inactive adolescent girls, found a positive effect of exercise on PSP, with the intervention group showing a more positive change in PSP compared to the control group (Lindwall & Lindgren, 2005).

A relevant question following these results is, what PSP domains does exercise have the largest impact on? A pattern from several of the above-mentioned intervention and cross-sectional studies seems to be that exercise has the largest positive impact on, or relationship with, the domain of physical conditioning (Fox & Corbin, 1989; Lindwall & Hassmén, 2004; Lindwall & Lindgren, 2005). By contrast, the body attractiveness subdomain has, in several studies, been revealed as the weakest link to exercise and has consequently been targeted as the PSP subdomain least susceptible to change as a function of exercise interventions (Fox, 1997).

Given the fact that physical appearance has consistently shown itself to be the strongest predictor of global self-esteem (Harter, 1993), and that the body subdomain has been shown to be the strongest predictor of physical self-worth (Fox, 1997), the question of why that domain of the physical self that is most highly linked to global self-esteem and physical self-worth is the most difficult one to change through exercise is of great significance. From a self-presentational perspective (Leary, 1992), it may be beneficial to consider how public the different domains of the physical self are. As stated by Fox (1998), the body (and hence physical appearance) could be perceived as a bridge between the inner mental world and the outer physical environment. Hence, the body and its appearance are constantly available for others to evaluate, whereas the more competence-based domains of the physical self (sport competence, physical conditioning and physical strength) reveal themselves more for scrutiny and feedback in specific contexts and situations. This could partially explain why the body and appearance aspects of the physical self are valued so highly and are linked so strongly to global self-esteem. The reason for why the body appears weakest in relation to exercise and sport may relate to the fact that the physical parameters linked to the body attractiveness subdomain (body weight, body mass index [BMI] and muscle tone) may simply be more difficult to change than the physical parameters that correspond to the perceived condition and strength subdomains (physical strength, general and specific fitness). In addition, the feedback of positive change is probably more direct and apparent for condition, strength and sport ability. That is, being able to lift more weights, running 10 km faster or being able to run for a longer distance, or performing better, at least technically, in sports, constitutes greater concrete evidence of successful changes than does a better looking body where the evaluation is more vague and dependent on the source. In addition, from the perspective of social comparison (Sonstroem, 1998), individuals probably more easily compare their progress with themselves as standards when it comes to condition, strength and sport, whereas the comparison with other fit bodies on display is often inevitable (Brownell, 1991a; Featherstone, 1991) and creates a tougher, and constantly changing, frame of reference (also labelled 'shifting goal posts phenomena'; Fox, 2000b).

Research examining body image and exercise

Together with low self-esteem, body dissatisfaction has revealed itself as one of the most consistent and robust predictors of eating pathology (Polivy & Herman, 2002; Stice, 2002). It seems pertinent to consider how sport and exercise participation may affect body image, given, on the one hand, the reported robust association between body image/dissatisfaction and eating disorders, and, on the other hand, the inconsistent results linking sport and exercise to eating disorders. The relationship between body image and exercise is complex, especially regarding females (Davis, 1997). For example, successful weight loss and moderate exercise may lead to enhanced body esteem and self-esteem (cf. the previously discussed EXSEM model), whereas excessive exercising in combination with eating pathology can involve very detrimental effects on body image and health for some individuals (Hausenblas & Carron, 1999; Hausenblas & Symons-Downs, 2002; Szabo, 2000; Thompson & Sherman, 2010), illustrating the potential 'dark side' of exercise and sport on health. Some studies investigating the link between body image and sport/exercise participation found no differences in body-image disturbances between exercisers and non-exercisers (Davis & Cowles, 1991), whereas others found that exercise is related to reductions in body-image disturbances, and more favourable evaluations of physical appearance, fitness and health (Bane & McAuley, 1996; McAuley, Bane, & Mihalko, 1995). Looking at the effect of the interaction between age and exercise on body satisfaction, satisfaction with bodily appearance has been shown to increase with age for moderately/highly physically active individuals but decrease for inactive individuals (Loland, 2000). Regarding gender differences in the relation between exercise and body image, it has been found that exercise behaviour predicts body satisfaction for males, whereas other factors, such as BMI, predicts body satisfaction for females more strongly (Hausenblas & Fallon, 2002; Loland, 2000). A meta-analytic review, incorporating 78 studies, demonstrated a small effect, indicating that athletes had a more positive body image than non-athletes (Hausenblas & Symons-Downs, 2001).

Research examining exercise and SPA

Overall, studies show that exercise and physical activity are related to levels of SPA (Hausenblas et al., 2004; Martin Ginis et al., 2007). Specifically, SPA has been linked to exercise participation, exercise attitudes (Crawford & Eklund, 1994; Lantz, Hardy, & Ainsworth, 1997; Spink, 1992) and reasons for exercise (Eklund & Crawford, 1994). Greater exercise has been shown to predict higher body satisfaction and lower SPA for males, whereas BMI seems to be a stronger predictor of SPA for females (Hausenblas & Fallon, 2002). However, the direction of the SPA–exercise relationship remains unclear as SPA has been identified both (a) as a potential barrier to exercise, due to concerns of showing one's physique to others in an exercise setting, and (b) as an incentive or motive to exercise to reduce SPA *via* the development of a fitter and more attractive physique (Martin Ginis & Leary, 2004).

Given the equivocal findings in studies examining the relation of physical activity and SPA, it has been suggested (Gammage, Martin Ginis, & Hall, 2004) that other variables, such as levels of self-presentational efficacy, may moderate or mediate this relationship.

Only a small number of studies have examined the effects of exercise intervention programmes on SPA. The results have, in general, shown that exercise interventions may reduce levels of SPA. For example, the Swedish intervention study described earlier also examined the effects of the exercise intervention programme on SPA in previously inactive adolescent girls (Lindwall & Lindgren, 2005). The exercise group revealed decreased SPA after 6 months of engaging in various exercise and sport activities twice a week, whereas the control group actually had increased their SPA level. Another intervention study conducted over 5 months demonstrated that exercise participation effectively reduced SPA, and that changes in efficacy and outcome expectations predicted reductions in physique anxiety for sedentary adults (McAuley et al. 1995). Similarly, women taking part in an aerobic exercise course significantly reduced their SPA and increased their body esteem over a 10-week period, whereas no such effects were found for the control group (Bartlewski, Van Raalte, & Brewer, 1996). Reduction of SPA has also been found in shorter (6-week) circuit training programmes (Williams & Cash, 2001). However, most of these studies have adopted quasi-experimental or pre-post designs, which constitute a threat to the validity of the results and render interpretation of the results more complex (Hausenblas et al., 2004). For example, the SPA levels of participants in control groups (enrolled in a developmental psychology course) and of participants in various exercise classes have been found to decrease to a similar degree (Diehl & Petrie, 1995). Hence, it is of great significance to search for those mechanisms in the exercise intervention that may account for the positive effects on SPA. Bartlewski et al. (1996) suggested three potential mediators of the effects of exercise on SPA and concerns about self-presentation. First, familiarity with the exercise setting may affect body concerns and SPA. Second, changes in SPA may be seen as a natural consequence of physiological changes resulting from the exercise programme, such as weight loss and increased muscle tone. Finally, positive SPA changes due to exercise may go hand in hand with changes in other psychological components, such as the self-concept (Fox, 2000a). The intervention study described before by Lindwall and Lindgren (2005) targeted several of these suggested mediators. First, the intervention programme was structured in a single-sex setting to avoid the potentially inhibitory effects of young males on the participant females with regards to their PSP and body image. Also, to enhance familiarity with the exercise setting and to create a supportive and safe (i.e. non-evaluative) atmosphere, the exercise participants were divided into four groups, each with its own exercise leader. In terms of the link between changes in physiological factors and SPA, there was no correlation between changes in BMI or physical fitness (submaximal oxygen uptake), indicating that changes in SPA and self-concept may be possible without accompanying physiological changes. Finally, as described earlier, for the exercise group, changes in other psychological components, in this case PSP, did follow the same trend as the changes in SPA. Moreover, social support, reductions in state anxiety following exercise and repeated exposure to sources of anxiety (e.g. other people in gyms or locker rooms or mirrors in the gym) have been mentioned as potential mediators of the exercise–SPA relationship (Carron, Burke, & Prapavessis, 2004; Hausenblas et al., 2004).

Mechanisms and a model

Several potential mechanisms for the positive effects of exercise on self-esteem and PSP have been suggested (Fox, 2000a, 2000b; Sonstroem, 1997a): (a) an unidentified psychophysiological factor that increases mood and self-regard; (b) enhanced body image, body satisfaction and body acceptance in relation to weight loss or increased muscle tone and fitness; (c) enhanced physical competence through improved skills, abilities and fitness; (d) increased sense of effectiveness, self-determination and control over body functioning and increased sense of autonomy; (e) enhanced self-acceptance; and (f) improved feelings of belonging to a group and having relationships within the exercise group.

In addition to this, several artificial, methodological factors linked to the research design may, at least partially, explain some of the effects of exercise on self-esteem (Morgan, 1997). Two such factors associated with the expectations of the experimenter are the Rosenthal effect and demand characteristics. The Rosenthal effect entails a self-fulfilling prophecy that tends to make participants improve with respect to the dependent variable due to expectations communicated by the experimenter, whereas demand characteristics involve the tendency for the participants themselves to identify the purpose of the study in order to accord with it. In addition to this, the Hawthorne effect, which refers to the improvement in a variable because participants received special attention and placebo effects (Desharnais, Jobin, Coté, Lévesque, & Godin, 1993; Ojanen, 1994), may also moderate any demonstrated effects.

A biopsychosocial model

To capture the complex and multilevel effects of exercise on the human psyche, and to be able to develop a broad foundation for the understanding of the mechanisms, how they function and how they interact to affect the individual, it is important to integrate psychophysiological/biological, psychological and sociocultural factors. As cited by Salmon (2001, p. 51), 'exercise is a complex psychobiological stimulus, which changes as its cultural significance changes'. Such a framework emphasises the effects of exercise on the physical self from micro-level to macro-level, recognising the roles of molecules as well and sociocultural norms and values. The biopsychosocial model presented here (Lindwall, 2004) should be perceived as a dynamic framework for future studies on the mechanisms of exercise on the physical self, rather than as a complete unifying theory. Overall, the model (see Figure 4.5)

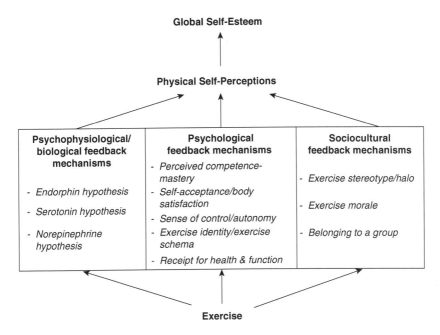

FIGURE 4.5 A biopsychosocial feedback model of mechanisms in the exercise–physical self relationship (Lindwall, 2004)

rests on the notion that various feedback systems linked to human functioning, occurring on different levels and through different channels, operate as active agents to make individuals feel better about themselves and their physiques when they exercise.

Starting with the psychophysiological/biological aspect, the three hypothesised mechanisms that seem to have received most empirical support, at least regarding effects on reducing anxiety and depression and elevating mood, are those relating to endorphin, serotonin and norepinephrine (Boecker et al., 2008; Chaouloff, 1997; Dishman, 1997; Hoffmann, 1997; Wipfli, Landers, Nagoshi, & Ringenbach, 2011). In short, the endorphin hypothesis focuses on the activation of endogenous opioid systems by exercise, whereas the serotonin and norepinephrine hypotheses highlight the interaction between physical activity and central serotonin (5-hydroxytryptamine [5-HT]) and changes in noradrenergetic activity after physical activity. The empirical support for these hypotheses rests on a combination of animal models and research on humans. The support for in particular the endorphin hypothesis has however been debated (Dishman & O'Connor, 2009).

Moving to the psychological factors, several variables have been suggested to account for the positive effects of exercise on the self, including increased perceived competence linked to the physical self and the body, enhanced self-acceptance and body satisfaction, increased sense of autonomy and control and exercise as a more pertinent aspect of one's identity, affecting the development of exercise-related schemas and subsequently information processing. In addition, strongly related to competence and sense of control, exercise may serve as a vital token of, or proof of, the healthy physical status of the individual in terms of bodily functions. That is, the cognitive and emotional interpretation and evaluation following an exercise bout (that one can trust the body and that it will not fail in terms of functions) may contribute significantly to enhanced PSP and subsequently to increased global self-esteem. This effect may be especially evident for individuals rehabilitating from various psychosomatic or stress-related health problems where experiences and memories of the body losing its normal functioning may linger for a long time after the incident and affect negatively the individual's general mental health. Furthermore, in accordance with the work of sociologists (Featherstone, 1991; Turner, 1992), we see the influence of general sociocultural value systems manifested in the modern Western world that are linked to the body and its role in general health and well-being. Overall, the exercise stereotype (Hodgins, 1992; Lindwall & Martin Ginis, 2006, 2008; Martin Ginis, Latimer, & Jung, 2003) supports the notion that exercise is accompanied by other attributes that are valued highly by other people, values that extend to non-physical attributes such as self-control and being a hard worker (i.e. the halo-effect; Cooper, 1981). Furthermore, given ideals and sociocultural pressures regarding the development and maintenance of both an attractive and aesthetically ideal body as well as a functional, fit and, most importantly, healthy physique (Brownell, 1991a, 1991b) free from pandemic modern day stress-related diseases, the communication to others that one subscribes to the prevalent ideals and practices regarding exercise may result in substantial positive feedback. In addition, the social support inherent in the social processes of, for example, an exercise programme group or recreational sport team also provides the individual with positive feedback that reflects positively on self-evaluations. Overall, as all the factors in the model co-develop, interact and overlap, and are more relevant in some situations and for some groups than others, a highly relevant challenge for future researchers is to outline when, under what circumstances and for whom the various factors are most active. Moreover, another relevant task for the future is to separate the effects of the mechanisms in the models from confounding factors such as various expectancy effects.

Future research

In addition to the recommendations offered above, future work should investigate the self, the physical self and their link to exercise from an interdisciplinary perspective, with cooperative contributions being made by scholars in biology, physiology, psychology and sociology. In addition, we need a better understanding of the dynamic nature of the physical self. Thus, longitudinal, prospective and experimental designs where conclusions regarding causes and effects can be drawn would be beneficial. Moreover, we need to know more about the moderating and mediating factors affecting the relation between exercise and self-concept. For example, for whom (e.g. men vs. women, younger vs. older, the mentally ill vs. healthy individual) and when (in what situations/settings) does exercise lead to improved self-concept? For example, it would be of interest to assess the role of exercise for self-perceptions and well-being in clinical groups of the depressed, burned-out and obese, or patients with eating disorders. Also, as most research has focused on aerobic-type activities, more research on various modalities would broaden the database. For example, studies examining various types of strength and conditioning regimes would be welcome.

Prospects: exercising the self in the field

To recapitulate, given the documented association of negative self-perceptions and low self-esteem with growing health problems such as depression and eating disorders, the positive relation of exercise to the physical self, documented in several studies as well as meta-analyses, should also be viewed from the broader perspective of applied mental health. Considering the robust scientific evidence that links exercise to general well-being, life adjustment and positive self-evaluation, it seems evident that exercise and physical activity have a lot to offer health practitioners as a complement to therapy and medication (e.g. Fox, Boutcher, Faulkner, & Biddle, 2000) regarding mental illness, whether viewed as a therapy for the treatment of mental illness or as an important tool in the prevention of mental illness or promotion of quality of life.

When translating the results of the research to an applied setting, the main message is that exercise is related to, and presumably leads to, more positive evaluations and perceptions of the physical self, especially for groups previously low in self-regard and self-esteem (e.g. females). Moreover, it seems that frequency of the activity, rather than the duration and intensity, is vital for the demonstrated significant effects on the physical self. In addition to demonstrating relationships between relevant variables in well-conducted studies, however, a vital task for exercise scientists is to 'spread the word' and communicate their results in a meaningful way to governing health bodies and practitioners in the field (cf. Fox, 2000b). It is, therefore, pertinent to ask what the reported statistical effects mean in terms of relevant behavioural changes (Kaplan, 1990; Sechrest, McKnight, & McKnight, 1996). Hence, the statistical effects need to be further translated and transferred into meaningful behavioural changes (e.g. what does the effects size of 0.21 for the SPA variable in the experiment group in a study mean in terms of changes in relevant behaviour, such as visits to the gym, despite the evaluation of others?). Some effects may be highly statistically significant but not practically relevant, while non-significant statistical trends (e.g. due to lack of power) may reveal themselves to be highly interesting and positive from a practical or clinical perspective, so it is essential to interpret the dependent variables and the size of the effects in studies from a practical perspective (Stoove & Andersen, 2003). From a clinical perspective, as exercise has been outlined as a 'double-edged' sword with the potential both to heal and harm, it is of the utmost importance that medical doctors, health professionals and strength and conditioning practitioners with the authority to prescribe exercise to patients and clients understand the effects and mechanisms of exercise on mental well-being and have correct information about suitable modes and types of activities, as well as levels of intensity, frequency and duration of the exercise activity.

Conclusions

This chapter started with a quite simple question: What role does regular exercise play in the shaping of, and evaluation of, individuals' self-perception? Based on the evidence from research, the answer to this question, however, appears to be quite multifaceted, complex and far from easy to answer. This said, however, the evidence we have so far from several meta-analyses and numerous studies do suggest that exercise and self-perceptions and self-esteem do relate in a reciprocal way. That is, the way individuals perceive and evaluate themselves linked to their body and its competence will most likely affect how they approach exercise (i.e. motives and motivation for exercising) and their engagement patterns (e.g. type of activity, frequency of activity, exercise setting and motives for engaging). On the other side, engaging in regular exercise will also have a positive effect on individuals' self-concept, probably first on more specific domains such as self-efficacy and PSP and later on broader concepts such as self-esteem. A number of moderating variables affect the exercise–self relationship, some of which have been better documented than others. For example, the effect will probably be larger if the individual goes into the exercise programme with lower self-esteem, lower physical fitness and a previous record of being sedentary. However, future research needs to further examine under what circumstances and for what groups and individuals the exercise–self relationship is strongest. The mechanisms underlying these complex relationships are likely a combination of biological/physiological, psychological and sociocultural factors that interrelate in a complex pattern. This notion calls for a biopsychosocial approach when trying to understand how individuals, after having stressed their bodies via an exercise bout in the gym or out in the woods, at the end of the day may go home and meet their gaze in the mirror with an increased smile, mirroring the inner feeling of increased general competence and self-liking.

Discussion questions

1. When (under what circumstances and for whom) is exercise effective in increasing people's self-perceptions and self-esteem and when may it instead be harmful?
2. Do you have any concrete examples of when exercise or sport made you feel better about yourself and when it instead made you feel worse?
3. What factors (environmental/material, psychological, social) in a typical exercise setting, such as a gym (or the place you normally visit), may increase the chance of a person experiencing enhanced or decreased competence and self-liking after an exercise bout?

4. How do values and norms in society affect how we value the appearance (i.e. how it looks) of our body versus its competence (i.e. what it can do)? What role do different actors have, such as media, parents, teachers, coaches and fitness instructors?

References

Alfermann, D., & Stoll, O. (2000). Effects of physical exercise on self-concept and well-being. *International Journal of Sport and Exercise Psychology, 30,* 47–65.

Aşçi, F. H. (2003). The effects of physical fitness training on trait anxiety and physical self-perceptions on female university students. *Psychology of Sport and Exercise, 4,* 255–264.

Aşçi, F. H., Aşçi, A., & Zorba, E. (1999). Cross-cultural validity and reliability of physical self-perception profile. *International Journal of Sport and Exercise Psychology, 30,* 399–406.

Aşçi, F. H., Kin, A., & Kosar, S. N. (1998). Effects of participation in an 8 week aerobic program on physical self-perception and body images satisfaction. *International Journal of Sport and Exercise Psychology, 29,* 366–375.

Bandura, A. (1977). Self-efficacy: Toward a unifying theory of behavioral change. *Psychological Review, 84,* 191–215.

Bandura, A. (1986). *Social foundations of thoughts and action.* Englewood Cliffs, NJ: Prentice Hall.

Bandura, A. (1997). *Self-efficacy: The exercise of control.* New York: Freeman.

Bane, S. M., & McAuley, E. (1996). Reducing social physique anxiety in college females. *Medicine and Science in Sport and Exercise, 28,* S85.

Bartlewski, P. P., Van Raalte, J. L., & Brewer, B. W. (1996). Effects of aerobic exercise on the social physique anxiety and body esteem of female college students. *Women in Sport and Physical Activity Journal, 5,* 49–62.

Baumeister, R. F. (1995). Self and identity: An introduction. In A. Tesser (Ed.), *Advanced social psychology* (pp. 51–99). New York: McGraw-Hill.

Biddle, S. J. H. (1997). Cognitive theories of motivation and the physical self. In K. R. Fox (Ed.), *The physical self: From motivation to well-being* (pp. 59–82). Champaign, IL: Human Kinetics.

Blaine, B., & Crocker, J. (1993). Self-esteem and self-serving biases in reaction to positive and negative events: An integrative review. In R. F. Baumeister (Ed.), *Self-esteem: The puzzle of low self-regard* (pp. 55–86). New York: Plenum Press.

Boecker, H., Sprenger, T., Spilker, M. E., Henriksen, G., Koppenhoefer, M., Wagner, K. J., . . . Tolle, T. R. (2008). The runner's high: Opioidergic mechanisms in the human brain. *Cerebral Cortex, 18,* 2523–2531.

Brownell, K. D. (1991a). Dieting and the search for the perfect body: Where physiology and psychology collide. *Behavior Therapy, 22,* 1–12.

Brownell, K. D. (1991b). Personal responsibility and control over our bodies: When expectations exceeds reality. *Health Psychology, 10,* 303–310.

Byrne, B. M. (1996). *Measuring self-concept across the lifespan: Issues and instrumentation.* Washington, DC: American Psychological Association.

Cafri, G., Thompson, K., Ricciardelli, L., McCabe, M., Smolak, L., & Yesalis, C. (2005). Pursuit of the muscular ideal: Physical and psychological consequences and putative risk factors. *Clinical Psychology Review, 25,* 215–239.

Campbell, A., & Hausenblas, H. A. (2009). Effects of exercise interventions on body image. *Journal of Health Psychology, 14,* 780–793.

Campbell, J. N., Trapnell, P. D., Heine, S. J., Katz, I. M., Lavalle, L. F., & Lehman, D. R. (1996). Self-concept clarity: Measurement, personality correlates and cultural boundaries. *Journal of Personality and Social Psychology, 70,* 141–156.

Campbell, R. N. (1984). *The new science: Self-esteem psychology.* Lanham, MD: University Press of America.

Carron, A. V., Burke, S. M., & Prapavessis, H. (2004). Self-presentation and group influences. *Journal of Applied Sport Psychology, 16*, 41–58.

Caruso, M. C., & Gill, D. L. (1992, December). Strengthening physical self-perception through exercise. *The Journal of Sport Medicine and Physical Fitness, 32*, 416–427.

Cash, T. F. (2004). Body image: Past, present, and future. *Body Image, 1*, 1–5.

Cash, T. F., & Pruzinsky, T. (Eds.). (2002). *Body image: A handbook of theory, research, and clinical practice*. New York: Guilford Press.

Chaouloff, F. (1997). The serotonin hypothesis. In W. P. Morgan (Ed.), *Physical activity and mental health* (pp. 179–198). London: Taylor & Francis.

Cooper, W. H. (1981). Ubiquitous halo. *Psychological bulletin, 90*, 218–244.

Crawford, S., & Eklund, R. C. (1994). Social physique anxiety, reasons for exercise and attitudes toward exercise settings. *Journal of Sport and Exercise Psychology, 16*, 70–82.

Crocker, J., & Wolfe, C. T. (2001). Contingencies of self-worth. *Psychological Review, 108*, 593–623.

Davis, C. (1997). Body image, exercise, and eating behaviors. In K. R. Fox (Ed.), *The physical self: From motivation to well-being* (pp. 143–174). Champaign, IL: Human Kinetics.

Davis, C., & Cowles, M. (1991). Body image and exercise: A study of relationships and comparisons between physically active men and women. *Sex Roles, 25*, 33–44.

Deci, E. L., & Ryan, R. M. (1985). *Intrinsic motivation and self-determination in human behavior.* New York: Plenum Press.

Desharnais, R., Jobin, J., Coté, C., Lévesque, L., & Godin, G. (1993). Aerobic exercise and the placebo effect: A controlled study. *Psychosomatic Medicine, 55*, 149–154.

Diehl, N., & Petrie, T. (1995). A longitudinal investigation of the effects of different exercise modalities on social physique anxiety [Abstract]. *Journal of Applied Sport Psychology, 7*, S55.

Dishman, R. K. (1997). The norepinephrine hypothesis. In W. P. Morgan (Ed.), *Physical activity and mental health* (pp. 199–212). London: Taylor & Francis.

Dishman, R. K., & O'Connor, P. J. (2009). Lessons in exercise neurobiology: The case of endorphins. *Mental Health and Physical Activity, 2*, 4–9.

Eagly, A. H., Ashmore, R. D., Makhijani, M. G., & Longo, L. C. (1991). What is beautiful is good, but...: A meta-analytic review of research on the physical attractiveness stereotype. *Psychological Bulletin, 110*, 109–128.

Eklund, R. C., & Crawford, S. (1994). Active women, social physique anxiety, and exercise. *Journal of Sport and Exercise Psychology, 16*, 431–448.

Featherstone, M. (1991). The body in consumer culture. In M. Featherstone, M. Hepworth, & B. S. Turner (Eds.), *The body: Social process and cultural theory*. London: Sage Publications.

Feingold, A. (1992). Good looking people are not what we think. *Psychological Bulletin, 111*, 304–341.

Fox, K. R. (1990). *The physical self-perception profile manual*. Dekalb, IL: Office for Health Promotion, Northern Illinois University.

Fox, K. R. (1997). The physical self and processes in self-esteem development. In K. R. Fox (Ed.), *The physical self: From motivation to well-being* (pp. 111–140). Champaign, IL: Human Kinetics.

Fox, K. R. (1998). Advances in the measurement of the physical self. In J. L. Duda (Ed.), *Advances in sport and exercise psychology measurement* (pp. 295–310). Morgantown, WV: Fitness Information Technology.

Fox, K. R. (2000a). Self-esteem, self-perceptions and exercise. *International Journal of Sport and Exercise Psychology, 31*, 228–240.

Fox, K. R. (2000b). The effects of exercise on self-perceptions and self-esteem. In S. J. H. Biddle, K. R. Fox, & S. H. Boutcher (Eds.), *Physical activity and psychological well-being* (pp. 88–118). London: Routledge.

Fox, K. R., Boutcher, S. H., Faulkner, G. E., & Biddle, S. J. H. (2000). The case for exercise in the promotion of mental health and psychological well-being. In S. J. H. Biddle, K.

R. Fox, & S. H. Boutcher (Eds.), *Physical activity, mental health and psychological well-being* (pp. 1–9). London: Routledge & Kegan Paul.

Fox, K. R., & Corbin, C. B. (1989). The physical self-perception profile: Development and preliminary validation. *Journal of Sport and Exercise Psychology, 11*, 408–430.

Fox, K. R., Corbin, C. B, & Couldry, W. H. (1985). Female physical estimation and attraction to physical activity. *Journal of Sport Psychology, 7*, 125–136.

Fredrickson, B. L., & Roberts, T.-A. (1997). Objectification theory: Toward understanding women's lived experience and mental health risks. *Psychology of Women Quarterly, 21*, 173–206.

Gammage, K. L., Martin Ginis, K. A., & Hall, C. R. (2004). Self-presentational efficacy: Its influences on social anxiety in an exercise class. *Journal of Sport and Exercise Psychology, 26*, 179–190.

Hagger, M., & Chatzisarantis, N. L. D. (2008). Self-determination theory and the psychology of exercise. *International Review of Sport and Exercise Psychology, 1*, 79–103.

Hart, E. A., Leary, M. R., & Rejeski, W. J. (1989). The measurement of social physique anxiety. *Journal of Sport and Exercise Psychology, 11*, 94–104.

Harter, S. (1978). Effectance motivation reconsidered: Toward a developmental model. *Human Development, 21*, 34–64.

Harter, S. (1990). Causes, correlates, and the functional role of global self-worth. In R. J. Sternberg, & J. Koligian, Jr. (Eds.), *Competence considered* (pp. 67–97). New Haven, CT: Yale University.

Harter, S. (1993). Causes and consequences of low self-esteem in children and adolescents. In R. F. Baumeister (Ed.), *Self-esteem: The puzzle of low self-regard* (pp. 87–116). New York: Plenum Press.

Harter, S. (1996). Historical roots of contemporary issues involving self-concept. In B. A. Bracken (Ed.), *Handbook of self-concept* (pp. 1–37). New York: Wiley.

Harter, S. (1999). *The construction of the self: A developmental perspective*. New York: Guilford Press.

Hausenblas, H. A., Brewer, B. W., & Van Raalte, J. L. (2004). Self-presentation and exercise. *Journal of Applied Sport Psychology, 16*, 3–18.

Hausenblas, H. A., & Carron, A. V. (1999). Eating disorder indices and athletes: An integration. *Journal of Sport and Exercise Psychology, 21*, 230–258.

Hausenblas, H. A., & Fallon, E. A. (2002). Relationship among body image, exercise behavior, and exercise dependence symptoms. *International Journal of Eating Disorders, 32*, 179–185.

Hausenblas, H. A., & Symons-Downs, D. (2001). Comparison of body image between athletes and nonathletes: A meta-analytic review. *Journal of Applied Sport Psychology, 13*, 323–339.

Hausenblas, H. A., & Symons-Downs, D. (2002). Exercise dependence: A systematic review. *Psychology of Sport and Exercise, 3*, 89–123.

Hodgins, M. (1992). A person-perception study of the 'healthy body–healthy mind' stereotype. *The Irish Journal of Psychology, 13*, 161–187.

Hoffmann, P. (1997). The endorphin hypothesis. In W. P. Morgan (Ed.), *Physical activity and mental health* (pp. 163–177). London: Taylor & Francis.

James, W. (1890). *Principles of psychology*. Chicago: Encyclopaedia Britannica.

Kaplan, R. M. (1990). Behavior as the central outcome in health care. *American Psychologist, 45*, 1211–1220.

Langlois, J. H., Kalakanis, L., Rubenstein, A. J., Larson, A., Hallam, M., & Smoot, M. (2000). Maxims or myths of beauty? A meta-analytic and theoretical review. *Psychological Bulletin, 3*, 390–423.

Lantz, C. D., Hardy, C. J., & Ainsworth, B. E. (1997). Social physique anxiety and perceived exercise behavior. *Journal of Sport Behavior, 20*, 83–94.

Leary, M. R. (1992). Self-presentation processes in exercise and sport. *Journal of Sport and Exercise Psychology, 14*, 339–351.

Levine, M. P., & Piran, N. (2004). The role of body images in the prevention of eating disorders. *Body Image, 1,* 57–70.

Lindwall, M. (2004). *Exercising the self: On the role of exercise, gender and culture for physical self-perceptions* (Unpublished doctoral dissertation). Department of Psychology, Stockholm University, Intellecta Docusys AB.

Lindwall, M., Aşçi, F. H., Palmeira, A., Fox, K. R., & Hagger, M. S. (2011). The importance of importance in the physical self: Support for the theoretically appealing but empirically elusive model of James. *Journal of Personality, 79,* 303–333.

Lindwall, M., & Hassmén, P. (2004). The role of exercise and gender for physical self-perceptions and importance ratings in Swedish university students. *Scandinavian Journal of Medicine and Science in Sports, 14,* 373–380.

Lindwall, M., & Lindgren, E.-C. (2005). The effects of a 6-month exercise intervention programme on physical self-perceptions and social physique anxiety in non-physically active adolescent Swedish girls. *Psychology of Sport and Exercise, 6,* 643–658.

Lindwall, M., & Martin Ginis, K. (2006). Moving towards a favorable image: The self-presentational benefits of exercise and physical activity. *Scandinavian Journal of Psychology, 47,* 209–217.

Lindwall, M., & Martin Ginis, K. (2008). Exercising impressive impressions: The exercise stereotype in male targets. *Scandinavian Journal of Medicine and Science in Sports.* doi:10.1111/j.1600-0838.2008.00869.x

Loland, N. W. (2000). The aging body: Attitudes toward bodily appearance among physically active and inactive women and men of different ages. *Journal of Aging and Physical Activity, 8,* 197–213.

Marsh, H. W. (1986a). Global self-esteem: Its relation to specific facets of self-concept and their importance. *Journal of Personality and Social Psychology, 51,* 1224–1236.

Marsh, H. W. (1986b). Causal ordering of self-concept and achievement: A multiwave, longitudinal panel analysis. *Journal of Educational Psychology, 82,* 646–656.

Martin Ginis, K. A., Latimer, A. E., & Jung, M. E. (2003). No pain no gain? Examining the generalizability of the exercise stereotype to moderately active and excessive active targets. *Social Behavior and Personality, 31,* 283–290.

Martin Ginis, K. A., & Leary, M. R. (2004). Self-presentational processes in health-damaging behavior. *Journal of Applied Sport Psychology, 16,* 59–74.

Martin Ginis, K. A., Lindwall, M., & Prapavessis, H. (2007). Who cares what other people think? Self-presentation in sport and exercise. In G. Tenenbaum, & R. Eklund (Eds.), *Handbook of sport psychology* (3rd ed., pp. 136–157). New York: Wiley.

McAuley, E., Bane, S. M., & Mihalko, S. L. (1995). Exercise in middle-aged adults: Self-efficacy and self-presentational outcomes. *Preventive Medicine, 24,* 319–328.

McAuley, E., Courneya, K. S., & Lettunich, J. (1991). Effects of acute and long-term exercise on self-efficacy responses in sedentary, middle-aged males and females. *The Gerontologist, 31,* 534–542.

McAuley, E., & Mihalko, S. L. (1998). Measuring exercise-related self-efficacy. In J. L. Duda (Ed.), *Advances in sport and exercise psychology measurement* (pp. 371–392). Morgantown, WV: Fitness Information Technology.

Morgan, W. P. (1997). Methodological considerations. In W. P. Morgan (Ed.), *Physical activity and mental health* (pp. 3–32). London: Taylor & Francis.

Murphy, G. (1947). *Personality: A biosocial approach to origins and structure.* New York: Harper & Row.

Ojanen, M. (1994). Can the true effects of exercise on psychological variables be separated from placebo effects? *International Journal of Sport Psychology, 25,* 63–80.

Page, A., Fox, A., McManus, A., & Armstrong, N. (1993, November 4–7). *Profiles of self-perception change following an eight week aerobic training program.* UK Sport: Partners in Performance. Book of Abstracts, Manchester.

Polivy, J., & Herman, C. P. (2002). Causes of eating disorders. *Annual Review of Psychology, 53,* 187–213.

Rosenberg, M. (1979). *Conceiving the self*. New York: Basic Books.

Ryan, R. M., & Deci, E. L. (2000). Self-determination theory and the facilitation of intrinsic motivation, social development, and well being. *American Psychologist, 55*, 54–56.

Salmon, P. (2001). Effects of physical exercise on anxiety, depression, and sensitivity to stress: A unifying theory. *Clinical Psychology Review, 21*, 33–61.

Schlenker, B. R., & Leary, M. R. (1982). Social anxiety and self-presentation: A conceptualization and model. *Psychological Bulletin, 92*, 641–669.

Schwartz, M. B., & Brownell, K. D. (2004). Obesity and body image. *Body Image, 1*, 43–56.

Sechrest, L., McKnight, P., & McKnight, K. (1996). Calibration of measures for psychotherapy outcome studies. *American Psychologist, 51*, 1065–1071.

Shavelson, R. J., Hubner, J. J., & Stanton, G. C. (1976). Self-concept: Validation of construct interpretations. *Review of Educational Research, 46*, 407–441.

Sonstroem, R. J. (1974). Attitude testing examining certain psychological correlates of physical activity. *Research Quarterly, 45*, 93–103.

Sonstroem, R. J. (1978). Physical estimation and attraction scales: Rationale and research. *Medicine and Science in Sports, 10*, 97–102.

Sonstroem, R. J. (1984). Exercise and self-esteem. *Exercise and Sport Sciences Reviews, 12*, 123–155.

Sonstroem, R. J. (1997a). The physical self-system: A mediator of exercise and self-esteem. In K. R. Fox (Ed.), *The physical self: From motivation to well-being* (pp. 3–26). Champaign, IL: Human Kinetics.

Sonstroem, R. J. (1997b). Physical activity and self-esteem. In W. P. Morgan (Ed.), *Physical activity and mental health* (pp. 127–144). Bristol: Taylor & Francis.

Sonstroem, R. J. (1998). Physical self-concept: Assessment and external validity. *Exercise and Sport Science Reviews, 26*, 133–164.

Sonstroem, R. J., Harlow, L. L., & Josephs, L. (1994). Exercise and self-esteem: Validity of model expansion and exercise associations. *Journal of Sport and Exercise Psychology, 16*, 29–41.

Sonstroem, R. J., & Morgan, W. P. (1989). Exercise and self-esteem: Rationale and model. *Medicine and Science in Sports and Exercise, 21*, 329–337.

Sonstroem, R. J., Speliotis, E. D., & Fava, J. L. (1992). Perceived physical competence in adults: An examination of the Physical Self-Perception Profile. *Journal of Sport and Exercise Psychology, 14*, 207–221.

Spence, J. C., McGannon, K. R., & Poon, P. (2005). The effect of exercise on global self-esteem: A quantitative review. *Journal of Sport and Exercise Psychology, 27*, 311–334.

Spink, K. S. (1992). Relation of anxiety about social physique to location of participation in physical activity. *Perceptual and Motor Skills, 74*, 1075–1078.

Stice, E. (2002). Risk and maintenance factors for eating pathology: A meta-analytic review. *Psychological Bulletin, 128*, 825–848.

Stoove, M. A., & Andersen, M. B. (2003). What are we looking at, and how big is it? *Physical Therapy in Sport, 4*, 93–97.

Szabo, A. (2000). Physical activity as a source of psychological dysfunction. In S. J. Biddle, K. R. Fox, & S. H. Boutcher (Eds.), *Physical activity and psychological well-being* (pp. 130–153). London: Routledge.

Taylor, S. E., & Brown, J. D. (1988). Illusion and well-being: A social-psychological perspective on mental health. *Psychological Bulletin, 193*, 193–210.

Tesser, A. (1988). Towards a self-evaluation maintenance model of social behavior. In L. Berkowitz (Ed.), *Advances in experimental social psychology* (*Vol. 21*, pp. 181–227). New York: Academic.

Thompson, J. K., Heinberg, L. J., Altabe, M., & Tantleff-Dunn, S. (1999). *Exacting beauty: Theory, assessment, and treatment of body image disturbance*. Washington, DC: American Psychological Association.

Thompson, R. A., & Sherman, R. T. (2010). *Eating disorders in sport*. New York: Routledge.

Tice, D. M. (1993). The social motivations of people with low self-esteem. In R. F. Baumeister (Ed.), *Self-esteem: The puzzle of low self-regard* (pp. 37–54). New York: Plenum Press.

Turner, B. S. (1992). *Regulating bodies: Essays in medical sociology.* London: Routledge.

White, R. W. (1959). Motivation reconsidered: The concept of competence. *Psychological Review, 66,* 297–333.

Williams, P. A., & Cash, T. F. (2001). Effects of a circuit training program on the body images of college students. *International Journal of Eating Disorders, 30,* 75–82.

Wipfli, B., Landers, D., Nagoshi, C., & Ringenbach, S. (2011). An examination of serotonin and psychological variables in the relationship between exercise and mental health. *Scandinavian Journal of Medicine and Science in Sports, 21,* 474–481.

5

RESISTANCE TRAINING AND MENTAL HEALTH

Shawn M. Arent and Devon L. Golem

RUTGERS UNIVERSITY, NEW JERSEY, USA

When applied appropriately, resistance training (RT) can produce significant increases in muscular strength, hypertrophy, and endurance (Feigenbaum, 2001; Kraemer & Ratamess, 2004). From a clinical standpoint, it also has the ability to positively impact numerous health conditions such as arthritis, Type II diabetes, and musculoskeletal dysfunction and injury (Graves & Franklin, 2001). In recent years, it has become increasingly apparent that RT can impact psychological outcomes as well as the physiological outcomes. While this effect has received considerably more support for aerobic exercise, the findings for RT have been encouraging (see Landers & Arent, 2007). For example, RT has been linked with improvements in depressive symptoms (e.g. North, McCullagh, & Tran, 1990), positive and negative affect (Arent, Landers, & Etnier, 2000), self-efficacy (Ewart, 1989), and quality of life (e.g. Ettinger et al., 1997). The purpose of this chapter is to provide a brief overview of the research addressing the psychological responses to acute RT. In addition to summarizing the extant literature, contemporary considerations in the RT–mental health relationship such as the conceptualization of intensity, dose–response issues, and potential mechanisms underlying the psychological benefits of RT will be addressed where sufficient evidence is available. Directions for future research will also be identified.

RT, anxiety, and affective responses: the influence of acute exercise

Single, acute bouts of aerobic exercise result in significant improvements in various transitory psychological states, including feelings of basic pleasure (Ekkekakis, Hall, & Petruzzello, 2005; Ekkekakis & Petruzzello, 1999), mood (Thayer, 2001), positive affect (Reed & Ones, 2006), and stress-related emotions such as state anxiety (SA; (Petruzzello, Landers, Hatfield, Kubitz, & Salazar, 1991). Findings from recent studies reveal that favorable changes in psychological states with acute exercise are related to established determinants of exercise behavior (Focht, 2009; Raedeke, Focht, & Scales, 2007; Rejeski, Gauvin, Hobson, & Norris, 1995) and predict future exercise adherence (Williams et al., 2008). Far less research has examined the psychological responses to single bouts of RT, and results of the few studies directly addressing the acute RT–affect relationship have yielded equivocal findings.

One of the first studies to examine the impact of RT on psychological states was conducted by Tharion, Harman, Kraemer, and Rauch (1991). They examined the effects of six different RT routines on mood state using a within-subjects design in 18 physically active college students who were recreational weight lifters. Sessions varied as a function of total work (low vs. high), training load (5RM vs. 10RM), and rest interval between each set (1 vs. 3 min). Mood was assessed immediately prior to and multiple times following each RT session. Significant elevations in mood disturbance were observed following sessions characterized by higher work-load, higher repetition range (10RM), and shorter rest intervals (1 min). It is worth noting that this particular RT protocol would likely have been the one to elicit the greatest lactate accumulation and stress hormone responses due to glycolytic demands and metabolic challenge.

Reductions in SA following acute aerobic exercise are one of the most common psychological benefits reported within the exercise psychology literature (Petruzzello et al., 1991; Raglin, 1997; Raglin, Turner, & Eksten, 1993). SA is characterized by feelings of tension, apprehension, or worry lasting anywhere from moments to hours in duration (Spielberger, Gorsuch, & Luschene, 1983). Acute aerobic exercise has been consistently linked with meaningful reductions in SA (Landers & Arent, 2007; Morgan, 1985; Petruzzello et al., 1991), and many of the earliest studies examining the effects of acute RT on psychological states focused upon changes in SA. Results indicated that acute RT resulted in either little to no change or elevations in SA responses. Raglin et al. (1993) examined SA responses to acute bouts of RT and stationary cycling in a sample of collegiate athletes. RT consisted of three sets of 6–10 repetitions at 70–80 percent of their individual 1RM while maintaining a 1–2 min rest interval between sets for 6–7 different strength training exercises. Stationary cycling was performed on a separate day for 30 min at 70–80 percent of age-predicted maximum heart rate (HR). Results indicated an increase in SA immediately following RT, and a significant post-exercise reduction in SA only emerged 60 min following the bout of stationary cycling. However, it is likely that these did not represent comparable intensities of exercise and that the RT was likely a much higher intensity bout, an issue that will be discussed later in this chapter.

Consistent with these findings, Koltyn, Raglin, O'Connor, and Morgan (1995) found no change in SA following a 50-min bout of recreational, self-selected intensity RT in college students. Similarly, Garvin, Koltyn, and Morgan (1997) found no significant differences in SA following an acute bout of RT performed at 70 percent of 1RM in college-age males. Due to these early findings, some researchers concluded that acute RT was not associated with anxiolytic benefits (Raglin, 1997; Raglin et al., 1993). Some studies have even found pronounced anxiogenic effects of RT. For example, increases in SA have been observed immediately following acute RT performed with loads $\geq$ 70 percent of 1RM (Bartholomew & Linder, 1998; Focht, 2002).

A number of studies, though, have observed improvements in SA and other relevant psychological states (Arent, Landers, Matt, & Etnier, 2005; Bartholomew, 1999; Bellezza, Hall, Miller, & Bixby, 2009; Bibeau, Moore, Mitchell, Vargas-Tonsing, & Bartholomew, 2010; Focht, 2002; Focht & Koltyn, 1999; Miller et al., 2009). Many of these studies also indicate that factors such as the type of RT routine performed, training load, and intensity may influence the psychological responses accompanying acute RT. These important programmatic variables and subject characteristics might help explain the results of some of the earlier work in this area and will be discussed next.

Training load and changes in psychological states following acute RT

As noted by Kraemer and Ratamess (2004): "Altering the training load can significantly affect the acute metabolic, hormonal, neural, and cardiovascular responses to training." Consistent with this, a growing number of investigations have documented improvements in psychological states following acute bouts of RT incorporating light to moderate training loads. O'Connor, Bryant, Veltri, and Gebhardt (1993) examined changes in SA following RT performed at 40, 60, and 80 percent of 10RM. There were reductions in SA at 90 and 120 min following only the 60 percent of 10RM RT session. Focht and Koltyn (1999) examined the effects of acute bouts of RT characterized by different loads and rest intervals, with participants completing either 12–20 repetitions/set at 50 percent of their 1RM while utilizing a 45–75 s rest interval between sets or completing 4–8 repetitions at 80 percent of their 1RM while resting 2–2.5 min between sets. Results revealed a significant reduction in SA only emerged following the 50 percent 1RM condition. However, transient increases in fatigue were also observed immediately following the 50 percent 1RM bout. The higher repetition range and shorter rest intervals which characterized the 50 percent 1RM condition may have also contributed to this bout eliciting a transitory post-exercise increase in fatigue. Similarly, Bibeau et al. (2010) manipulated load (50–55 percent 1RM vs. 80–85 percent 1RM) and rest intervals (30 vs. 90 s) in college students participating in a weight training class and found that only the "low-long" group (i.e. the lowest intensity) reported significantly higher positive affect than the control at 5 min post. All load/rest combinations resulted in increased SA immediately post-exercise, though this was most pronounced in the "high-short" group (i.e. the highest intensity). All groups had reductions in SA at 20 and 40 min post. However, the authors acknowledge that they may not have adequately implemented a high-intensity protocol which may explain the pattern of affective responses. One notable limitation of this study was the use of only four exercises which is inconsistent with any of the current recommendations on proper RT program design. This same methodological issue was also evident in a study by Miller et al. (2009) that attempted to determine whether three different modes of RT focusing on either concentric (CE), eccentric

(EE), or traditional concentric/eccentric (TE) contractions produced different HR, rating of perceived exertion (RPE), and affective responses. Load as a percentage of 10RM (80, 100, and 120 percent) was manipulated within each of three sets of the four exercise protocol, making intensity inferences that much more difficult. Despite slightly lower RPE and HR responses for the EE condition, all three conditions had similar affective benefits as reflected by increased pleasantness for the 60 min recovery as well as an initial, transient increase in activation.

Focht (2002) compared a traditional multiple-set RT bout to a circuit RT bout. The circuit RT, which consisted of a load equal to 50 percent of 1RM for 1 set of 12 different exercises (10–20 repetitions/set) and a 30–45 s rest interval between sets, produced reduced SA. On the other hand, the traditional multiple set routine (i.e. 75 percent of 1RM, three sets of 6–10 repetitions, 1–2 min rest interval between sets) yielded no significant changes. Ratings of perceived exertion were significantly higher during the multiple set routine relative to the circuit routine session. It should be noted that in each of the aforementioned studies (Focht, 2002; Focht & Koltyn, 1999; O'Connor et al., 1993) some post-exercise assessments of psychological states were obtained after individuals were permitted to resume normal daily activities. Factors other than the RT itself may have contributed to the psychological responses observed, and this possibility should clearly be considered when interpreting the findings of these investigations (Landers & Arent, 2007). Arent, Alderman, Short, and Landers (2007) found that allowing subjects to leave the testing environment following completion of an RT session at 50 percent of 1RM produced different patterns of affective responses compared to those required to stay in the environment for up to 120-min postexercise, though both groups had favorable affective responses within 60 min post.

Transient increases in SA have been found immediately following 20 min of acute RT at 75–85 percent of 1RM (Bartholomew & Linder, 1998). However, 20 min of RT at 40–50 percent of 1RM resulted in a significant reduction in SA that was observed within 20-min postexercise. Unfortunately, a notable methodological problem limits interpretability. The investigators used a time limit to control the protocol. It is likely that subjects completed a different number of exercises and total sets for each condition. Without controlling for volume, trying to make conclusions regarding load or "intensity" (as defined by %1RM) is difficult at best. It is apparent that differences in methodology and the assignment of program design variables have been a hallmark of this area of study and have limited the ability to adequately make direct comparisons across studies. It is also important to acknowledge that several acute RT–affect studies incorporated programmatic characteristics that likely required participants to complete at least some sets to the point of momentary muscular failure (Bartholomew & Linder, 1998; Focht, 2002; Focht & Koltyn, 1999; Garvin et al., 1997; Raglin et al., 1993). This could clearly impact how one feels in response to acute RT participation. Overall, the findings strongly suggest that load assignment may be an important programmatic factor that influences the psychological responses to acute RT. Furthermore, this factor may be even more important if the concept of "momentary failure" is taken into account as an indicator of overall intensity (Arent et al., 2005).

It is also worth noting that in the prior investigations that either failed to document anxiolytic benefits following acute RT (Garvin et al., 1997; Koltyn et al., 1995; Raglin et al., 1993) or reported delayed reductions in SA (Focht, 2002; Focht & Koltyn, 1999; O'Connor et al., 1993) participants reported baseline SA values that were considerably lower than age-related normative values. Thus, it is possible that low initial values created a floor effect making it less likely to observe reductions in SA soon after the cessation of activity, and the potential influence of such floor effects has been readily acknowledged in past acute aerobic exercise research (O'Connor, Petruzzello, Kubitz, & Robinson, 1995; Raglin, 1997; Raglin et al., 1993).

Dose–response effects of acute RT: reconsidering the role of intensity

It is important to recognize that prior investigations have been characterized by marked differences in load determination and assignment, total volume, repetition ranges, and rest intervals between sets. As Arent et al. (2005) point out, the inconsistency in prescription and lack of control over volume-load evident in these past investigations precludes the ability to draw firm conclusions regarding the dose–response relationship between acute RT and psychological responses. In an attempt to directly examine the role of intensity while controlling for volume, Arent et al. (2005) examined the affective responses to acute RT performed at 40, 70, and 100 percent of 10RM in a sample of 31 college-age men and women. SA, positive and negative affect, and feelings of energy, calmness, tiredness, and tension were assessed prior to and several times within the hour following each acute RT session. Results revealed that the moderate-intensity bout (70 percent of 10RM) resulted in the greatest improvement in SA, positive and negative affect, energy, and calmness. These responses emerged immediately following the 70 percent of 10RM condition and were found to persist for an hour post-exercise. Additionally, the high-intensity condition (100 percent of 10RM) was accompanied by unfavorable psychological responses including increases in SA, negative affect, and tension. These findings demonstrate that, when properly defining intensity and controlling for RT volume, acute moderate-intensity RT results in more favorable psychological responses relative to either low- or high-intensity bouts of RT. Furthermore, these intensity considerations are now consistent with the most recent American College of Sports Medicine (ACSM, 2010) definitions of RT intensity which also focus on RPE. This study currently represents the definitive dose–response investigation of the psychological responses to acute RT and should be used to guide the design of future research examining the role of intensity in the acute RT–affect relationship.

Future directions for acute RT–affect research

While more recent findings suggest acute RT results in meaningful improvements in psychological states (Arent et al., 2005; Bartholomew, 1999; Bartholomew & Linder, 1998; Focht, 2002; Focht & Koltyn, 1999; O'Connor et al., 1993), the overall extant literature remains mixed, with some studies documenting no change (Garvin et al., 1997; Koltyn et al., 1995) and others reporting negative psychological responses (Bartholomew & Linder, 1998; Raglin et al., 1993; Tharion et al., 1991). Inconsistencies in methodology limit the ability to adequately make comparisons across existing studies or generate comprehensive conclusions regarding the influence of RT upon psychological states. The differences in methodology, prescription, and psychological measures employed in investigations likely contribute to the equivocal results that have been observed in this area of research. Nonetheless, taken collectively, prior investigations into the psychological responses to acute RT have provided a solid empirical foundation for future investigations. Additionally, when we consider the results of Arent et al. (2005) and the implications for properly defining RT intensity, many of the outcomes in this area of research become remarkably consistent and make theoretical sense. Given that most of the earlier studies (and even some of the more recent ones) likely had participants lifting to momentary or volitional failure, the transient increases in SA often seen in these studies would support the notion that it is not so much about "how much" weight is lifted, but rather "how" that weight is lifted. It appears that there are independent and synergistic effects that load, volume, and training to momentary failure may have upon the psychological responses to acute RT and this clearly requires further investigation.

A number of important methodological and conceptual considerations must be addressed to make significant advances in the understanding of the RT–affect relationship. The measurement of psychological states is one methodological issue that warrants consideration. Many studies have focused primarily upon changes in SA following acute RT. However, to more adequately determine the breadth and scope of psychological states that may be positively influenced by acute RT, it is necessary to expand beyond exclusively assessing changes in stress-related emotions such as SA. Advances in the conceptualization and measurement of dimensional (Ekkekakis & Petruzzello, 1999; Thayer, 2001) and hierarchical models of affect (Raedeke et al., 2007; Tellegen, Watson, & Clark, 1999; Watson, 2002) provide innovative frameworks and strategies that allow for a more comprehensive evaluation of the affective states experienced in conjunction with acute exercise and should, accordingly, be used to help guide the selection of assessments incorporated in future studies of the psychological responses to RT. An additional measurement consideration is the need to document changes in psychological states that emerge *during* acute RT. Given that in-task responses may be markedly different from those observed post-exercise (Ekkekakis et al., 2005) and how one feels during acute RT may contribute to determining both training responses and motivation to continue regular strength training participation, assessments of psychological responses during acute RT should be incorporated in future inquiry exploring this relationship. A recent study examined in-task and post-task affective responses to RT utilizing different exercise orders and found differences in Feeling Scale responses during the exercise bout (Bellezza et al., 2009). Despite potential intensity confounds in this particular study, the approach clearly warrants further investigation.

Though theoretical focus has been placed on the in-task exercise experience as it relates to adherence, researchers must begin to recognize that the goals of the individual likely impact adherence as well and take this into account when designing interventions. For example, if a person desires increased strength or changes in body composition, many of the protocols used in the available literature would be insufficient to induce such changes. There needs to be a concerted effort by researchers to actually use well-designed RT programs.

Other relevant methodological and conceptual considerations involve the study of potential dose–response effects of acute RT. Arent et al. (2005) convincingly argued for the need to consider, and control for, multiple programmatic factors that shape the intensity of RT when investigating the dose–response effects of acute RT on affective responses. It is clear that many aspects of the RT stimulus other than load (i.e. volume, rest intervals between sets, set termination criteria: volitional fatigue versus momentary muscular failure) that are commonly manipulated to optimize the training effect directly influence RT intensity. Modifications of these programmatic factors can influence intensity, energy expenditure, and effort sense, and it is quite likely that they also have a meaningful impact upon the psychological responses to acute RT. There are also a host of individual participant characteristics such as training status, training goals, activity preference, RT-related self-efficacy beliefs, and exertional preference and tolerance that may influence how one responds psychologically to a given bout of RT. As noted previously in the exercise psychology literature (Arent et al., 2005; Landers & Arent, 2007), Chrousos and Gold (1992) have proposed that there may be a family of dose–response curves involving the affective responses to RT of different intensities. Systematic investigation of the potential moderating role of these participant and RT characteristics is required to elucidate the family of dose–response curves that are observed with the psychological responses to acute RT.

A final, related conceptual consideration is the pressing need to directly address the mechanisms underlying the acute RT–affect relationship. Although several biological (endorphin, serotonin, hypothalamic-pituitary-adrenal [HPA] axis) and psychological (distraction, mastery) hypotheses have been proposed to explain the psychological benefits of acute exercise, empirical support for these mechanisms remains sparse. Arent et al. (2005) demonstrated support for the role of HPA axis involvement in that high-intensity RT (100 percent of 10RM) elicited negative affective responses that were accompanied by concomitant elevations in salivary cortisol level. Bellezza et al. (2009) attempted to examine the role of lactate on affective responses to different exercise orders. However, theoretical support for this mechanism was poorly developed, and the methodological design did very little to allow direct testing of lactate as a determinant of affective responses.

In summary, while the overall literature examining the psychological responses to acute RT has yielded relatively mixed findings, recent research provides compelling evidence that this mode of exercise can produce meaningful improvements in an array of psychological states. Although some progress has been made in the investigation of the effects of acute RT on psychological responses, inquiry into the

RT–affect relationship is still relatively limited and there are many methodological and conceptual issues that warrant attention if we are to advance our understanding of the psychological benefits of acute RT. There has been very little systematic inquiry, and researchers need to make a concerted effort to utilize well-designed programs, pay attention to key programmatic variables, and properly define intensity. There has also been a very unfortunate trend to modify multiple programmatic variables from study to study, which has severely limited our ability to synthesize the existing literature. Even studies following the work of Arent et al. (2005) have often failed to pay attention to issues surrounding the definition of intensity and acknowledge established physiological responses.

RT and general well-being

The concept of "well-being" typically encompasses a number of variables including, but not limited to, quality of life, mental and physical health, and self-perception. It is well established that physical activity and exercise are associated with physical and mental health (Blumenthal et al., 1989; Colcombe et al., 2003; K. R. Fox, 1999; McAuley, Kramer, & Colcombe, 2004; Revnic, Nica, & Revnic, 2007; Yasunaga et al., 2006). Aerobic exercise has been the primary mode of physical activity in the majority of studies evaluating the effect of exercise on general well-being. Recently, RT has received more attention in this topic of study.

It is important to note the "ceiling effect" that is mentioned numerous times throughout the current literature. Individuals who begin an intervention with higher scores for general well-being and cognitive function have little room for improvement and will certainly experience smaller effects in these categories compared to individuals who begin with lower feelings of general well-being and cognitive function scores. Keeping this concept in mind, it is vital to consider the subject populations that are involved in the reviewed studies. However, it is important to note that *all* individuals may reap significant benefits from RT interventions, though healthy, physically fit, highly motivated individuals may psychologically respond to the least degree to RT. Because of this, research and interpretation of that research needs to emphasize determination of a *meaningful* level of improvement.

RT and quality of life

Older adults are often the focal population in research involving quality of life as age-related declines in physical and mental capacity have enormous impacts on functionality, life satisfaction, and feelings of self-efficacy (Blumenthal et al., 1989). Research has shown that RT is appropriate for older adults as it reverses the typical age-related muscle loss and consequent loss of strength (Blumenthal et al., 1989). Furthermore, studies combining RT with aerobic exercise revealed increased self-efficacy and positive moods (Ewart, 1989).

Most of the studies evaluating the effects of RT on quality of life have used elderly subject populations (i.e., greater than 60 years old; Cassilhas et al., 2007;

Kimura et al., 2010; Singh, Clements, & Fiatarone, 1997), though some studies included subjects 40 years and above (Grant, Todd, Aitchison, Kelly, & Stoddart, 2004; Levinger et al., 2009; Levinger, Goodman, Hare, Jerums, & Selig, 2007). Singh et al. (1997) evaluated the effect of a 10-week RT program on quality of life in depressed, sedentary older adults. Compared to the non-exercising control group, those who completed RT three times per week had increased quality of life scores. Perhaps more importantly, the scores of the RT group improved to age-matched standard levels. As well, the RT group had significant improvements in overall morale and in their attitude toward aging compared to the non-exercising control group (Singh et al., 1997). RT was also found to improve quality of life in sedentary elders that were not depressed compared to non-exercising controls (Kimura et al., 2010). This finding indicates that the positive effects of RT on quality of life are not limited to depressed individuals.

Obese individuals are another subject population at risk for lower quality of life scores (Han, Tijhuis, Lean, & Seidell, 1998) and are a population that may benefit both physiologically and psychologically from RT as observed in a 12-week study by Grant et al. (2004). Overweight, sedentary females aged 55–70 years improved life satisfaction scores after a 12-week RT program compared to the non-exercise controls (Grant et al., 2004). When comparing the effects of RT on individuals with low metabolic risks to those with high metabolic risks, Levinger et al. (2007) observed that only the high-risk group showed significant improvement in quality of life scores.

The appearance of greater improvement in quality of life among depressed, overweight, and high metabolic risk individuals compared to healthy or low-risk individuals is consistent with the concept of a ceiling effect mentioned earlier. However, the loads and intensities (among other programmatic factors) of the interventions within these studies may have differed. Cassilhas et al. (2007) compared the effects of a low-load (50 percent 1RM) and a high-load (80 percent 1RM) RT program on quality of life in older males. Both conditions were effective at improving general health scores compared to a no-overload control group, yet only the lower load condition was effective in significantly improving the vitality scores compared to the control group. Strength significantly increased in both RT groups, but to a greater degree in the high-load group (Cassilhas et al., 2007). It is possible that longer programs emphasizing strength or hypertrophy modes of RT (consistent with an 80 percent 1RM load) would produce greater physiological gains that could translate to improved activities of daily living. This could translate to greater improvements in quality of life. Unfortunately, few studies have taken a more "long-term" approach to RT and these conclusions are speculative at this stage. Future research should emphasize adequate and *appropriately designed* RT programs in order to maximally impact physical and psychological variables that may influence quality of life.

RT and physical self-perception

Physical self-perception is a dimension of self-concept that is further described in the Expanded Exercise and Self-Esteem Model (EXSEM; Sonstroem, 1998). The tool typically used to assess physical self-perception is the Physical Self-Perception Scale (PSPP; K. Fox & Corbin, 1989). The PSPP evaluates five subscales of physical self: Sports Competence, Body Attractiveness, Physical Condition, Physical Strength, and Overall Physical Self-Worth. There are also versions that have been revised to more appropriately assess older and younger populations (PSPP for older adults and the children and youth PSPP, respectively; Whitehead, 1995).

The previously mentioned study by Grant et al. (2004) that found an improvement in life satisfaction among older, overweight females participating in 12 weeks of RT also evaluated physical self-perception. The findings revealed that both the non-exercising control group and the RT group improved body attractiveness scores, yet no other significant improvements were observed. However, the control group showed a decrease in total physical self-worth scores while these scores did not change in the RT group (Grant et al., 2004). The authors discussed the possibility that, due to low adherence, low statistical power may have explained the absence of a difference between the groups. However, it is important to note that functional improvements in performance were not observed in RT compared to the control group, therefore the RT program may have needed to be reconstructed to promote physical performance improvements.

Jones, Matthews, Murray, Van Raalte, and Jensen (2010) also evaluated the effects of a 12-week RT program on physical self-perception on college-age female athletes. All subjects participated in the intervention, therefore a no-exercise control was not used. A significant increase in physical strength scores of the PSPP were observed after training, but there were no changes in the other subscales (Jones et al., 2010), potentially due to a ceiling effect. As athletes, these subjects began with high scores in these subscales compared to the established standards (K. Fox & Corbin, 1989). An important result from this study is the positive correlation between strength gains and perceived physical strength scores (Jones et al., 2010).

A recent study conducted in our laboratory evaluated the effects of RT on physical self-perception in Hispanic adolescents (Velez, Golem, & Arent, 2010). Both males and females participated in either a 12-week RT program or attended physical education classes as the control group. The RT group had significant improvements in total physical self-perception, physical condition, body attractiveness, and global self-worth compared to the control group (Velez et al., 2010). As well, the RT group not only had significant strength gains, but also exhibited significant decrease in percent body fat and increase in lean body mass compared to the control group, thus suggesting a possible correlation between increased strength, improved body composition, and improved physical self-perception (Velez et al., 2010).

The three previous studies are difficult to directly compare as they evaluated different subject populations and used different RT interventions. However, the latter two studies indicated an improvement of physical self-perception with RT that was effective at promoting strength gains. The results from Velez et al. (2010) suggest that future research should further evaluate the correlation between body compositional changes along with strength changes and physical self-perception.

Furthermore, physically efficacious RT programs should be designed in these studies in order to maximize impact on psychological correlates.

RT and self-efficacy

Self-efficacy specifically focuses on an individual's perception of their own capacity to perform a specific task (Bandura, 1977). According to the EXSEM (Sonstroem, 1998), self-efficacies are very specific self-perceptions that make up more general self-concepts. The effect of RT on self-efficacy has been evaluated in depressed older adults (Singh et al., 1997). Although there was an increase in total morale after 10 weeks of RT, these older subjects did not have significant change in self-efficacy scores related to lifting, climbing, jogging, push-ups, and walking (Singh et al., 1997). Improvement was noted as a trend in lifting, push-ups, and jogging self-efficacy in the RT group compared to the no-exercise control group, yet these changes were not significant. It is possible that a longer or more intense protocol would have produced greater physiological changes and potentially resulted in corresponding psychological responses.

Similar-aged individuals that were not depressed were the subject base for another study evaluating the effects of different RT intensities (Low: 55–65 percent 1RM vs. High: 75–85 percent 1RM) on self-efficacy and self-competence (Tsutsumi, Don, Zaichkowsky, & Delizonna, 1997). Strength gains and improved self-efficacy were significantly related to RT intensity. Both RT groups improved strength, self-efficacy for lifting and push-ups, and physical self-competence compared to a non-exercise control group (Tsutsumi et al., 1997). The high-intensity group improved to a greater degree than the low-intensity group, indicating a potential dose–response effect.

Taken as a whole, it appears that RT has positive effects on self-perception and self-efficacy. Further research is needed to examine the relationship between these variables and the physiological changes that occur with RT. The difference in these relationships among different populations should also be evaluated. Whether these variables continue to increase with continued, long-term progressive RT is another question that has arisen from the given literature. More comparison studies between the effects of aerobic versus anaerobic exercise versus a combination of the two should be evaluated in depth.

RT and cognitive function

It is now well accepted that physical exercise has positive effects on cognitive functioning (see Landers & Arent, 2007, for a review). Many early studies focused primarily on the effects of aerobic exercise on cognition, but RT has recently begun to receive attention. Although much more research is needed on this particular topic, the available evidence provides many directions for future research on the effects of RT on cognitive function.

Most studies in this area have focused on the elderly as the subject population, primarily due to the fact that cognitive function declines with age (Cepeda, Kramer, & Gonzalez de Sather, 2001; Verhaeghen & Cerella, 2002). Some cognitive functions, such as memory, attention, and executive function, are particularly susceptible to deterioration with age (van Dam & Aleman, 2004). It has even been suggested that there is a temporal association between exercise earlier on in the life cycle and the decreased risk of dementia or Alzheimer's disease later in life (Fratiglioni, Paillard-Borg, & Winblad, 2004; Rovio et al., 2005).

Kimura et al. (2010) found that 12 weeks of RT in elderly men and women resulted in improvements in the mental health aspects of quality of life, but did not produce changes in cognition, compared to a control group. Similar effects were seen following another 12-week RT study by Tsutsumi et al. (1997). Despite increased strength and self-efficacy, no change in cognitive function was observed. Contrary to these findings, another study evaluating cognitive effects of RT on an elderly sample revealed that 8 weeks of RT improved word list recognition scores (immediate and delayed) compared to a no-exercise control group (Perrig-Chiello, Perrig, Ehrsam, Staehelin, & Krings, 1998). However, there were no differences in memory or cognitive speed compared to the control group. A possible explanation for the lack of significant effects in these studies may have to do with duration of intervention.

Cassilhas et al. (2007) compared the effects of two different RT intensities (50 vs. 80 percent 1RM) on cognitive function in older adults. However, the duration of the intervention was 24 weeks. Compared to the no-overload control group, both intensity groups significantly improved cognitive function to similar degrees (Cassilhas et al., 2007). However, strength was improved to a greater degree in the high-intensity group and quality of life was improved to a greater degree in the low-/moderate-intensity group (Cassilhas et al., 2007), as mentioned previously.

Besides intensity, the impact of frequency of RT (1 × /week vs. 2 × /week) on the cognitive effects of elderly females has also been evaluated (Liu-Ambrose et al., 2010). After 52 weeks of intervention, it was observed that RT at both frequencies resulted in improved attention compared to the control (Liu-Ambrose et al., 2010). Unfortunately, intensity was not specified in this study and therefore cannot be directly compared to the above studies. However, only one of the three studies mentioned above with a duration shorter than 24 weeks revealed a treatment effect on cognitive function. Therefore, longer duration studies may be necessary to examine the effects of RT on cognition in the elderly.

Conclusions

After extensive review of the literature revolving around the effects of RT on affect, general well-being, and cognitive function, it is apparent that much more research is needed. The current literature generally lacks a progressive coherency that would enable the work to build upon itself. The resulting observations touch on many of the important aspects of the topic, such as duration and intensity of the training, but they tend to stand-alone rather than build toward a body of research that can guide policy. The conflicting results of the available research are often due to the variability in methodology. The research currently lacks the depth and validity needed to provide a strong platform for the creation of guidelines and practical application.

Not only does the coherence of the methodology and training interventions need to be improved, but the general approach to examining the impact of RT on mental health needs to be more systematic and logical. In other words, if the effects of training duration are being studied, only the duration of an existing intervention should be varied. Other variables should be held constant. Changing the intensity, subject population, load, frequency, and outcome measures along with the duration does not provide the needed extension of evidence to progressively learn about this topic. The duration of RT interventions presented in the literature range from a single session to several weeks to 3 years. The frequency of sessions range from once to four times per week. The loads are either self-selected (sometimes not measured) or 40–90 percent of 1RM, or a percentage of RM. The number of sets and repetitions vary considerably, sometimes emphasizing muscular endurance, muscular strength, or muscular hypertrophy. More recently, the ACSM (2010) guidelines for RT (for the specific subject populations) are being incorporated to promote consistency, but the selection of exercises varies in number and on emphasis of upper, lower, or total body. It is worth noting that the complexity of RT prescription exceeds that of aerobic exercise tremendously. There are significantly more variables to consider when structuring an appropriate RT bout or program. These variables include, but are not limited to, repetitions, sets, load, rest intervals, exercise order, supersets, compound sets, EE versus CE emphasis, speed of movement, body part training split, and frequency. It is precisely because of this complexity, though, that researchers must begin to apply a more systematic approach to the examination of RT effects.

Despite the incongruent nature of the available literature, there is encouraging evidence for the psychological benefits of RT. Further research in this area and on the unique benefits of RT is clearly warranted. However, researchers must begin to make a concerted effort to utilize adequate RT programs and pay attention to key design variables. Furthermore, there must be a more coherent effort to systematically advance the studies being conducted on the mental health effects of RT. The approach to this point has been largely atheoretical and disjointed. Researchers must begin to examine the mechanisms underlying the psychological effects of RT if we hope to move toward a causal model and begin to formulate recommendations that can guide public policy.

Practical applications

Based on the available literature, it appears that optimal RT prescription for mental health benefits may not necessarily be the same prescription for optimal physical benefits. However, these outcomes are not mutually exclusive, particularly when applied to training programs rather than acute exercise. Long-term changes in strength, body composition, and overall musculoskeletal fitness appear to be related to positive changes in general well-being and self-perception. There is also a modest effect for improved cognitive functioning, though the evidence for a dose–response effect is minimal. This is clearly an area warranting more research. Moderate-intensity RT, when properly defined, appears to be efficacious for improving acute affective states. Furthermore, there is good preliminary support for the role of the stress response (i.e. HPA axis) as a potential mechanism driving these responses. The efficacy of both acute and chronic RT is seen across many subject populations, but appears to be particularly pronounced for individuals that potentially have the most to gain from a functional standpoint. Practitioners and researchers alike should be encouraged to pay attention to the manipulation of RT-related variables during program design to accurately and adequately control intensity and achieve the desired outcomes consistent with the participants' needs. Regardless of the short-comings inherent in the current work on the mental health benefits of RT, it is apparent that this modality of exercise has the potential to positively impact a number of psychological constructs and is a useful tool for improving both physical and psychological health.

Discussion questions

1. How did early classifications of "intensity" potentially lead to conclusions that RT did not have anxiolytic effects?
2. What are some current strengths and weaknesses of the literature regarding the effects of acute bouts of RT on affect and SA?
3. Why is it important to establish dose–response effects for RT and mental health? What does future research need to do to address this issue?
4. How might individual differences (i.e. health status, training history) influence psychological responses to RT?

References

American College of Sports Medicine. (2010). *ACSM guidelines for exercise testing and prescription* (8th ed.). Philadelphia: Lippincott Williams & Wilkins.

Arent, S. M., Alderman, B. L., Short, E. J., & Landers, D. M. (2007). The impact of the testing environment on affective changes following acute resistance exercise. *Journal of Applied Sport Psychology, 19*, 1533–1571.

Arent, S. M., Landers, D. M., & Etnier, J. L. (2000). The effects of exercise on mood in older adults: A meta-analytic review. *Journal of Aging and Physical Activity, 8*, 407–430.

Arent, S. M., Landers, D. M., Matt, K. S., & Etnier, J. (2005). Dose–response and mechanistic issues in the resistance training and affect relationship. *Journal of Sport and Exercise Psychology, 27*, 92–110.

Bandura, A. (1977). Self-efficacy: Toward a unifying theory of behavioral change. *Psychological Review, 84*, 191–215.

Bartholomew, J. B. (1999). The effect of resistance exercise on manipulated preexercise mood states for male exercisers. *Journal of Sport and Exercise Psychology, 21*, 39–51.

Bartholomew, J. B., & Linder, D. E. (1998). State anxiety following resistance exercise: The role of gender and exercise intensity. *Journal of Behavioral Medicine, 21*, 205–219.

Bellezza, P. A., Hall, E. E., Miller, P. C., & Bixby, W. R. (2009). The influence of exercise order on blood lactate, perceptual, and affective responses. *Journal of Strength and Conditioning Research, 23*, 203–208.

Bibeau, W. S., Moore, J. B., Mitchell, N. G., Vargas-Tonsing, T., & Bartholomew, J. B. (2010). Effects of acute resistance training of different intensities and rest periods on anxiety and affect. *Journal of Strength and Conditioning Research, 24*, 2184–2191.

Blumenthal, J., Emery, C., Madden, D., George, L., Coleman, E., Riddle, M., ... Williams, R. S. (1989). Cardiovascular and behavioral effects of aerobic exercise training in healthy older men and women. *Journal of Gerontology, 44*, 147–157.

Cassilhas, R. C., Viana, V. A., Grassmann, V., Santos, R. T., Santos, R. F., Tufik, S., & Mello, M. T. (2007). The impact of resistance exercise on the cognitive function of the elderly. *Medicine and Science in Sports and Exercise, 39*, 1401–1407.

Cepeda, N. J., Kramer, A. F., & Gonzalez de Sather, J. C. (2001). Changes in executive control across the life span: Examination of task-switching performance. *Developmental Psychology, 37*, 715–730.

Chrousos, G. P., & Gold, P. W. (1992). The concepts of stress and stress system disorders: Overview of physical and behavioral homeostasis. *The Journal of the American Medical Association, 267*, 1244–1252.

Colcombe, S. J., Erickson, K. I., Raz, N., Webb, A. G., Cohen, N. J., McAuley, E., & Kramer, A. F. (2003). Aerobic fitness reduces brain tissue loss in aging humans. *Journals of Gerontology Series A: Biological Sciences & Medical Sciences, 58*, 176.

Ekkekakis, P., Hall, E. E., & Petruzzello, S. J. (2005). Variation and homogeneity in affective responses to physical activity of varying intensities: An alternative perspective on dose–response based on evolutionary considerations. *Journal of Sports Sciences, 23*, 477–500.

Ekkekakis, P., & Petruzzello, S. J. (1999). Acute aerobic exercise and affect: Current status, problems and prospects regarding dose–response. *Sports Medicine, 28*, 337–374.

Ettinger, W. H., Jr., Burns, R., Messier, S. P., Applegate, W., Rejeski, W. J., Morgan, T., ... Craven, T. (1997). A randomized trial comparing aerobic exercise and resistance exercise with a health education program in older adults with knee osteoarthritis: The fitness arthritis and seniors trial (FAST). *The Journal of the American Medical Association, 277*, 25–31.

Ewart, C. K. (1989). Psychological effects of resistive weight training: Implications for cardiac patients. *Medicine and Science in Sports and Exercise, 21*, 683–688.

Feigenbaum, M. S. (2001). Rationale and review of current guidelines. In J. E. Graves, & B. A. Franklin (Eds.), *Resistance training for health and rehabilitation* (pp. 13–32). Champaign, IL: Human Kinetics.

Focht, B. C. (2002). Pre-exercise anxiety and the anxiolytic responses to acute bouts of self-selected and prescribed intensity resistance exercise. *The Journal of Sports Medicine and Physical Fitness, 42*, 217–223.

Focht, B. C. (2009). Brief walks in outdoor and laboratory environments: Effects on affective responses, enjoyment, and intentions to walk for exercise. *Research Quarterly for Exercise and Sport, 80*, 611–620.

Focht, B. C., & Koltyn, K. F. (1999). Influence of resistance exercise of different intensities on state anxiety and blood pressure. *Medicine and Science in Sports and Exercise, 31*, 456–463.

Fox, K., & Corbin, C. (1989). The physical self-perception profile: Development and preliminary validation. *Journal of Sport and Exercise Psychology, 11*, 408–430.

Fox, K. R. (1999). The influence of physical activity on mental well-being. *Public Health Nutrition, 2*(3A), 411–418.

Fratiglioni, L., Paillard-Borg, S., & Winblad, B. (2004). An active and socially integrated lifestyle in late life might protect against dementia. *Lancet Neurology, 3*, 343–353.

Garvin, A. W., Koltyn, K. F., & Morgan, W. P. (1997). Influence of acute physical activity and relaxation on state anxiety and blood lactate in untrained college males. *International Journal of Sports Medicine, 18*, 470–476.

Grant, S., Todd, K., Aitchison, T. C., Kelly, P., & Stoddart, D. (2004). The effects of a 12-week group exercise programme on physiological and psychological variables and function in overweight women. *Public Health, 118,* 31–42.

Graves, J. E., & Franklin, B. A. (2001). *Resistance training for health and rehabilitation.* Champaign, IL: Human Kinetics.

Han, T. S., Tijhuis, M. A., Lean, M. E., & Seidell, J. C. (1998). Quality of life in relation to overweight and body fat distribution. *American Journal of Public Health, 88,* 1814–1820.

Jones, M. T., Matthews, T. D., Murray, M., Van Raalte, J., & Jensen, B. E. (2010). Psychological correlates of performance in female athletes during a 12-week off-season strength and conditioning program. *Journal of Strength and Conditioning Research, 24,* 619–628.

Kimura, K., Obuchi, S., Arai, T., Nagasawa, H., Shiba, Y., Watanabe, S., & Kojima, M. (2010). The influence of short-term strength training on health-related quality of life and executive cognitive function. *Journal of Physiological Anthropology, 29,* 95–101.

Koltyn, K. F., Raglin, J. S., O'Connor, P. J., & Morgan, W. P. (1995). Influence of weight training on state anxiety, body awareness and blood pressure. *International Journal of Sports Medicine, 16,* 266–269.

Kraemer, W. J., & Ratamess, N. A. (2004). Fundamentals of resistance training: Progression and exercise prescription. *Medicine and Science in Sports and Exercise, 36,* 674–688.

Landers, D. M., & Arent, S. M. (2007). Physical activity and mental health. In G. Tenenbaum, & R. C. Eklund (Eds.), *Handbook of sport psychology* (pp. 469–491). Hoboken, NJ: Wiley & Sons.

Levinger, I., Goodman, C., Hare, D. L., Jerums, G., Morris, T., & Selig, S. (2009). Psychological responses to acute resistance exercise in men and women who are obese. *Journal of Strength and Conditioning Research, 23,* 1548–1552.

Levinger, I., Goodman, C., Hare, D. L., Jerums, G., & Selig, S. (2007). The effect of resistance training on functional capacity and quality of life in individuals with high and low numbers of metabolic risk factors. *Diabetes Care, 30,* 2205–2210.

Liu-Ambrose, T., Nagamatsu, L. S., Graf, P., Beattie, B. L., Ashe, M. C., & Handy, T. C. (2010). Resistance training and executive functions: A 12-month randomized controlled trial. *Archives of Internal Medicine, 170,* 170–178.

McAuley, E., Kramer, A. F., & Colcombe, S. J. (2004). Cardiovascular fitness and neurocognitive function in older adults: A brief review. *Brain, Behavior, and Immunity, 18,* 214–220.

Miller, P. C., Hall, E. E., Chmelo, E. A., Morrison, J. M., DeWitt, R. E., & Kostura, C. M. (2009). The influence of muscle action on heart rate, RPE, and affective responses after upper-body resistance exercise. *Journal of Strength and Conditioning Research, 23,* 366–372.

Morgan, W. P. (1985). Affective beneficence of vigorous physical activity. *Medicine and Science in Sports and Exercise, 17,* 94–100.

North, T. C., McCullagh, P., & Tran, Z. V. (1990). Effect of exercise on depression. *Exercise and Sport Sciences Reviews, 18,* 379–415.

O'Connor, P. J., Bryant, C. X., Veltri, J. P., & Gebhardt, S. M. (1993). State anxiety and ambulatory blood pressure following resistance exercise in females. *Medicine and Science in Sports and Exercise, 25,* 516–521.

O'Connor, P. J., Petruzzello, S. J., Kubitz, K. A., & Robinson, T. L. (1995). Anxiety responses to maximal exercise testing. *British Journal of Sports Medicine, 29,* 97–102.

Perrig-Chiello, P., Perrig, W. J., Ehrsam, R., Staehelin, H. B., & Krings, F. (1998). The effects of resistance training on well-being and memory in elderly volunteers. *Age and Ageing, 27,* 469–475.

Petruzzello, S. J., Landers, D. M., Hatfield, B. D., Kubitz, K. A., & Salazar, W. (1991). A meta-analysis on the anxiety-reducing effects of acute and chronic exercise: Outcomes and mechanisms. *Sports Medicine, 11,* 143–182.

Raedeke, T. D., Focht, B. C., & Scales, D. (2007). Social environmental factors of psychological responses to acute exercise for socially physique anxious females. *Journal of Sport and Exercise Psychology, 8,* 463–476.

Raglin, J. S. (1997). Anxiolytic effects of physical activity. In W. P. Morgan (Ed.), *Physical activity and mental health* (pp. 107–126). Washington, DC: Taylor & Francis.

Raglin, J. S., Turner, P. E., & Eksten, F. (1993). State anxiety and blood pressure following 30 min of leg ergometry or weight training. *Medicine and Science in Sports and Exercise, 25,* 1044–1048.

Reed, J., & Ones, D. (2006). The effect of acute aerobic exercise on positive activated affect: A meta-analysis. *Psychology of Sport and Exercise, 7,* 477–514.

Rejeski, W. J., Gauvin, L., Hobson, M. L., & Norris, J. L. (1995). Effects of baseline responses, in-task feelings, and duration of activity on exercise-induced feeling states in women. *Health Psychology, 14,* 350–359.

Revnic, C. R., Nica, A. S., & Revnic, F. (2007). The impact of physical training on endocrine modulation, muscle physiology and sexual functions in elderly men. *Archives of Gerontology and Geriatrics, 44*(Suppl. 1), 339–342.

Rovio, S., Kareholt, I., Helkala, E. L., Viitanen, M., Winblad, B., Tuomilehto, J., … Kivipelto, M. (2005). Leisure-time physical activity at midlife and the risk of dementia and Alzheimer's disease. *Lancet Neurology, 4,* 705–711.

Singh, N. A., Clements, K. M., & Fiatarone, M. A. (1997). A randomized controlled trial of progressive resistance training in depressed elders. *The Journals of Gerontology Series A: Biological Sciences and Medical Sciences, 52,* M27–M35.

Sonstroem, R. J. (1998). Physical self-concept: Assessment and external validity. *Exercise and Sport Sciences Reviews, 26,* 133–164.

Spielberger, C. E., Gorsuch, R. L., & Luschene, R. E. (1983). *Manual for the state-trait anxiety inventory.* Palo Alto, CA: Consulting Psychologists Press.

Tellegen, A., Watson, D., & Clark, L. A. (1999). On the dimensional and hierarchical structure of affect. *Psychological Science, 10,* 297–303.

Tharion, W. J., Harman, E. A., Kraemer, W. J., & Rauch, T. M. (1991). Effect of different weight training routines on mood states. *Journal of Applied Sport Science Research, 5,* 60–65.

Thayer, R. E. (2001). *Calm energy: How people regulate mood with food and exercise.* New York: Oxford University Press.

Tsutsumi, T., Don, B. M., Zaichkowsky, L. D., & Delizonna, L. L. (1997). Physical fitness and psychological benefits of strength training in community dwelling older adults. *Applied Human Science: Journal of Physiological Anthropology, 16,* 257–266.

van Dam, P. S., & Aleman, A. (2004). Insulin-like growth factor-I, cognition and brain aging. *European Journal of Pharmacology, 490,* 87–95.

Velez, A., Golem, D. L., & Arent, S. M. (2010). The impact of a 12-week resistance training program on strength, body composition, and self-concept of Hispanic adolescents. *Journal of Strength and Conditioning Research, 24,* 1065–1073.

Verhaeghen, P., & Cerella, J. (2002). Aging, executive control, and attention: A review of meta-analyses. *Neuroscience and Biobehavioral Reviews, 26,* 849–857.

Watson, D. (2002). Positive affectivity. In C. R. Snyder, & S. J. Lopez (Eds.), *Handbook of positive psychology* (pp. 106–119). New York: Oxford University Press.

Whitehead, J. (1995). A study of children's physical self-perceptions using an adapting physical self-perception questionnaire. *Pediatric Exercise Science, 7,* 133–152.

Williams, D. M., Dunsiger, S., Ciccolo, J. T., Lewis, B. A., Albrecht, A. E., & Marcus, B. H. (2008). Acute affective response to a moderate-intensity exercise stimulus predicts physical activity participation 6 and 12 months later. *Psychology of Sport and Exercise, 9,* 231–245.

Yasunaga, A., Togo, F., Watanabe, E., Park, H., Shephard, R. J., & Aoyagi, Y. (2006). Yearlong physical activity and health-related quality of life in older Japanese adults: The Nakanojo study. *Journal of Aging and Physical Activity, 14,* 288–301.

6

EXERCISE DEPENDENCE

Dave Smith

MANCHESTER METROPOLITAN UNIVERSITY, CREWE, UK

Bruce D. Hale

PENN STATE BERKS, READING, PA, USA

Introduction

It is ironic that in this day and age that, while most exercise researchers are investigating ways to get more people exercising regularly and reducing overweight and obese bodies, other researchers are interested in understanding why a smaller percentage of the population exercise excessively. Though all medical practitioners agree that regular exercise should be an important part of a healthy lifestyle, some individuals develop an obsessive approach to it that can be damaging physiologically, psychologically and socially. The addictive qualities of exercise have been known to researchers for at least 40 years, since the work of Baekeland (1970). As part of his sleep deprivation research, Baekeland wanted to explore the effects of exercise deprivation. He had to abandon this part of his research, however, as he found participants impossible to recruit. Despite offering large sums of money, he could not persuade enough participants to forego regular exercise for several weeks. His observations led him to conclude that many of these individuals were addicted to exercise.

Exercise dependence defined

Since the time of Baekeland, psychologists have paid this phenomenon a great deal of attention. Though various terms have been used to describe this construct, including exercise addiction, obligatory exercise and compulsive exercise, we will use the term 'exercise dependence' throughout this chapter. Exercise dependence can be defined as 'a process that compels an individual to exercise in spite of obstacles, and results in physical and psychological symptoms when exercise is withdrawn' (Pierce, 1994, p. 149). Essentially, therefore, it is a condition where moderate to vigorous exercise becomes compulsive (Hausenblas & Symons Downs, 2002b).

Pierce's definition describes exercise dependence as a unidimensional construct. More recently other researchers (e.g. Hausenblas & Symons Downs, 2002b; Veale, 1995) have defined exercise dependence as a multidimensional maladaptive pattern of exercise behaviour. Specifically, it has been defined as 'a craving for leisure time physical activity that results in uncontrollable excessive exercise behaviour and that manifests in physiological symptoms (e.g., tolerance, withdrawal) and/or psychological symptoms (e.g., anxiety, depression)' (Hausenblas & Symons Downs, 2002a, p. 90).

The aim of this chapter is to examine exercise dependence in those engaged in weight training. First, the consequences of exercise dependence will be explored, then its psychological and behavioural antecedents and correlates will be examined. Based on current knowledge, we will provide suggestions to sport and exercise psychologists, strength and conditioning specialists and other health professionals involved in this field for working with individuals who display signs of exercise dependence. Finally, we will suggest future research directions for those wishing to study this construct further.

Measurement of exercise dependence in weight trainers

Problems with measurement accuracy and validity have dominated this area of psychological inquiry. Most early measures were unidimensional, involved interviewing participants (Sachs & Pargman, 1979), lacked proper psychometric validation, focused primarily on aerobic activity (running) and lacked any theoretical basis (Hausenblas & Symons Downs, 2002a). In the last decade, attempts to measure this elusive concept have involved multidimensional self-report inventories based on theoretical and clinical constructs, and several attempts to categorize exercisers as 'at risk' or 'asymptomatic' in exercise dependence. For aerobic activity, Ogden, Veale, and Summers (1997) created the Exercise Dependence Questionnaire (EDQ), a 29-item self-report that produced eight subscales (Social–Occupational Interference, Positive Reward, Withdrawal Symptoms, Exercise for Weight Control, Insight into Problems, Exercise for Social Reasons, Exercise for Health Reasons, Stereotyped Behaviour) under a total score. Hausenblas and Symons Downs (2002a) and Symons Downs, Hausenblas, and Nigg (2004) concluded that one subscale (i.e. Stereotyped Behaviour) is psychometrically unsound and five subscales appear to measure exercise attitudes, benefits and social aspects, not exercise dependence. More recently, Hausenblas and colleagues (Hausenblas & Symons Downs, 2002b; Symons Downs et al., 2004) have produced a more psychometrically valid instrument to measure multidimensional exercise dependence based on all seven criteria (Tolerance, Withdrawal Effects, Continuance, Lack of Control, Reductions in Other Activities, Time, Intention) for substance dependence identified in DSM-IV (*Diagnostic and Statistical Manual for Mental Disorders*, 4th Edition; American Psychiatric Association, 1994). Even more recently, Terry, Szabo, and Griffiths (2004) have presented a short screening inventory consisting of one item for each of the seven dependence criteria, the Exercise Addiction Inventory (EAI), which purports to be able to accurately identify people at risk for exercise addiction. While these questionnaires do a better job of measuring the multidimensional concept of exercise dependence, none was constructed specifically to measure exercise dependence in exercise in an anaerobic setting (i.e. weight training).

To determine how common bodybuilding dependence is, as well as to determine its psychological antecedents, correlates and consequences, it is necessary to be able to accurately measure it. Therefore, we developed the nine–item Likert-scored Bodybuilding Dependence Scale (BDS; Smith, Hale, & Collins, 1998). This was based on the symptoms of exercise dependence noted in the previous literature, and exploratory factor analysis indicated that it comprised three subscales. One subscale (Social Dependence) appeared to reflect the need to be in the bodybuilding social environment. Another subscale (Training Dependence) seemed to reflect the need to engage in regular weight training. The third subscale (Mastery Dependence) appeared to measure the need to exert control over training schedules. Results (Smith et al., 1998) appeared to strongly support the internal reliability of all three subscales and construct validity of the Social Dependence subscale, but were less supportive of the validity of the other two subscales. We concluded that it appears to be a combination of personality dispositions and the social nature of bodybuilding training that individuals can become dependent upon, rather than the actual activity of lifting weights. Interestingly, there were significant differences between different weight training populations on the different subscales (e.g. on the Social Dependence subscale, bodybuilders scored higher than Olympic weightlifters and fitness weight trainers, whereas on the Mastery Dependence subscale the weightlifters scored higher than the bodybuilders). This suggests that different aspects of exercise dependence may be more salient for certain weight training populations. Perhaps the positive social feedback from bodybuilding peers on increased muscle size drives bodybuilding dependence, whereas powerlifters are more motivated by goals of mastering various lifts with increased resistance.

A follow-up study (Hurst, Hale, & Smith, 2000) examined differences between experienced and inexperienced bodybuilders in BDS scores, and examined the construct and concurrent validity of the scale. The findings supported the concurrent and construct validity of all three BDS subscales, with experienced bodybuilders scoring significantly higher than inexperienced bodybuilders and weightlifters on these subscales and on the Social Support Survey – Clinical Form (Richman, Rosenfeld, & Hardy, 1993). In addition, significant correlations were found between all three BDS subscales and the Social Physique Anxiety (SPA) Scale (Hart, Leary, & Rejeski, 1989) and a bodybuilding-specific version of the Athletic Identity Measurement Scale (Cornelius, 1999). These findings contrast with a recent study (Smith, Wright, & Winrow, 2010) where no relationship was found between SPA and exercise dependence in runners. Smith et al. hypothesized that these contrasting findings may be due to a difference in the motives for participation in the two activities, a hypothesis that warrants further investigation. They suggested that bodybuilders are more likely than runners to train specifically to enhance appearance, and that compared to exercise-dependent bodybuilders it is less likely that those who develop an obsessive approach to running do so because of its effects on their physique.

Overall, these early findings were supportive of the validity and reliability of the BDS. More importantly, they shed light upon some of the psychosocial and motivational antecedents of exercise dependence in bodybuilders. For example, Smith et al. (1998) and Hurst et al. (2000) supported the idea that many bodybuilders begin training to reduce feelings of low self-esteem and poor body image, and as their self-esteem and body image improve through their training they can apparently become dependent upon it to feel positive about themselves. The importance of self-esteem as an antecedent of exercise dependence was also examined by Groves, Biscomb, Nevill, and Matheson (2008), who found a relationship between these two variables that is mediated by identity such that exercise dependence was more prevalent in environments where identity was more likely to be reinforced through sport and exercise. Clearly, the weights gym is such an environment. Hurst et al. (2000) also found that social support was an important antecedent of bodybuilding dependence. It seems that immersion and acceptance in the gym social scene, and the social bonding that goes along with it, is central to most cases of exercise dependence in bodybuilders.

Smith and Hale (2004) performed a confirmatory factor analysis to re-examine the factor structure of the BDS more thoroughly, and also examined the effects of competitive status and gender on bodybuilding dependence. The findings strongly supported the three-factor model of bodybuilding dependence described by Smith et al. (1998). In terms of between-group differences, competitive bodybuilders scored higher on all three BDS subscales than non-competitive bodybuilders, but there were no significant gender differences. This study also found a relationship between bodybuilding dependence and 'muscle dysmorphia (MD)' (a newly described subcategory of body dysmorphic disorder involving excessive weightlifting to increase muscle bulk). Thus, this finding supports the notion that exercise dependence is an important part of the pattern of behaviour that characterizes the muscle dysmorphic individual.

Smith and Hale (2005) examined social and psychological antecedents of bodybuilding dependence (life satisfaction, socioeconomic status, marital status and parental status) and also examined the test–retest reliability of the BDS, using a sample of 181 male bodybuilders. Pearson correlations revealed high test–retest reliability for all three subscales ($r = 0.94$, 0.96 and 0.94 for Social Dependence, Training Dependence and Mastery Dependence, respectively). Pearson correlations also revealed significant negative correlations between all three BDS subscales and scores on the Satisfaction with Life Scale (Diener & Lucas, 1991). For the analysis of socioeconomic status, participants were classified into managerial and professional class (e.g. lawyers, accountants), intermediate class (e.g. nurses) and working class (e.g. production line workers, shop assistants) according to the UK Government's National Statistics Socio-Economic Classification (NS-SEC; Office for National Statistics, 2001). Working class participants scored higher on all three BDS subscales than intermediate class participants who, in turn, scored higher than professional class participants. Participants who were not currently involved in a romantic relationship scored significantly higher on all BDS subscales than those who were romantically involved. Parents scored significantly higher than non-parents on Social and Mastery Dependence, but not on Training Dependence. Thus, these results demonstrate that life satisfaction, socioeconomic status, marital status and parental status can successfully predict BDS scores. More specifically, the 'typical' male bodybuilder in the United Kingdom who displays symptoms of dependence will be single, childless or of intermediate or low socioeconomic status, and will have a relatively low level of subjective well-being. Therefore, clinical attention should be paid to the possibility of bodybuilding dependence if a bodybuilder with such a demographic profile presents to a physician or psychologist with apparent symptoms of overtraining and/or obsessive/compulsive behaviour.

So far, therefore, this line of research has yielded a simple, quick, valid and reliable measurement tool and lots of interesting and potentially useful information regarding the psychological and psychosocial issues surrounding exercise dependence in bodybuilders. The only other validated measure of exercise dependence in an anaerobic exercise population is the Exercise Dependence Scale (EDS) of the Muscle Dysmorphia Inventory (MDI) created by Rhea, Lantz, and Cornelius (2004). This scale has been primarily used to identify other behavioural correlates in dysmorphic samples and compare different types of lifting samples.

Incidence of exercise dependence

In today's western societies struggling with huge increases in obesity and sedentary behaviour, it is ironic that exercise scientists have tried to also measure the prevalence of excessive exercise habits. In fact, several studies (Garman, Hayduk, Crider, & Hodel, 2004; Zmijewski & Howard, 2003) have reported that between 22 and 46 per cent of their undergraduate college exercise samples were at risk for exercise dependence, while other researchers (Hale, Roth, Delong, & Briggs, 2010; Hildebrandt, Schlundt, Langenbucher, & Chung, 2006) have found 15 and 17 per cent of their weightlifting sample showed strong clinical symptoms of exercise dependence and MD (see Reel & Galli, this volume, for more information), respectively. In contrast, other recent studies (Allegre, Souville, Therme, & Griffiths, 2006; Hausenblas & Symons Downs, 2002a; Terry et al., 2004) have reported that the exercise dependence prevalence in their samples was more conservatively in the 3–13 per cent range, and that MD prevalence was estimated at 10 per cent among the weightlifting population (Pope & Katz, 1994). It remains unclear as to what the actual prevalence really is, but the concepts of exercise dependence and the obsession with body image remain a hotbed of research inquiry in the twenty-first century.

To cloud the situation further, Szabo (2000) has suggested that exercise dependence prevalence in active older participants may be lower, and results by Kjelsas and Augestad (2003) support this hypothesis with their finding that younger women scored significantly higher on the EDQ (Ogden et al., 1997) than older female runners. Recently, Edmunds, Ntoumanis, and Duda (2006) provided evidence that participants grouped into two younger cohorts (less than 24 years old, 25–34 years) were significantly higher in Total Exercise Dependence scores on the EDS (Hausenblas & Symons Downs, 2002b; Symons Downs et al., 2004) than those above 35 years of age. Other evidence by Weik and Hale (2009) found prevalence rates in male and female adult exercisers (mean age of approximately 40 years) that were similar to those of published undergraduate samples (Hausenblas & Symons Downs, 2002a). Finally, most recently Hale et al. (2010) reported no significant differences on the EDS between 18–24 and 25–55 age cohorts. Even with better validated questionnaires like the EDS, it appears that more research is necessary to see if any true age difference exists.

Early efforts in exercise psychology to identify any possible gender differences in exercise dependence seem unclear and again were determined by the quality of the questionnaire used. Early research using unidimensional questionnaires either found no gender differences (Furst & Germone, 1993; Triola, 1996) or women scoring higher in exercise dependence (Masters & Lambert, 1989; Pierce, Rohaly, & Fritchley, 1997).

Clearer trends in possible gender differences appear when studies using the multidimensional questionnaires are scrutinized. For the EDQ, Kjelsas and Augestad (2003) and Zmijewski and Howard (2003) reported that women scored significantly higher on the Exercise for Weight Control, Health Reasons and Withdrawal Symptoms subscales, while men scored higher on the Insight into Problems subscale. The opposite trend appears for gender differences in studies using the EDS. Hausenblas and Fallon (2002) and Hausenblas and Symons Downs (2002c) reported that undergraduate men showed higher means on 6 out of 7 subscales of the EDS. Then Symons Downs et al. (2004) reported that almost three times as many undergraduate males were categorized as being 'at risk' for exercise dependence as females. Recently Weik and Hale (2009) also reported results supporting this gender-specific finding where males scored higher in exercise dependence on the EDS, and women scored higher in exercise dependence on the EDQ. All of the above studies have examined possible gender differences in primarily aerobic exercisers. To date, only Smith and Hale (2004) compared gender differences in weightlifters on the BDS with a small cohort of female bodybuilders and reported no significant gender differences. Efforts to identify any possible gender differences in exercise dependence still seem unclear and again based on the quality of the questionnaire used. More research needs to be undertaken to determine whether the items of recent questionnaires are gender-biased for specific items (Weik & Hale, 2009).

Consequences of exercise dependence

There was some early debate in the literature as to whether exercise dependence should be viewed as a positive or negative phenomenon. Glasser (1976) classified regular physical activity as a 'positive addiction', due to the positive effects on health and psychological well-being resulting from regular exercise. Glasser contrasted this with negative addictions, such as drug abuse, which can be physiologically and psychologically debilitating. Sachs and Pargman (1979) interviewed a sample of male runners and found that some of them displayed withdrawal symptoms such as anxiety and guilt when they were deprived of their running. Despite such withdrawal symptoms, these authors saw dependence upon exercise as a positive phenomenon, and even suggested ways of promoting it. Similarly, Thaxton (1982) reported that participants who ran at least 5 days/week experienced increased depression and increased galvanic skin response when asked to abstain from a run. She concluded that, given the addictive effects of running, obsessive–compulsive personality disorders may be successfully treated using this form of exercise. Thaxton hypothesized that, as obsessive personalities tend to have high anxiety levels, running might be a productive outlet for compulsiveness as well as a release from tension.

However, most exercise psychologists currently believe that exercise dependence can be harmful socially, psychologically and physically. Morgan (1979) noted that addicted runners let their exercise interfere with family, work and social responsibilities. He behaviourally defined 'negative addiction' as: exercising when vocationally, socially and medically contraindicated; needing daily exercise to cope; not being able to live without running; and experiencing withdrawal symptoms without regular exercise. For example, in such individuals, running may take on vocational overtones, and the individual's job will thus be seen as much less important, possibly even jeopardizing his or her employment. Also, loved ones and friends may be relegated to roles of insignificance. Chan and Grossman (1988) reported that consistent runners suffered withdrawal symptoms of psychological distress when they were unable to run. Unlike Sachs and Pargman (1979) and Thaxton (1982), Chan and Grossman (1988) saw this level of exercise as problematic due to the negative affect which may occur if such an individual is forced to discontinue running (e.g. due to injury). More recently, Aidman and Woollard (2003) also reported that self-reported addicted runners suffered emotional distress when forced to miss a scheduled training session. According to Grant (1988), when exercise addicts are unable to run for long periods of time, they suffer symptoms such as: depression; lack of energy; decreased self-confidence and self-esteem; loss of interest in eating, sex and other activities; insomnia; and weight loss or gain. DeBenedette (1990), Wichmann and Martin (1992) and Adams and Kirby (2002) have noted that excessive exercise can lead to severe injuries and health problems. For example, the risk of multiple overuse injuries is greatly increased by excessive exercise. In addition, overexercising can cause fatigue, muscle atrophy, depressed immune system, early degenerative arthritic changes and kidney damage.

It also appears that there is a link between excessive exercise and mortality. Paffenbarger, Hyde, Wing, and Hsieh (1986) found in their study of Harvard alumni that death rate from all causes declined as the level of calories expended per hour of leisure activity rose up to a certain point. However, among subjects who exercised excessively, expending more than 3,500 kcal/week, the death rate increased. More recently, researchers have shown life-threatening cardiac changes (right ventricle dysfunction) as a result of repetitive, prolonged exercise such as that performed by endurance athletes (Ector et al., 2007).

Therefore, exercise dependence, and the associated excessive exercise, can be harmful physically, psychologically and socially. Those engaging in weight training, particularly bodybuilders, often appear to exhibit characteristics of exercise dependence, and in our early work, we chronicled a great deal of anecdotal evidence to this effect (see, e.g., Smith et al., 1998). Chronic overtraining, potentially harmful dieting, drug use and a general obsession with the 'bodybuilding lifestyle' to the exclusion of other important aspects of life such as work, relationships and family life appeared common. Indeed, anyone who trains in a bodybuilding gym probably knows a number of people who display symptoms of an exercise dependence disorder. However, some examples may serve to illustrate just how serious this problem can be. In his autobiography, former bodybuilding champion Sam Fussell (1991) chronicled a lifestyle which was entirely geared around the sport. After losing his job (indirectly due to his obsession with bodybuilding), he devoted his life to the gym. Time which was not spent lifting was spent preparing for it. This behaviour was clearly detrimental to his health. For example, he noted that when preparing for an important competition,

> Thanks to the rigors of my training, my hands were more ragged, callused and cut than any longshoreman's. Thanks to the drugs and my diet, I couldn't run more than 20 yards without pulling up and gasping for air. My ass cheeks ached from innumerable steroid injections, my stomach whined for sustenance, my whole body throbbed from gym activities and enforced weight loss. Thanks to the competition tan, my skin was breaking out everywhere.

Interestingly, Fussell claims that this lifestyle was common amongst the Southern Californian bodybuilding community. And such behaviour does not appear to be confined to this bodybuilding Mecca. For example, some very revealing comments were made in a UK radio documentary *Iron Maidens* (H. Thompson & Mares, 1993), in which several top British female bodybuilders discussed their lifestyles and their attitudes towards the sport. One former British champion stated that bodybuilding was her whole life; her commitment to her training even led to the breaking off of her engagement to her fiancé. Another woman's daily training programme involved such long weight training and aerobic workouts that it left virtually no time for her to do anything else. When faced with injuries which forced her to withdraw from an important competition and temporarily cease training, she suffered from severe withdrawal symptoms:

> I was dead depressed and really down about the whole thing. All this year I've been training for this competition and now I'm not doing it everything has just totally stopped. My life has just fell apart really because I have been training non-stop and I just don't know what to do with myself now. I'm lost.

The obsessive attitude which many bodybuilders have towards their training was summed up nicely by bodybuilding journalist T. C. Luoma (Luoma & Mentzer, 1995): 'Many bodybuilders do nothing else. They spend every living hour, every minute of the day building their muscles, to the exclusion of any kind of life.' Indeed, in a study of professional female bodybuilders, Fisher (1997) found that, on average, the women spent 5–6 hours/day in bodybuilding-related activities, and another 6 hours thinking about bodybuilding. As one woman put it: 'The great majority of women I know that are involved with it are obsessed with their weight…just compulsive about it.' In 2000, Pope, Phillips, and Olivardia also began documenting case examples of the potential psychological and medical problems associated with MD or what they called 'the Adonis Complex'. Many other anecdotal examples could be given of apparent dependence upon bodybuilding, but hopefully these will suffice to illustrate the degree of dependence.

A full understanding of this phenomenon is important for all those involved in working with people who regularly engage in weight training. However, most of the exercise dependence research to date has focused on aerobic activities, particularly running. Based on the research collected by Hausenblas and Fallon (2002), for example, less than 10 per cent of studies had been focused exclusively on weight training. Noting this lack of research, we reasoned that research needed to examine this phenomenon in weight trainers, with particular need for a valid and reliable measurement tool. Since 1998, we have undertaken a series of studies focused on developing and validating the BDS that were described earlier. The following section, however, will examine other relevant research that has helped shed light on the psychological antecedents and correlates of exercise dependence in the weight training population.

Correlates of exercise dependence

In this section, we present several concepts that are closely related to or are correlates of exercise dependence reported in the weightlifting research.

Eating disorders

Initially in the addictions literature (McCreary & Sadava, 2001), adolescent girls were found to have a higher prevalence of eating disorders and symptomology (body image disturbances, excessive exercise patterns) than adolescent boys. But other researchers (Pope et al., 2000) have suggested that adolescent boys also have similar behavioural problems (poor body image and self-esteem, use of anabolic steroids, eating disorders and excessive exercise behaviours) that revolve around the drive to be more muscular that is reinforced in western culture. In any attempt to link exercise dependence with eating disorders, Hausenblas and Symons Downs (2002a) and Veale (1995) suggest that 'primary exercise dependence' (no underlying eating disorder) must be distinguished from 'secondary exercise dependence' (part of an eating disorder).

Yates, Leehey, and Shisslak (1983) first proposed in their 'anorexia analogue hypothesis' that eating disorders are a common behavioural characteristic in obligatory male runners and female anorexics. Their findings showed limited support for the notion that these cohorts share similar compulsive personality characteristics and that both were using running to control weight. Most research undertaken in the last decade usually attempts to differentiate primary from secondary exercise dependence by assessing the potential for concurrent eating disorders.

Drive for muscularity

More recently, McCreary and Sasse (2000) have suggested that men and boys in western society have developed significant body concerns that cause them to generate a 'drive for muscularity' to meet a perceived high societal standard for a muscular physique. This drive for muscularity among primarily young boys and men involves a strong body image concern that they are not as muscular as the average male body shape (McCreary & Sadava, 2001).

Since the primary goal of bodybuilding is the development of a hypermesomorphic physique and that of powerlifting is to enhance strength, it seems logical to suggest that bodybuilders could also be higher in the drive for muscularity. But research findings to date show no clear pattern regarding this hypothesis. Hallsworth, Wade, and Tiggemann (2005) reported that, while bodybuilders placed a greater emphasis on the importance of appearance in their self-esteem than powerlifters, there was no significant difference with powerlifters on their non-validated measure of drive for muscularity. Similarly, Pickett, Lewis, and Cash (2005) also reported that both competitive bodybuilders and 'non-competitive weight trainers' were equally more 'appearance-invested' than active athletic controls who did not weightlift (no measure of drive for muscularity was taken). In contrast, Lantz, Rhea, and Mayhew (2001) reported that bodybuilders had significantly higher concerns regarding the size and shape of their physique than powerlifters (again, no measure drive for muscularity was assessed). Most recently, Hale et al. (2010) reported that powerlifters were found to be significantly higher on *Drive for Muscularity Scale* (DMS; McCreary & Sasse, 2000) Total and Muscle Development Behaviours scales than bodybuilders. The DMS is a 15-item questionnaire designed to measure males' and females' attitudes about their muscularity and their desire to be more muscular. It has two subscales: the Muscle Development Behaviours (BEH) scale (seven items) and the Muscularity-Oriented Body Image Attitude (ATT) scale (seven items), which can be calculated for men; regression results suggested that exercise dependence may be directly related to the drive for muscularity.

While studies (Litt & Dodge, 2008; McCreary & Sasse, 2000) have shown that males high in drive for muscularity spend more time lifting weights than those with lower levels of this drive, only two studies to date (Chittester & Hausenblas, 2009; Hale et al., 2010) have explored the relationship between drive for muscularity and exercise dependence in weightlifters. Chittester and Hausenblas found a significant correlation of the EDS with muscle-oriented body image (ATT; 0.35) and Muscularity-related Behaviour scales (BEH; 0.57) of the DMS. More recently Hale et al. found that total DMS score significantly predicted total EDS score but none of the BDS scores across a combined sample of bodybuilders, powerlifters and fitness lifters. Future analyses need to separately compare the relationship of drive for muscularity and exercise dependence in pure bodybuilding or powerlifting samples in order to clearly determine whether the reasons differ among lifting types.

Muscular dysmorphia

Based on several anecdotal (Fussell, 1991; Klein, 1993) and clinical ('reverse anorexia' or 'bigorexia'; Pope, Gruber, & Choi, 1997; Pope et al., 2000) reports, Lantz et al. (2001) developed a model that asserts that exercise dependence is a critical component of a multidimensional psychobehavioural syndrome known as muscular dysmorphia (MD). MD is thought to be an obsessive–compulsive body image disorder that involves incessant thoughts where individuals perceive that their body is not muscular enough. Components of MD include: body image distortion/dissatisfaction, dietary constraints, pharmacological aids, dietary supplements, exercise dependence, physique concealment and low self-esteem. Exercise dependence is one of the symptoms of MD that is measured on a scale of the MDI created by Rhea et al. (2004).

Antecedents of exercise dependence

Carron, Hausenblas, and Estabrooks' (2003) exercise psychology text provides the most comprehensive summary to date of potential causes of exercise dependence categorized under three major areas: psychological, physiological and psychobiological.

Psychological

Their first explanation categorizes several potential causes that could result from psychological personality traits, concurrent addictive behaviours and the mood enhancement effects of exercise.

Exercise-dependent individuals are thought to differ in certain personality traits which may motivate them to engage in dependent behaviours. Research has supported the hypothesis that traits such as perfectionism (Coen & Ogles, 1993; Hagan & Hausenblas, 2003; Hausenblas & Symons Downs, 2002b), obsessive–compulsiveness (Davis, Kennedy, Ravelski, & Dionne, 1994), neuroticism and high trait anxiety (Coen & Ogles, 1993; Rudy & Estok, 1989) and low self-esteem (Hurst et al., 2000; Rudy & Estok, 1989) are correlated with exercise dependence. Findings on the trait of narcissism are less clear (Davis & Fox, 1993; Spano, 2001).

Other researchers have examined relationships between perfectionism and exercise dependence in weight training populations. For example, Kuennen and

Waldron (2007) found a significant relationship between perfectionism scores and scores on the exercise dependence subscale of the MDI. This result concurs with previous research suggesting a link between perfectionism and exercise dependence in aerobic exercise (Coen & Ogles, 1993; Hagan & Hausenblas, 2003; Hausenblas & Symons Downs, 2002b). Perfectionism can lead to obsessive behaviour as perfectionists are rarely satisfied with their efforts or achievements, and this can manifest itself in the weights gym as an obsessive approach to exercise.

We have already discussed the anorexia analogue hypothesis of Yates et al. (1983). Although there are little data (Powers, Schocken, & Boyd, 1998) suggesting a common psychopathology between exercise dependence and eating disorders, it is clear that many weightlifters with prior eating disorders also suffer from exercise dependence (Pope et al., 2000).

Finally, hundreds of studies have shown that exercise leads to positive mental states, and cessation of exercise regimens may lead to negative mental states (Landers & Arent, 2001). These researchers are suggesting that weightlifters like aerobic exercisers can become dependent on exercise since it produces a regular, beneficial psychological mood enhancement after exercise and reduces depression, stress and anxiety.

Finally, some researchers (Hurst et al., 2000; Smith et al., 1998) have provided evidence that the weightlifting fraternity and environment provide social acceptance after repeated episodes of prior failure to gain approval from others and regularly offer a powerful social support network from peers that helps participants successfully cope with daily stressors. This 'social cocoon' can become a psychological crutch in the daily lives of some dependent lifters.

Physiological

Some early psychologists (J. Thompson & Blanton, 1987) hypothesized that individuals could get 'addicted' to exercise because during a workout natural opiates (e.g. beta endorphins, endocannabinoids) are produced. To date, only one study (Pierce, Eastman, Tripathi, Olson, & Dewey, 1993) has produced any results that have not supported this hypothesis. Another biochemical explanation (Pope et al., 2000) suggests that individuals with obsessive–compulsive disorders are inherently lower in brain serotonin levels, which leads to compulsive behaviours. Many psychiatrists have reported success in treating body dysmorphics (MD is considered a type of this obsessive–compulsive disorder) with serotonin uptake-inhibitor drugs (Phillips & Hollander, 2008).

A more plausible physiological explanation involves J. Thompson and Blanton's (1987) sympathetic arousal response cycle. It proposes that initial fitness leads to greater efficiency during exercise, so exercisers need a greater intensity to produce their desired arousal level over time. This gradual need for improvement leads to dependent-lifting behaviours because lifters must continually do higher intensity workouts to produce the desired arousal response. This hypothesis has not yet been tested with an extensive longitudinal study.

Psychobiological

This explanation suggests that psychological and physiological factors interact to produce a predisposition for dependent behaviours (Jacobs, 1986). Two major factors (subjective aversion and situational influence) are necessary to produce this predisposition. First, an individual must experience either a depressed or overly excited psychological state, and be characterized by feelings of inadequacy and rejection caused by childhood experiences. This predisposition for dependent behaviours occurs in a limited number of individuals and remains inactive until the individual experiences a situation (e.g. successful workout) that results in an alteration of their physiological state and reduction of their aversive psychological state. Over time this regular occurrence leads to dependent behaviour. Only one study (Beh, Mathers, & Holden, 1996) to date has indirectly tested this explanation with partial support in an electroencephalography (EEG) study.

A psychobiological explanation for bodybuilding dependence

In our first paper on this topic (Smith et al., 1998), we noted that many scientific studies have shown weight training can significantly enhance self-esteem (see, e.g., Tucker, 1983a, 1983b, 1987). This increase in subjective self-evaluation is not surprising given that many males are unhappy with their physiques, and regular weight training can produce quite dramatic improvements in appearance. Therefore, it makes sense that, as individuals increase the size of their muscles through weight training, they will begin to view themselves more favourably.

As individuals successfully use weight training to improve their self-esteem and body image, some may begin to rely exclusively on their training to feel good about themselves. This increase is most likely to occur in those who have low self-esteem in most or all of the areas of their lives that they feel are important to them (Smith, Hale, Rhea, Olrich, & Collier, 2009). For such individuals, the time they spend in the gym may be the only time they feel a high degree of self-worth. Because of this situation-specific increase, they try to spend as much time in there as possible. In this way, they become compulsive about their training, placing a higher priority on it than on other activities, and neglecting other responsibilities in order to train. Anyone who trains in a weights gym probably knows a number of people who display symptoms of an exercise dependence disorder such as the anecdotal examples mentioned earlier in this chapter.

Differences in exercise dependence between lifting types

Most researchers studying anaerobic activities realized early on that different kinds of weightlifters may have different goals for their workouts, which may impact their susceptibility to exercise dependence and drive for muscularity behaviours. Since powerlifters and Olympic lifters train to lift as much as possible in one repetition and are not as concerned with muscular development, it has been hypothesized (Hallsworth et al., 2005; Lantz, Rhea, & Cornelius, 2002) that they may be less likely to develop obsessive overtraining routines designed to satisfy body image concerns. On the other hand, since bodybuilders train to develop a hypermesomorphic physique and do so to overcome body image and self-esteem weaknesses (Hildebrandt et al., 2006; Hurst et al., 2000; Olivardia, Pope, & Hudson, 2000; Pope et al., 2000), they may be more susceptible to excessive exercise routines, obsessive eating disturbances and steroid usage.

The research findings to date are unclear regarding these hypothesized exercise dependence differences in lifters. Hurst et al. (2000) reported that experienced bodybuilders scored significantly higher on the Social, Training and Mastery dependence subscales of the BDS and SPA (Hart et al., 1989) than their powerlifting sample. In contrast, Lantz et al. (2002) found no significant differences between competitive bodybuilders and powerlifters on the Exercise Dependence subscale of the MDI (Rhea et al., 2004). Furthermore, on a non-validated measure of exercise dependence with a small sample of 14 powerlifters, Pierce and Morris (1998) reported that the sample seemed to have a high degree of exercise dependence. Most recently, Hale et al. (2010) found that bodybuilders and powerlifters were significantly higher than fitness lifters on EDS Total, the seven EDS scales and the three BDS scales. In summary, these contrasting findings suggest that different lifting types need to be clearly identified, and psychometrically valid measures of exercise dependence should be used to investigate possible comparisons in the future.

Helping individuals experiencing or at risk of bodybuilding dependence

This section will use this present state of knowledge to provide suggestions to sport and exercise psychologists, strength and conditioning professionals and health professionals for working with individuals displaying potential symptoms of exercise dependence.

Warning signals for exercise dependence

Since individual weightlifters can suffer devastating short- and long-term medical, vocational, social and psychological injuries and debilitation from the effects of exercise dependence, it is critical that coaches, trainers, health care specialists, sport and exercise psychologists, clinical psychologists and psychiatrists all become familiar with possible behavioural warning signals falling into personality, behavioural and eating disorder categories.

From a personality trait perspective, it appears that individuals scoring high in perfectionism, obsessive–compulsive behaviours, SPA and the drive for muscularity, and low in body image and physical self-esteem, may be highly at risk for developing exercise dependence in a weightlifting programme. When participants begin to show little interest in family, work and relationships, and their sole focus seems to be on their daily workout(s), then practitioners must be wary of potential negative behaviours dominating their lifestyle. Lifters whose thoughts are dominated by their daily workout and who suffer guilt and withdrawal behavioural responses when they cannot work out for a day or so should immediately draw the attention of helping professionals in their arena.

The regular observation of various behavioural responses should also alert professionals that the lifter may need a quick intervention to deter the negative consequences of exercise dependence. Personal trainers, coaches or fitness professionals may notice that potentially dependent individuals often undertake multiple daily workouts (1–3 hours per session, often twice a day) at approximately the same time and place at their gym facility. Although elite and highly committed athletes may also follow this multiple routine, questioning of the individual may reveal a dependent person who has no or few long-term competitive goals and feels he/she must undergo this tightly controlled regimen to keep at bay feelings of low self-esteem and poor body image. In addition, these individuals suffer an abnormal amount of overuse injuries resulting from this excessive workout programme. Furthermore, they can be found in the gym working out when injured so badly that a physician has forbade them from exercising or when they are so sick that they should be at home resting. They don't feel right if they miss an exercise session for any reason.

Finally, since the evidence to date suggests that male lifters are more likely to suffer from exercise dependence linked to weightlifting, observers will likely notice that potentially dependent individuals have a tight, social support group of fellow lifters who always work out together in the same fitness facility. Male lifters, especially bodybuilders, seem to encourage each other to spend exorbitant time at the gym working on getting bigger by using an intense, closely monitored workout regimen and dietary control. This group exerts a very powerful group motivation to focus all of an individual's daily efforts on lifting more weight and gaining more muscle.

The last category, and perhaps the most obvious, is that the health care helper may notice that the individual shows symptoms of extreme dietary control and possible eating disorders before and after gym workouts. Individuals with potential exercise dependence may be observed to be always on a diet, which consists of little variety, high protein and little fat content. These individuals will be seen ingesting numerous supplements including vitamins, protein shakes and other questionable nutritional aids, and sometimes may be seen buying or using illegal or banned anabolic supplements (steroids, growth hormone) as part of their quest to obtain body perfection. They will also obtain pain killers which allow them to work out harder and longer, and diuretics that allow them to eliminate water weight for that 'cut look' especially immediately before a competition. If the helper sees other obvious signs of a possible eating disorder (starvation, bingeing and purging, extreme body image disturbances), he/she should counsel the individual to seek immediate help from a specialized clinician who can treat such disorders.

Possible interventions for exercise dependence

Both weight training participants and health care specialists need to become more aware of the potential dangers of exercise dependence, its symptoms occurring in weightlifters and various potential interventions available to minimize its impact or reduce its occurrence. Berger, Pargman, and Weinberg (2007), in their popular exercise psychology text, offer three main categories of interventions: educational, behavioural and clinical.

Educational information about the causes, consequences and symptoms should be made available to all weightlifters, bodybuilders, trainers, coaches and health care specialists who come in contact with potential exercise-dependent lifters. Like other addictive behaviours, if people are familiar with the warning signals and outward symptoms, often participants can change their own behaviours or external helpers can recommend changes in workout patterns to avoid the short- and long-term deleterious effects of exercise dependence. Helpers who spot highly regulated work-out regimens, notice unhealthy eating patterns or pervasive withdrawal responses, or hear out loud regular compulsive thoughts and words about exercise need to be aware of the potential for addictive behaviours in these individuals. Even gym managers and personal trainers should be educated to clearly identify this set of behaviours and attitudes and have intervention or referral strategies available for their local weightlifting clientele. An ounce of prevention does go a long way.

Participants also need to be responsible for monitoring their own thoughts and behaviours. If you know you have an obsessive–compulsive personality, may suffer from low body image and self-esteem, have prior problems with an eating disorder or have a history of obesity as a child, you may be a likely candidate for exercise dependence. A family history of obsessive–compulsive disorders or eating disorders may also warrant some concern. If constant thoughts of working out dominate your daily train of thought, and you cannot seem to control and limit your work-out motivation, then perhaps you are at risk for exercise dependence. Proactive awareness may help keep exercisers from transforming from being a committed exerciser to becoming a dependent exerciser.

Participants and helpers must also use behavioural strategies to try to avoid or limit exercise dependence effects. Berger et al.'s (2007) list of strategies includes: keeping exercise workouts limited to 3–4 times/week for 30–60 minutes, training with alternating hard and easy days to avoid overuse injuries, finding a workout partner who is not obsessed with exercise, scheduling rest days as a regular part of the weekly cycle, setting realistic short- and long-term goals and, when injured, making sure the participant is fully recovered before restarting.

To this list, we would add that moderation is the key to all activities to avoid addiction. Building in a cross-training component (e.g. including totally aerobic workouts) to a regimen that avoids the same repetitive, high-intensity anaerobic workout can help control compulsive addictive behaviours and limit physiological and psychological damage. Trainers or coaches could also model other non-compulsive behaviours that could help lifters to realize that other workout or coping strategies are available. Participants must become responsible for learning self-monitoring skills for their workout behaviours, practise coping strategies for dealing with stress and develop behaviours for improving relationships and encouraging interests outside of the gym.

Serious exercise dependence and eating disorder behaviours warrant serious clinical and counselling interventions. While weightlifters may not suffer from the early life-threatening damage that many anorexics do, the continuous damage caused by years of excessive exercise, overuse of legal and illegal ergogenic aids, poor dietary practices and social and psychological isolation could lead to a premature demise. When health care helpers notice clients with potentially damaging behaviours, attitudes and cognitions, they need to encourage these lifters to seek professional help and counselling or make a referral for these individuals. Referrals could be made to specially trained nutritionists, specialized coaches and trainers or physical therapists, sport and exercise psychologists or physicians, clinical and counselling psychologists and psychiatrists.

Dependent and addictive behaviours may be difficult to totally eliminate, but with proper help, they can be controlled. The first step is awareness and education in both participant and helper. Although many professionals may believe that exercise dependence is a minor concern in the face of the obesity and sedentary epidemic of the twenty-first century, it is a behavioural disorder that can have serious consequences for weightlifters. It is our hope that this information will reduce its prevalence and lead to more effective interventions in the future.

Future research on exercise dependence in weightlifters

While much information about exercise dependence in exercisers has been produced in the last two decades of research, very little is known about the prevalence, possible causes, behavioural correlates and long-term consequences of exercise dependence. In this chapter, we have attempted to elucidate some of these topics, but many remain open to investigation. In particular, more research needs to test various models (e.g. Jacobs' [1986] psychobiological addictions model and J. Thompson and Blanton's [1987] physiological model of exercise dependence) to see which seems to predict resulting exercise dependence behaviours more accurately. Unlike Rhea, Lantz, and Trail's (2000) detailed conceptual framework for MD, no one in the exercise dependence literatures has yet proposed a fully developed model of exercise dependence including lists of antecedents, behaviours and consequences. In fact, more research needs to be taken to understand how exercise dependence becomes a critical component of MD over time.

Although progress has been made in measuring exercise dependence, questions about validity and reliability of measures still remain. Are the EDS and EDQ measuring gender-biased components of exercise dependence in differing constructs? Does the BDS accurately measure exercise dependence in bodybuilders and powerlifters or is exercise commitment being measured? Are new measures of exercise dependence (Exercise Addictions Inventory, Terry et al., 2004; EDS of the MDI, Rhea et al., 2004) as valid and reliable as the EDS and BDS?

With better measures, more progress needs to be made on accurately describing the prevalence of exercise dependence in weightlifters and other related syndromes (e.g. MD). With more data, researchers can determine whether the incidence and potential for exercise dependence is high (Garman et al., 2004; Pope & Katz, 1994; Zmijewski & Howard, 2003) or more moderate (Hale et al., 2010; Hildebrandt et al., 2006). One half of the population has been virtually ignored in this area because a lower percentage of exercise-dependent female weightlifters is assumed to exist. With the exception of Fisher's (2001) groundbreaking qualitative research on female bodybuilders and Smith and Hale's (2004) study on gender differences on the BDS, little research has examined the incidence and antecedents of exercise dependence in women. This small sample of bodybuilders should be carefully examined for all components of the exercise dependence model.

Finally, the potential influences of drugs such as anabolic steroids on exercise dependence and the relationship of eating disorders to exercise dependence need to be more fully examined from both theoretical and treatment perspectives. Researchers and practitioners need to better understand how steroids and other drugs reinforce addictive behaviours in the weight room and lead to more self-destructive consequences. In addition, grant funding is becoming available to investigate how exercise and eating disorders are related. The nature of primary versus secondary exercise dependence is still unclear and little is known about eating disorders in males, especially in the weightlifting domain.

Discussion questions

1. How is exercise dependence related to other weightlifting psychological problems (MD, eating disorders, steroid use)?
2. How does exercise dependence differ from exercise commitment in elite athletes?
3. Is the drive for muscularity a reliable predictor of future exercise dependence behaviours in weightlifters?
4. Are common exercise dependence questionnaires (EDQ, EDS, EAI) measuring the same behaviours or different components of the construct? Are they valid? Are they reliable?
5. Can these questionnaires be used to predict exercise dependence and MD in later weightlifting behaviours? Can clinicians and practitioners use these questionnaires with confidence to measure the potential for exercise dependence?
6. Are bodybuilders more susceptible to exercise dependence than powerlifters?
7. Can counselling and drug therapies be used to counter the negative medical and psychological consequences of exercise dependence in weightlifters?
8. Which antecedents are the most powerful predictors of later exercise dependence symptoms in weightlifters?

References

Adams, J., & Kirby, R. J. (2002). Excessive exercise as an addiction: A review. *Addiction research, 30*, 415–437.

Aidman, E., & Woollard, S. (2003). The influence of self-reported exercise addiction on acute emotional and physiological responses to brief exercise addiction. *Psychology of Sport and Exercise, 4*, 225–236.

Allegre, B., Souville, M., Therme, P., & Griffiths, M. (2006). Definitions and measures of exercise dependence. *Addiction Research and Theory, 14*, 631–646.

American Psychiatric Association. (1994). *Diagnostic and statistical manual of mental disorders* (4th ed.). Washington, DC: Author.

Baekeland, F. (1970). Exercise deprivation: Sleep and psychological reactions. *Archives of General Psychiatry, 22*, 365–369.

Beh, H. C., Mathers, S., & Holden, J. (1996). EEG correlates of exercise dependency. *International Journal of Psychophysiology, 23*, 121–128.

Berger, B., Pargman, D., & Weinberg, R. (2007). *Foundations of exercise psychology* (4th ed.). Morgantown, WV: Fitness Institute Technology.

Carron, A. V., Hausenblas, H. A., & Estabrooks, P. A. (2003). *The psychology of physical activity.* New York: McGraw-Hill.

Chan, C. S., & Grossman, H. Y. (1988). Psychological effects of running loss on consistent runners. *Perceptual and Motor Skills, 66*, 875–883.

Chittester, N. I., & Hausenblas, H. A. (2009). Correlates of the drive for muscularity: The role of anthropometric measures and psychological factors. *Journal of Health Psychology, 14*, 872–877.

Coen, S., & Ogles, B. (1993). Psychological characteristics of the obligatory runner: A critical examination of the anorexia analogue hypothesis. *Journal of Sport and Exercise Psychology, 15*, 338–354.

Cornelius, A. (1999, May). *The Athletic Identity Measurement Scale: Unidimensional or multidimensional?* Paper presented at the annual conference for Athletic Counselling, Springfield College, 1000, Springfield, MA.

Davis, C., & Fox, J. (1993). Excessive exercise and weight preoccupation in women. *Addictive Behaviours, 18*, 201–211.

Davis, C., Kennedy, S. H., Ravelski, E., & Dionne, M. (1994). The role of physical activity in the development and maintenance of eating disorders. *Psychological Medicine, 24*, 957–967.

DeBenedette, V. (1990). Are your patients exercising too much? *The Physician and Sportsmedicine, 18*(8), 119–122.

Diener, E., & Lucas, R. E. (1991). Subjective emotional well-being. In M. Lewis, & J. M. Haviland (Eds.), *Handbook of emotions* (2nd ed., pp. 325–327). New York: Guilford.

Ector, J., Ganame, J., van der Nerwe, N., Adriaeneesens, B., Pison, L., Willems, R., . . . Heidbuchel, H. (2007). Reduced right ventricular ejection fraction in endurance athletes presenting with ventricular arrhythmias: A quantitative angiographic assessment. *European Heart Journal, 28*, 345–353.

Edmunds, J., Ntoumanis, N., & Duda, J. L. (2006). Examining exercise dependence symptomology from a self-determination perspective. *Journal of Health Psychology, 11*, 887–903.

Fisher, L. A. (1997). Building one's self up: Bodybuilding and the construction of identity among professional female bodybuilders. In P. L. Moore (Ed.), *Building bodies* (pp. 135–164). New Brunswick, NJ: Rutgers University Press.

Fisher, L. A. (2001). Case studies of female bodybuilders: Culture gone awry? *Proceedings of the Association for the Advancement of Applied Sport Psychology* (pp. 8–9). Denton, TX: Ronjon.

Furst, D. M., & Germone, K. (1993). Negative addiction in male and female runners and exercisers. *Perceptual and Motor Skills, 77*, 192–194.

Fussell, S. (1991). *Muscle: Confessions of an unlikely bodybuilder.* London: Abacus.

Garman, J. F., Hayduk, D. M., Crider, D. A., & Hodel, M. M. (2004). Occurrence of exercise dependence in a college-aged population. *Journal of American College Health, 52*, 221–227.

Glasser, W. (1976). *Positive addiction.* New York: Harper & Row.

Grant, E. (1988). The exercise fix: What happens when fitness fanatics just can't say no? *Psychology Today, 22*(2), 26–27.

Groves, M., Biscomb, K., Nevill, A., & Matheson, H. (2008). Exercise dependence, self-esteem and identity reinforcement: A comparison of three universities in the United Kingdom. *Sport in Society, 11*, 59–73.

Hagan, A. L., & Hausenblas, H. A. (2003). The relationship between exercise dependence symptoms and perfectionism. *American Journal of Health Studies,* Spring–Summer, 1–6.

Hale, B. D., Roth, A., Delong, R., & Briggs, M. (2010). Exercise dependence and the drive for muscularity in male bodybuilders, power lifters, and fitness lifters. *Body Image, 7*, 234–239.

Hallsworth, L., Wade, T., & Tiggemann, M. (2005). Individual differences in male body image: An examination of self-objectification in recreational bodybuilders. *British Journal of Health Psychology, 10*, 453–465.

Hart, E. A., Leary, M. R., & Rejeski, W. J. (1989). The measurement of social physique anxiety. *Journal of Sport and Exercise Psychology, 11*, 94–104.

Hausenblas, H., & Fallon, E. (2002). Relationship among body image, exercise behaviour, and exercise dependence symptoms. *International Journal of Eating Disorders, 32*, 179–185.

Hausenblas, H., & Symons Downs, D. (2002a). Exercise dependence: A systematic review. *Psychology of Sport and Exercise, 3*, 89–123.

Hausenblas, H., & Symons Downs, D. (2002b). How much is too much? The development and validation of the exercise dependence scale. *Psychology and Health, 17*, 387–404.

Hausenblas, H., & Symons Downs, D. (2002c). Relationship among sex, imagery, and exercise dependence symptoms. *Psychology of Addictive Behaviors, 16*, 169–172.

Hildebrandt, T., Schlundt, D., Langenbucher, J., & Chung, T. (2006). Presence of muscle dysmorphia symptomology among male weightlifters. *Comprehensive Psychiatry, 47*, 127–135.

Hurst, R., Hale, B. D., & Smith, D. (2000). Exercise dependence in bodybuilders and weight lifters. *British Journal of Sports Medicine, 11*, 319–325.

Jacobs, D. (1986). A general theory of addictions: A new theoretical model. *Journal of Gambling Behaviour, 2*, 15–31.

Kjelsas, E., & Augestad, L. B. (2003). Gender differences in competitive runners and their motive for physical activity. *European Journal of Psychiatry, 17*, 157–171.

Klein, A. M. (1993). *Little big men.* Albany: State University of New York Press.

Kuennen, M. R., & Waldron, J. J. (2007). Relationships between specific personality traits, fat free mass indices, and the muscle dysmorphia inventory. *Journal of Sport Behaviour, 30*, 453–470.

Landers, D. M., & Arent, S. M. (2001). Physical activity and mental health. In R. N. Singer, H. A. Hausenblas, & C. Janelle (Eds.), *Handbook of research on sport psychology* (2nd ed., pp. 740–765). New York: Wiley.

Lantz, C. D., Rhea, D. J., & Cornelius, A. E. (2002). Muscle dysmorphia in elite-level power lifters and bodybuilders: A test of differences within a conceptual model. *Journal of Strength and Conditioning Research, 16*, 649–655.

Lantz, C. D., Rhea, D. J., & Mayhew, J. L. (2001). The drive for size: A psycho-behavioral model of muscle dysmorphia. *International Sport Journal, 5*, 71–85.

Litt, D., & Dodge, T. (2008). A longitudinal investigation of the Drive for Muscularity Scale: Predicting use of performance enhancing substances and weightlifting among males. *Body Image, 5*, 346–351.

Luoma, T. C. (interviewer), & Mentzer, M. (interviewee). (1995). *Muscle Media 2000 audio tape interview series: Mike Mentzer part 3.* Golden, CO: Muscle Media 2000.

Masters, K. S., & Lambert, M. J. (1989). On gender comparison and construct validity: An examination of the commitment to running scale in a sample of marathon runners. *Journal of Sport Behaviour, 12*, 196–202.

McCreary, D. R., & Sadava, S. W. (2001). Gender differences in relationships among perceived attractiveness, life satisfaction, and health in adults as a function of body mass index and perceived weight. *Psychology of Men and Masculinity, 2*, 108–116.

McCreary, D. R., & Sasse, D. K. (2000). An exploration of the drive for muscularity in adolescent boys and girls. *Journal of American College Health, 48*, 297–304.

Morgan, W. P. (1979). Negative addiction in runners. *The Physician and Sports Medicine, 7*, 57–77.

Office for National Statistics. (2001). *The ESRC review of government social classifications.* London: Author.

Ogden, J., Veale, D., & Summers, Z. (1997). The development and validation of the Exercise Dependence Questionnaire. *Addiction Research, 5*, 343–356.

Olivardia, R., Pope, H. G., & Hudson, J. (2000). Muscle dysmorphia in male weightlifters: A case control study. *American Journal of Psychiatry, 157*, 1291–1296.

Paffenbarger, R. S., Jr., Hyde, R. T., Wing, A. L., & Hsieh, C. C. (1986). Physical activity, all-cause mortality, and longevity of college alumni. *New England Journal of Medicine, 314*, 605–613.

Phillips, K. A., & Hollander, E. (2008). Treating body dysmorphic disorder with medication: Evidence, misconceptions, and a suggested approach. *Body Image, 5*, 13–27.

Pickett, T. C., Lewis, R. J., & Cash, T. F. (2005). Men, muscles, and body image: Comparisons of competitive bodybuilders, weight trainers, and athletically active controls. *British Journal of Sports Medicine, 39*, 217–222.

Pierce, E. (1994). Exercise dependence syndrome in runners. *Sports Medicine, 18*, 149–155.

Pierce, E., Eastman, N., Tripathi, H., Olson, K., & Dewey, W. (1993). B-endorphin response to endurance exercise: Relationship to exercise dependence. *Perceptual and Motor Skills, 77*, 767–770.

Pierce, E., & Morris, J. T. (1998). Exercise dependence among competitive power lifters. *Perceptual and Motor Skills, 86*, 991–994.

Pierce, E., Rohaly, K., & Fritchley, B. (1997). Sex differences on exercise dependence for men and women in a marathon road race. *Perceptual and Motor Skills, 84*, 991–994.

Pope, H. G., Gruber, A. J., & Choi, P. (1997). Muscle dysmorphia: An under-recognized form of body dysmorphic disorder. *Psychosomatics, 38*, 548–557.

Pope, H. G., & Katz, D. L. (1994). Psychiatric and medical effects of anabolic-androgenic steroids: A controlled study of 160 athletes. *Archives of General Psychiatry, 51*, 375–382.

Pope, H. G., Phillips, K. A., & Olivardia, R. (2000). *The Adonis complex: The secret crisis of male body obsession.* New York: Free Press.

Powers, P., Schocken, D., & Boyd, E. (1998). Comparison of habitual runners and anorexia nervosa patients. *International Journal of Eating Disorders, 23*, 133–143.

Rhea, D. J., Lantz, C. D., & Cornelius, A. E. (2004). Development of the Muscle Dysmorphia Inventory (MDI). *The Journal of Sports Medicine and Physical Fitness, 44*, 428–435.

Rhea, D. J., Lantz, C. D., & Trail, G. T. (2000). Muscle dysmorphia: A confirmatory test of a new model. *Research Quarterly for Exercise and Sport, 71* (Supplement 1), A–94.

Richman, J. M., Rosenfeld, L. B., & Hardy, C. J. (1993). The social support survey: An initial evaluation of a clinical measure and practice model of the social support process. *Research in Social Work Practice, 3*, 288–311.

Rudy, E., & Estok, P. (1989). Measurement and significance of negative addiction in runners. *Journal of Nursing Research, 11*, 548–558.

Sachs, M. L., & Pargman, D. (1979). Running addiction: A depth interview examination. *Journal of Sport Behaviour, 2*, 143–155.

Smith, D., & Hale, B. D. (2004). Validity and factor structure of the Bodybuilding Dependence Scale. *British Journal of Sports Medicine, 38*, 177–181.

Smith, D., & Hale, B. D. (2005). Exercise dependence in bodybuilding: Antecedents and reliability of measurement. *Journal of Sports Medicine and Physical Fitness, 45*, 401–408.

Smith, D., Hale, B. D., Rhea, D., Olrich, T., & Collier, K. (2009). Big, buff and dependent: Exercise dependence, muscle dysmorphia and steroid use in bodybuilding. In F. Columbus (Ed.), *Men and addictions* (pp. 1–36). New York: Nova Science.

Smith, D., Wright, C., & Winrow, D. (2010). Exercise dependence and social physique anxiety in runners. *International Journal of Sport and Exercise Psychology, 8,* 61–69.

Smith, D., Hale, B. D., & Collins, D. J. (1998). Measurement of exercise dependence in bodybuilders. *Journal of Sport Medicine and Physical Fitness, 38,* 66–74.

Spano, L. (2001). The relationship between exercise and anxiety, obsessive-compulsiveness, and narcissism. *Personality and Individual Differences, 30,* 87–93.

Symons Downs, D., Hausenblas, H., & Nigg, C. R. (2004). Factorial validity and psychometric examination of the Exercise Dependence Scale – Revised. *Measurement in Physical Education and Exercise Science, 8,* 183–201.

Szabo, A. (2000). Physical activity as a source of psychological dysfunction. In S. J. Biddle, K. R. Fox, & S. H. Boutcher (Eds.), *Physical activity and psychological well-being* (pp. 130–153). London: Routledge.

Terry, A., Szabo, A., & Griffiths, M. (2004). The Exercise Addiction Inventory: A new brief screening tool. *Addiction Research and Theory, 12,* 489–499.

Thaxton, L. (1982). Physiological and psychological effects of short-term exercise addiction on habitual runners. *Journal of Sport Psychology, 4,* 73–80.

Thompson, H. (Writer and Presenter), & Mares, A. (Producer). (1993). *Iron maidens.* Manchester, UK: BBC Radio 4.

Thompson, J., & Blanton, P. (1987). Energy conservation and exercise dependence: A sympathetic arousal hypothesis. *Medicine and Science in Sports and Exercise, 19,* 91–99.

Triola, D. P. (1996). *Commitment to physical activity and body image distortion in college students* (Unpublished master's thesis). Springfield College, Springfield, MA.

Tucker, L. A. (1983a). Effect of weight training on self-concept: A profile of those influenced most. *Research Quarterly for Exercise and Sport, 54,* 389–397.

Tucker, L. A. (1983b). Weight training: A tool for the improvement of self and body concepts of males. *Journal of Human Movement Studies, 9,* 31–37.

Tucker, L. A. (1987). Effect of weight training on body attitudes: Who benefits most? *Journal of Sports Medicine and Physical Fitness, 27,* 70–78.

Veale, D. (1995). Does exercise dependence really exist? In J. Annett, B. Cripps, & H. Steinberg (Eds.), *Exercise addiction: Motivation for participation in sport and exercise.* Leicester, UK: British Psychological Society.

Weik, M., & Hale, B. D. (2009). Contrasting gender differences on two measures of exercise dependence. *British Journal of Sports Medicine, 43,* 204–207.

Wichmann, S., & Martin, D. R. (1992). Exercise excess: Treating patients addicted to fitness. *The Physician and Sportsmedicine, 20*(5), 193–200.

Yates, A., Leehey, K., & Shisslak, C. (1983). Running – An analogue of anorexia? *New England Journal of Medicine, 308,* 251–255.

Zmijewski, C. F., & Howard, M. O. (2003). Exercise dependence and attitudes toward eating among young adults. *Eating Behaviours, 4,* 181–195.

7

DRIVE FOR MUSCULARITY

Christian Edwards and Gyozo Molnar

UNIVERSITY OF WORCESTER, UK

David Tod

ABERYSTWYTH UNIVERSITY, UK

Todd G. Morrison

UNIVERSITY OF SASKATCHEWAN, CANADA

The contemporary ideal male physique is large and muscular, and has become more so over the last 40 years (Pope, Phillips, & Olivardia, 2000). This ideal is a prevalent and socially constructed image in today's Western societies (Baghurst, Hollander, Nardella, & Haff, 2006). In addition to aesthetic advantages, some individuals perceive that males with muscular physiques possess various positive traits and experience success in other domains of life (Ryckman, Butler, Thornton, & Lindner, 1997). Given the prevalence of this ideal and the importance it is accorded, it is unsurprising that significant numbers of Western males perceive discrepancies between their current and desired muscularity levels (Frederick et al., 2007).

The disjunction between current and ideal muscularity levels, and the belief individuals with muscular physiques accrue certain advantages, may induce a drive for muscularity (DM) in certain men. Although only subject to recent investigation, research on this drive is vibrant. As characteristic of many emerging areas, researchers have explored numerous possible correlates. The findings of many studies need to be replicated, and there have been few sustained efforts to test theory. A review appears timely as a way to consolidate research trends and identify useful future investigations. The current chapter includes (a) a DM definition, (b) an overview of scales commonly used to measure this drive, (c) an overview of existing theories that help describe the emergence of this drive in some men, (d) identification of future research and (e) practical applications for helping people whose DM might interfere with their lives.

Drive for muscularity

A psychological drive is an aroused state of tension arising from a need and motivates individuals to act to reduce that tension. Regarding the DM, the tension may surface from individuals' perceptions that they are insufficiently muscular

(McCreary & Sasse, 2000), which may result in preoccupations with behaviours directed at increasing muscularity and reducing perceived discrepancies between current and ideal physiques (Bergeron & Tylka, 2007). These two ideas appear in contemporary definitions of the DM (Nowell & Ricciardelli, 2008).

Although the drive definition helps identify key dimensions, the DM is probably not a drive in the conventional sense (Morrison, Morrison, & McCann, 2006). Most theories present the DM as a socially constructed desire. It was labelled a drive to help create a parallel with the drive for thinness, a much researched female body image topic (Morrison et al., 2006).

The DM exists along a low-to-high continuum. Some level of the drive may be healthy, due to the benefits associated with resistance training (O'Donovan et al., 2010). High levels have often been portrayed as unhealthy because of links with excessive exercise, drug abuse, unsafe dietary practices and social impairment. It is unclear what scores on questionnaires are required to differentiate healthy from unhealthy levels, particularly as relationships between the DM and behaviour have not always been strong. Researchers need to identify what levels of the drive are associated with health and well-being.

Measurement of the drive for muscularity

To date, three instruments designed to measure the DM have received psychometric testing in multiple studies: the Drive for Muscularity Scale (DMS: McCreary & Sasse, 2000), the Drive for Muscularity Attitudes Questionnaire (DMAQ: Morrison, Morrison, Hopkins, & Rowan, 2004) and the Swansea Muscularity Attitudes Questionnaire (SMAQ: Edwards & Launder, 2000). The psychometric properties of each of these measures will be outlined briefly, with emphasis placed on studies not appearing in an earlier review of the DM literature (Morrison et al., 2006).

Drive for Muscularity Scale

The DMS consists of 15 items (e.g. 'I think that I would look better if I gained 10 pounds in bulk') and uses a six-point Likert-type response format (*never* to *always*). In the original development and validation study, McCreary and Sasse (2000) generated a list of motivations to become muscular using information obtained from 'weight-training enthusiasts' (p. 298) and a content analysis of weight-training magazines. The face validity of these motivations was assessed by men and women involved in weight training and the DMS was subsequently created. The authors did not over-sample content domain by generating a large number of items, and then reducing the item pool. Presumably, the authors felt these 15 items were the best exemplars of the DM.

The DMS and other instruments (e.g. the Rosenberg Self-Esteem Scale, RSE: Rosenberg, 1989) were administered to 197 Canadian high-school students. Scale score reliability coefficients for the DMS were satisfactory ($\alpha = 0.84$ for boys;

$\alpha = 0.78$ for girls). Also, as hypothesised, boys' DM correlated negatively with their level of self-esteem and positively with their level of depression. Neither correlation was statistically significant for girls. It is unclear whether this non-significance reflects differential salience, as proposed by the authors, or restriction of range (i.e. on 11 out of 15 items, females' mean scores were < 2.0 on a scale, where $1 =$ never). With respect to the scale's discriminant validity, findings were mixed. No statistically significant correlations were obtained between girls' DM and two indices of the drive for thinness (the Eating Attitudes Test and the Body Dissatisfaction subscale of the Eating Disorders Inventory). Contrary to the authors' prediction, however, a significant positive correlation was obtained between boys' scores on the Eating Attitudes Test and the DMS ($r = 0.37$).

Dimensionality

The authors conceptualised the DM as unidimensional, although they did not examine the measure's factor structure. McCreary, Sasse, Saucier, and Dorsch (2004) attempted to address this limitation by conducting a Principal Components Analysis (PCA) with varimax rotation on DMS data provided by 630 Canadian high-school and university students. Findings for the 'lower order' component analysis revealed a two-component solution for male participants, with the first component representing muscularity-oriented body image (MBI: seven items) and the second component purportedly focusing on behaviours engaged in by men to become more muscular (MB: seven items). Although the MB is routinely conceptualised as behavioural, some items are cognitive in nature, measuring guilt and the perception that weight training interferes with one's life. Further, some items map onto content found in measures designed to assess muscle dysmorphia (e.g. 'Other people think I work out with weights too often'). One question ('I think about taking anabolic steroids') failed to load on either component; it was recommended that this item 'not be included in the calculation of the overall DMS score' (p. 55). Another item ('I feel guilty if I miss a weight-training session') cross-loaded (0.35 on Factor 1 and 0.70 on Factor 2); however, McCreary et al. (2004) did not address this issue.

For females, a four-component solution was obtained. Based on the 'scree test and factor [sic] interpretability' (p. 52), the authors suggested a two-component solution offered the best representation of the data. Component loadings revealed that an attitudinal/behavioural distinction was viable for women, with some questions measuring attitudes towards muscularity (six items) and other questions measuring muscularity-oriented behaviours (four items). Similar to male participants, the steroid item did not load on either component.

A 'higher order' PCA with varimax rotation then was conducted using the seven-item MBI and seven-item MB identified for male participants as input variables. A single-component solution was obtained for both male and female participants.

As Morrison et al. (2006) noted, it is unclear why McCreary et al. (2004) used PCA rather than exploratory factor analysis (EFA), as the latter is recommended for structure detection (Fabrigar, Wegener, MacCallum, & Strahan, 1999). In addition, the rationale for employing varimax rotation, which constrains factors/components to be uncorrelated (Finch & West, 1997), is not readily apparent; such a constraint would appear inappropriate when applied to a scale whose items (purportedly) assess a common latent construct: namely, the DM. Indeed, researchers have documented consistently that scores on the MBI and MB correlate between 0.35 and 0.55 (Bergeron & Tylka, 2007; Dodge, Litt, Seitchik, & Bennett, 2008; Giles & Close, 2008; McCreary et al., 2004; McPherson, McCarthy, McCreary, & McMillan, 2010). Given that oblique rotation permits, but does not require, components/factors to be intercorrelated, it affords 'a more accurate and realistic representation of how constructs are likely to be related to one another' (Fabrigar et al., 1999, p. 282). Also, the suitability of using PCA or EFA to identify higher-order factors has been questioned (Rubio, Berg-Weger, & Tebb, 2001). Finally, the authors combined data for high-school and university participants, without conducting separate analyses to determine whether the resultant component solutions were similar. Most of the high-school students were enrolled in grades 9 or 10 and were likely between 14 and 16 years of age. In contrast, the university students, most of whom were first year, were probably 18 or 19 years old.

Underscoring the possible importance of developmental factors vis-à-vis the DM, Smolak and Stein (2006) distributed the DMS and other measures to 287 middle-school American boys ranging in age from 11 to 15. To ensure compatibility with the analysis conducted by McCreary et al. (2004), these authors used PCA with varimax rotation. A three component solution was obtained, although the eigenvalue for the third component was only slightly greater than 1.0. Inspection of the component loadings revealed that eight items cross-loaded (i.e. they had two or more loadings ≥ 0.30). Recently, McPherson et al. (2010) factor analysed the DMS using a more suitable technique: principal axis factor analysis with oblique rotation. Parallel analysis was employed to assist in factor retention; a superior choice to scree plot inspection or the problematic eigenvalue greater than 1.0 'rule'. Respondents were 594 Scottish men participating in a community running event. Results indicated that a two-factor solution provided a suitable representation of the data. However, the steroid item loaded on the MB factor, and the item 'I lift weights to build up muscle' double loaded.

We are unaware of additional factor analytic work published on the DMS. At present, it is unclear whether the DM, as represented by this scale, is best conceptualised as a single 'higher order' factor or as two modestly correlated factors. The possibility that a more complicated configuration emerges for specific age groups cannot be discounted at this point in time (see Smolak & Stein, 2006). As well, the composition of the factors appears to be somewhat unstable (e.g. the steroid item loads in some studies, but not in others).

Reliability

Available evidence suggests that reliability coefficients for the DMS and its two subscales are good (Dodge et al., 2008; Giles & Close, 2008; Kelley, Neufeld, &

Musher-Eizenman, 2010; McPherson et al., 2010; Wojtowicz & von Ranson, 2006). Item-total correlations are satisfactory, with the possible exception of the item, 'I think that my legs are not muscular enough', which fell below the 0.30 cut-off (Wojtowicz & von Ranson, 2006). Test–retest reliability of the DMS also has been investigated. Resultant *r* values range from good to excellent (Litt & Dodge, 2008; McPherson et al., 2010).

Validity coefficients

Based on available evidence, it is difficult to form a coherent picture of the validity of MBI and MB scale scores. Dodge et al. (2008) found that scores on the MB correlated with current use of performance-enhancing substances (PES), willingness to use a fictitious PES and current status as an intercollegiate athlete (i.e. yes/no). Scores on the MBI, however, did not correlate significantly with any of these variables. Given that the MB contains items that focus on PES (e.g. 'I use protein or energy supplements'), the correlations may have been inflated due to content overlap. Addressing the absence of research focusing on the relationship between anthropometric measures (e.g. fat-free mass index) and the DM, Chittester and Hausenblas (2009) examined the weight, height and body fat of 113 college-aged American males. Contrary to Dodge et al. (2008), supplement use correlated significantly with the MB and MBI (although the latter *r* was appreciably stronger). Exercise dependence correlated with both subscales whereas weightlifting did not (i.e. it correlated with the MB only). However, given that the MB contains items measuring weightlifting, it is not surprising that this subscale correlates with indices of exercise. Finally, none of the anthropometric measures (e.g. fat-free mass index, body mass index [BMI] and body fat percentage) emerged as significant predictors of total DMS.

Focusing on psychological variables, Bergeron and Tylka (2007) reported that scores on the MBI were associated with indices of distress, depression, self-esteem and use of proactive coping, whereas scores on the MB were not. Wojtowicz and von Ranson (2006) identified a significant positive correlation between the MBI and the Body Dissatisfaction subscale of the Eating Disorder Inventory (EDI; the correlation for the MB was not statistically significant). Neither the MBI nor MB correlated significantly with the EDI Drive for Thinness subscale. Examining the relationship between exposure to men's lifestyle publications (i.e. 'lad' magazines) and the DM, Giles and Close (2008) found that both DMS subscales correlated significantly with awareness and internalisation of the idealistic standards of male appearance disseminated by media. Surprisingly, the MB subscale correlated more strongly with exposure to lad magazines than did the MBI. Finally, McPherson et al. (2010) noted that Scottish participants who reported currently altering their food intake for the purpose of gaining muscle mass evidenced significantly higher scores on both the MBI and MB in comparison to those who had not modified their food intake. When participants were categorised on the basis of whether they were or were not dieting to *lose* weight, no differences on the MBI and MB were observed.

Wojtowicz and von Ranson (2006) reported that total DMS scores were positively associated with the drive for thinness in males, but not females. (No statistically significant association was observed between scores on the DMS and scores on a measure of body dissatisfaction.) These authors also furnished concurrent validity evidence; scores on the DMS correlated significantly with the SMAQ. Kelley et al. (2010) found that the DMS significantly predicted problematic eating attitudes and behaviours, body esteem and body inadequacy for male but not female participants. The DMS was a significant predictor of body compulsivity (the perceived need to maintain one's exercise regimen) in males and females as well as body preoccupation (females only). However, DMS did not emerge as a statistically significant predictor of body anxiety in either males or females. Daniel and Bridges (2010) identified positive correlations between the DMS and internalisation of idealistic standards of male appearance and body surveillance (i.e. the degree to which individuals evaluate their appearance as outside observers). No association was obtained between DMS scores and body shame; and a counterintuitive inverse correlation was reported between the DMS and body objectification (i.e. individuals who were more likely to evaluate their body in aesthetic terms evidenced a lower DM). Among a group of young boys, Smolak and Stein (2006) noted that statistically significant predictors of the DM were: perceived influence of muscular images in media, engagement in social comparison and investment in the strength and athleticism dimensions of traditional masculine gender roles. Finally, Gordon and Dombeck (2010) reported that the DMS correlated significantly with the EDI Bulimia and Drive for Thinness subscales as well as grandiose narcissism and the extent to which participants' self-esteem was contingent on their physical appearance.

Drive for Muscularity Attitudes Questionnaire

The DMAQ contains eight items (e.g. 'Muscularity is important to me') and uses a five-point Likert-type response format (*strongly disagree* to *strongly agree*). Two items are reverse scored to control for response set bias; however, the usefulness of this practice has been questioned (Barnette, 2000).

In developing this measure, Morrison et al. (2004) generated 41 items that assessed men's attitudes towards muscularity. In creating these items, relevant literature on the DM was reviewed. The item pool was distributed to 412 Canadian male undergraduate students. PCA with oblique rotation was used for item reduction purposes. To reduce the number of items, stringent retention criteria were employed (i.e. only items loading on the first component at ≥ 0.50, but not crossloading on any other component at ≥ 0.30, were retained). Scale score reliability analysis also was used for item reduction purposes (i.e. any question with an item-total correlation coefficient lower than 0.30 or higher than 0.70 was deleted). Eight items were retained.

Dimensionality

The unidimensionality of the DMAQ has been documented consistently using PCA, EFA and confirmatory factor analysis (CFA). For example, using data provided by 304 Canadian male undergraduates, Morrison et al. (2004) conducted a PCA on the eight-item DMAQ. A single-component solution was obtained. This analysis was complemented by a CFA with a different sample ($N = 250$). Based on several fit indices, a unidimensional solution offered a satisfactory representation of the data (e.g. robust comparative fit and goodness of fit indices were 0.95). Finally, Morrison and Harriman (2005) conducted a principal axis factor analysis of DMAQ data provided by 202 male undergraduate students. Again, a unidimensional solution was obtained.

Reliability

Published research indicates that the DMAQ's scale score reliability is good, with coefficients typically falling in the low- to mid-80s (Bergeron & Tylka, 2007; McDonagh, Morrison, & McGuire, 2008; Morrison & Harriman, 2005). To date, the measure's test–retest reliability has not been investigated.

Validity coefficients

Available evidence suggests that the DMAQ possesses convergent validity. For example, scores on this measure correlate positively with body image self-consciousness during physical intimacy, vanity, psychological distress, depression, engagement in universalistic social comparison, exposure to men's health and fitness magazines, the muscularity of the physique one would like to achieve (as determined by a figural rating scale) steroid contemplation, consumption of protein to increase muscle mass and weight training (Bergeron & Tylka, 2007; McDonagh et al., 2008; Morrison, Morrison, & Hopkins, 2003; Morrison et al., 2004). Inverse associations were observed between DMAQ scores and satisfaction with current level of muscularity, self-esteem, both general and appearance specific, and use of proactive coping (Bergeron & Tylka, 2007; Morrison & Harriman, 2005; Morrison et al., 2004). The DMAQ did not correlate significantly with a measure of social desirability bias, even after corrections were made for attenuation in *r* due to measurement error (Morrison & Harriman, 2005). Finally, as evidence of con-current validity, Bergeron and Tylka (2007) reported that the DMAQ correlates significantly with the MBI and MB subscales of the DMS.

Swansea Muscularity Attitudes Questionnaire

The SMAQ consists of 20 items (e.g. 'Being muscular gives me confidence') and uses a seven-point Likert-type response format (*definitely* to *definitely not*). In their article outlining the SMAQ's construction, Edwards and Launder (2000) conducted two preliminary studies (*N*s = 112 and 152), but details were not provided. Findings from these studies were used to create a 'refined' 32-item version, which then was distributed to a third sample ($N = 303$). To examine the dimensionality of this version, an unspecified form of factor analysis with varimax rotation was used. As per the authors' expectations, a two-factor solution was deemed suitable, with 20 items retained. Ten items loaded on the first factor (Drive for Muscularity [SMAQ-DFM]), and ten items loaded on the second factor (Positive Attributes of Muscularity [SMAQ-PAM]). The former represents the desire to achieve a more muscular physique whereas the latter assesses beliefs concerning the purported benefits of being muscular. Scale score reliability coefficients on the SMAQ-DFM and SMAQ-PAM were high (αs = 0.94 and 0.91, respectively). No additional psychometric testing of the SMAQ was conducted by Edwards and Launder (2000).

Dimensionality

Morrison and Morrison (2006) noted that some of the statistical choices made by Edwards and Launder (2000) were not optimal. First, the authors used orthogonal rather than oblique rotation. Given that the SMAQ-DFM and SMAQ-PAM are strongly intercorrelated (e.g. r = 0.71 in Tylka, Bergeron, & Schwartz, 2005), constraining factors to be uncorrelated is inappropriate. Second, Edwards and Launder (2000) relied on the eigenvalue greater than one 'rule' to determine factor retention. This method is problematic because it may result in factor over-extraction (Hayton, Allen, & Scarpello, 2004). Finally, the authors retained items that loaded on more than one factor (e.g. 'Being muscular gives me confidence': 0.46, SMAQ-DFM, and 0.68, SMAQ-PAM).

To address these limitations, Morrison and Morrison (2006) conducted an EFA (maximum-likelihood estimation) with oblique rotation. Parallel analysis was used to assist in factor retention. A convenience sample of 250 men attending a Canadian post-secondary institution served as participants. A three-factor solution was identified, with items denoting the intention to become more muscular (eight items), engagement in muscle-building activities (two items) and positive beliefs about muscularity (ten items). A CFA with an independent sample (N = 304) revealed that this tridimensional model provided a good representation of the data. However, modification indices suggested that one item ('Men with small muscles are less masculine than men with larger muscles') should be deleted. To date, no researchers have attempted to replicate this three-factor model.

Reliability

Alpha coefficients for the SMAQ and its two subscales are typically high. For example, Jung, Forbes, and Chan (2010) reported strong alpha coefficients for samples of college men recruited from the United States (αs = 0.90 for the SMAQ-DFM and SMAQ-PAM) and Hong Kong-China (αs = 0.90 for the SMAQ-DFM and 0.83 for the SMAQ-PAM). Excellent alpha coefficients (α > 0.85) also were obtained by Barlett and Harris (2008), Martin, Kliber, Kulinna, and Fahlman (2006) and Tylka et al. (2005). In contrast, Wojtowicz and von Ranson (2006) reported a good alpha coefficient for the SMAQ-DFM but an unsatisfactory one for the SMAQ-PAM. Warranting mention is their finding that, for the SMAQ-PAM, Cronbach's alpha was < 0.50 for a small sample of male weightlifters ($n = 27$). We are unaware of any studies that have examined the test–retest reliability of the SMAQ.

Validity coefficients

The available literature suggests that the SMAQ and its subscales correlate in the anticipated direction with other measures of the DM. For example, Morrison and Morrison (2006) found that scores on the SMAQ-PAM were positively associated with scores on the DMAQ. These authors also reported that what they labelled the Intention and Engagement subscales of the SMAQ correlated significantly with the DMAQ. Further evidence of concurrent validity is provided by Tylka et al. (2005); that is, DMS–MBI (McCreary et al., 2004) correlated with the SMAQ-DFM and the SMAQ-PAM. The DMS–MB subscale was significantly associated with the SMAQ-DFM, but not the SMAQ-PAM.

Mixed evidence exists for convergent validity. Wojtowicz and von Ranson (2006) reported that, for male participants only, scores on the SMAQ-DFM and SMAQ-PAM correlated significantly with the EDI Drive for Thinness subscale. The nature of this relationship suggests simultaneous desires for greater musculature and lower body fat; a physique which better approximates the muscular ideal. Neither the SMAQ-DFM nor the SMAQ-PAM correlated with the EDI Body Dissatisfaction subscale. Among a small sample of American male college students ($N = 98$), Martin et al. (2006) found that the SMAQ-PAM correlated with social physique anxiety (anxiety triggered by the belief others are negatively assessing one's appearance) as well as appearance evaluation (how satisfied individuals are with their appearance) and appearance orientation (the importance individuals place upon their appearance). The SMAQ-DFM, however, only correlated significantly with appearance orientation. In contrast, Barlett and Harris (2008) found that neither the SMAQ-DFM nor the SMAQ-PAM were associated with scores on the physical appearance, physical condition and upper body strength subscales of the Body Esteem Scale. Jung et al. (2010) obtained similar non-significant correlations for both American and Hong Kong-Chinese subsamples. These authors also found that, contrary to Martin et al. (2006), appearance evaluation did not correlate with the drive for, and beliefs about, muscularity, as measured by the SMAQ. Tylka et al. (2005) also reported non-significant correlations between scores on a measure of maladaptive eating attitudes and behaviours (EAT-26) and the SMAQ-DFM and SMAQ-PAM.

Limited research has examined the relationship between anthropometric measures such as per cent body fat and the SMAQ. However, akin to what has been observed for the DMS, available data suggest that these indices do not correlate with each other (e.g. Martin et al., 2006).

Summary

Evidence suggests none of the DM measures is a gold-standard instrument. The most commonly used scale, the DMS, possesses key limitations compromising its utility. As mentioned earlier, McCreary and Sasse (2000) did not generate an exhaustive pool of items. Instead, they created and retained a small number of questions, which has implications for the content validity of the measure. Reviewing the items on the DMS reveals that the MB subscale contains a mixture of statements measuring beliefs and behaviours, with some content overlapping with indices of muscle dysmorphia. Correlating the DMS with behavioural 'manifestations' of the DM (e.g. weightlifting and protein consumption) is problematic as the DMS also examines engagement in behaviours to increase muscle mass. Thus, due to item redundancy, correlations may be inflated. Finally, although the DMS has been distributed to female participants (e.g. McCreary et al., 2004), it remains unknown whether this scale is suitable for use with women. Mean item scores tend to be very low and words such as 'bulk' and 'mass' may have different connotations for men and women (Morrison et al., 2003).

Given the narrow scope of the DMS, DMAQ and SMAQ, some researchers have argued in favour of measures that provide a more comprehensive assessment of men's bodies. For example, the Male Body Attitudes Scale (MBAS: Tylka et al., 2005) examines dissatisfaction stemming primarily from perceived deficiencies in muscularity, body fat and height. Ryan, Morrison, Roddy, and McCutcheon (2010) provide evidence suggesting that a modified version of the MBAS has promising psychometric properties. Also, the Male Body Dissatisfaction Scale (MBDS), recently developed by Ochner, Gray, and Brickner (2009), may prove useful for researchers wishing to go 'beyond muscles' when investigating men's attitudes towards their physical appearance. Importantly, the MBDS also permits respondents to specify the relative importance of each item on a scale from 1 (no importance) to 10 (great importance). Additional research is needed to determine whether scales such as the MBDS and MBAS complement existing DM measures or serve as more sophisticated proxies.

Theoretical discussion of the drive for muscularity

One of the most commonly used theoretical frameworks in the DM literature is Festinger's (1954) social comparison theory, which argues that individuals compare themselves to others to process social information and establish their social selves (i.e. when evaluating the self, one compares it to others as part of the identity formation process). Festinger (1954) hypothesised that the drive exists in all humans to evaluate opinions and abilities, both of which bear on behaviour. To underpin the significance of social comparison, he added that 'the holding of incorrect opinions and/or inaccurate appraisals of one's abilities can be punishing or even fatal' (p. 117), which bears relevance to when one compares his/her corporeality to an ideal (body) type.

All societies have certain norms, values and acceptable behaviour patterns which are hegemonically manufactured and perpetuated (Ingham & Hardy, 1993). People internalise these values and behaviours in the socialisation process via key socialising agencies (Giddens, 2006). One of these socialising agencies is the mass media

(Berger, 1995), which has the cultural power to confer status on public issues/ images and to legitimise and enforce norms, views and social practices (Grieve, 2007). As part of social integration, individuals are exposed to, learn from and internalise what is considered normal/acceptable appearance and behaviour (Shaw & Waller, 1995). More importantly, people also learn that deviating from the norm has consequences. For us to know whether we deviate from the norm and, if so, to what extent, we compare ourselves – in this case, our physical self – to what we perceive to be the social ideal as presented in the dominant discourse. This social comparative process often results in frustration, leading to an amplified drive to develop and possess a mesomorphic male body.

As the above indicates, there are many factors and socialising agencies influencing men's DM. So far, 'existing theoretical discussions have adopted biopsychological perspectives' (Tod & Lavallee, 2010, p. 3) when interpreting some of these factors. Therefore, in addition to approaches already in use, we suggest that the sociology of the body literature should be explored with the view of broadening the theoretical horizon of the DM field. Admixing could include Bourdieu's habitus and symbolic capital and Foucault's representations of power (for overviews see Shilling, 1993; Turner, 2007).

Major research findings

To help synthesise research, we used Cash's (2002) body image model to group variables into meaningful clusters. According to Cash, four historical factors influence body image attitudes: cultural socialisation, interpersonal experiences, physical attributes and personality characteristics. When placed in situations triggering body image attitudes, individuals experience various behaviours, cognitions and emotions. We also added a section labelled eating disorders/disorders.

The majority of studies have been descriptive, and causality has not been established. Below, we present some variables as antecedents and others as consequences of the DM. The positioning of these variables reflects our thinking and not empirical evidence. Researchers will advance knowledge by adopting designs allowing causality to be determined.

Social culturalisation

Based on most perspectives, viewing muscular images should correlate with an increased DM. Although supportive results exist (Duggan & McCreary, 2004; Harrison & Bond, 2007), in most studies non-significant findings have emerged (Hatoum & Belle, 2004; Hobza & Rochlen, 2009; Tiggemann, 2005). Based on available literature, a meaningful association between exposure to muscular images and the DM is not apparent. Meta-analyses have yielded negative associative and causal relationships between exposure to media images and body image perceptions, but these studies were not focused on DM (Barlett, Vowels, & Saucier, 2008; Blond, 2008).

A more consistent pattern emerges between media image interpretation and the DM. For example, the DM is correlated positively with individuals' internalisation of media-conveyed attitudes and media acceptance, endorsement or investment (e.g. Daniel & Bridges, 2010; Giles & Close, 2008; Karazsia & Crowther, 2009; Smolak & Stein, 2006). Not all results have been concordant, however. Petrie, Greenleaf, Carter, and Reel (2007) found that the DM was related to perceived weight pressures from the movies and magazines for male athletes symptomatic for eating disorders, but not those asymptomatic (classification was based on the Questionnaire for Eating Disorder Diagnoses).

The social culturalisation findings make intuitive sense. If exposure to muscular images increased the DM, then all males would have high levels because such images are common in today's Western society. Instead, the degree to which individuals perceive these images as providing a standard against which to compare themselves more consistently correlates with the DM, an idea compatible with theorising in more general male body image literature (Ryan & Morrison, 2010).

Interpersonal experience

Few studies have included interpersonal experience-related measures, although many results have been consistent with theoretical expectations. For example, having been teased about appearance, weight or muscularity by parents or peers, along with having experienced negative comments about appearance, is related with DM attitudes, but not behaviours (Nowell & Ricciardelli, 2008; Smolak & Stein, 2006). Similarly, a tendency to engage in social comparison is also related with the DM (Smolak & Stein, 2006). Finally, perceived pressure from parents, friends, romantic partners and sports personnel (coaches and teammates) to achieve or maintain a certain body size and/or weight has been correlated with the DM (Petrie et al., 2007).

There is scope to expand knowledge of the interpersonal experiences associated with the DM. Petrie et al.'s (2007) findings, for example, may indicate that relationships between interpersonal experiences and the DM are moderated by other variables (e.g. eating disorder symptoms). In addition, some of the variables measured, such as interpersonal sensitivity and distrust, have not yielded statistically significant relationships (Maida & Armstrong, 2005), and the associations that have emerged with DM behaviours are not in agreement with measures of attitudes (Nowell & Ricciardelli, 2008; Smolak & Stein, 2006).

Personality characteristics

Researchers have investigated the associations between several characterological variables and the DM. The ones receiving most attention are: the drive for thinness, drive for leanness, body- and self-esteem and gender role orientation. Findings relevant to each of these variables are detailed below.

Drive for thinness and drive for leanness

There have been mixed findings when examining the correlation between drive for thinness and DM (Martins, Tiggemann, & Kirkbride, 2007; Mussap, 2008; Zelli, Lucidi, & Mallia, 2010). Mixed findings suggest thinness and muscularity represent incompatible goals. One paper demonstrated positive correlations between drive for leanness and DM (Smolak & Murnen, 2008). This observation makes conceptual sense because individuals with high levels of the DM also would probably aim for a lean body and is compatible with the finding that hypermesomorphic bodies are not regarded as ideal (Ryan & Morrison, 2010).

Body- and self-esteem

Generally, self-esteem has correlated negatively with the DM (Chittester & Hausenblas, 2009; Smolak & Stein, 2006). Various other esteem-related variables have been examined. Some correlate positively with the DM, such as male body image esteem and trait male body esteem (Barlett & Harris, 2008), whereas others appear to have associations that are: (a) inconsistent (e.g. upper body strength esteem, body esteem); (b) negative (e.g. genital esteem, physical appearance self-esteem); or (c) not statistically significant (e.g. sexual self-esteem, state male body esteem). Aside from self-esteem, most esteem variables have been examined infrequently.

Gender role

McCreary, Saucier, and Courtenay (2005) proposed muscularity was important to many males because muscular males are perceived to be more masculine. Supporting this conjecture, numerous male gender role-typed variables (e.g. traditional attitudes towards men, conformity to masculine norms and masculine gender role stress) have correlated positively with the DM for both genders (Mahalik et al., 2003; McCreary et al., 2005; Mussap, 2008; Smolak & Stein, 2006). In these studies, female-typed traits were not significantly correlated with this drive (McCreary et al., 2005; Smolak & Murnen, 2008).

Other personality characteristics

Although many other personality variables have been examined in relation to the DM, these variables have seldom been studied more than once. Some of these variables have correlated positively with the DM, such as neuroticism, perfectionism, focus on appearance, fear of negative evaluation, overall psychological distress and fitness orientation (Bergeron & Tylka, 2007; Davis, Karvinen, & McCreary, 2005; Kyrejto, Mosewich, Kowalski, Mack, & Crocker, 2008). Other personality variables have negatively correlated (e.g. coping and vanity), and some factors have provided mixed findings (e.g. hardiness and public self-consciousness). These mixed findings may be due to: (a) differences between genders (e.g. Kyrejto et al. [2008]

found public self-consciousness was correlated with the DM in females but not males) and/or (b) use of different measures of the DM (Bergeron and Tylka [2007] found hardiness was correlated with the DM when measured using the DMS, but not when using the DMAQ).

Physical and demographic attributes

Gender

In 95 per cent of studies, males had a significantly stronger DM than females, perhaps unsurprising given the different societal expectations for men and women. Not all results have been unanimous, however. Regarding DM behaviours, no differences emerged between males and females who weight trained (Robert, Munroe-Chandler, & Gammage, 2009), indicating some females may have a strong DM (Gruber, 2007).

Body composition

Typically, non-significant correlations occur between the DM and various body composition measures (Martin Ginis, Eng, Arbour, Hartman, & Phillips, 2005; McCreary, Karvinen, & Davis, 2006). Conceptually, the DM is a psychological variable likely to be correlated more strongly with perceived rather than actual body composition (Martin Ginis et al., 2005). In addition, the DM focuses on high muscle and low fat levels, and not necessarily other body composition variables (Grabarek & Cooper, 2008). These non-significant correlations may also be explained by differences in the way participants interpret objective physical changes in body fat (Martin Ginis et al., 2005), an idea explored in more detail later in the chapter.

Physical strength and size

Studies typically reveal non-significant relationships between strength variables and the DM. Researchers, however, have examined students (McCreary et al., 2006) and sedentary individuals (Martin Ginis et al., 2005). It may be that these populations are primarily concerned with the appearance of their muscularity, rather than their actual muscular strength (Martin Ginis et al., 2005). Athletic populations may provide a different pattern of results due to functional strength being required for sports performance.

Other physical and demographic variables

Other physical and demographic variables that have received little attention include age, school grade, place of residence, stage of transsexual adjustment and sexual orientation. Mixed results are often reported with statistically significant correlations emerging on occasion (e.g. Nowell and Ricciardelli [2008] reported that age was negatively correlated with the drive). Further research is required on these variables to clarify their relationship with the DM.

Cognitions

Body satisfaction

The DM is negatively correlated with individuals' satisfaction with their current muscularity levels (Morrison & Harriman, 2005). There have been equivocal findings with respect to other body attributes such as: facial satisfaction, appearance satisfaction and body-specific satisfaction (Petrie et al., 2007). The relationship between DM and body part satisfaction may be influenced by the body part under scrutiny and whether the participants evidence eating disorders symptomatology (e.g. Petrie et al., 2007). Given the limited work, additional research is needed.

Body dissatisfaction

Most studies report positive relationships between global body dissatisfaction and DM attitudes (Arbour & Martin Ginis, 2006; Tylka et al., 2005), but not DM behaviours or combined attitude and behaviour scores (Grabarek & Cooper, 2008; McCreary & Sasse, 2000; Tylka et al., 2005). These results suggest dissatisfaction may not result necessarily in behaviour change.

Positive correlations have been documented between the DM and dissatisfaction with current levels of muscularity (Bergeron & Tylka, 2007; Tylka et al., 2005). Individuals evidencing a stronger DM also tend to report greater dissatisfaction with their upper and lower body (Martins et al., 2007). Less clear trends emerge with other body dissatisfaction related variables, however (Grabarek & Cooper, 2008; Jones & Crawford, 2005). For example, there was no significant correlation with current body fat dissatisfaction and mixed evidence for a relationship with height dissatisfaction (Bergeron & Tylka, 2007; Cafri & Thompson, 2004; Tylka et al., 2005). Height and body fat may be perceived by individuals as separate to muscle-oriented variables.

Body perception

Across different measures of body perception equivocal findings are noted. For example, there are mixed results for the relationship between DM and perceived muscularity (Cafri & Thompson, 2004; Martin Ginis et al., 2005). Some individuals may be cognisant of, but unconcerned with, the discrepancy between actual and ideal muscularity, and others may be more concerned about other components of body image. For example, Martin Ginis et al. (2005) obtained a significant positive correlation between the DM and perceived body fat in sedentary males, but no significant correlation with perceived level of muscle. Both large muscle mass and low body fat contribute to displaying high levels of muscularity. Sedentary individuals compared to active populations often have higher body fat levels (Kohrt, Malley, Dalsky, & Holloszy, 1992). Individuals with high levels of fat also often have higher levels of muscularity to support their fat mass (Kyle, Schutz, Dupertuis, & Pichard, 2003). Sedentary individuals may focus more on their perceived fat levels rather than their muscle mass because their fat levels may be concealing their muscularity.

Other cognitive variables

A number of other cognitive variables have been explored, although findings are seldom replicated. These variables may be grouped into three broad categories: (a) weight and shape concern, (b) doping attitudes and (c) other body-related attitudes and cognitions. First, generally positive correlations exist between weight and shape concerns and the DM in male populations, and unsupportive studies have typically examined females, or have used DM indices that have been modified in an ad hoc fashion (Grossbard, Lee, Neighbors, & Larimer, 2009; Jones & Crawford, 2005). Second, the DM is positively correlated with the contemplation of using (Morrison et al., 2004), positive attitudes towards (Zelli et al., 2010), willingness to use (Dodge et al., 2008) and intentions to use (Zelli et al., 2010) doping substances. These relationships exist, in some cases, regardless of participants' sporting levels or gender (Zelli et al., 2010). The remaining cognitive variables, classified as other body attitudes and cognitions, have received limited attention. Many of these variables appear to correlate positively with the DM and include appearance intolerance (Hildebrandt, Langenbucher, & Schlundt, 2004), body surveillance (Martins et al., 2007) and compulsivity about workout schedules (Kelley et al., 2010). Mixed findings exist for other variables such as self-objectification, body inadequacy and body preoccupation (Hallsworth, Wade, & Tiggemann, 2005; Martins et al., 2007).

Emotions

Results suggest that the DM is positively associated with self-reported negative emotions, including trait anxiety, body anxiety, social physique anxiety and appearance anxiety (Chandler, Grieve, Derryberry, & Pegg, 2009; Duggan & McCreary, 2004; Hallsworth et al., 2005; Hildebrandt et al., 2004; Kelley et al., 2010; Kyrejto et al., 2008; Maida & Armstrong, 2005; Martin Ginis et al., 2005; Martin et al., 2006; McCreary & Saucier, 2009; Petrie et al., 2007). Body shame is another negative emotion that has typically been correlated with the drive on multiple occasions (Daniel & Bridges, 2010; Hallsworth et al., 2005; Martins et al., 2007; Smolak & Murnen, 2008).

The remaining emotional variables have received scant attention, but typically, although not unanimously, the results indicate that the DM is associated with negative moods and emotions. Petrie et al. (2007), for example, found that depressed, sad, stressed and guilty moods were related to the drive in individuals reporting eating disorder symptoms, but not in asymptomatic participants. Maida and Armstrong (2005) found that the DM was related with hostility, but not maturity fears.

Psychological disorders

Body dysmorphic disorder and muscle dysmorphia

The DM is positively correlated with body dysmorphic disorder in males (Hallsworth et al., 2005; Maida & Armstrong, 2005). Positive correlations are also evident between symptoms of muscle dysmorphia and the DM, as measured by the DMS attitudes subscale (Robert et al., 2009) and total score (Chandler et al., 2009; Grieve & Helmick, 2008), but not the behaviour subscale.

Obsessive–compulsive disorder and depression

Generally positive correlations exist between the DM and obsessive–compulsive disorder (Hildebrandt et al., 2004; Maida & Armstrong, 2005). In most cases, depression is positively correlated with DM attitudes (Bergeron & Tylka, 2007). Only one study has examined the correlation between depression and DM behaviours, with no statistically significant correlation reported (Bergeron & Tylka, 2007).

Eating disorders and concerns

Individuals with a stronger DM may experience eating concerns, restrict food intake and engage in selective eating strategies (Mussap, 2008; Tylka et al., 2005). Furthermore, people who diet to gain weight report a significantly stronger DM than those who diet to lose weight (McCreary & Sasse, 2002). Dieting and avoiding types of food that are perceived as unhealthy may constitute a healthy behaviour due to the relevant health benefits that result from these strategies (Esposito et al., 2011). However, individuals with a strong DM may also engage in negative food and weight control strategies (Mussap, 2008; Petrie et al., 2007). For example, the DM is related to indicants of bulimia such as purging (Hallsworth et al., 2005; Hildebrandt et al., 2004; Mussap, 2008).

Behaviour

Supplement and PES use

Supplement use is generally positively correlated with the DM (Chittester & Hausenblas, 2009; Hildebrandt et al., 2004; Litt & Dodge, 2008). One study examined actual drug use and found no significant relationship with a composite DM questionnaire (Cafri, van den Berg, & Thompson, 2006), a finding discordant with the observation that the drive correlated with the contemplation of use (Morrison et al., 2004). It is likely that the DM is just one influence on drug use.

Sports and exercise participation

Athletes and bodybuilders generally report a stronger DM compared to non-athletes (Dodge et al., 2008; Morrison et al., 2004; Zelli et al., 2010) and non-bodybuilders (Hallsworth et al., 2005). Furthermore, a stronger DM is associated with exercise dependence (Chittester & Hausenblas, 2009; Hale, Roth, DeLong, & Briggs, 2010). Some individuals may consider sport and physical activity engagement as a way of achieving an ideal body. It is unsurprising that muscle-building activities significantly correlate with the DM (Chittester & Hausenblas, 2009;

Litt & Dodge, 2008; Morrison & Morrison, 2006). Positive correlations also have been reported with cardiovascular exercise (Hallsworth et al., 2005; Morrison et al., 2004), suggesting individuals with a stronger DM may aim to simultaneously increase muscle and reduce body fat. The DM is related more strongly with weightlifting than cardiovascular exercise (Morrison et al., 2004).

Other behaviours

Individuals with a stronger DM are more likely to engage in conversations about muscularity and appearance (Jones & Crawford, 2005). Also, the DM correlates with body-checking behaviours achieved through visual comparison, but not with comparisons made via physical manipulations (e.g. pinching/measuring the bicep to examine fat levels and muscularity; Hildebrandt, Alfano, & Langenbucher, 2010).

Summary

Research generally supports theoretical propositions. Through societal norms and interpersonal experiences, some people (typically male) become convinced their physiques are insufficiently muscular. People with low self-esteem may be especially vulnerable to perceiving they are inadequate, and their efforts to build muscle may be an attempt to address low self-perceptions. Although weight training may improve self-esteem (Tucker & Mortell, 1993), developing muscularity may not always address feelings of inadequacy. Also, the DM may be associated with thoughts, feelings and behaviours resulting in lowered quality of life and unpleasant health and well-being.

Future research

Establishing questionnaire psychometrics

In addition to establishing the psychometric properties of DM measures, as mentioned above, normative data will assist in the interpretation of individuals' scores. For example, cut-off scores do not exist; it is unknown what is a low, medium or high DM score. Similarly, no measures have been calibrated against behaviours in people's lives. Calibration involves representing DM scores in understandable, meaningful and interpretable metrics (Andersen, McCullagh, & Wilson, 2007). For example, how large do differences between scores need to be before a demonstrable difference in steroid use can be expected?

Sample selection

The average sample size in drive for muscularity studies is 218 (SD = 218), and participants' average age is 21.68 years (SD = 5.97 years). Just 4 per cent of studies have classified participants' sexual orientation, and one study examined racial differences. Echoing earlier discussion regarding gender, in some studies, the populations examined may not be those associated with a high drive. To illustrate, 64 per cent of samples have involved college students and 13 per cent have examined high-school students. In 6.6 per cent of studies, recreational weight trainers have been examined. Competitive lifters and bodybuilders (4.4 per cent) are not often examined – the types of individuals who likely have high levels of the drive. Furthermore, just 4 per cent of studies have classified participants as competitive athletes. In studies examining sporting and weight training populations, students have often been utilised as comparison samples, but their training background is often unreported. Training background seems a possible confounding variable needing to be addressed in some manner.

Theory development and research design

Researchers have identified numerous correlates of the DM. One challenge is to examine ways these correlates interact with each other and the DM. For example, body composition measures have not correlated consistently with the DM, but it is possible the interactions they have with other psychological variables may influence the drive. Researchers could examine frameworks that organise existing correlates into meaningful patterns. Alternatively, investigators might draw on existing theories to flesh out their understanding of the DM. For example, examining self-determination theory's psychological needs (i.e. competence, relatedness, autonomy; Ryan & Deci, 2000) may expand understanding about relationships between the DM and social culturalisation variables.

Typically, investigators have adopted descriptive designs. Alternative methods will add to knowledge. Experiments, for example, will help provide evidence regarding causality. Qualitative studies will provide insights into what life is like for individuals with strong DM.

Intervention research

Current research provides some support that the DM is a mental health issue. Stronger levels of the drive may be associated with thoughts, feelings and behaviours resulting in impaired functioning or reduced quality of life. Finding ways to prevent individuals becoming consumed by the DM or help them reduce their drive may have beneficial consequences. To date, there has been limited examination of possible prevention or treatment interventions. Cognitive–behavioural therapeutic approaches have the most evidence for resolving body image disturbances (Cash, 2008). Given that the DM is a body image-related construct, cognitive–behavioural principles may be effective in helping individuals reduce their drives.

Practical implications

Professionals in strength and conditioning contexts may come across individuals with a strong DM. Knowledge about the drive may assist them in identifying and directing individuals whose health and well-being are potentially adversely affected towards suitable help. Raising the topic, however, can be tricky. A significant proportion of individuals – and males in particular – will not readily admit to appearance motives. There seem to be taboos against expressing appearance anxieties in males (Pope et al., 2000). Repeated attempts to discuss the topic will probably strain practitioner–client relationships. Clients may raise the issue in the future, perhaps after their appearance concerns have influenced their lives negatively. If clients raise the issue, professionals may help them locate suitable mental health practitioners. If practitioners consider that other health issues are present then they may need to approach a mental health professionals for advice on how to proceed. Unless suitably qualified to help with psychological distress, professionals need to refer clients to another practitioner.

The majority of people wishing to exercise to look better are not greatly upset about their appearance. Well-designed strength and conditioning programmes can invoke changes in body composition and raise body image. Strength and conditioning coaches can help many individuals who wish to look better, but whose lives are not influenced negatively by their dissatisfaction. Explaining to clients what is and is not possible may help address unrealistic expectations. Body image changes appear to result from moderate- to high-intensity exercise. Following programme design guidelines laid out by professionals organisations, such as the National Strength and Conditioning Association, will likely lead to safe and effective training regimes.

Strength and conditioning coaches often work out, may have bodies closer to the ideal physique than their clients and may influence their clients' body image attitudes. There are ways practitioners can help promote healthy attitudes. Practitioners, for example, can reflect on their own body image and beliefs about how important appearance is in life. With increased self-awareness, practitioners are in better positions to change any negative beliefs and prevent these beliefs from influencing their clients' attitudes.

One message practitioners can portray is acceptance of people regardless of their appearance. Another message is that the media-displayed ideal physique is not necessary for well-being or a fulfilling life. A third message is that success in life, however defined, is influenced by many factors over which clients have control (e.g. work ethic) rather than variables over which they have less control (e.g. their looks). A fourth message is that the pursuit of the ideal physique can be damaging to physical, mental and social health when it leads to extreme measures such as cosmetic surgery, regimented diets and lifestyles, excessive exercise and drug abuse (see Pope et al., 2000, for more discussion).

Conclusions

In this chapter, we have reviewed existing research and offered ways to expand current understanding. We hope that investigators continue to examine the construct and expand knowledge, particularly in directions that lead to strategies for helping prevent or ameliorate the unhealthy physical, psychological and social effects that a preoccupation with muscularity may have on individuals.

Discussion questions

1. What behaviours, verbal statements and emotions do you observe in people who have a strong DM?
2. In what ways do your observations parallel and differ from research?
3. What factors in typical strength and conditioning settings may trigger a strong DM?
4. In what ways may these factors be modified?
5. What socialising agents influence how we value our appearance?
6. Which ones seem most likely to influence a DM?
7. Which DM questionnaire seems to have the most promise in becoming a 'gold-standard measure'?

References

Andersen, M. B., McCullagh, P., & Wilson, G. J. (2007). But what do the numbers really tell us? Arbitrary metrics and effect size reporting in sport psychology research. *Journal of Sport and Exercise Psychology, 29,* 664–672.

Arbour, K. P., & Martin Ginis, K. A. (2006). Effects of exposure to muscular and hypermuscular media images on young men's muscularity dissatisfaction and body dissatisfaction. *Body Image, 3,* 153–161.

Baghurst, T., Hollander, D. B., Nardella, B., & Haff, G. G. (2006). Change in sociocultural ideal male physique: An examination of past and present action figures. *Body Image, 3,* 87–91.

Barlett, C. P., & Harris, R. J. (2008). The impact of body emphasizing video games on body image concerns in men and women. *Sex Roles, 59,* 586–601.

Barlett, C. P., Vowels, C. L., & Saucier, D. A. (2008). Meta-analyses of the effects of media images on men's body-image concerns. *Journal of Social and Clinical Psychology, 27,* 279–310.

Barnette, J. J. (2000). Effects of stem and Likert response option reversals on survey internal consistency: If you feel the need, there is a better alternative to using those negatively worded items. *Educational & Psychological Measurement, 60,* 361–370.

Berger, A. A. (1995). *Essentials of mass communication theory.* London: Sage.

Bergeron, D., & Tylka, T. L. (2007). Support for the uniqueness of body dissatisfaction from drive for muscularity among men. *Body Image, 4,* 288–295.

Blond, A. (2008). Impacts of exposure to images of ideal bodies on male body dissatisfaction: A review. *Body Image, 5,* 244–250.

Cafri, G., & Thompson, J. K. (2004). Evaluating the convergence of muscle appearance attitude measures. *Assessment, 11,* 224–229.

Cafri, G., van den Berg, P., & Thompson, J. K. (2006). Pursuit of muscularity in adolescent boys: Relations among biopsychosocial variables and clinical outcomes. *Journal of Clinical Child and Adolescent Psychology, 35,* 283–291.

Cash, T. F. (2002). Cognitive-behavioral perspectives on body image. In T. F. Cash, & T. Pruzinsky (Eds.), *Body image: A handbook of theory, research, & clinical practice* (pp. 38–46). New York: Guilford.

Cash, T. F. (2008). *The body image workbook: An eight-step program for learning to like your looks* (2nd ed.). Oakland, CA: New Harbinger Publications.

Chandler, C. G., Grieve, F. G., Derryberry, W. P., & Pegg, P. O. (2009). Are anxiety and obsessive-compulsive symptoms related to muscle dysmorphia? *International Journal of Men's Health, 8,* 143–154.

Chittester, N. I., & Hausenblas, H. A. (2009). Correlates of drive for muscularity. *Journal of Health Psychology, 14,* 872–877.

Daniel, S., & Bridges, S. K. (2010). The drive for muscularity in men: Media influences and objectification theory. *Body Image*, 7, 32–38.

Davis, C., Karvinen, K., & McCreary, D. R. (2005). Personality correlates of a drive for muscularity in young men. *Personality and Individual Differences*, 39, 349–359.

Dodge, T., Litt, D., Seitchik, A., & Bennett, S. (2008). Drive for muscularity and beliefs about legal performance enhancing substances as predictors of current use and willingness to use. *Journal of Health Psychology*, 13, 1173–1179.

Duggan, S. J., & McCreary, D. R. (2004). Body image, eating disorders, and the drive for muscularity in gay and heterosexual men: The influence of media images. *Journal of Homosexuality*, 47, 45–58.

Edwards, S., & Launder, C. (2000). Investigating muscularity concerns in male body image: Development of the Swansea Muscularity Attitudes Questionnaire. *International Journal of Eating Disorders*, 28, 120–124.

Esposito, K., Di Palo, C., Maiorino, M. I., Petrizzo, M., Bellastella, G., Siniscalchi, I., & Giugliano, D. (2011). Long-term effect of Mediterranean-style diet and calorie restriction on biomarkers of longevity and oxidative stress in overweight men. *Cardiology Research and Practice*, 5, Article ID 293916.

Fabrigar, L. R., Wegener, D. T., MacCallum, R. C., & Strahan, E. J. (1999). Evaluating the use of exploratory factor analysis in psychological research. *Psychological Methods*, 4, 272–299.

Festinger, L. (1954). A theory of social comparison processes. *Human Relations*, 7, 117–140.

Finch, J. F., & West, S. G. (1997). The investigation of personality structure: Statistical models. *Journal of Research in Personality*, 31, 439–485.

Frederick, D. A., Buchanan, G. M., Sadehgi-Azar, L., Peplau, L. A., Haselton, M. G., Berezovskaya, A., & Lipinski, R. E. (2007). Desiring the muscular ideal: Men's body satisfaction in the United States, Ukraine, and Ghana. *Psychology of Men & Masculinity*, 8, 103–117.

Giddens, A. (2006). *Sociology* (5th ed.). London: Polity.

Giles, D. C., & Close, J. (2008). Exposure to 'lad magazines' and drive for muscularity in dating and non-dating young men. *Personality and Individual Differences*, 44, 1610–1616.

Gordon, K. H., & Dombeck, J. J. (2010). The associations between two facets of narcissism and eating disorder symptoms. *Eating Behaviors*, 11, 288–292.

Grabarek, C., & Cooper, S. (2008). Graduate students' social and emotional functioning relative to characteristics of eating disorders. *The Journal of General Psychology*, 135, 425–451.

Grieve, F. G. (2007). A conceptual model of factors contributing to the development of muscle dysmorphia. *Eating Disorders*, 15, 63–80.

Grieve, R., & Helmick, A. (2008). The influence of men's self-objectification on the drive for muscularity: Self-esteem, body satisfaction and muscle dysmorphia. *International Journal of Men's Health*, 7, 288–298.

Grossbard, J. R., Lee, C. M., Neighbors, C., & Larimer, M. E. (2009). Body image concerns and contingent self-esteem in male and female college students. *Sex Roles*, 60, 198–207.

Gruber, A. J. (2007). A more muscular female body ideal. In J. K. Thompson, & G. Cafri (Eds.), *The muscular ideal: Psychological, social, and medical perspectives* (pp. 217–234). Washington, DC: American Psychological Association.

Hale, B. D., Roth, A. D., DeLong, R. E., & Briggs, M. S. (2010). Exercise dependence and the drive for muscularity in male bodybuilders, power lifters, and fitness lifters. *Body Image*, 7, 234–239.

Hallsworth, L., Wade, T., & Tiggemann, M. (2005). Individual differences in male body-image: An examination of self-objectification in recreational body builders. *British Journal of Health Psychology*, 10, 453–465.

Harrison, K., & Bond, B. J. (2007). Gaming magazines and the drive for muscularity in pre-adolescent boys: A longitudinal examination. *Body Image*, 4, 269–277.

Hatoum, I. J., & Belle, D. (2004). Mags and abs: Media consumption and bodily concerns in men. *Sex Roles*, 51, 397–407.

Hayton, J. C., Allen, D. G., & Scarpello, V. (2004). Factor retention decisions in exploratory factor analysis: A tutorial on parallel analysis. *Organizational Research Methods, 7*, 191–205.

Hildebrandt, T., Alfano, L., & Langenbucher, J. W. (2010). Body image disturbance in 1000 male appearance and performance enhancing drug users. *Journal of Psychiatric Research, 44*, 841–846.

Hildebrandt, T., Langenbucher, J., & Schlundt, D. G. (2004). Muscularity concerns among men: Development of attitudinal and perceptual measures. *Body Image, 1*, 169–181.

Hobza, C. L., & Rochlen, A. B. (2009). Gender role conflict, drive for muscularity, and the impact of ideal media portrayals on men. *Psychology of Men & Masculinity, 10*, 120–130.

Ingham, A. G., & Hardy, S. (1993). Introduction: Sport studies through the lens of Raymond Williams. In A. G. Ingham, & J. W. Loy (Eds.), *Sport in social development* (pp. 1–19). Champaign, IL: Human Kinetics.

Jones, D. C., & Crawford, J. K. (2005). Adolescent boys and body image: Weight and muscularity concerns as dual pathways to body dissatisfaction. *Journal of Youth and Adolescence, 34*, 629–636.

Jung, J., Forbes, G. B., & Chan, P. (2010). Global body and muscle satisfaction among college men in the United States and Hong Kong-China. *Sex Roles, 63*, 104–117.

Karazsia, B. T., & Crowther, J. H. (2009). Social body comparison and internalization: Mediators of social influences on men's muscularity-oriented body dissatisfaction. *Body Image, 6*, 105–112.

Kelley, C. C. G., Neufeld, J. M., & Musher-Eizenman, D. R. (2010). Drive for thinness and drive for muscularity: Opposite ends of the continuum or separate constructs? *Body Image, 7*, 74–77.

Kohrt, W. M., Malley, M. T., Dalsky, G. P., & Holloszy, J. O. (1992). Body composition of healthy sedentary and trained, young and older men and women. *Medicine & Science in Sports & Exercise, 24*, 833.

Kyle, U. G., Schutz, Y., Dupertuis, Y. M., & Pichard, C. (2003). Body composition interpretation: Contributions of the fat-free mass index and the body fat mass index. *Nutrition, 19*, 597–604.

Kyrejto, J. W., Mosewich, A. D., Kowalski, K. C., Mack, D. E., & Crocker, P. R. E. (2008). Men's and women's drive for muscularity: Gender differences and cognitive and behavioral correlates. *International Journal of Sport and Exercise Psychology, 6*, 69–84.

Litt, D., & Dodge, T. (2008). A longitudinal investigation of the Drive for Muscularity Scale: Predicting use of performance enhancing substances and weightlifting among males. *Body Image, 5*, 346–351.

Mahalik, J. R., Locke, B. D., Ludlow, L. H., Diemer, M. A., Scott, R. P., Gottfried, M., & Freitas, G. (2003). Development of the conformity to masculine norms inventory. *Psychology of Men & Masculinity, 4*, 3–25.

Maida, D. M., & Armstrong, S. L. (2005). The classification of muscle dysmorphia. *International Journal of Men's Health, 4*, 73–91.

Martin, J. J., Kliber, A., Kulinna, P., & Fahlman, M. (2006). Social physique anxiety and muscularity and appearance cognitions in college men. *Sex Roles, 55*, 151–158.

Martin Ginis, K. A., Eng, J. J., Arbour, K. P., Hartman, J. W., & Phillips, S. M. (2005). Mind over muscle? Sex differences in the relationship between body image change and subjective and objective physical changes following a 12-week strength-training program. *Body Image, 2*, 363–372.

Martins, Y., Tiggemann, M., & Kirkbride, A. (2007). Those speedos become them: The role of self-objectification in gay and heterosexual men's body image. *Personality and Social Psychology Bulletin, 33*, 634–647.

McCreary, D. R., Karvinen, K., & Davis, C. (2006). The relationship between the drive for muscularity and anthropometric measures of muscularity and adiposity. *Body Image, 3*, 145–152.

McCreary, D. R., & Sasse, D. K. (2000). An exploration of the drive for muscularity in adolescent boys and girls. *Journal of American College Health, 48*, 297–304.

McCreary, D. R., & Sasse, D. K. (2002). Gender differences in high school students' dieting behavior and their correlates. *International Journal of Men's Health, 1*, 195–213.

McCreary, D. R., Sasse, D. K., Saucier, D. M., & Dorsch, K. D. (2004). Measuring the drive for muscularity: Factorial validity of the drive for muscularity scale in men and women. *Psychology of Men & Masculinity, 5*, 49–58.

McCreary, D. R., & Saucier, D. M. (2009). Drive for muscularity: Body comparison, and social physique anxiety in men and women. *Body Image, 6*, 24–30.

McCreary, D. R., Saucier, D. M., & Courtenay, W. H. (2005). The drive for muscularity and masculinity: Testing the associations among gender-role traits, behaviours, attitudes, and conflict. *Psychology of Men & Masculinity, 6*, 83–94.

McDonagh, L. K., Morrison, T. G., & McGuire, B. E. (2008). The naked truth: Development of a scale designed to measure male body image self-consciousness during physical intimacy. *The Journal of Men's Health, 16*, 253–265.

McPherson, K. E., McCarthy, P., McCreary, D. R., & McMillan, S. (2010). Psychometric evaluation of the Drive for Muscularity Scale in a community-based sample of Scottish men participating in an organised sporting event. *Body Image, 7*, 368–371.

Morrison, T. G., & Harriman, R. L. (2005). Additional evidence for the psychometric soundness of the drive for muscularity attitudes questionnaire (DMAQ). *The Journal of Social Psychology, 145*, 618–620.

Morrison, T. G., & Morrison, M. A. (2006). Psychometric properties of the Swansea muscularity attitudes questionnaire (SMAQ). *Body Image, 3*, 131–144.

Morrison, T. G., Morrison, M. A., & Hopkins, C. (2003). Striving for bodily perfection? An exploration of the drive for muscularity in Canadian men. *Psychology of Men & Masculinity, 4*, 111–120.

Morrison, T. G., Morrison, M. A., Hopkins, C., & Rowan, E. T. (2004). Muscle mania: Development of a new scale examining the drive for muscularity in Canadian men. *Psychology of Men & Masculinity, 5*, 30–39.

Morrison, T. G., Morrison, M. A., & McCann, L. (2006). Striving for bodily perfection? An overview of the drive for muscularity. In M. V. Kindes (Ed.), *Body image: New research* (pp. 1–34). New York: Nova Science.

Mussap, A. J. (2008). Masculine gender role stress and the pursuit of muscularity. *International Journal of Men's Health, 7*, 72–89.

Nowell, C., & Ricciardelli, L. A. (2008). Appearance-based comments, body dissatisfaction and drive for muscularity in males. *Body Image, 5*, 337–345.

Ochner, C. N., Gray, J. A., & Brickner, K. (2009). The development and initial validation of a new measure of male body dissatisfaction. *Eating Behaviours, 10*, 197–201.

O'Donovan, G., Blazevich, A., Boreham, C., Cooper, A. R., Crank, H., Ekelund, U., … Stamatakis, E. (2010). The ABC of physical activity for health: A consensus statement from the British Association of Sport and Exercise Sciences. *Journal of Sports Sciences, 28*, 573–591.

Petrie, T. A., Greenleaf, C., Carter, J. E., & Reel, J. J. (2007). Psychological correlates of disordered eating among male collegiate athletes. *Journal of Clinical Sport Psychology, 1*, 340–357.

Pope, H. G., Jr., Phillips, K. A., & Olivardia, R. (2000). *The Adonis complex: The secret crisis of male body obsession*. New York: The Free Press.

Robert, C. A., Munroe-Chandler, K. J., & Gammage, K. L. (2009). The relationship between the drive for muscularity and muscle dysmorphia in male and female weight trainers. *Journal of Strength and Conditioning Research, 23*, 1656–1662.

Rosenberg, M. (1989). *Society and the adolescent self-image* (reprint ed.). Middletown, CT: Wesleyan University Press.

Rubio, D. M., Berg-Weger, M., & Tebb, S. S. (2001). Using structural equation modelling to test for multidimensionality. *Structural Equation Modelling, 8*, 613–626.

Ryan, R. M., & Deci, E. L. (2000). Self-determination theory and the facilitation of intrinsic motivation, social development, and well-being. *American Psychologist, 55*, 68–78.

Ryan, T. A., & Morrison, T. G. (2010). Psychometric properties of the Muscle Appearance Satisfaction Scale among Irish and British men. *Body Image, 7*, 246–250.

Ryan, T. A., Morrison, T. G., Roddy, S., & McCutcheon, J. (2010). Psychometric properties of the Revised Male Body Attitudes Scale among Irish men. *Body Image, 8*, 64–69.

Ryckman, R. M., Butler, J. C., Thornton, B., & Lindner, M. A. (1997). Assessment of physique subtype stereotypes. *Genetic, Social, and General Psychology Monographs, 123*, 101–128.

Shaw, J., & Waller, G. (1995). The media's impact on body image: Implications for prevention and treatment. *Eating Disorders: The Journal of Treatment & Prevention, 3*, 115–123.

Shilling, C. (1993). *The body and social theory.* London: Sage.

Smolak, L., & Murnen, S. K. (2008). Drive for leanness: Assessment and relationship to gender, gender role and objectification. *Body Image, 5*, 251–260.

Smolak, L., & Stein, J. A. (2006). The relationship of drive for muscularity to sociocultural factors, self-esteem, physical attributes, gender role, and social comparison in middle school boys. *Body Image, 3*, 121–129.

Tiggemann, M. (2005). Television and adolescent body image: The role of program content and viewing motivation. *Journal of Social and Clinical Psychology, 24*, 361–381.

Tod, D., & Lavallee, D. (2010). Towards a conceptual understanding of muscle dysmorphia development and sustainment. *International Review of Sport and Exercise Psychology, 3*, 111–131.

Tucker, L. A., & Mortell, R. (1993). Comparison of the effects of walking and weight training programs on body image in middle-aged women: An experimental study. *American Journal of Health Promotion, 8*, 34–42.

Turner, B. S. (2007). *The body and society: Explorations in social theory* (3rd ed.). London: Sage.

Tylka, T. L., Bergeron, D., & Schwartz, J. P. (2005). Development and psychometric evaluation of the Male Body Attitudes Scale (MBAS). *Body Image, 2*, 161–175.

Wojtowicz, A. E., & von Ranson, K. M. (2006). Psychometric evaluation of two scales examining muscularity concerns in men and women. *Psychology of Men & Masculinity, 7*, 56–66.

Zelli, A., Lucidi, F., & Mallia, L. (2010). The relationships among adolescents' drive for muscularity, drive for thinness, doping attitudes, and doping intentions. *Journal of Clinical Sport Psychology, 4*, 39–52.

8

EATING DISORDERS IN SPORT

Justine J. Reel

UNIVERSITY OF UTAH, USA

Nick Galli

CALIFORNIA STATE UNIVERSITY, NORTHRIDGE, USA

Christy Henrich, an Olympic gymnast hopeful, died from an eating disorder in 1992 after being told by a judge to lose weight to gain a competitive edge (Ryan, 1995). Eating disorders yield the highest mortality rate of any psychiatric disorder among female adolescents (Casiero & Frishman, 2006). Individuals with eating disorders are suffering from physical and mental health consequences, and eating disorders have been declared a public health threat (Reel et al., 2011). Eating disorders are no longer viewed merely as a glorified diet or a means to secure a higher score, faster time, or a more aesthetically pleasing physique. This chapter will explore types of eating disorders, athletes who experience more risk of developing eating disorders, and how a strength and conditioning coach can help prevent eating disorders.

Types of eating disorders

Eating disordered behaviors are generally classified across a spectrum of eating symptoms (Beals, 2004) ranging from severe clinical cases to subclinical eating behaviors that may not fit diagnostic criteria for eating disorders but could still be considered disordered eating. Although the American Psychiatric Association (APA, 2000a) is in the process of preparing the fifth edition of the *Diagnostic Statistical Manual of Mental Disorders – 4th Edition* (DSM-IV-TR), eating disorders have been typically diagnosed using three main categories: anorexia nervosa (AN), bulimia nervosa (BN), or eating disorder not otherwise specified (EDNOS) (APA, 2000a). These categories are mainly used for the purpose of identification of the problem and diagnosing clients to provide a code for insurance support for treatment.

Anorexia nervosa

AN represents a refusal to gain weight or maintain 85 percent of one's expected body weight for his or her age and height. AN clients are easy to recognize from their skeletal appearance that results from restricting caloric intake to unhealthy levels. AN may be accompanied with occasional purging (e.g. vomiting) which would receive a purging subtype classification, but many anorexics will fall under a restricting subtype in which weight loss is accomplished through restricting, dieting, and exercising. AN clients report a fear of gaining weight and a fear of fatness that seems irrational to everyone else due to their emaciated appearance. Amenorrhea, the absence of a menstrual cycle for at least three cycles, is a requisite for the diagnosis of AN (Pinheiro et al., 2007), and menstrual irregularities (e.g. infrequent or inconsistent menstrual period) may be observed as a first sign of detection of disordered eating for a female athlete.

Prevalence studies have indicated that approximately 1 percent of the female population who are adolescents or adults meet the diagnostic criteria for AN. However, onset of this disorder rarely occurs in women over the age of 40. Incidence rates for males are expected to be lower than females by 3–12 times, with incidence rates of less than 0.3 percent for males who meet full criteria for AN (APA, 2000b). AN is most prevalent in industrialized nations where citizens who are thin are considered to be attractive within one's culture.

Follow-up studies with hospitalized AN populations indicated that 44 percent of clients were able to restore weight and resume menstruation which was classified as a "good" outcome. However, 24 percent were rated "poor" (unable to restore weight and menstruation), 28 percent rated between "poor" and "good," and 5 percent had died (premature mortality; APA, 2000b). Mortality rates for AN are staggering, as individuals with AN have a 12-fold greater risk of death and a 57-fold greater risk of suicide (Keel et al., 2003; Zucker, Losh, Bulik, LaBar, & Pelphrey, 2007).

Psychological characteristics that have been associated with AN include perfectionism, being goal-oriented, and having an achievement orientation. Despite showing strong academic accomplishments or performing well in athletics or other areas, AN clients tend to exhibit low self-esteem (Beals, 2004). Unfortunately qualities of the body and weight changes are directly connected to one's self-worth. The AN individual may feel secretly rewarded or reinforced for unhealthy restricting behaviors when one comments "you look so thin." Owens, Allen, and Spangler (2010) found that females were significantly more sensitive to visual images, while undergoing functional magnetic resonance imaging (MRI) scanning, compared to men. While females demonstrated greater body dissatisfaction and brain activation when exposed to both overweight and thin images, males remained largely unaffected by the exposure (Owens et al., 2010). Body image differences between males and females have been widely documented; however, body image disturbances in males (e.g. muscle dysmorphia [MD]) exist and will be discussed later in the chapter (Petrie & McFarland, 2009).

Bulimia nervosa

Bulimic individuals may be more difficult to identify strictly based upon one's physical appearance. Individuals who exhibit clear behavioral symptoms (i.e. binge and purge episodes) as well as the psychological characteristics (e.g. body image concern) will receive the diagnosis for BN. Binge eating episodes are typically compensated with purging episodes at a frequency of twice a week for at least 3 months (APA, 2000a). Binge eating episodes are characterized by eating more than most people would eat within a discrete time period (e.g. within a 2-hour period) and may be associated with feeling overfull or stuffed. Binge episodes are characterized by having a sense of lack of control (e.g. feeling like one cannot stop eating or is compelled to have a particular food). Binge episodes typically include forbidden foods or trigger foods and may involve eating foods high in fat, carbohydrates, or sugar content. In some cases, BN clients will drive from one fast food restaurant to another in search of binge foods.

Binge eating episodes are met with feelings of shame and guilt. The only way a BN individual can regain control is through engaging in compensatory behaviors in attempts to prevent weight gain and "purge" guilt. Purging methods may include vomiting, laxative abuse, diet pills, enemas, or excessive exercise. Like AN, once a diagnosis of BN is provided, the clinician should specify whether the individual meets the criteria for purging or nonpurging subtype. To qualify for purging subtype, the BN individual must use vomiting or laxative purging behavior regularly. The nonpurging classification would represent the BN individual who would be more likely to use restricting or excessive exercise as a compensatory method (Mitchell & Peterson, 2005).

Prevalence rates for BN are estimated at 1–3 percent of U.S. women with a lower 0.13–0.96 percent for males (Carter & Rudd, 2005). Prognosis for BN may be slightly better than AN according to outcome data. A 50–70 percent short-term success rate was reported for BN individuals who received treatment (Herzog, Nussbaum, & Marmor, 1996). In a study that followed BN patients 6 years after intensive treatment, 60 percent of outcomes were rated as "good," 29 percent were between "good" and "poor," and 10 percent were rated "poor" (Fichter & Quadflieg, 1997).

BN individuals also face body image disturbances and concern with one's shape and size. BN individuals are often described as having poor impulse control and are often paralleled with other addictions (e.g. substance abuse). In fact, substance abuse has been identified in 30–37 percent of BN clients. Both AN and BN patients may also exhibit co-morbid conditions such as mood disorders (e.g. major depression), anxiety disorders, or obsessive–compulsive disorders (as high as 25 percent in AN clients; APA, 2000b).

Eating disorder not otherwise specified

The final diagnostic category that appears in the DSM-IV-TR is the EDNOS. This "catch-all" category includes all eating disorders that do not fit the full criteria for either AN or BN. In some cases, an individual exhibits characteristics of AN but presenting symptoms are viewed as below the threshold for diagnosis due to the presence of menses (Mitchell & Peterson, 2005). In other cases, the individual presents with symptoms of both bulimia and anorexia fairly evenly. Binge eating disorder (BED) has fit within the EDNOS category and is discussed in the research section of the current DSM; however, it is expected that BED will be a separate eating disorder diagnosis in the next version. BED includes binge eating episodes characteristic of BN without the compensatory behavior. BED has been found to be more common in certain populations (e.g. African-American females) than either AN or BN (Ackard, Fulkerson, & Neumark-Sztainer, 2007; J. Y. Taylor, Caldwell, Baser, Faison, & Jackson, 2007).

Prevalence rates of EDNOS are higher than for AN or BN. Kjelsas, Bjornstrom, and Gotestam (2004) discovered a life-time prevalence of 14.6 percent for the Norwegian adolescent females with EDNOS compared with lower rates (i.e. 2.5 percent) of females who met full criteria for other clinical EDs. McNulty (1997) reported that 5–9.4 percent of males in the general population met criteria for EDNOS when less than 1 percent of males met the criteria for either anorexia or BN.

Prevalence of eating disorders in sport

Although eating disorders may occur in a variety of individuals, certain subpopulations are at greater risk than others. Because of the mental and physical demands of sport, competitive athletes are one subpopulation who are particularly vulnerable to the development of eating disorders. The results of several studies have shown that athletes are more likely than nonathletes to suffer symptoms of eating disorders. A review of 34 studies conducted between 1975 and 1997 revealed that elite athletes from a variety of sports were at a higher risk for eating disorders than nonathletes (Smolak, Murnen, & Ruble, 2000). The difference between athletes and nonathletes was especially apparent when comparing elite athletes in lean sports (e.g. distance running, gymnastics) with nonathletes. Similarly, in their review of 92 studies, Hausenblas and Carron (1999) found that athletes scored higher on indices of bulimia and anorexia than nonathletes. Sundgot-Borgen and Torstveit (2004) compared eating disorder symptomology in a large sample of elite Norwegian athletes to symptomology in an age-matched sample of control participants. Whereas 4.6 percent of the nonathletes exhibited symptoms of a subclinical or clinical eating disorder, 13.5 percent of the athletes reported such symptoms. Most recently, a multisite investigation of female and male Division I National Collegiate Athletic Association (NCAA) athletes revealed that 19.2 percent of males and 25 percent of females could be classified as symptomatic for an eating disorder (Greenleaf, Petrie, Carter, & Reel, 2009; Petrie, Greenleaf, Reel, & Carter, 2008).

Proponents of the physical and psychosocial health benefits of sport participation may be surprised at the aforementioned research findings. In fact, the results of some studies have indicated that sport participation may serve as a buffer for eating disorder development (e.g. Petrie, 1996; Wilkins & Boland, 1991). For example, Wilkins and Boland (1991) found that the collegiate athletes in their study reported significantly less dieting, were less likely to perceive themselves as overweight, had higher body esteem, and had more confidence in their bodies than nonathletes. Similar findings were obtained by DiBartolo and Shaffer (2002), as the female athletes in their study reported less eating disorder symptomology, more positive affect, and greater emotional well-being than a matched sample of nonathletes. A recent study comparing elite Norwegian high school athletes with an age-matched nonathlete control group showed that the nonathletes exhibited more dieting and a higher incidence of disordered eating compared to the athletes (Martinsen, 2010).

Conflicting findings with regard to eating disorder risk between athletes and nonathletes indicate that the relationship between sport participation and eating disorders is not as simple as it may seem. Indeed, an extensive review revealed that, depending on several factors, sport participation can either reduce or increase athletes' risk for an eating disorder (Smolak et al., 2000). Gender, sport type, and competitive level are three of the most important factors to consider when evaluating athletes' risk for an eating disorder.

Gender

Similar to eating disorders in the general population, female athletes are generally thought to be at a heightened risk for eating disorders compared to males. Most research supports this contention. In a study of rowers, Sykora, Grilo, Wilfley, and Brownell (1993) found that female rowers had more maladaptive eating patterns than males, and had tried vomiting as a weight loss practice more than males. Reel and Gill (1998) found that female cheerleaders reported a higher drive for thinness and body dissatisfaction (two variables associated with eating disorder symptoms) than male cheerleaders. In a large-scale examination of eating disorders in intercollegiate athletes, Johnson, Powers, and Dick (1999) found that 1.1 percent of female and 0 percent of male athletes met the criteria for AN. In addition, 9.2 percent of females and 0.01 percent of males classified as having clinically significant problems with bulimia, and 5.52 percent of females and 2.04 percent of males, reported purging on a weekly or greater basis. A more recent study by Engel et al. (2003) revealed that Division I female athletes had more body dissatisfaction, endorsed purging more, and restricted their caloric intake more than Division I male athletes.

A particular concern for lean-sport female athletes is known as the *female athlete triad*. Previously defined as the presence of disordered eating, amenorrhea, and osteoporosis, the American College of Sports Medicine recently revised the triad criteria to provide a more comprehensive view (Beals, Brey, & Gonyou, 1999; Nattiv et al., 2007). The new criteria explain the interrelationships among the three components of the triad, and view each component along a spectrum from "health" to "disease" (Nattiv et al., 2007). Thus, the former triad criteria represent the extreme "disease" pole of each triad component, with the new criteria acknowledging that less serious manifestations of each component, such as low energy availability, menstrual dysfunction, and low bone mineral density, should also be considered problems for female athletes.

Adolescents have been suggested as particularly at risk for components of the triad, due to the physical, psychological, and social changes that occur during this developmental period. Using the revised triad criteria as a guide, Hoch et al. (2009) compared triad components between high school student-athletes and sedentary students. A considerable proportion (78 percent) of the athletes and nonathletes (65 percent) exhibited at least one triad component. Other studies have revealed that the triad is a concern for all physically active females, including intercollegiate and elite-level adult athletes (e.g. Reel, SooHoo, Doetsch, Carter, & Petrie, 2007; Ye Vian, Bee Koon, Lai Oon, & Mohd Ismail, 2009).

Findings of female-specific issues such as the triad, and higher eating disorder risk in female as opposed to male athletes, have led to a proliferation of research focused solely on female athletes. However, researchers and practitioners have recently begun to more closely explore body image, weight concerns, and eating disorders in male athletes (e.g. Baum, 2006; Glazer, 2008). Petrie et al. (2008) examined the prevalence of eating disorders and related symptoms in 203 Division I male athletes. Although none of the athletes were classified as suffering from an eating disorder, nearly 20 percent could be considered symptomatic. Although few male athletes may experience an eating disorder, the psychological profile of those that do is still not well understood. It appears that the psychological correlates of eating disorders present in female athletes (e.g. body image concerns, negative affect) do not have the same salience for males (Petrie, Greenleaf, Carter, & Reel, 2007).

Male athletes in power sports

Although it is clear that female athletes experience eating disorders at a higher rate than males, it may be that the signs and symptoms associated with traditional eating disorders are not indicative of the body and weight concerns of many male athletes. Recent research suggests that male athletes in power sports such as football, baseball, and track and field may be at risk for pathological behaviors related to *gaining* weight (e.g. Galli & Reel, 2009; MacKinnon et al., 2003). Males' desire to gain weight in the form of increased muscle mass has become a major area of focus for body image and eating disorder researchers in recent years. Researchers have found that, although men may develop some of the traditional disordered eating behaviors (e.g. restricting, purging) as they pursue weight loss and becoming leaner (similar to what women do), they may also face pressure to increase their body size and muscularity (Cafri et al., 2005; McCreary & Sasse, 2000). This concern with muscularity may lead to MD, a preoccupation with gaining muscle coupled with an irrational belief that they are too small and weak (Pope, Katz, & Hudson, 1993). These beliefs can result in behaviors such as compulsive exercise, body cleansing, low or no fat diets, and the use of anabolic substances to promote muscle growth (Lantz, Rhea, & Mayhew, 2001; Pope et al., 1993; Pope, Phillips, & Olivardia, 2000).

Although the prevalence of MD in athletes and nonathletes is still unknown, Lantz et al. (2001) suggested that athletes involved in sports predicated on muscular size, strength, and power might be particularly at risk. Not surprisingly, MD has been revealed as a problem in some competitive bodybuilders (e.g. Lantz, Rhea, & Cornelius, 2002; Mosley, 2009). Unfortunately, little research has been conducted on MD in more traditional sports. Muller, Dennis, Schneider, and Joyner (2004) compared a model of MD between male weight lifters/bodybuilders and male athletes in contact and noncontact sports. Their results showed that the lifters reported significantly more MD behaviors than the athletes, including use of supplements, avoidance of high fat foods, using a tape measure to assess their body, and thinking about using steroids. Baghurst and Lirgg (2009) similarly compared MD symptoms between natural bodybuilders, nonnatural bodybuilders, recreational weight lifters, and collegiate football players. Although the football players scored the lowest on nearly all of the dimensions of MD, they scored the highest on physique protection, and indicated the second highest use of pharmacological substances (behind nonnatural bodybuilders). The authors suspected that one reason for the lack of MD symptoms in the athletes may have been due to the questionnaire not being designed to measure a wide range of different populations. The finding of high scores on physique protection may indicate that the tight-fitting attire worn by the athletes causes some concern for the players, and that they were concerned with exhibiting the "look" of an intercollegiate athlete (Galli & Reel, 2009). Further research with varying samples of male athletes is clearly needed to fully understand the prevalence, predictors, and consequences of MD in the sport setting.

Sport type

As suggested earlier with regard to male athletes, the demands of the particular sport that athletes participate in may determine their eating disorder risk. Two meta-analytic reviews conducted several years ago revealed that athletes involved in aesthetic sports (e.g. dance, gymnastics, diving) are more likely to suffer from eating disorders than athletes in other sports (Hausenblas & Carron, 1999; Smolak et al., 2000). The results of other studies have revealed that athletes in endurance and weight class sports are also particularly at risk for eating disturbances (e.g. Lakin, Steen, & Oppliger, 1990; Weight & Noakes, 1987). The following sections summarize research findings related to each of the three high-risk sport types (i.e. aesthetic, endurance, weight class), as well as athletes in ball game sports.

Aesthetic sports

Because much of their success depends on their appearance in addition to their skill, athletes in aesthetic sports such as dance, figure skating, gymnastics, and diving have been suggested as a high-risk subgroup of athletes by eating disorder researchers. The results of numerous studies highlight the risks associated with competing in such sports. Gymnastics has been perhaps the most frequently studied aesthetic sport in relation to eating disorders. In one of the earliest studies documenting disordered eating in athletes, Rosen and Hough (1988) found that all 42 of the gymnasts in their study were dieting, and 62 percent reported using at least one pathogenic weight loss strategy. Over half (60 percent) of the collegiate gymnasts in Petrie's (1993) study were symptomatic for an eating disorder. The gymnasts in a study by de Bruin, Oudejans, and Bakker (2007) reported dieting more than a group of non-aesthetic sport participants. Interestingly, the nongymnasts were more negative about their body, indicating that the gymnasts' dieting was more a factor of performance and coach pressure than body image concern.

Figure skaters are another subgroup of athletes who have been identified as at risk for eating disorders. Similar to the de Bruin et al. (2007) study, Ziegler et al. (1998) found that the adolescent skaters in their study dieted despite having a relatively positive body image, and exhibited symptoms of the female athlete triad such as inadequate energy intake and delayed menarche. G. M. Taylor and Ste-Marie (2001) compared eating disorder symptomology between Canadian female figure skaters and a matched control group, and found that the skaters' profile on the Eating Disorder Inventory was more similar to an eating disorder population than the controls. In a study of female collegiate dancers, Reel, SooHoo, Jamieson, and Gill (2005) found that, although the dancers exhibited lower eating disorder symptomology than nondancers, they did report significant weight pressures related to their costume, the mirror, and performance. In one of the few eating disorder studies involving divers, Haase, Prapavessis, and Owens (2002) examined differences in disordered eating correlates between female team (i.e. soccer, volleyball, and netball) and aesthetic-based individual (i.e. diving and sport aerobics) athletes. The individual sport athletes exhibited higher social physique anxiety and bulimic behaviors than the team sport athletes.

Endurance sports

Concern for eating disorders in endurance athletes dates back nearly 25 years to Wheeler, Wall, Belcastro, Conger, and Cumming's (1986) study examining anorexic tendencies in high mileage runners. Although the runners did not show significantly more anorexic behaviors than nonrunners in the Wheeler et al. study, research in this area has continued. Because of the high training volume and pressure to be thin for endurance sports such as running, some researchers have suggested that individuals with an eating disorder may be attracted to participate in such sports (Beals, 2004). Although no researchers have been able to deduce whether it is endurance sports that cause eating disorders, or whether individuals with eating disorders are attracted to endurance sports, there is some evidence endurance athletes are at a heightened risk for eating disorders. In a study of body image disturbances in runners, Pasman and Thompson (1988) found that the runners had significantly greater eating disturbances than sedentary controls. More recently, Hulley and Hill (2001) investigated the presence of eating disorder symptoms in elite British female distance runners. The runners had a higher prevalence of eating disorders and related symptomology than would be expected in the general population, as 16 percent had an eating disorder. In a study of male cyclists, Riebl, Subudhi, Broker, Schenck, and Berning (2007) found that cyclists scored significantly higher on a measure of eating disorder symptomology than a control group. Interestingly, the cyclists demonstrated an inadequate knowledge of nutritional demand, thus placing them at an increased risk for unhealthy eating practices.

Weight class sports

Similar to endurance and aesthetic sport athletes, athletes in weight class sports have been identified as an at-risk subgroup. Males and females in sports such as wrestling and rowing are often compelled to engage in unhealthy weight loss behaviors to "make weight" for competition. Such weight cycling may have a detrimental effect on the physiological and psychological health of athletes (Brownell, Steen, Rodin, & Wilmore, 1992; Choma, Sforzo, & Keller, 1998). Those associated with the sport of wrestling have historically endorsed unhealthy practices such as excessive running, sitting in saunas, and wearing vapor-impermeable suits to drop down to a lower weight class for competition (Alderman, Landers, Carlson, & Scott, 2004). Although recent rule changes have helped to curb drastic weight loss measures in wrestling, athletes in other weight class sports are also at risk (Oppliger, Utter, Scott, Dick, & Klossner, 2006). Karlson (2001) found that female rowers exhibited significantly more restrained eating and diuretic use than either runners or controls. Professional horse jockeys have reported food avoidance, sauna use, laxative abuse, and even self-induced vomiting as a way to meet the low-weight demands of their sport (King & Mezey, 1987). Depalma, Koszewski, Case, and Barile (1993) explored the weight control practices of lightweight football players, and found that 74 percent reported binge eating, 66 percent had fasted, and 17 percent had used self-induced vomiting to control their weight.

Ball game sports

Although less attention has been paid to ball sport athletes, there is evidence of eating and body image disturbances in these athletes. Harris and Foltz (1999) found that, although the young women tennis players in their study exhibited normal eating patterns, they did feel that their weight was very important to them. As previously mentioned, males in power sports such as football may experience some weight-related pressure. Indeed, MacKinnon et al. (2003) found that lower body fat was related to more positive self-esteem in high school football players. Sundgot-Borgen and Torstveit (2004) identified eating disorders in 16 percent of elite ball game athletes, and called attention to the problem of eating disorders and the female athlete triad in female football players (Sungot-Borgen & Torstveit, 2007).

Competitive level

The level of competition has been suggested as an important determinant of eating disorder risk. Sundgot-Borgen (1994) suggested that, because of the pressures associated with high-level sports, elite athletes might be at greater risk than athletes who compete at lower levels. The meta-analytic findings of Smolak et al. (2000) supported Sundgot-Borgen's belief, as elite lean-sport athletes were identified as a particular at-risk group. Picard (1999) found that Division I athletes exhibited more signs of disordered eating than Division III athletes or nonathletes. In a study of disordered eating in Chinese and Japanese runners and gymnasts, a higher competitive level was associated with the development of disordered eating (Okano et al., 2005). Other studies, however, have not revealed higher level athletes to have a higher risk for eating disorders. Hausenblas and Carron (1999) suggested that perhaps athletes with eating disorders are "selected out" at elite levels, as they would not be able to meet the more strict performance demands of a higher competitive level. No significant differences were found between club and varsity athletes on body dissatisfaction and bulimic symptomology (Holm-Denoma, Scaringi, Gordon, Van Orden, & Joiner, 2009). Similarly, Ferrand and Brunet (2004) found no differences between elite, national, and regional level cyclists on eating attitudes. Equivocal findings with regard to eating disorder risk and competitive level suggest that other factors, such as gender, sport type, personality, and perceived weight pressure, might be more important to consider in future research.

Summary

Although more research is necessary to more accurately determine which athletes are at greatest risk for an eating disorder, present findings suggest that female athletes who compete in aesthetic, endurance, or weight class sports are a high-risk group for traditional eating disorders such as AN and BN. Males in power sports such as football may be at risk for symptoms of MD. Although conflicting findings exist with regard to the influence of competitive level on eating disorder risk, strength and conditioning coaches should be aware of the additional weight pressures that higher levels of competition pose.

Eating disorder triggers in the sport environment

Although it is informative to know which athletes warrant extra concern with regard to eating disorders, it is perhaps more critical to understand how and why athletes develop eating disorders. Researchers suggest that the etiology of eating disorders in athletes is complex, and cannot be completely explained by any single factor. Instead, a multitude of biological, sociodemographic, psychological, and environmental factors work together to influence athletes' risk for an eating disorder (Beals, 2004; Dosil, 2008). As researchers explore exactly how different factors interact to cause eating disorders in athletes, the sport environment has been revealed as particularly influential (Dosil, 2008). Weight pressures in the form of weight-related comments, weight requirements, or uniform concerns can trigger negative body image and/or the use of pathogenic weight control behaviors in athletes (see Galli & Reel, 2009; Galli, Reel, Petrie, Greenleaf, & Carter, 2011; Reel & Gill, 2001; Reel, SooHoo, Petrie, Greenleaf, & Carter, 2010).

Of all the significant others in an athlete's environment that may have a negative impact on their risk for an eating disorder, coaches perhaps have the most profound effect. As athletes' chief source of information, instruction, and motivation, coaches' actions can be a strong trigger for the development of eating disorders in athletes (Thompson & Sherman, 1999a). In an early study of coaches' influence on pathogenic weight control behaviors in female gymnasts, Rosen and Hough (1988) found that 75 percent of gymnasts who were told by their coaches that they were too heavy resorted to pathogenic behaviors such as fasting, laxative use, or vomiting. A more recent study by Kerr, Berman, and de Souza (2006) revealed that gymnasts who had received disparaging remarks regarding their body from coaches were significantly more likely than those athletes who did not hear such remarks to believe that they needed to lose weight, engage in pathogenic weight loss behaviors, and report having an eating disorder. Recent efforts to develop psychometrically valid tools to measure weight pressures in athletes have revealed coaches as one of the underlying dimensions of weight pressures in both male and female intercollegiate athletes (see Galli et al., 2011; Reel et al., 2010). Although the vast majority of coaches acknowledge that eating disorders are a problem for athletes (e.g. Vaughan, King, & Cottrell, 2004), it appears that few coaches recognize the emotional impact that weight- and body-related comments can have for athletes. The following quote from a study by Galli and Reel (2009) was made by a male collegiate golfer, and illustrates the unintended consequences of a seemingly harmless remark regarding his weight:

> I've had my coach say I'm a little bigger than I should be. He didn't call me fat or anything, but I've had coaches make plenty of jokes. I mean, it's not completely true – I just laugh and walk away. But you get home and you think, "Do I really [need to lose weight]?" (p. 101)

In addition to critical comments, coaches impact athletes' eating disorder risk in other ways. Perhaps the most damaging practice for athletes' body image weight behaviors is the use of group weigh-ins. For male and female athletes, group weigh-ins can turn body weight into a competition between teammates (Thompson & Sherman, 1999b). Athletes may resort to pathogenic behaviors in an effort to avoid being "called out" as the lightest or heaviest athlete on the team. As such, researchers and practitioners have argued strongly against the use of group weigh-ins for athletes (e.g. Reel & Galli, 2006; Thompson & Sherman, 1999a). Suggestions for alternative approaches to weight monitoring are offered later in this chapter.

A final possible eating disorder trigger in the sport environment is the team uniform. Athletes in aesthetic sports such as figure skating, gymnastics, or diving may experience weight pressure due to the revealing nature of their uniform. The uniform was the most often reported weight pressure in a sample of female collegiate swimmers (Reel & Gill, 2001). Similarly, Greenleaf (2004) found that 67.4 percent of the collegiate synchronized skaters in her sample believed that their uniform made them conscious of their bodily appearance. In a more recent study, Reel et al. (2010) found that 34.3 percent of a sample of female intercollegiate athletes from a variety of sports (including both lean and nonlean sports) reported pressure related to their team uniform. It should be noted that male athletes are not immune to uniform pressures. Galli et al. (2011) found that 84 percent of swimmers, 57 percent of track and field athletes, and 47 percent of football players reported that their team uniform made them aware of their build. Improvements in technology have led to uniforms for swimmers and track athletes that are tighter and more revealing than ever. Although performance may be enhanced by adopting the latest uniform style, coaches should take the aforementioned studies into consideration when considering uniform modifications for their team.

Applied implications

Identification of eating disorders among athletes

Athletes will likely be in denial about engaging in disordered eating behaviors. Therefore, it is unlikely they will come forward of their own volition to ask for help. It is important for strength and conditioning coaches and other sport professionals to recognize the signs and symptoms of eating disorders so that appropriate referrals can be made to get the athlete's support.

Warning signs for athletes with eating disorders

Individuals who work with athletes but who do not necessarily treat eating disorders on a regular basis can learn the psychological signs and physical symptoms to look for in their clients. For example, an athletic trainer may notice sudden weight gain or loss while working with injury rehabilitation with an athlete or a strength coach may detect a decrement of strength, endurance, or overall energy. Other physical signs could include but are not limited to: complaints about gastrointestinal distress (e.g. bloating, constipation), brittle nails and hair, intolerance to cold when temperature is not extreme, frequent musculoskeletal injuries (e.g. stress fractures), slow recovery and long healing time for wounds or injuries, and increased bruising. Athletes with eating disorders may also complain about sleep disturbances, especially insomnia. It is not uncommon for dental professionals to detect BN symptoms among their patients who exhibit tooth decay and gum erosion (DeBate, Shuman, & Tedesco, 2007; DeBate, Tedesco, & Kerschbaum, 2005).

Psychological signs include mood swings or irritability, depression, or social withdrawal (Beals, 2004). Coaches, teammates, family members, or athletic trainers may report that an athlete has become difficult to work with or is highly sensitive to criticism. Common behavioral signs may include avoiding social events that involve food, increased physical activity, using the bathroom immediately following a meal, and showing a preoccupation with food, calories, or body weight (e.g. an athlete may report weighing oneself several times a day). Athletic trainers or physicians may detect a noticeable drop in blood pressure or body temperature (C. J. Johnson, 2003). An extensive list of warning signs and symptoms can be found on the National Collegiate Athletic Association website (www.ncaa.org).

An individual who is working with an athlete who is displaying some or many of these warning signs can continue to build trust with that person. It may be helpful to keep questions general such as the following ones to avoid putting an athlete on the defensive:

- How are you feeling today?
- How has your energy been lately?
- How has your sleep been?
- Do you have any medical complaints?

Once the professional has collected adequate data he/she can decide whether he/she is the appropriate person to confront the athlete about disordered eating concerns. How to approach an athlete and provide appropriate treatment referrals will be discussed in the next section.

Referral strategies for sport professionals

With the variety of eating disorders and body image disturbances evident in the sport community, it is important to know how to manage these conditions once they have been identified. Management of disordered eating and eating disorders involves confronting the athlete, offering resources and referral options, communicating with the athlete's treatment team, and helping the athlete with the transition back into sport if they must cease participation during weight restoration and treatment (Thompson & Sherman, 2010).

To best assist an athlete with disordered eating or an eating disorder, it is important to develop an eating disorder resource network BEFORE any problems emerge. First, an individual specializing in eating disorder treatment or someone who has in-depth knowledge of community resources should be identified. At the middle and high school level, a school counselor may be the first contact. If no school counselor is available, the web should be checked for community resources (www.edreferral.com or www.nationaleatingdisorders.org are good places to start).

At the university level, a counseling center may offer some specialized resources and support. However, many of the general mental health facilities have begun to refer eating disorder clients to eating disorder specialists or treatment centers across the world. There are some teams and universities that have a multidisciplinary treatment team (physician, mental health professional, dietitian, strength coach) that handle almost all eating disorder cases for that particular school or team. Strength coaches serve as front-line detection of a problem and facilitate getting the athlete necessary support usually beginning with a physician referral for vital signs and medical monitoring (Joy, Wilson, & Varechok, 2003). An athlete will likely receive additional support from a dietitian, mental health professional, and a sport psychology consultant.

How to approach an athlete

It is important to be delicate when approaching an athlete who is suspected of having an eating disorder because she may be in strong denial and may react to others with heightened sensitivity. Sport professionals should understand that athletes have an intense fear of losing control of their unhealthy eating behaviors because of the perception that weight gain will occur. Upon initial confrontation, one should expect the athlete to deny identified behaviors and make every attempt to hide "symptoms" in the future.

Approaching the athlete with disordered eating concerns is a challenge in any setting. The potential for success will increase if the atmosphere is athlete-centered (i.e. if rapport is established between the sport professional and the athlete). Ohio State University's athletic department (Hill, 2001) issued one of the first eating disorder policies with the following suggestions for how to approach a student-athlete about disordered eating:

- The individual (e.g. coach, staff member) who has the best rapport with the student-athlete should arrange a private meeting.
- In a respectful tone, specific observations that led to concern should be mentioned, making sure to give the athlete time to respond.
- "I" statements should be chosen over "You" statements to avoid placing the athlete on the defensive. For example, saying "I've noticed you've been fatigued lately and I'm concerned about you" is preferable to "You need to eat and everything will be fine."
- Realize that there are no simple solutions (e.g. "Just eat something") to a complex problem. Suggesting simple solutions will only encourage the student-athlete to hide the behavior from you in the future.
- Implications of an eating disorder on team participation should not be discussed. Instead, professionals should affirm that the student-athlete's role on the team will not be jeopardized by an admission to a problem. The team may be the athlete's only diversion from her disordered eating. By eliminating this opportunity for social support, the athlete may dive into further pathology without the supervision of a coach or trainer.
- Regardless of whether the student-athlete responds with denial or hostility, it is important to encourage the athlete to meet with a professional for an assessment. Acknowledge that seeking outside help is often beneficial and is not a sign of weakness.

Due to the serious medical consequences associated with eating disorders, including death, it is essential that an athlete suffering from an eating disorder initiate treatment as soon as possible. Furthermore, there appears to be a relationship between the duration of the eating disorder prior to treatment and the length of time it takes for the patient to recover (Hall & Ostroff, 1999).

The decision whether an athlete should continue to compete during treatment is complex and should be considered on a case-by-case basis. Generally, the athlete should remain under medical supervision if she is even contemplating athletic participation (Thompson & Sherman, 2010). However, if the athlete agrees to seek treatment for disordered eating, there are benefits and risks involved with allowing her to compete.

If an athlete is removed from the team as a disciplinary measure, she may become further socially isolated, and will miss out on the potentially helpful guidance and supervision from coaches, athletic trainers, and teammates. Missing the team experience may contribute to generalized feelings of loss and rejection that may serve to aggravate disordered eating symptoms (Beals, 2004). Moreover, the team can provide an invaluable source of self-esteem, social support, and hopefulness for the disordered eating athlete (Thompson & Sherman, 2010).

Unfortunately, continuing to compete may jeopardize treatment if the athlete is not closely monitored. It is important for the athlete to realize that her health is more important than her athletic performance. By competing, the athlete may receive mixed messages from a coach who asks the athlete how she is feeling in practice and focuses on winning at all costs during competition. Therefore, the entire coaching staff and teammates need to be informed about the deleterious effects of giving inconsistent messages to the athlete. In addition, continuing to compete may distract the athlete from devoting full attention to treatment. She may use athletic participation as an excuse to engage in more intensive physical expenditures, deviate from prescribed nutritional plans, or miss psychotherapy appointments for a practice or game (Beals, 2004; Thompson & Sherman, 2010).

Ultimately, both the benefits and risks should be considered when negotiating whether an athlete will continue to compete. Similarly to an injured athlete, an athlete with an eating disorder should be encouraged to maintain her sport identity by attending all team meetings and practices (Dosil, 2008). Only under close medical supervision should an athlete engage in competitions. Coaches and other sport/health professionals should maintain close contact with medical personnel to ensure the athlete's continued safety.

The role of the strength and conditioning coach in eating disorder prevention

Just as coaches, including strength and conditioning coaches, can contribute to the development of eating disorders in athletes, they can also take measures to prevent eating disorders from occurring. As discussed previously in this chapter, disparaging remarks or jokes regarding an athlete's body weight, shape, and size should *never* occur. Further, strength and conditioning coaches should refrain from publicly comparing athletes' bodies, or applying sport-specific body stereotypes to athletes. For example, not all distance runners should be expected to be ultra-thin, and not all offensive linesmen should be expected to weigh 300 pounds. Not only can body-related comments embarrass the athlete, they may signal to other athletes on the team that it is acceptable to make similar comments to their teammates in the locker room or on the playing field. Coaches may choose to create a "No Tolerance" policy with regard to body-related talk, such that athletes who engage in banter regarding a teammate's body will be punished. If there is an issue with an athlete's weight, coaches should address their concerns privately and without ridicule.

Strength and conditioning coaches may be charged with monitoring athletes' weight. As discussed previously in this chapter, the manner in which weigh-ins are conducted can have consequences for athletes' body esteem and weight change behaviors. Weigh-ins and body composition assessments should be conducted in private, and athletes should be made readily aware of the purpose of such measures (Reimers, 2000). Although weigh-ins can be important for monitoring athletes' hydration and caloric intake, athletes may need these reasons explained to them to understand the benefits of such measurements. Imposing weight and body fat standards without justification may promote dangerous weight change behaviors such as fasting, overeating, or overexercise. Finally, weight and body fat standards should be created on an athlete-to-athlete basis rather than based upon generic standards for a given sport. Strength and conditioning coaches should monitor athletes carefully to determine the optimal body weight and composition for their health and performance. As mentioned previously, all athletes are not created equal, and a body weight that works for one athlete will not necessarily work, or even be possible, for another. Athletes' health should always take precedent when making decisions regarding body standards.

For athletes that are attempting to lose or gain weight, the strength and conditioning coach should provide them with the resources necessary to manage their weight healthfully and effectively (Reimers, 2000). Athletes who are not provided with assistance in the weight management process may resort to unhealthy and dangerous dieting practices in an effort to lose or gain weight as quickly as possible. Although such practices aren't in themselves indicative of an eating disorder, they may lead to an eating disorder in the future (Fairburn, Cooper, Doll, & Davies, 2005). Ideally, athletes and teams will have access to a Registered Dietitian (RD) trained in sports nutrition. The RD should be the go-to person for any diet or dietary supplement question that athletes have. In the absence of such an individual, strength and conditioning coaches should educate athletes on basic principles of safe and effective dieting. However, it should never be the role of the strength and conditioning coach to prescribe specific diets to athletes, as this is usually outside the realm of their training.

Promoting a healthful training environment

The efforts of the strength and conditioning coach should extend beyond prevention and toward promoting an environment conducive to healthy living and sport participation. First, as athletes' primary source of training information, it is imperative that volume and intensity be closely monitored to prevent overtraining. Most athletes (as people with eating disorders) are perfectionists, and often subscribe to the theory that "more is better" (Thompson & Sherman, 1999b). As such, coaches should ensure that athletes are not completing additional unauthorized training outside of regularly scheduled lifting and conditioning sessions. Athletes should be assured that rest is indeed an integral part of their training. Second, allow athletes some autonomy in selecting their workouts. For example, if two exercises such as the deadlift and squat will both help athletes achieve their strength and conditioning goals, then allowing them to select their preference may enhance their sense of autonomy. Giving athletes more choice in the structure of their workouts will enhance motivation, and help prevent staleness and burnout. Finally, be proactive by providing athletes with ideas for healthy and affordable snacks and recipes on a weekly or monthly basis. Coaches might even enlist the assistance of a trained sports dietitian for this project. Recipes can be e-mailed or texted to athletes so as to not waste any time in the gym. By emphasizing the importance of a balanced and wholesome diet, athletes are more likely to make healthy eating a priority.

Future research directions

Alternative research designs and a focus on diverse athletic populations are necessary to further advance coaches' understanding of eating disorders in athletes. Complex models of eating disorder development, encompassing a wide range of psychosocial, environmental, and biological variables (e.g. Petrie et al., 2007), should be tested on diverse samples of athletes. The testing and refinement of sport-specific eating disorder models will further elucidate the nature of eating disorders in athletes, and inform the practice of coaches. Although such models can be tested through cross-sectional designs, it is time to implement more longitudinal studies wherein the dynamic process of eating disorder development is examined over the course of months or years.

Just as model testing will provide a clearer picture of how difference variables interact to increase or decrease athletes' risk for developing an eating disorder, qualitative studies can increase our understanding of athletes' eating disorder experiences. Although the use of qualitative research designs in eating disorder research is not new, few studies have focused in depth on athletes that currently have or formerly had an eating disorder. Giving a voice to athletes who have actually experienced an eating disorder can provide a powerful perspective for researchers and coaches. The use of group interviews and case studies can provide additional information not obtainable through "paper-and-pencil" measures.

In addition to athletes who have actually suffered an eating disorder, other understudied populations include male, ethnic minority female, disabled, senior, and retired athletes. Virtually everything that is known about eating disorders in athletes is specific to able-bodied young adult White females who participate in aesthetic or endurance sports at an elite level. Researchers would be remiss to ignore the experiences of the sport participants who do not fit the "typical" profile of someone with an eating disorder. Because little is known about body image and eating disorders in diverse populations, perhaps qualitative methods should first be employed to gain an in-depth understanding of the experiences of these individuals. The results of qualitative studies could be used to create conceptual models of eating disorder development, which could then be quantitatively tested.

Discussion questions

1. Which athletes may be more at risk for developing eating disorders? What factors exist within the sport environment that may contribute to an athlete feeling the pressure to lose, gain, or maintain an unhealthy weight?
2. How does the team uniform influence athletes' body image?
3. What are some key warning signs for athletes with eating disorders?
4. How should a sport professional approach an athlete who is showing signs of an eating disorder?
5. How can strength and conditioning coaches promote healthful behaviors and prevent eating disorders?

References

Ackard, D. M., Fulkerson, J. A., & Neumark-Sztainer, D. (2007). Prevalence and utility of DSM-IV eating disorder diagnostic criteria among youth. *International Journal of Eating Disorders*, 40, 409–417.

Alderman, B. L., Landers, D. M., Carlson, J., & Scott, J. R. (2004). Factors related to rapid weight loss practices among international-style wrestlers. *Medicine & Science in Sports & Exercise*, 36, 249–252.

American Psychiatric Association. (2000a). *Diagnostic statistical manual of mental disorders* (4th ed., text rev.). Washington, DC: Author.

American Psychiatric Association. (2000b). *Practice guideline for the treatment of patients with eating disorders*. Arlington, VA: Author.

Baghurst, T., & Lirgg, C. (2009). Characteristics of muscle dysmorphia in male football, weight training, and competitive natural and non-natural bodybuilding samples. *Body Image*, 6, 221–227.

Baum, A. (2006). Eating disorders in the male athlete. *Sports Medicine*, 36, 1–6.

Beals, K. A. (2004). *Disordered eating among athletes: A comprehensive guide for health professionals*. Champaign, IL: Human Kinetics.

Beals, K. A., Brey, R. A., & Gonyou, J. B. (1999). Understanding the female athlete triad: Eating disorders, amenorrhea, and osteoporosis. *Journal of School Health*, 69, 337–340.

Brownell, K. D., Steen, S. N., Rodin, J., & Wilmore, J. H. (1992). Weight cycling in athletes: Effects on behavior, physiology, and health. In K. D. Brownell, J. Rodin, & J. H. Wilmore (Eds.), *Eating, body weight, and performance in athletes: Disorders of modern society* (pp. 159–171). Philadelphia, PA: Lea & Febiger.

Cafri, G., Thompson, J. K., Ricciardelli, L., McCabe, M., Smolak, L., & Yesalis, C. (2005). Pursuit of the muscular ideal: Physical and psychological consequences and putative risk factors. *Clinical Psychology Review*, 25, 215–239.

Carter, J. E., & Rudd, N. A. (2005). Disordered eating assessment for college student-athletes. *Women in Sport and Physical Activity Journal*, 14, 62–75.

Casiero, D., & Frishman, W. H. (2006). Cardiovascular complications of eating disorders. *Cardiology in Review, 14*, 227–231.

Choma, C. W., Sforzo, G. A., & Keller, B. A. (1998). Impact of rapid weight loss on cognitive function in collegiate wrestlers. *Medicine & Science in Sports & Exercise, 30*, 746–749.

DeBate, R., Shuman, D., & Tedesco, L. A. (2007). Eating disorders in the oral health curriculum. *Journal of Dental Education, 71*, 655–663.

DeBate, R., Tedesco, L. A., & Kerschbaum, W. E. (2005). Knowledge of oral and physical manifestations of anorexia and bulimia nervosa among dentists and dental hygienists. *Journal of Dental Education, 69*, 346–354.

de Bruin, A. P., Oudejans, R. D., & Bakker, F. C. (2007). Dieting and body image in aesthetic sports: A comparison of Dutch female gymnasts and non-aesthetic sport participants. *Psychology of Sport and Exercise, 8*, 507–520.

Depalma, M. T., Koszewski, W. M., Case, J. G., & Barile, R. J. (1993). Weight control practices of lightweight football players. *Medicine & Science in Sports & Exercise, 25*, 694–701.

DiBartolo, P. M., & Shaffer, C. (2002). A comparison of female college athletes and non-athletes: Eating disorder symptomatology and psychological well-being. *Journal of Sport & Exercise Psychology, 24*, 33–41.

Dosil, J. (2008). *Eating disorders in athletes.* Hoboken, NJ: Wiley.

Engel, S. G., Johnson, C., Powers, P. S., Crosby, R. D., Wonderlich, S. A., Wittrock, D. A., & Mitchell, J. E. (2003). Predictors of disordered eating in a sample of elite Division I college athletes. *Eating Behaviors, 4*, 333–343.

Fairburn, C. G., Cooper, Z., Doll, H. A., & Davies, B. A. (2005). Identifying dieters who will develop an eating disorder: A prospective, population-based study. *The American Journal of Psychiatry, 162*, 2249–2255.

Ferrand, C., & Brunet, E. (2004). Perfectionism and risk for disordered eating among young French male cyclists of high performance. *Perceptual and Motor Skills, 99*, 959–967.

Fichter, M. M., & Quadflieg, N. (1997). Six-year course of bulimia nervosa. *International Journal of Eating Disorders, 22*, 361–384.

Galli, N., & Reel, J. J. (2009). Adonis or Hephaestus? Exploring body image in male athletes. *Psychology of Men & Masculinity, 10*, 95–108.

Galli, N., Reel, J. J., Petrie, T. P., Greenleaf, C., & Carter, J. (2011). Preliminary development and validation of the weight pressures in sport scale for male athletes. *Journal of Sport Behavior, 34*, 47–68.

Glazer, J. L. (2008). Eating disorders among male athletes. *Current Sports Medicine Reports, 7*, 332–337.

Greenleaf, C. (2004). Weight pressure and social physique anxiety among collegiate synchronized skaters. *Journal of Sport Behavior, 27*, 260–276.

Greenleaf, C., Petrie, T. A., Carter, J., & Reel, J. J. (2009). Female collegiate athletes: Prevalence of eating disorders and disordered eating behaviors. *Journal of American College Health, 57*, 489–496.

Haase, A. M., Prapavessis, H., & Owens, R. G. (2002). Perfectionism, social physique anxiety and disordered eating: A comparison of male and female elite athletes. *Psychology of Sport and Exercise, 3*, 209–222.

Hall, L., & Ostroff, M. (1999). *Anorexia nervosa: A guide to recovery.* Carlsbad, CA: Gurze.

Harris, M. B., & Foltz, S. (1999). Attitudes toward weight and eating in young women tennis players, their parents and their coaches. *Eating Disorders: The Journal of Treatment and Prevention, 7*, 191–205.

Hausenblas, H. A., & Carron, A. V. (1999). Eating disorder indices and athletes: An integration. *Journal of Sport & Exercise Psychology, 21*, 230–258.

Herzog, D. B., Nussbaum, K. M., & Marmor, A. K. (1996). Comorbidity and outcome in eating disorders. *Psychiatry Clinical North America, 19*, 843–859.

Hill, L. (2001). The Ohio State University Department of Athletics eating disorder policy 2001 [Online]. Retrieved from http://ehe.osu.edu/sportsnut/policy/ED.pdf

Hoch, A. Z., Pajewski, N. M., Moraski, L., Carrera, G. F., Wilson, C. R., Hoffmann, R. G., … Gutterman, D. D. (2009). Prevalence of the female athlete triad in high school athletes and sedentary students. *Clinical Journal of Sport Medicine, 19*, 421–424.

Holm-Denoma, J. M., Scaringi, V., Gordon, K. H., Van Orden, K. A., & Joiner, T. E., Jr. (2009). Eating disorder symptoms among undergraduate varsity athletes, club athletes, independent exercisers, and nonexercisers. *International Journal of Eating Disorders, 42*, 47–53.

Hulley, A. J., & Hill, A. J. (2001). Eating disorders and health in elite women distance runners. *International Journal of Eating Disorders, 30*, 312–317.

Johnson, C., Powers, P. S., & Dick, R. (1999). Athletes and eating disorders: The National Collegiate Athletic Association Study. *International Journal of Eating Disorders, 26*, 179–188.

Johnson, C. J. (2003). Current challenges in recognizing and treating eating disorders. *Minnesota Medicine, 86*, 34–39.

Joy, E. A., Wilson, C., & Varochok, S. (2003). The multidisciplinary team approach to the outpatient treatment of disordered eating. *Current Sports Medicine Reports, 2*, 331–336.

Karlson, K. A. (2001). Prevalence of eating disordered behavior in collegiate lightweight women rowers and distance runners. *Clinical Journal of Sport Medicine, 11*, 32–37.

Keel, P. K., Dorer, D. J., Eddy, K. T., Franko, D., Charatan, D. L., & Herzog, D. B. (2003). Predictors of mortality in eating disorders. *Archives of General Psychiatry, 60*, 170–183.

Kerr, G., Berman, E., & de Souza, M. J. (2006). Disordered eating in women's gymnastics: Perspectives of athletes, coaches, parents, and judges. *Journal of Applied Sport Psychology, 18*, 28–43.

King, M. B., & Mezey, G. (1987). Eating behaviour of male racing jockeys. *Psychological Medicine: A Journal of Research in Psychiatry and the Allied Sciences, 17*, 249–253.

Kjelsas, E., Bjornstrom, C., & Gotestam, K. G. (2004). Prevalence of eating disorders in female and male adolescents (14–15 years). *Eating Behavior, 5*, 13–25.

Lakin, J. A., Steen, S. N., & Oppliger, R. A. (1990). Eating behaviors, weight loss methods, and nutrition practices among high school wrestlers. *Journal of Community Health Nursing, 7*, 223.

Lantz, C. D., Rhea, D. J., & Cornelius, A. E. (2002). Muscle dysmorphia in elite-level power lifters and bodybuilders: A test of differences within a conceptual model. *Journal of Strength & Conditioning Research, 16*, 649–655.

Lantz, C. D., Rhea, D. J., & Mayhew, J. L. (2001). The drive for size: A psycho-behavioral model of muscle dysmorphia. *International Sports Journal, 5*, 71–86.

MacKinnon, D. P., Goldberg, L., Cheong, J., Elliot, D., Clarke, G., & Moe, E. (2003). Male body esteem and physical measurements: Do leaner, or stronger, high school football players have a more positive body image? *Journal of Sport & Exercise Psychology, 25*, 307–322.

Martinsen, M. (2010). Dieting to win or to be thin? A study of dieting and disordered eating among adolescent elite athletes and non-athlete controls. *British Journal of Sports Medicine, 44*, 70–76.

McCreary, D. R., & Sasse, D. K. (2000). An exploration of the drive for muscularity in adolescent boys and girls. *Journal of American College Health, 48*, 297.

McNulty, P. A. (1997). Prevalence and contributing factors of eating disorder behaviors in active duty men. *Military Medicine, 162*, 753–758.

Mitchell, J. E., & Peterson, C. B. (Eds.). (2005). *Assessment of eating disorders*. New York, NY: Guilford Press.

Mosley, P. E. (2009). Bigorexia: Bodybuilding and muscle dysmorphia. *European Eating Disorders Review, 17*, 191–198.

Muller, S. M., Dennis, D. L., Schneider, S. R., & Joyner, R. L. (2004). Muscle dysmorphia among selected male college athletes: An examination of the Lantz, Rhea, and Mayhew model. *International Sports Journal, 8*, 119–124.

Nattiv, A., Loucks, A. B., Manore, M. M., Sanborn, C. F., Sundgot-Borgen, J., & Warren, M. P. (2007). American College of Sports Medicine position stand: The female athlete triad. *Medicine & Science in Sports & Exercise, 39*, 1867–1882.

Okano, G., Holmes, R. A., Mu, Z., Yang, P., Lin, Z., & Nakai, Y. (2005). Disordered eating in Japanese and Chinese female runners, rhythmic gymnasts and gymnasts. *International Journal of Sports Medicine, 26*, 486–491.

Oppliger, R. A., Utter, A. C., Scott, J. R., Dick, R. W., & Klossner, D. (2006). NCAA rule change improves weight loss among national championship wrestlers. *Medicine & Science in Sports & Exercise, 38*, 963–970.

Owens, T. E., Allen, M. D., & Spangler, D. L. (2010). A fMRI study of self-reflection about body image: Sex differences. *Personality and Individual Differences, 48*, 849–854.

Pasman, L., & Thompson, J. K. (1988). Body image and eating disturbance in obligatory runners, obligatory weightlifters, and sedentary individuals. *International Journal of Eating Disorders, 7*, 759–769.

Petrie, T. A. (1993). Disordered eating in female collegiate gymnasts: Prevalence and personality/attitudinal correlates. *Journal of Sport & Exercise Psychology, 15*, 424–436.

Petrie, T. A. (1996). Differences between male and female college lean sport athletes, nonlean sport athletes, and nonathletes on behavioral and psychological indices of eating disorders. *Journal of Applied Sport Psychology, 8*, 218–230.

Petrie, T. A., Greenleaf, C., Carter, J. E., & Reel, J. J. (2007). Psychosocial correlates of disordered eating among male collegiate athletes. *Journal of Clinical Sport Psychology, 1*, 340–357.

Petrie, T. A., Greenleaf, C., Reel, J., & Carter, J. (2008). Prevalence of eating disorders and disordered eating behaviors among male collegiate athletes. *Psychology of Men & Masculinity, 9*, 267–277.

Petrie, T. A., & McFarland, M. (2009). Men and muscles: The increasing objectification of the male body. In J. J. Reel, & K. A. Beals (Eds.), *Hidden faces of eating disorders and body image*. Reston, VA: AAHPERD/NAGWS.

Picard, C. L. (1999). The level of competition as a factor for the development of eating disorders in female collegiate athletes. *Journal of Youth and Adolescence, 28*, 583–594.

Pinheiro, A., Thornton, L. M., Plotonicov, K. H., Tozzi, F., Klump, K. L., Berrettini, W. H., … Bulik, C. M. (2007). Patterns of menstrual disturbances in eating disorders. *International Journal of Eating Disorders, 40*, 424–434.

Pope, H. G., Katz, D. L., & Hudson, J. I. (1993). Anorexia nervosa and "reverse anorexia" among 108 male bodybuilders. *Comprehensive Psychiatry, 34*, 406–409.

Pope, H. G., Phillips, K. A., & Olivardia, R. (2000). *The Adonis complex*. New York: Touchstone.

Reel, J. J., Ashcraft, C., Lacy, R., Bucciere, R. A., SooHoo, S., Richards, D., & Mihalopoulos, N. (2011). "Full of Ourselves PLUS": Lessons learned when implementing an eating disorder and obesity prevention program. *Journal of Sport Psychology in Action, 3*, 20–28.

Reel, J.J., & Galli, N. (2006). Should coaches be the "weight" police? *JOPERD, 6–7*, 85.

Reel, J. J., & Gill, D. L. (1998). Weight concerns and disordered eating attitudes among male and female college cheerleaders. *Women in Sport and Physical Activity Journal, 7*, 79–94.

Reel, J. J., & Gill, D. L. (2001). Slim enough to swim? Weight pressures for competitive swimmers and coaching implications [Electronic version]. *Sport Journal, 4*. Retrieved from http://www.thesportjournal.org/article/slim-enough-swim-weight-pressures-competitive-swimmers-and-coaching-implications

Reel, J. J., SooHoo, S., Doetsch, H., Carter, J. E., & Petrie, T. A. (2007). The female athlete triad: Is the triad a problem among Division I female athletes? *Journal of Clinical Sport Psychology, 1*, 358–370.

Reel, J. J., SooHoo, S., Jamieson, K. M., & Gill, D. L. (2005). Femininity to the extreme: Body image concerns among college female dancers. *Women in Sport and Physical Activity Journal, 14*, 39–51.

Reel, J. J., SooHoo, S., Petrie, T. A., Greenleaf, C., & Carter, J. E. (2010). Slimming down for sport: Developing a weight pressures in sport measure for female athletes. *Journal of Clinical Sport Psychology, 4*, 99–111.

Reimers, K. (2000). Eating disorders and obesity. In T. R. Baechle, & R. W. Earle (Eds.), *Essentials of strength and conditioning* (2nd ed., pp. 259–271). Champaign, IL: Human Kinetics.

Riebl, S. K., Subudhi, A. W., Broker, J. P., Schenck, K., & Berning, J. R. (2007). The prevalence of subclinical eating disorders among male cyclists. *Journal of the American Dietetic Association, 107*, 1214–1217.

Rosen, L. W., & Hough, D. O. (1988). Pathogenic weight-control behaviors of female college gymnasts. *Physician & Sportsmedicine, 16*, 140–143, 146.

Ryan, J. (1995). *Little girls in pretty boxes: The making and breaking of elite gymnasts and figure skaters.* New York: Warner.

Smolak, L., Murnen, S. K., & Ruble, A. E. (2000). Female athletes and eating problems: A meta-analysis. *International Journal of Eating Disorders, 27*, 371–380.

Sundgot-Borgen, J. (1994). Risk and trigger factors for the development of eating disorders in female elite athletes. *Medicine & Science in Sports & Exercise, 26*, 414–419.

Sundgot-Borgen, J., & Torstveit, M. K. (2004). Prevalence of eating disorders in elite athletes is higher than in the general population. *Clinical Journal of Sport Medicine, 14*, 25–32.

Sundgot-Borgen, J., & Torstveit, M. K. (2007). The female football player, disordered eating, menstrual function and bone health. *British Journal of Sports Medicine, 41*, i68–i72.

Sykora, C., Grilo, C. M., Wilfley, D. E., & Brownell, K. D. (1993). Eating, weight, and dieting disturbances in male and female lightweight and heavyweight rowers. *International Journal of Eating Disorders, 14*, 203–211.

Taylor, G. M., & Ste-Marie, D. M. (2001). Eating disorders symptoms in Canadian female pair and dance figure skaters. *International Journal of Sport Psychology, 32*, 21–28.

Taylor, J. Y., Caldwell, C. H., Baser, R. E., Faison, N., & Jackson, J. S. (2007). Prevalence of eating disorders among Blacks in the national survey of American life. *International Journal of Eating Disorders, 40*, S10–S14.

Thompson, R. A., & Sherman, R. T. (1999a). Athletes, athletic performance, and eating disorders: Healthier alternatives. *Journal of Social Issues, 55*, 317–337.

Thompson, R. A., & Sherman, R. T. (1999b). "Good athlete" traits and characteristics of anorexia nervosa: Are they similar? *Eating Disorders: The Journal of Treatment & Prevention, 7*, 181–190.

Thompson, R. A., & Sherman, R. T. (2010). *Eating disorders in sport.* New York: Routledge.

Vaughan, J. L., King, K. A., & Cottrell, R. R. (2004). Collegiate athletic trainers' confidence in helping female athletes with eating disorders. *Journal of Athletic Training, 39*, 71–76.

Weight, L. M., & Noakes, T. D. (1987). Is running an analog of anorexia? A survey of the incidence of eating disorders in female distance runners. *Medicine & Science in Sports & Exercise, 19*, 213–217.

Wheeler, G. D., Wall, S. R., Belcastro, A. N., Conger, P., & Cumming, D. C. (1986). Are anorexic tendencies prevalent in the habitual runner? *British Journal of Sports Medicine, 20*, 77–81.

Wilkins, J. A., & Boland, F. J. (1991). A comparison of male and female university athletes and nonathletes on eating disorder indices. *Journal of Sport Behavior, 14*, 129–143.

Ye Vian, Q., Bee Koon, P., Lai Oon, N., & Mohd Ismail, N. (2009). The female athlete triad among elite Malaysian athletes: Prevalence and associated factors. *Asia Pacific Journal of Clinical Nutrition, 18*, 200–208.

Ziegler, P. J., Khoo, C. S., Sherr, B., Nelson, J. A., Larson, W. M., & Drewnowski, A. (1998). Body image and dieting behaviors among elite figure skaters. *International Journal of Eating Disorders, 24*, 421–427.

Zucker, N. L., Losh, M., Bulik, C. M., LaBar, K. S., & Pelphrey, K. A. (2007). Anorexia nervosa and autism spectrum disorders: Guided investigation of social cognitive endophenotypes. *Psychological Bulletin, 133*, 976–1006.

9

THE MISUSE OF ANABOLIC–ANDROGENIC STEROIDS

Susan H. Backhouse

CARNEGIE RESEARCH INSTITUTE, LEEDS METROPOLITAN UNIVERSITY, UK

Anabolic–androgenic steroids (AAS)[1] are substances related to the male hormone testosterone. Although their use is legitimised for medical reasons, some individuals self-administer these substances to enhance performance or improve physique. Accordingly, more has been written about AAS than almost any other performance- or image-enhancing substance of its time and the public's recognition of illegal AAS use for performance gains dates back to the 1988 Seoul Olympics when Canadian sprinter Ben Johnson tested positive for Stanozolol. Over two decades later, androgens remain the most commonly used ergogenic aid in organised sport. Specifically, in 2008, anabolic agents contributed 59 per cent of all reported adverse analytical findings (World Anti-Doping Agency [WADA], 2008), with Nandrolone and Stanozolol the most common drugs within this class. This figure was significantly higher than the next prohibited drugs class, Cannabinoids, which comprised 9 per cent of adverse findings. Therefore, the misuse of AAS continues despite the tacit acceptance, in most quarters, of a relationship between misuse and negative health reactions (Kanayama, Hudson, & Pope, 2010). Thus, the self-administration of AAS remains a cosmopolitan issue as its use spreads across continents.

Most of the medical case reports and cross-sectional research studies published in relation to AAS use involve bodybuilders. Indeed, the two regimes have shared a long historical association. This emphasis on bodybuilders suggests individuals interested in augmenting muscular development and strength are more likely to misuse AAS than any other population group and estimate figures support this assertion. Moreover, bodybuilders and associated strength and power athletes have been found to use AAS in ways (e.g. higher doses, longer duration, administering an array of drugs) that put them at greater risk for a range of negative health reactions (Friedl, 2000). Therefore, this chapter will seek to draw together the body of knowledge available in relation to the: (a) evolution and incidence of AAS use, (b) motives for AAS use and attitudes towards illicit AAS use, (c) portrait of AAS users,

(d) effects of non-prescribed AAS use, (e) potential for psychological and physical dependency, and (f) treatment and prevention. Throughout, the focus will be on examining findings drawn from bodybuilding sub-cultures. It is worth pointing out at this stage that the aim of this chapter is not to support, condone or argue against AAS use but to provide a balanced account of the literature.

Introduction to the AAS family of hormones

Synthetically derived, AAS are variants of the naturally occurring male hormone, testosterone. Testosterone is a steroid hormone produced by various tissues in the human body, although it is mainly the product of the endocrine glands (e.g. testes, ovaries, adrenal glands). It promotes the development and maintenance of secondary male sexual characteristics (androgenic) and promotes muscular growth (anabolic) (Thiblin & Petersson, 2005). Thus, the properties of the synthetic drug give rise to its name – AAS. AAS are legally prescribed to treat a number of medical conditions, including those which result in steroid hormone deficiency (i.e. delayed puberty) and lean muscle mass loss (i.e. HIV and cancer). In the United Kingdom, AAS are Class C controlled drugs which means it is legal to possess and to consume AAS, but illegal to import, sell or supply them without a licence. In contrast, their possession is a criminal offence in the United States and Australia, and the British Government has been considering changing the law to this effect for some time (Korkia, 1994).

In light of their anabolic effects, these substances are sometimes abused in the quest for enhanced sporting performance or physical appearance, and users can develop complicated polydrug regimes. Typically, users engage in two common patterns of AAS use: 'cycling' and 'stacking'. In order to achieve the effect desired, strict cycling regimes are adhered to which involve intermittent use of AAS over a period of weeks or months, followed by a holiday period. Generally, supraphysiological doses of AAS are taken for 4–18 weeks followed by a drug-free phase approximating 1–12 months (Congeni & Miller, 2002). In addition, 'pyramiding' is frequently undertaken whereby users taper off at the end of a stacking cycle to reduce side effects and withdrawal symptoms.

Stacking involves multi-drug use in progressively increasing doses over a short period of time and is adopted in order to maximise the effectiveness of each of the drugs administered. On average, AAS users have been noted to administer five different synthetic drugs at the same time (Sturmi & Diorio, 1998). However, little scientific evidence exists to support the concept of stacking or cycling (Basaria, 2010; Sturmi & Diorio, 1998). As a rule, AAS are consumed orally or administered via intra-muscular injection, although, in recent times, gels and creams have become the administration route of choice by elite athletes as they attempt to circumvent doping controls (Basaria, 2010). Regardless of the delivery mechanism, AAS users tend to exceed the typical medical doses by 40–100 or more times (Sturmi & Diorio, 1998).

Evolution and incidence of AAS use

The culture of consuming pharmacologically active substances to improve performance dates back centuries, with the ancient Greeks purported to use testicular extracts to bolster courage or libido (Kochakian, 1990). One thousand years later, French physiologist Charles E. Brown-Sequard (1889) reported the first public claims of the effects of AAS in the *Lancet*. He described the anabolic effect of dog and guinea pig testicular extract on himself, when injected subcutaneously, and concluded that his strength and intellect increased and that his constipation was relieved. Since this time, synthetic variants of testosterone in the form of AAS have been developed, and in the late 1930s and early 1940s, they were introduced into the medical community as possible therapeutic agents. Allegedly, Hitler's troops were administered AAS in order to make them more aggressive in battle (Wade, 1972) and these powerful doping agents were soon discovered by elite athletes as reports of increased muscle mass were cascaded (Wade, 1972). It follows that the first confirmed report of the non-medical use of AAS was in preparation for the 1954 Vienna weightlifting championships. It was during this competition that the Soviet Union scooped numerous gold medals and the team doctor revealed their use of testosterone in an attempt to enhance performance (Yesalis, Courson, & Wright, 1993). Subsequently, the US team doctor introduced the drugs to athletes in the United States and their penetration has been witnessed since this time (Pederson & Wichstrom, 2001).

Nevertheless, drug-testing procedures for AAS were not introduced into the Olympics until the 1976 Montreal Games. Its misuse was further propagated as AAS experimentation was recounted and ergogenic effects documented through the 'underground press', such as the late Dan Duchaine's (US bodybuilder) *Underground Steroid Handbook* (1989). Contrastingly, such 'lived' accounts were at odds with the prestigious and influential American College of Sports Medicine's (ACSM, 1977) official position stand, which stated that 'there is no conclusive scientific evidence that extremely large doses of anabolic-androgenic steroids either aid or hinder athletic performance'. However, a decade later, this official line was reversed and the position stand stated that in the presence of an adequate diet AAS can contribute to increases in body weight, often in the lean mass compartment (ACSM, 1987). Kanayama, Hudson, et al.'s (2010) assertion that the failure of the science and medicine community to recognise the efficacy of AAS use could explain the reluctance of AAS users to engage with medical professionals in relation to their AAS use (Dawson, 2001).

Uncovering a secret national system of athlete hormone doping in East Germany initially brought the systemic and planned nature of AAS abuse in sport into public consciousness following the publication of top secret doctoral theses and scientific reports by eminent professors and physicians (Werner & Berendonk, 1997). The extent of the systematic doping practices of several thousand East German athletes between 1965 and 1989 (Franke & Berendonk, 1997) was detailed during trials in Germany of doctors and officials who perpetrated this programme and some shocking declarations emerged. While the former athletes of this system provided testimonies of the performance gains, they also noted the acute and chronic side effects they experienced as a consequence of AAS use. Furthermore, the unforeseen effect of AAS use during their athletic careers on their offspring (e.g. chronic ailments directly related to the use of illegal medications) was also noted as women and adolescent girls were heavily targeted for androgen treatment during the doping regime.

Generally, when we hear about AAS, it is because a professional sportsperson has tested positive for its use, and the 1990s saw the release of the Dubin report (Dubin, 1990). This publication documented the findings of a Canadian Government-led investigation which highlighted the pervasive use of AAS to enhance sports performance was acknowledged across sport types, sporting levels and age groups. Similarly, the 409-page Mitchell (2007) report on US baseball named 85 players in its performance-enhancing drug use roll call and the Bay Area Laboratory Cooperative (BALCO) designer steroid scandal dominated global news headlines because of the number of international athletes and support staff involved (Fainaru-Wada & Williams, 2006). Yet, athletes involved in amateur and recreational sports and exercise activities outnumber the figure of top-level athletes in the abuse of AAS (American Medical Association [AMA], 1990) and doping practices are no longer the province of elite athletes. For this reason, it is claimed that AAS use is becoming a public health concern (British Medical Association [BMA], 2002; Kanayama, Hudson, et al., 2010).

Today, recreational users are the most rapidly expanding user group and this could be due to the fact that AAS use facilitates a short cut to improved functionality and aesthetic profile (Skarberg, Nyberg, & Engstrom, 2008). To illustrate, the Swedish anti-doping hotline received 40,000 AAS-related calls from 1993 to 2000 and noted that the largest group (30 per cent) were callers connected with gyms (Eklof, Thurelius, Garle, Rane, & Sjoqvist, 2003). In short, AAS users represent a wider population group who simply want to look good and be 'fit for work' – they can include your local fireman, nightclub bouncer, aerobics instructor, favourite television celebrity or friend's teenage son.

Prevalence studies first appeared in North America in the late 1980s, but it wasn't until the end of the 1990s that such reports appeared in Europe. Today, while it is universally accepted that the use of AAS has spread beyond the athletic field, the change in prevalence rates over the last decade is contested (Kanayama, Boynes, Hudson, Field, & Pope, 2007). While some reports suggest an increasing use of AAS by young people and adolescents (van Amsterdam, Opperhuizen, & Hartgens, 2010), others challenge this belief owing to methodological shortcomings in prevalence recording (Kanayama et al., 2007). Therefore, experts worldwide caution that prevalence statistics should be interpreted with these limitations in mind.

Findings from the 'Monitoring the Future' study, an annual survey of drug use behaviour among US secondary school students, has suggested that since 1993 there has been an increase of AAS use of approximately 38–50 per cent (van Amsterdam, Opperhuizen, & Hartgens, 2010). Moreover, based on the current prevalence statistics available, it is estimated that the total number of AAS users worldwide is in the millions (Kanayama, Hudson, et al., 2010), with the great majority of users being male. Focusing on the adolescent population, the bulk of published surveys suggest that 3–12 per cent of adolescent males living in Western societies admit to lifetime or present use of AAS, with adolescent females typically displaying a lower prevalence rate of 1–2 per cent. Currently, knowledge on prevalence is heavily guided by studies from North America, and it is important for the field to supplement this data by conducting large-scale and nationally representative studies from sites outside North America (Striegel et al., 2006).

From a UK perspective, the only national study of AAS use was commissioned by the Department of Health and published in 1993 (Korkia & Stimson, 1993). At this time, the authors found that AAS use was evenly distributed throughout the Home Countries when needle exchanges and gyms were examined. More recently, surveys of private gymnasia in the West Glamorgan area of Wales have reported a 32 per cent increase in AAS use over a 10-year period, with the most recent figures from 2006 recording a 70 per cent AAS usage rate (Baker, Graham, & Davies, 2006). Findings from the latest British Crime Survey, 2008–2009 (Hoare, 2009), shows that declared lifetime prevalence of AAS misuse for those aged between 15 and 59 years stood at 1.1 per cent for men and 0.1 per cent for women (0.6 per cent prevalence in total). These represent similar statistics to the misuse of opioids (0.9 per cent lifetime prevalence) and heroin (0.7 per cent lifetime prevalence). It is notable that the misuse of AAS was highest in the age group 25–34 years (1.7 per cent males, 0.2 per cent females) and the data suggests that the 16–34 year age group is most at risk of AAS misuse.

Prior research has shown that much higher estimates of the misuse of AAS can be found in strength and power sport groups such as bodybuilders and weightlifters (Korkia, 1994; Kutscher, Lund, & Perry, 2002; Thiblin & Petersson, 2005; Wichstrom & Pedersen, 2001). Kutscher et al. (2002) noted that 55 per cent of elite powerlifters reported lifetime use of these drugs and this dovetails with Wagman, Curry, and Cook (1995) who noted 67 per cent of elite US powerlifters declared a lifetime use of AAS. With a focus on strength gain, powerlifters, bodybuilders and weightlifters appear to be a group particularly at risk of AAS abuse (Korkia, 1994).

In sum, while epidemiological studies are more commonplace, estimates of use remain problematic because of the clandestine nature of AAS. Moreover, AAS users are a challenging group to engage in research (Larance, Degenhardt, Copeland, & Dillon, 2008), which leads to small sample sizes in the majority of studies and a limited ability to then generalise the findings to the wider population. In addition, respondents to prevalence surveys may under- or over-report use owing to a misunderstanding and a lack of knowledge about the substances they have actually used.

Motives for AAS use and attitudes towards illicit AAS use

AAS are positively projected in the media, with the term 'on steroids' commonly used to market many products ranging from the Chevrolet Matiz to Post-It Notes.

While medical researchers have cited the health risks associated with AAS use, there appears to be a growing impetus to misuse these drugs. In some sports, particularly those that covet speed and power, athletes who do not want to use AAS often believe that they cannot be competitive without them. Indeed, this coercive argument can lead to the belief that failure to use performance-enhancing substances will render the competitor unable to compete effectively because 'everyone else is doing it' (Dubin, 1990). Although our normative beliefs may not accurately represent the playing field in which we compete, they can be a significant motivator, especially in professional sports where an athlete's future often depends on outperforming others (Backhouse, Atkin, McKenna, & Robinson, 2007).

While the pressure of sports competition and the belief of doping practices can be a motivator for AAS use, there is a growing recognition of society's vulnerability to cultural and media representations of femininity and masculinity. Therefore, motivation does not just originate from a pressure to achieve sporting prowess, it also comes from an evaluation of our mirror reflections. The body has become an object through which people achieve individual self-identity, and modifications of size, shape and appearance are easily witnessed. Historically, body image research has focused on females, and eating disorders have been the pathological state most commonly related to body image disorders. Nevertheless, in the last 30 years, there appears to have been a cultural shift in beliefs regarding the ideal male body image (Goldfield & Woodside, 2009).

Muscles are now depicted as an art form in popular culture; one only has to look at advertising and film to witness this shift. We are bombarded with the 'buff' body images (rippling six packs and bulging biceps) of male models and film stars such as Daniel Craig, Matt Damon and Vin Diesel as their sculpted physiques are used to great effect in order to sell products or overcome villains. Further evidence of physique expectations draws from the profound morphological changes of the figures of our toy shop 'Action Heroes'. Specifically, Pope, Olivardia, Gruber, and Borowiecki (1999) noted a marked increase in the size of GI Joe, particularly in the bicep and chest regions. The authors point out that such heroic figures give a very clear indication of the changing perceptions of what the 'perfect' male should look like. However, Pickett, Lewis, and Cash (2005) argue that current media images of masculinity are beyond reach for most men and therefore it is not surprising that the media's exacting projection of masculinity has been linked to muscle dysmorphia (MD; Leit, Pope, & Gray, 2001).

Ordinarily, men and women differ in respect to their ideal body image; women idealise a thinner, toned appearance, whereas men desire a muscular, yet lean appearance (Choi, Pope, & Olivardia, 2002b). Accordingly, in the early 1990s, the terms 'reverse anorexia' or 'bigorexia' were coined in order to account for a growing shift from an obsession with becoming increasingly smaller to a chronic preoccupation with muscularity and leanness (Pope, Katz, & Hudson, 1993). The concept of MD then emerged, which is a form of body dysmorphic disorder and a type of obsessive compulsive disorder. In essence, the obsession is accruing large amounts of lean muscle mass, and the compulsion is the engagement in behaviours to achieve such high levels of muscularity (Dawes & Mankin, 2004). Ironically, this disorder is often accompanied with skewed body images and a perception of being thin and weak when the opposite is true (Choi, Pope, & Olivardia, 2002a). Ultimately, it can be genetically impossible to achieve a hypermesomorphic shape through diet and exercise alone and this situation creates an opportunity for the misuse of performance- and image-enhancing substances.

The acknowledged relationship between AAS and increased strength, fat-free mass and decreased body fat is highly appealing to a population of individuals who exhibit body image pathology such as a desperate need to increase their size. Hence, there is a growing literature base implicating body image as a possible predictor or consequence of AAS use (Goldfield & Woodside, 2009) and evidence is available to support the argument that individuals with MD are more likely to use AAS and have a higher lifetime use of other substances (Kanayama, Pope, Cohane, & Hudson, 2003). To illustrate, body image disturbance has been acknowledged in heavy AAS users (Kanayama, Barry, Hudson, & Pope, 2006) and Goldfield and Woodside (2009) noted a greater drive for thinness, body dissatisfaction, ineffectiveness and perfectionism in current bodybuilding users compared to former AAS users and non-users. Furthermore, bodybuilders have been found to self-report the greatest use of AAS and a greater body dissatisfaction, higher drive for bulk, elevated perfectionism and lower self-esteem compared to runners and martial artists (Blouin & Goldfield, 1995). At the present time it is not clear if it is a cause or effect relationship between MD and AAS use as not all users exhibit body image pathology (Kanayama et al., 2006). However, in view of the perceptions of MD sufferers, the potential for extreme cycling and stacking regimes in order to eliminate negative self-perceptions is tenable.

In order to explore motives for use, Monaghan (2002) adopted a different perspective and conducted an ethnographic study which allowed the voices of AAS-using bodybuilders to be heard. The study illuminated the power of justification over excuse in this sample as physique enhancement was the end goal and AAS use was seen as instrumental in achieving that goal. Users asserted that there was no high to be gained from AAS misuse. Instead, use was qualified as an adjunct to a demanding bodybuilding lifestyle, supporting previous research by Olrich and Ewing (1999). Monaghan also reported users' negative evaluations of those that refuted the use of AAS (which he termed 'condemnation of condemners'), with one bodybuilding user offering the example of a refuter talking negatively of AAS users while holding a beer in one hand and a cigarette in the other. Further, the sample voiced a 'denial of injury' – a belief that everything is okay in moderation. To many bodybuilders, their adherence to low-fat diets and a regular exercise habit buttresses their view that they are 'healthier' than the average person, despite their AAS experimentation. All things considered, bodybuilding AAS users view their use of self-technologies as part of a strategy for self-enhancement and in that sense they are paralleling the medicalisation of society, defined as a preoccupation with 'quick fixes' and exemplified by a daily diet of the latest pills and potions in the hope of improved human functioning (Waddington, 2000).

In short, lifestyle and participation activities ultimately define the goals of those who choose to use AAS and the literature converges on three common motives for AAS use. They are: (a) performing better in sports, (b) looking good and (c) becoming stronger (Ehrnborg & Rosén, 2009; Wichstrom & Pedersen, 2001). Consequently, there appears to be at least two distinct groups of user: those that take AAS to achieve their competitive goals and those driven by an image of the self that is inexorably linked to their physical appearance or capabilities.

Portrait of AAS users

Lifetime prevalence of AAS use is typically higher among men in their 20s and 30s and virtually all supraphysiological users of AAS perform weight training in order to maximise the substance effects (Kanayama, Hudson, & Pope, 2009). Historically, these predictors have been complemented by risk profiles including being a polysubstance abuser who has low self-esteem and poor school performance (Bahrke, Yesalis, Kopstein, & Stephens, 2000; DuRant, Ecobedo, & Heath, 1995; Kanayama, Pope, et al., 2003). However, a changing AAS user portrait has recently been painted by Cohen, Collins, Darkes, and Gwartney (2007) based on the findings of a study which recruited a generous sample of North American male AAS users via AAS-related internet websites. They found that 'typical' users were Caucasian, approximately 30 years old, highly educated, gainfully employed earning an above-average wage and not active in organised sports. Yet, motives for use fell in line with previous research as increases in skeletal muscle mass, strength and physical attractiveness were once again reported. These findings call into question the commonly held views of the typical AAS user and further research is required in order to ensure appropriately targeted prevention programmes are designed in the future. It is also worth stating that poor relationships with fathers (Kanayama, Pope, et al., 2003) and immigrant status (Kindlundh, Hagekull, Isacson, & Nyberg, 2001) are two further factors found to display significant independent associations with the use of AAS.

AAS users report the most common sources of AAS information as being internet sites (62 per cent) and friends (55 per cent) (Larance et al., 2008). Both these sources are unqualified to offer health-related advice, and given the prescription requirement for legal AAS use and the health risks associated with unsupervised use, it is notable that only 22 per cent of the sample listed their doctor as a source of information. Furthermore, Pope, Kanayama, Ionescu-Pioggia, and Hudson (2004) established that 56 per cent had never revealed their AAS use to a doctor. While Striegel et al. (2006) suggest that the public health system is strongly involved in supporting and monitoring AAS use, other authors assert the common mistrust of medical professionals and a lack of use disclosure to this community. This credibility gap may in part be due to the fact that members of the medical community originally claimed that AAS use was ineffective in improving musculature and strength (Pope et al., 2004).

In light of this mistrust and the legal ramifications of AAS misuse, the internet and an unregulated black market caters for AAS procurement (Larance et al., 2008).

A recent Google search for 'buy anabolic androgenic steroids' produced about 192,000 hits and the companies listed offered numerous anabolic agents with a tag line of 'no prescription required'. These companies typically operate out of the Far East and for a relatively inexpensive price they are willing to ship worldwide and deliver to the buyer's door in a matter of days. Most companies flood their sites with disclaimers highlighting the dangers of buying AAS and most assert the importance of consulting with a doctor before buying AAS. However, in view of the medical community mistrust already described, these disclaimers appear superficial.

Concerningly, the internet is a bulging source of unfettered information, and the demand for appearance- and performance-enhancing substances is leading to an expanding counterfeit market (Graham et al., 2009). Illegal laboratories are opening for business, concocting and naming their own products and infusing the market with a large proportion of counterfeit AAS injectables (Graham et al., 2009). Coupled with this increase, Thevis et al. (2008) found that 35 per cent of confiscated black market compounds labelled AAS did not contain or did not *only* contain the declared ingredients. Supplements are also on the radar of risk because an International Olympic Committee (IOC)-funded study demonstrated that nearly 20 per cent of a sample of 240 supplements sold in the United States contained undeclared AAS (Geyer et al., 2004). This presence is significant for an athlete, subject to drug testing, as it could give rise to a positive dope test and a subsequent ban from sport under the concept of strict liability.

Effects of non-prescribed AAS use

Clinical trials documenting long-term physiological effects of supraphysiological doses of AAS are notably absent from the literature. Thus, the basis of what is known of AAS effects has largely developed from case reports and cross-sectional designs which do not allow causality to be inferred (Kanayama, Hudson, et al., 2010). Still, AAS are defined as psychosomatic drugs because their effects are systemic, since no tissues are devoid of androgen receptors and all androgen receptors distributed throughout the body possess some level of binding affinity for a particular steroid (Shahidi, 2001). As a result, physiological and psychological effects follow their use and abuse.

The reported AAS contraindications described in the medical and behavioural science literature are wide-ranging, from relatively 'minor' cosmetic effects such as hair loss and acne, to potentially lethal effects such as liver tumours and cardiovascular disease. Hence, Friedl (2000) asserts that it is an oversimplification to reduce such risks to a single list and he emphasises the importance of context. While some contraindications may be perceived as negative to some, they may resonate as useful to other users (e.g. temporary infertility, weight gain). The most common side effects reported by AAS users ($n = 4{,}339$) on a telephone hotline (1996–2000) were aggression (835), depression (829), acne (770), worries (657), gynecomastia (637) and potency problems (413) (Eklof et al., 2003). Importantly, these commonly reported effects are generally reversible with cessation of AAS (Friedl, 2000).

However, the most recent reviews speculate that the most harmful adverse effects of AAS misuse are those that affect the cardiovascular and reproductive systems (Kanayama, Hudson, & Pope, 2008; Parssinen & Seppala, 2002; Tan & Scally, 2009). Hepatic and neurological system effects are also well documented. Although a number of adverse effects will be considered here, it is beyond the scope of this chapter to examine all the potential effects in detail. Therefore, the reader is referred to reviews by Modlinski and Fields (2006), Payne, Kotwinski, and Montgomery (2004) and Kanayama et al. (2008) for more in-depth analysis.

Performance effects

Wood (2008) stated that there is no longer any question that AAS work as performance-enhancing substances and the general consensus is that AAS have positive skeletal muscle-enhancing effects when combined with an appropriate diet and strength training regime (ACSM, 1987). Still, the efficacy of clinical studies on subsequent athletic performance benefits have been contested (Kennedy & O'Sullivan, 1997). This is in part due to the methodological challenges of studying the effects of AAS (Kennedy & O'Sullivan, 1997). Specifically, ensuring that participants are blind to their experimental treatment is difficult because of the potential for weight and size gain, acne, testicular atrophy, etc. on the AAS trial. This difficulty remains a significant issue for the field. Typically, short-term studies (3–10 weeks) document a 3–5 kg weight gain (Friedl, 2000). Prior to the landmark studies by Bhasin and colleagues (Bhasin et al., 1996; Bhasin, Woodhouse, & Storer, 2001), many thought the positive effects associated with AAS use were due to increased aggression and drive (Bahrke & Yesalis, 2004). However, Bhasin and colleagues, findings have challenged this view.

The research team randomised 43 healthy eugonadal weightlifters to one of four groups (testosterone with or without exercise, placebo with or without exercise) and results from the 40 men who completed the study showed that a significant increase in body mass, fat-free mass, muscle hypertrophy and muscular strength occurred following the 10-week regime of injecting testosterone enanthate. The effects were exacerbated when progressive resistance training accompanied this programme. Again, placebo effects due to being able to identify the active drug and current use of AAS in this population were highlighted and caution was emphasised when interpreting the findings (Kennedy & O'Sullivan, 1997). Taking these anabolic findings into account, it is unsurprising that individuals with an eye on strength gains and musculature development (weightlifters, bodybuilders, powerlifters) are the predominant misusers of AAS.

To date, the specific biological mechanisms responsible for changes in strength and body composition following AAS use are far from clear (Bahrke & Yesalis, 2004). However, it is interesting to note that nearly every study that has documented positive findings has done so using a one repetition maximum (RM) strength test (Friedl, 2000) and it has been repeatedly demonstrated that 10mg/d (or more) of methandienone (Dianabol) will produce an improved 1 RM. However, whether these effects transfer to improvements in end points relating to specific strength training regimes or actual sports performance remains to be seen.

Adverse somatic effects

The cardiac effects of long-term AAS use remain inadequately characterised (Baggish et al., 2010) and epidemiological studies are notably absent. However, Baggish et al. (2010) compared cardiac parameters in weightlifters reporting long-term AAS use to otherwise similar weightlifters without prior AAS exposure. The authors concluded that cardiac dysfunction in long-term AAS users appears more severe than previously reported, and may be sufficient to increase the risk of heart failure. Indeed, there is an emerging consensus that chronic AAS abuse may be associated with an increased risk of sudden cardiac death and cardiac hypertrophy (Fineschi et al., 2007; Melchert & Welder, 1995). However, this is a topic of much debate as the compelling evidence is based on case reports of AAS abusers and causality cannot yet be inferred. Therefore, the underlying mechanism of cardio-vascular toxicity is poorly understood. However, it is conceivable that demographic trends may begin to emerge as long-term users who initiated self-administration in their 20s approach middle age (Kanayama, Hudson, et al., 2010) because AAS-induced disease states may begin to surface (Kanayama, Brower, Wood, Hudson, & Pope, 2009a). While many AAS users would argue that they represent a low-risk group for heart disease because of their commitment to strenuous exercise, avoidance of smoking and maintenance of relatively low body fat (Friedl, 2000), their typical polypharmacy diet of substances could override these protective factors. Presently, the synergistic health effects of this common practice are unknown.

Although the somatic effects of AAS misuse are highly debated, there appears to be universal acceptance of a direct relationship between AAS use and lipoprotein profile. Specifically, a reduction in high-density lipoprotein cholesterol (HDLC) is consistently observed following AAS misuse (Kanayama, Hudson, et al., 2010) and this decreased profile is typically in the region of 40–70 per cent (Glazer, 1991). Such a pronounced profile adaptation is thought to be an aetiological risk factor for premature coronary heart disease (CHD) (Glazer, 1991) and therefore AAS misuse is a public health risk factor worthy of acknowledgement. However, the exact role of androgens in CHD is still the source of much debate, largely due to the nature of the studies from which this evidence base is founded. Furthermore, current evidence suggests that these lipid effects are often reversed following AAS discontinuation (Shahidi, 2001).

Attention will now be turned to the reproductive effects of AAS misuse. As synthetic analogues of testosterone, AAS act via a negative feedback loop to suppress the hypothalamic-pituitary-adrenal (HPA) axis in males (hypogonadotropic hypogonadism) leading to a dose-dependent suppression of gonad-stimulating hormones (Pope & Brower, 2009). In males, this medical condition results in infertility through decreased sperm counts, decreased sperm motility and testicular atrophy. Also, sexual functioning is influenced by AAS effects bringing about increased or decreased libido (Tan & Scally, 2009). These reproductive effects appear to be dose dependent in males and they generally reverse with discontinuation of use (Pope & Brower, 2009; Tan & Scally, 2009). In light of the purported transient male fertility effects, a large multi-centre trial funded by the World Health Organization (WHO) was undertaken, and initial findings note the long-term effectiveness of testosterone enanthate administration as a male contraceptive in carefully screened males (Wu, Farley, Peregoudov, & Waites, 1996). However, there appears to be variability in the participants' return to normal, with reports ranging from 5 to 18 months (Gazvani et al., 1997; Menon, 2003). Hypogonadism can also lead to major depressive episodes, and therefore users who attempt to withdraw from abusing AAS are at risk of developing an addiction to this drug in order to alleviate the symptoms that ensue when administration is ceased (Brower, 2002).

Last, there appears to be little question that administering C-17-alkylated oral forms of AAS increases the risk of liver tumours in men (Wood, 2008) and that AAS users are susceptible to musculoskeletal injuries, such as ruptured tendons, ligaments or muscles (Kanayama, Hudson, et al., 2010). Given the suggestion from some quarters that AAS use in adolescents is also on the rise, it is concerning to note that AAS misuse can induce premature closure of the growth plates and therefore prevent teens from obtaining their genetically predetermined height (Wood, 2008).

Adverse psychological effects

Although the effects of exogenous androgens on the soma are expansively documented, the scope of investigations of psychological effects of AAS has been narrow, with a particular focus on mood disorders (Goldfield & Woodside, 2009). This restricted view is largely due to the fact that research in this field is complex. More specifically, the variety of agents used (content and purity), duration of use, participant access restrictions, user personality profiles, assortment of psychological assessment and the concomitant use of other drugs (Bahrke, 2000) makes for a challenging research environment. Consequently, the relationship between androgens and psychiatric symptoms, such as human aggression, remains tenuous. It is true that a large number of animal experimental studies have established a clear association between testosterone levels, dominance and aggressive behaviour, but this relationship is more complex in the study of human behaviour (Thiblin & Parlklo, 2002). Still, there is converging evidence from case studies, cross-sectional studies and a small number of longitudinal studies that suggests some users are susceptible to developing bouts of aggression and mood disturbance.

Case studies

Anecdotal reports of indiscriminate, unprovoked attacks ('roid rage') by AAS users are widely publicised and sensationalised. While AAS misuse is believed to play a role in the aetiology of violent behaviours and several cases of apparent AAS-induced crimes have been reported in the media and the scientific literature, the research community have not fully established the psychiatric risk of AAS use. However, one of the earliest reports of this association outlined a case of three men, with no previous psychiatric or anti-social histories, who impulsively committed crimes, including murder, while taking AAS (Pope & Katz, 1990). Following further investigations, the same principal authors concluded that AAS use 'may occasionally be a significant, although uncommon, factor in criminal behaviour' (Pope, Kouri, Powell, Campbell, & Katz, 1996, p. 256). Further, Thiblin, Lindquist, and Rajs (2000) outline a case for AAS users being at risk of 'dying a violent death' because of the maladaptive behaviours associated with AAS use. More specifically, Thiblin et al. (2000) investigated the deaths of 34 male AAS users and noted that nine were victims of murder, 11 had committed suicide and 12 died of accidental causes.

Recently in the United Kingdom, the violent crimes of Raoul Moat, a bodybuilder and former nightclub bouncer, have been blamed on AAS abuse leading to a volatile personality. Indeed, in July 2010, national newspapers were awash with headlines associating AAS use with the murder of his ex-girlfriend's boyfriend. As an illustration, the *Guardian* newspaper (6 July 2010) referred to Moat as a 'steroid-addicted bodybuilder' and 'prone to unpredictable outbursts'. Further, the Moat rampage drew comparisons to that of AAS-abusing American bodybuilder David Bieber who murdered a policeman in the United Kingdom in 2003. In both cases, the self-administration of other psychoactive drugs alongside AAS is unknown, and it is unclear whether these individuals were prone to violence or anti-social behaviour before their AAS misuse. Moreover, it has been reported that bodybuilding AAS users do not believe in 'roid rage' and see this discourse for violence and crime as an excuse (Monaghan, 2002).

Cross-sectional studies

Increased aggression as a consequence of non-prescribed AAS use has been indicated in cross-sectional studies where users typically report higher scores on self-administered aggression-hostility scales. Kouri, Pope, Katz, and Oliva (1995) noted that moderately high doses of testosterone cypionate were associated with increased aggressive responding in individuals who had not used AAS before. Similarly, Parrott, Choi, and Davies (1994) examined 21 AAS-using male amateur athletes who attended a needle-exchange clinic and observed that AAS use periods coincided with the reporting of significantly higher levels of aggression, irritability, anxiety and negativism compared with non-use periods. Further, Galligani, Renck, and Hansen (1996) reported that current AAS users scored significantly higher on verbal aggression than past or never AAS users, and increased violence by AAS users towards wives and girlfriends has also been accounted (Choi & Pope, 1994).

Latterly, Lundholm, Käll, Wallin, and Thiblin (2010) have noted that 26 per cent of participants reported lifetime experience of AAS in two remand prisons in Stockholm ($n = 3,597$). In this setting, they observed an overrepresentation of violent crime among persons who had reported AAS experience, independent of age and sex. Thus, the findings support earlier research that has demonstrated an increased risk for violent crime in AAS users after controlling for substance abuse (Beaver, Vaughn, Delisi, & Wright, 2008; Klotz, Petersson, Isacson, & Thiblin, 2007). Equally, these findings are irrespective of the temporal relationship between the violent crime and AAS use and the authors propose that the effects of AAS use may be long lasting and lower the threshold for violent acts. Alternatively, they posit that AAS use may be overrepresented in individuals who demonstrate particularly strong risk taking or impulsive behaviour.

Longitudinal studies

The most recent studies which have typically employed 'gold standard' experimental designs have provided contrasting and less compelling evidence than that provided by case studies and cross-sectional reports. Bhasin et al. (1996) reported no effects on mood or behaviour after 10 weeks of high-dose testosterone treatment which brought about a four to five times greater than normal increase in circulating testosterone levels. Further checks were also employed in this investigation, as participant self-report of psychological status was triangulated with peer observations (partner, spouse or parent) of participant behaviour during the study period.

The wider application of testosterone as a male contraceptive agent has prompted renewed interest, and longitudinal studies have emerged to examine the actions and safety of androgens. O'Connor, Archer, and Wu (2004) provided 28 eugonadal men with a single administration of 1,000 mg of testosterone undecanoate in a double blind, placebo-controlled cross-over design. They found that, while this long-acting exogenous testosterone raised plasma testosterone concentrations into the supraphysiological range, only relatively minor mood changes were detected and there was no change in aggressive behaviour. The authors concluded that the absence of behavioural effects could be due to the relatively short time during which testosterone was elevated and further emphasised that the increase was in the range likely to be used for hormonal contraception, not AAS misuse. Typically, AAS misusers expose themselves to extremely high doses of AAS (e.g. > 1,000 mg/week), often in combination with other poorly documented anabolic agents (Parkinson & Evans, 2006; Parrott et al., 1994; Pope, Kouri, & Hudson, 2000).

In contrast, Su et al. (1993) conducted a double blind, placebo-controlled cross-over study and found that increased doses of methyltestosterone over a 2-week period correlated with increased irritability, mood swings, violent feelings and hostility. Similarly, Pope et al. (2000) injected participants with 600 mg/week of testosterone cypionate for 6 weeks, followed by no treatment for 6 weeks and then placebo for 6 weeks. They reported significant increases in mania and aggression during the androgen phase but they concluded that the responses were highly variable. More specifically, 84 per cent reported minimal to no psychiatric effects, 12 per cent became mildly hypomanic and 4 per cent markedly hypomanic. Thus, supraphysiological doses appear to contribute to psychiatric dysfunction in susceptible individuals but effects do not appear to be uniformly expressed.

Pagonis, Angelopoulos, Koukoulis, and Hadjichristodoulou (2006) attempted to employ an ecologically valid experimental design in order to examine psychiatric reactions to increasing AAS dosing. In the experimental group, users self-administered and self-obtained their anabolic agents (and associated substances) and were classified according to their regime. Specifically, 28 were classified as 'light' abusers, 59 as 'medium' abusers and 73 as 'heavy' abusers. In contrast, 80 participants administered self-directed regimens of placebo compounds and 80 participants acted as a control group – they abstained from any substance abuse whatsoever. The authors examined an array of psychological problems and psychopathological symptoms and observed a significant increase in all subscales of the Symptom Checklist-90 (SC-90) and the Hostility and Direction of Hostility Questionnaire (HDHQ). Specific states affected include obsessive compulsive disorder, depression, anxiety, hostility, self-criticism and guilt. This study demonstrated that stratifying AAS use led to escalating side effects as the abuse pattern intensified. Thus a dose response relationship is supported. This finding supports the assertion of Pope and Katz (1996) that psychiatric symptoms are more common and severe as the AAS dose increases. Time after time, psychotic symptoms associated with AAS use occur among individuals consuming more than 1,000 mg/week (Pope and Katz, 1996).

Pagonis, Angelopoulos, Koukalis, Hadjichristodoulou, and Toli (2006) have also conducted a novel experiment of AAS effects using two pairs of male monozygotic twins with total genome similarity. One of the twins of each pair self-administered a multiple combination of AAS (doses were 5–10 times greater than those used in controlled studies) over a 12 week cycle, while the other did not. Both followed a common training and nutrition regime and they were subjected to two random and unexpected doping control tests in order to monitor drug levels. This study demonstrated significant changes in aggressiveness, hostility and anxiety, and these changes were noted in the twins who used AAS, with the non-using twins showing no deviation from their initial baseline status.

On balance, the findings discussed above do not necessarily help to elucidate the effects of self-administration of AAS in quantities that are 10–100 times the therapeutic dose and, to date, it has not been possible to prove a causal link between AAS use and maladaptive behaviours, such as aggression. A high level of bias accompanies self-reported side effect research (Bahrke, 2000) and, in line with other drugs, some individuals will be fine self-administrating AAS and others will experience side effects. Furthermore, Bahrke states that 'concerns about adverse effects of moderate doses (200 mg/wk) of exogenous testosterone on male aggressive behaviour have perhaps been overstated, particularly by the media' (p. 256). All things considered, this research field occupies a difficult position because AAS regimes in controlled studies may be inadequate to reveal significant psychiatric effects and it is unethical to test the doses suspected to be in use (Wood, 2008). Therefore, this brings about an absence of evidence and this could be perceived by users as evidence of absence.

Exploring the potential for psychological and physical dependence

By definition, dependence refers to the inability to control or stop using a substance despite adverse consequences and a desire or several attempts to do so (Brower, 2009). Brower (2009) conceives that abuse may precede the development of dependence and, currently, there is no evidence in the published literature that abuse or dependence develops from therapeutic use of AAS (Kanayama, Cohane, Weiss, & Pope, 2003). However, Brower and colleagues were amongst the first researchers to associate AAS misuse and dependence in the late 1980s. Recently, Brower (2009) reported that at least 254 instances of AAS dependence have been documented in peer-reviewed medical journals. The reported cases are predomi-nantly among bodybuilders who chronically self-administer supraphysiological doses of AAS alongside a strict weight training and diet regime. Further, it has been estimated that up to one-third of users become dependent on AAS based on analy-sis across dependency studies (Kanayama, Brower, Wood, Hudson, & Pope 2009a).

Psychiatrists have very specific definitions for 'psychoactive substance depen-dence' caused by using drugs that alter mood, thinking or behaviour. Consequently, the *Diagnostic and Statistical Manual of Mental Disorders*, Fourth Edition (DSM-IV) substance dependence criteria has been interpreted for diagnos-ing AAS dependence (Kanayama, Brower, Wood, Hudson, & Pope, 2009b). To meet the psychiatric criteria for AAS dependency, a user must have at least three of the following symptoms occurring at any time in the same 12-month period before a clinical diagnosis of dependency is made – the individual: (a) takes the substance in larger amounts or over a longer period than intended; (b) wants to stop or cut down use but is unable to do so; (c) spends a lot of time on substance-related activity; (d) replaces social, work or leisure activities with substance use; (e) continues substance use despite the problems caused or worsened by use; (f) exhi-bits tolerance; and (g) experiences withdrawal symptoms.

Typically, AAS abusers experience positive effects at the onset of their use and for many users this coincides with them feeling at their best; their self-esteem is high, their strength and body bulk is noticeable and they are receiving positive peer recog-nition (Skarberg et al., 2008). However, such positive experiences can eventually be outweighed by the negative side effects that can ensue in some individuals. The conti-nuation of AAS despite deleterious effects (Brower, 2002) could be explained by the fact that, for many current users, body image is tied to their use of AAS and the results in terms of developing a muscular body and achieving a lean muscle mass often pro-vides the stimulus to keep using AAS despite the side effects (Skarberg et al., 2008). In fact, AAS dosage and dissatisfaction with body image were the best predictors of dependence (Brower, Blow, Young, & Hill, 1991) and users report and accept the potential dependency effects of AAS use (Monaghan, 2002). However, for those who cease AAS use, common withdrawal symptoms include depressed mood, fatigue, body image dissatisfaction and craving more AAS (Brower et al., 1991).

The mechanism of AAS dependence is largely unknown, and van Amsterdam (2010) has cautioned that AAS dependence may be confounded by factors like exercise dependence and multi-drug use. Of late, Kanayama, Hudson, et al. (2010) have proposed a theoretical model depicting how AAS dependence can develop through three primary (direct stimulation on the brain) and secondary (reinforce-ment) hypothesised effects. The 'anabolic effect' proposes that the modulating factor is a body image disorder and the mechanism of addiction is through a negative reinforcement mechanism via a fear of losing supraphysiological muscle size. A slow-recovering HPA axis and a predisposition to depression when hypogonadal are the hypothesised modulating factors of the 'androgenic effects' hypothesis. In this instance, the mechanism of addiction is hypothesised to relate to negative reinforcement pertaining to loss of sexual function, fatigue and other hypogonadal symptoms and depression. Finally, the 'hedonic effects' mechanism is hypothesised to be modulated by an impulsive, risk-taking endophenotype, and the mechanism of action is hypothesised to be positive reinforcement through classical addiction via pathways similar to opioid addiction. This proposed model appears to be an extension of a two-stage model first put forward by Brower (2002).

Treatment and prevention

Reflected in the volume of published research in the field of dependence, treatment and prevention is a lack of funding for AAS-related research. At the same time, effective treatment practices could become increasingly important as prevalence rates suggest a trend of increasing AAS use and the AAS user group who initiated self-administration in the 1980s begin to embark on middle age. Importantly, recent developments in the field have led to the proposal of a six-goal treatment programme by Kanayama et al. (2010). The six goals that should underscore any programme are: (a) build motivation to initiate and maintain abstinence from AAS and all other addictive substances as well as non-medical use of prescription medications; (b) assist initiation of abstinence by alleviating distressing withdrawal symptoms, which may require pharmacological intervention; (c) address substance-induced and co-occurring medical and psychiatric disorders, including MD and persistent suppression of the HPA axis; (d) develop a social support system that favours recovery; (e) improve coping skills and self-efficacy for managing stress that may increase risk for relapse; and (f) balance exercise-related behaviours with alternative rewarding activities (p. 10). The challenge for the treatment of AAS dependence in the future could centre on the assertions that AAS users do not consider their AAS use as pathological. Instead, they justify this practice as a positive step towards bettering themselves physically (Cohen et al., 2007; Monaghan, 2002), and education programmes are encouraged to recognise this perspective in their intervention mapping phase.

Evidence on the effectiveness of AAS primary prevention is limited. While it is true that you can now easily acquire a text entitled *10 Part Steroid University Course* from an online website (this course is not affiliated to a university, despite the title of the volume), the same cannot be said of access to preventive education. The key to abating AAS abuse is preventing it. So, more time and energy should be invested in developing educational programmes for young children and adolescents in order to develop their protective armour from AAS misuse in the future. Going forward, primary prevention programmes need to target those at risk of AAS use by addressing the vulnerabilities related to body image as well as the social environment that might reinforce use (such as a focus on winning and physical attractiveness).

It is becoming increasingly clear that detection–deterrence policies, in the form of drug testing, are not the long-term solution to this societal issue. There are many loopholes in this approach – it does not address the root causes of the behaviour and, as recently proven in the sporting domain, athletes can employ the most advanced scientists to circumvent the system (Fainaru-Wada & Williams, 2006). Furthermore, it is costly and, given the limited reach of current drug-testing policies, it will not serve to abate increased AAS use in the wider population. Moreover, we must be reticent of the fact that AAS users have minimised the importance of side effects relative to the positively perceived body image effects. This is often accompanied by a justification of use relative to other alternative unhealthy 'acceptable' behaviours (such as alcohol consumption) (Monaghan, 2002).

Following withdrawal, AAS-induced weight increases tend to decline over time (Forbes, Porta, Herr, & Griggs, 1992). Therefore, the potential for long-term abuse is real. Often users who have not experienced side effects don't rely on objective evidence until it is too late and the case of the infamous Gregg Valentino illustrates this point. A recent documentary (www.greggvalentino.net) showed how Valentino became a minor celebrity because he was recorded to have the world's biggest biceps and the media showcased this individual as a 'true freak'. His chronic AAS abuse became an obsession which he believes originates from his small stature; AAS allowed him to transform his physique into something seemingly beyond the body's capability. Unfortunately, his use was so extreme that he ended up with an infection in his bicep which required emergency surgery. The issue for the future revolves around the potentially long latencies of AAS effects and what Pope terms the 'steroid time bomb'.

Final remarks and future research

Having completed this selective review of the literature on the misuse of AAS, it is time to summate. At least some of the reasons behind the divergent assessments of the prevalence of AAS use and its subsequent adverse effects are hopefully a little more apparent. On the one hand, there is consistency in the evidence that the use of this performance- and image-enhancing drug has spread to the broadest reaches of society. The misuse of AAS is no longer the prefecture of elite athletes – society is witnessing the emergence of striving for perfection and this has brought about the birth of the 'mirror athlete'. However, the extent of this reach is the source of debate. Further, there is a growing archive of case reports and cross-sectional research associating AAS use with deleterious somatic, behavioural and psychiatric effects. Having said this, there continues to be a tangled web of interpretations offered on the adverse effects of AAS misuse, made worse by a relatively limited pool of research studies and designs (Friedl, 2000). The misuse of AAS may bring about chronic side effects, but such effects appear dose dependent and idiosyncratic responses typify the research findings. Moreover, the quality of the evidence, for the most part, is not optimal (Kanayama, Brower, et al., 2010). The fact that participants are volunteers and most psychological outcomes are self-reported and, therefore, subject to expectancy bias, in conjunction with ethical issues of administering supraphysiological doses of AAS and the inability to implement a 'placebo' drug control, make it practically impossible to design a 'definitive' longitudinal intervention study. Thus, the research field is far from reaching a position whereby causal relationships can be declared. Despite this, there are methodological steps that can bring future studies at least closer to this unattainable ideal: careful selection of outcome measures and protocols, randomisation, polydrug assessment, intention-to-treat analyses, blinding of outcome assessors and adequate intervention and follow-up periods. Additionally, a number of authors have questioned the methodological shortcomings and contradictions of much of the current evidence base and have lamented at the fact that the majority of the work is positioned in a positivist epistemology (Monaghan, 2002). Therefore, it is time to look beyond the medical models if we are to fully understand the context in which AAS misuse occurs.

Currently, the exact AAS dosing required to bring about strength gains, recovery effects and performance advantages does not exist. As a result, users experiment with varying doses and different types of AAS without any known upper limits (Friedl, 2000). Given the difficulties of receiving ethical clearance for administering supraphysiological doses of AAS, alongside a multi-pharmacy of substances to counter the adverse effects, the only way that research is likely to realise higher dose effects is from prospective studies of such users. Bodybuilders who experience significant weight gains can respond with a desire to get bigger, and it is unclear how 'big enough' is determined. While AAS have recently been classified as an illicit drug with a relatively low harm (van Amsterdam, Opperhuizen, Koeter, & van den Brink, 2010), it is impossible to conclude that there is a safe way to use AAS because the long-term consequences of AAS use have not been investigated and are simply unknown. In the long run, AAS misuse may prevent the very things that they are supposed to enhance (Hall & Chapman, 2005).

Discussion questions

1. Psychological factors are associated with increased risk of misusing AAS. Discuss.
2. How are changes in society influencing the patterns of AAS use?
3. What do we know about the effects of illicit AAS use?
4. Should the use of AAS for non-medical purposes be a stigmatised practice? Why or why not?
5. How might an AAS misuse prevention programme be developed?

Note

1 For the purpose of this chapter, AAS use refers to self-administration of the drugs without prescription.

References

American College of Sports Medicine. (1977). Position statement on the use and abuse of anabolic–androgenic steroids in sports. *Medicine and Science in Sports and Exercise, 9*(4), xi–xiii.

American College of Sports Medicine. (1987). Position stand on the use of anabolic–androgenic steroids in sports. *Medicine and Science in Sports and Exercise, 19*, 534–539.

American Medical Association. (1990). Medical and nonmedical uses of anabolic–androgenic steroids. Council on Scientific Affairs. *Journal of the American Medical Association, 264*(22), 2923–2927.

Backhouse, S. H., Atkin, A., McKenna, J., & Robinson, S. (2007). *International literature review: Attitudes, behaviours, knowledge and education – Drugs in sport: Past, present and future.* Montreal: World Anti-Doping Agency. Retrieved from www.wada-ama.org/Documents/Education_Awareness/SocialScienceResearch/Funded_Research_Projects/2006/Backhouse_et_al_Full_Report.pdf

Baggish, A. L., Weiner, R. B., Kanayama, G., Hudson, J. I., Picard, M. H., Hutter, A. M., Jr., & Pope, H. G., Jr. (2010). Long term anabolic–androgenic steroid use is associated with left ventricular dysfunction. *Circulation and Heart Failure, 3*, 472–476.

Bahrke, M. S. (2000). Psychological effects of endogenous testosterone and anabolic–androgenic steroids. In C. E. Yesalis (Ed.), *Anabolic steroids in sport and exercise* (2nd ed.). Champaign, IL: Human Kinetics.

Bahrke, M. S., & Yesalis, C. E. (2004). Abuse of anabolic androgenic steroids and related substances in sport and exercise. *Current Opinion in Pharmacology, 4*(6), 614–620.

Bahrke, M. S., Yesalis, C. E., Kopstein, A. N., & Stephens, J. A. (2000). Risk factors associated with anabolic–androgenic steroid use among adolescents. *Sports Medicine, 29*(6), 397–405.

Baker, J. S., Graham, M., & Davies, B. (2006). Steroid and prescription medicine abuse in recreational gym users: A regional study. *European Journal of Internal Medicine, 17*(7), 479–484.

Basaria, S. (2010). Androgen abuse in athletes: Detection and consequences. *Journal of Clinical Endocrinology and Metabolism, 95*(4), 1533–1543.

Beaver, K. M., Vaughn, M. G., Delisi, M., & Wright, J. P. (2008). Anabolic–androgenic steroid use and involvement in violent behavior in a nationally representative sample of young adult males in the United States. *American Journal of Public Health, 98*(12), 2185–2187.

Bhasin, S., Storer, T. W., Berman, N., Callegari, C., Clevenger, B., Phillips, J., … Casaburi, R. (1996). The effects of supraphysiologic doses of testosterone on muscle size and strength in normal men. *New England Journal of Medicine, 335*(1), 1–7.

Bhasin, S., Woodhouse, L., & Storer, T. W. (2001). Proof of the effect of testosterone on skeletal muscle. *Journal of Endocrinology, 170*, 27–38.

Blouin, A. G., & Goldfield, G. S. (1995). Body image and steroid use in male bodybuilders. *International Journal of Eating Disorders, 18*(2), 159–165.

British Medical Association. (2002). *Drugs in sport: The pressure to perform.* Board of Science and Education. London, UK: Author.

Brower, K. J. (2002). Anabolic steroid abuse and dependence. *Current Psychiatry Reports, 4*(5), 377–387.

Brower, K. J. (2009). Anabolic steroid abuse and dependence in clinical practice. *Physician and Sportsmedicine, 37*(4), 131–140.

Brower, K. J., Blow, F. C., Young, J. P., & Hill, E. M. (1991). Symptoms and correlates of anabolic androgenic steroid dependence. *British Journal of Addiction, 86*, 759–768.

Brown-Sequard, C. E. (1889). The effects produced on man by subcutaneus injections of liquid obtained from the testicles of animals. *The Lancet, 2*, 105–107.

Choi, P. Y., & Pope, H. G., Jr. (1994). Violence toward women and illicit androgenic–anabolic steroid use. *Annals of Clinical Psychiatry, 6*(1), 21–25.

Choi, P. Y., Pope, H. G., Jr., & Olivardia, R. (2002a). Muscle dysmorphia: A new syndrome in weightlifters. *British Journal of Sports Medicine, 36*(5), 375–376; discussion 377.

Choi, P. Y., Pope, H. G., Jr., & Olivardia, R. (2002b). Muscle dysmorphia: A new syndrome in weightlifters. *British Journal of Sports Medicine, 36*(5), 375–376.

Cohen, J., Collins, R., Darkes, J., & Gwartney, D. (2007). A league of their own: Demographics, motivations and patterns of use of 1,955 male adult non-medical anabolic steroid users in the United States. *Journal of the International Society of Sports Nutrition, 4*, 12.

Congeni, J., & Miller, S. (2002). Supplements and drugs used to enhance performance. *Pediatric Clinics of North America, 49*(2), 435–461.

Dawes, J., & Mankin, T. (2004). Muscle dysmorphia. *Strength and Conditioning Journal, 26*, 24–25.

Dawson, R. T. (2001). Drugs in sport – The role of the physician. *Journal of Endocrinology, 170*(1), 55–61.

Dubin, C. (1990). *Commission of inquiry into the use of drugs and banned practices intended to increase athletic performance.* Ottawa, ON: Canadian Government Privy Council Office.

Duchaine, D. (1989). *Underground steroid handbook II.* Venice: HLR Technical Books.

DuRant, R. H., Ecobedo, J. G., & Heath, G. W. (1995). Anabolic steroid use, strength training, and multiple drug use among adolescents in the United States. *Pediatrics, 96*(1), 23–28.

Ehrnborg, C., & Rosén, T. (2009). The psychology behind doping in sport. *Growth Hormone & IGF Research, 19*(4), 285–287.

Eklof, A. C., Thurelius, A. M., Garle, M., Rane, A., & Sjoqvist, F. (2003). The anti-doping hot-line, a means to capture the abuse of doping agents in the Swedish society and a new service function in clinical pharmacology. *European Journal of Clinical Pharmacology, 59*(8–9), 571–577.

Fainaru-Wada, M., & Williams, L. (2006). *Game of shadows: Barry bonds, BALCO, and the steroids scandal that rocked professional sports.* New York: Gotham Books.

Fineschi, V., Riezzo, I., Centini, F., Silingardi, E., Licata, M., Beduschi, G., & Karch, S. B. (2007). Sudden cardiac death during anabolic steroid abuse: Morphologic and toxicologic findings in two fatal cases of bodybuilders. *International Journal of Legal Medicine, 121*(1), 48–53.

Forbes, G.B., Porta, C.R., Herr, B.E., & Griggs, R.C. (1992). Sequence of changes in body composition induced by testosterone and reversal of changes after drug is stopped. *Journal of the American Medical Association, 267*, 397–399.

Franke, W. W., & Berendonk, B. (1997). Hormonal doping and androgenization of athletes: A secret program of the German Democratic Republic government. *Clinical Chemistry, 43*(7), 1262–1279.

Friedl, K. E. (2000). Effects of anabolic steroids on physical health. In C. E. Yesalis (Ed.), *Anabolic steroids in sport and exercise* (2nd ed.). Champaign, IL: Human Kinetics.

Galligani, N., Renck, A., & Hansen, S. (1996). Personality profile of men using anabolic androgenic steroids. *Hormones and Behaviour, 30*(2), 170–175.

Gazvani, M. R., Buckett, W., Luckas, M. J. M., Aird, I. A., Hipkin, L. J., & Lewis-Jones, D. I. (1997). Conservative management of azoospermia following steroid abuse. *Human Reproduction, 12*(8), 1706–1708.

Geyer, H., Parr, M. K., Mareck, U., Reinhart, U., Schrader, Y., & Schanzer, W. (2004). Analysis of non-hormonal nutritional supplements for anabolic–androgenic steroids – Results of an international study. *International Journal of Sports Medicine, 25*(2), 124–129.

Glazer, G. (1991). Atherogenic effects of anabolic steroids on serum lipid levels: A literature review. *Archives of Internal Medicine, 151*(10), 1925–1933.

Goldfield, G. S., & Woodside, D. B. (2009). Body image, disordered eating, and anabolic steroids in male bodybuilders: Current versus former users. *Physician and Sportsmedicine, 37*(1), 111–114.

Graham, M. R., Ryan, P., Baker, J. S., Davies, B., Thomas, N. E., Cooper, S. M., … Kicman, A. T. (2009). Counterfeiting in performance- and image-enhancing drugs. *Drug Testing and Analysis, 1*(3), 135–142.

Hall, R. C., & Chapman, M. J. (2005). Psychiatric complications of anabolic steroid abuse. *Psychosomatics, 46*(4), 285–290.

Hoare, J. (2009). *Drug misuse declared: Findings from the 2008/09 British crime survey.* London: Home Office.

Kanayama, G., Barry, S., Hudson, J. I., & Pope, H. G., Jr. (2006). Body image and attitudes toward male roles in anabolic–androgenic steroid users. *American Journal of Psychiatry, 163*(4), 697–703.

Kanayama, G., Boynes, M., Hudson, J. I., Field, A. E., & Pope, H. G., Jr. (2007). Anabolic steroid abuse among teenage girls: An illusory problem? *Drug and Alcohol Dependence, 88*(2–3), 156–162.

Kanayama, G., Brower, K. J., Wood, R. I., Hudson, J. I., & Pope, H. G., Jr. (2009a). Anabolic-androgenic steroid dependence: An emerging disorder. *Addiction, 104*(12), 1966–1978.

Kanayama, G., Brower, K. J., Wood, R. I., Hudson, J. I., & Pope, H. G., Jr. (2009b). Issues for DSM-V: Clarifying the diagnostic criteria for anabolic–androgenic steroid dependence. *American Journal of Psychiatry, 166*(6), 642–645.

Kanayama, G., Brower, K. J., Wood, R. I., Hudson, J. I., & Pope, H. G., Jr. (2010). Treatment of anabolic–androgenic steroid dependence: Emerging evidence and its implications. *Drug and Alcohol Dependence, 109*(1–3), 6–13.

Kanayama, G., Cohane, G. H., Weiss, R. D., & Pope, H. G., Jr. (2003). Past anabolic-androgenic steroid use among men admitted for substance abuse treatment: An under-recognized problem? *Journal of Clinical Psychiatry, 64*(2), 156–160.

Kanayama, G., Hudson, J. I., & Pope, H. G., Jr. (2008). Long-term psychiatric and medical consequences of anabolic–androgenic steroid abuse: A looming public health concern? *Drug and Alcohol Dependence, 98*(1–2), 1–12.

Kanayama, G., Hudson, J. I., & Pope, H. G., Jr. (2009). Features of men with anabolic-androgenic steroid dependence: A comparison with nondependent AAS users and with AAS nonusers. *Drug and Alcohol Dependence, 102*(1–3), 130–137.

Kanayama, G., Hudson, J. I., & Pope, H. G., Jr. (2010). Illicit anabolic–androgenic steroid use. *Hormones and Behavior, 58*(1), 111–121.

Kanayama, G., Pope, H. G., Jr., Cohane, G., & Hudson, J. I. (2003). Risk factors for anabolic–androgenic steroid use among weightlifters: A case-control study. *Drug and Alcohol Dependence, 71*(1), 77–86.

Kennedy, M. C., & O'Sullivan, A. J. (1997). Do anabolic–androgenic steroids enhance sporting performance? *Medical Journal of Australia, 166*(2), 60–61.

Kindlundh, A. M. S., Hagekull, B., Isacson, D. G. L., & Nyberg, F. (2001). Adolescent use of anabolic–androgenic steroids and relations to self-reports of social, personality and health aspects. *European Journal of Public Health, 11*(3), 322–328.

Klotz, F., Petersson, A., Isacson, D., & Thiblin, I. (2007). Violent crime and substance abuse: A medico-legal comparison between deceased users of anabolic androgenic steroids and abusers of illicit drugs. *Forensic Science International, 173*(1), 57–63.

Kochakian, C. D. (1990). History of anabolic androgenic steroids. In G. Lin, & L. Erinhoff (Eds.), *Anabolic steroid abuse.* Rockville, MD: National Institute on Drug Abuse.

Korkia, P. (1994). Anabolic steroid use in Britain. *International Journal of Drug Policy, 5*, 6–10.

Korkia, P., & Stimson, G. (1993). *Anabolic steroid use in Great Britain: An exploratory investigation.* London: The Centre for Research on Drugs and Health Behaviour.

Kouri, E. M., Pope, H. G., Jr., Katz, D. L., & Oliva, P. (1995). Fat-free mass index in users and nonusers of anabolic–androgenic steroids. *Clinical Journal of Sports Medicine, 5*(4), 223–228.

Kutscher, E. C., Lund, B. C., & Perry, P. J. (2002). Anabolic steroids: A review for the clinician. *Sports Medicine, 32*(5), 285–296.

Larance, B., Degenhardt, L., Copeland, J., & Dillon, P. (2008). Injecting risk behaviour and related harm among men who use performance- and image-enhancing drugs. *Drug and Alcohol Review, 27*(6), 679–686.

Leit, R. A., Pope, H. G., Jr., & Gray, J. J. (2001). Cultural expectations of muscularity in men: The evolution of playgirl centerfolds. *International Journal of Eating Disorders, 29*(1), 90–93.

Lundholm, L., Käll, K., Wallin, S., & Thiblin, I. (2010). Use of anabolic androgenic steroids in substance abusers arrested for crime. *Drug and Alcohol Dependence, 111*(3), 222–226.

Melchert, R. B., & Welder, A. A. (1995). Cardiovascular effects of androgenic–anabolic steroids. *Medicine and Science in Sports and Exercise, 27*(9), 1252–1262.

Menon, D. K. (2003). Successful treatment of anabolic steroid-induced azoospermia with human chorionic gonadotropin and human menopausal gonadotropin. *Fertility and Sterility, 79*(3), 1659–1661.

Mitchell, G. (2007). *Report to the Commissioner of Baseball of an independent investigation into the illegal use of steroids and other performance enhancing substances by players in Major League Baseball.* New York: Office of the Commissioner of Baseball.

Modlinski, R., & Fields, K. B. (2006). The effect of anabolic steroids on the gastrointestinal system, kidneys, and adrenal glands. *Current Sports Medicine Reports, 5*(2), 104–109.

Monaghan, L. F. (2002). Vocabularies of motive for illicit steroid use among bodybuilders. *Social Science and Medicine, 55*(5), 695–708.

O'Connor, D. B., Archer, J., & Wu, F. C. W. (2004). Effects of testosterone on mood, aggression and sexual behavior in young men: A double-blind, placebo-controlled, cross-over study. *Journal of Clinical Endocrinology and Metabolism, 89*, 2837–2845.

Olrich, T. W., & Ewing, M. E. (1999). Life on steroids: Bodybuilders describe their perceptions of the anabolic androgenic steroid use period. *The Sport Psychologist, 13*, 299–312.

Pagonis, T. A., Angelopoulos, N. V., Koukoulis, G. N., & Hadjichristodoulou, C. S. (2006). Psychiatric side effects induced by supraphysiological doses of combinations of anabolic steroids correlate to the severity of abuse. *European Psychiatry, 21*(8), 551–562.

Pagonis, T. A., Angelopoulos, N. V., Koukoulis, G. N., Hadjichristodoulou, C. S., & Toli, P. N. (2006). Psychiatric and hostility factors related to use of anabolic steroids in monozygotic twins. *European Psychiatry, 21*(8), 563–569.

Parkinson, A. B., & Evans, N. A. (2006). Anabolic androgenic steroids: A survey of 500 users. *Medicine and Science in Sports and Exercise, 38*(4), 644–651.

Parrott, A. C., Choi, P. Y., & Davies, M. (1994). Anabolic steroid use by amateur athletes: Effects upon psychological mood states. *Journal of Sports Medicine and Physical Fitness, 34*(3), 292–298.

Parssinen, M., & Seppala, T. (2002). Steroid use and long-term health risks in former athletes. *Sports Medicine, 32*(2), 83–94.

Payne, J. R., Kotwinski, P. J., & Montgomery, H. E. (2004). Cardiac effects of anabolic steroids. *Heart, 90*(5), 473–475.

Pederson, W., & Wichstrom, L. (2001). Adolescents, doping agents and drug use: A community study. *Journal of Drug Issues, 31*, 517–542.

Pickett, T. C., Lewis, R. J., & Cash, T. F. (2005). Men, muscles, and body image: Comparisons of competitive bodybuilders, weight trainers, and athletically active controls. *British Journal of Sports Medicine, 39*(4), 217–222.

Pope, H. G., Jr., & Brower, K. J. (2009). Anabolic–androgenic steroid-related disorders. In B. J. Sadock, V. A. Sadock, & P. Ruiz (Eds.), *Comprehensive textbook of psychiatry* (9th ed., pp. 1419–1431). Philadelphia, PA: Lippincott Williams & Wilkins.

Pope, H. G., Jr., Kanayama, G., Ionescu-Pioggia, M., & Hudson, J. I. (2004). Anabolic steroid users' attitudes towards physicians. *Addiction, 99*(9), 1189–1194.

Pope, H. G., Jr., & Katz, D. L. (1990). Homicide and near-homicide by anabolic steroid users. *Journal of Clinical Psychiatry, 51*(1), 28–31.

Pope, H. G., Jr., Katz, D. L., & Hudson, J. I. (1993). Anorexia nervosa and 'reverse anorexia' among 108 male bodybuilders. *Comprehensive Psychiatry, 34*(6), 406–409.

Pope, H. G., Jr., Kouri, E. M., & Hudson, J. I. (2000). Effects of supraphysiologic doses of testosterone on mood and aggression in normal men: A randomized controlled trial. *Archives of General Psychiatry, 57*(2), 133–140; discussion 155–156.

Pope, H. G., Jr., Kouri, E. M., Powell, K. F., Campbell, C., & Katz, D. L. (1996). Anabolic–androgenic steroid use among 133 prisoners. *Comprehensive Psychiatry, 37*(5), 322–327.

Pope, H. G., Jr., Olivardia, R., Gruber, A., & Borowiecki, J. (1999). Evolving ideals of male body image as seen through action toys. *International Journal of Eating Disorders, 26*(1), 65–72.

Shahidi, N. T. (2001). A review of the chemistry, biological action, and clinical applications of anabolic–androgenic steroids. *Clinical Therapeutics, 23*(9), 1355–1390.

Skarberg, K., Nyberg, F., & Engstrom, I. (2008). The development of multiple drug use among anabolic–androgenic steroid users: Six subjective case reports. *Substance Abuse Treatment Prevention and Policy, 3*, 24.

Striegel, H., Simon, P., Frisch, S., Roecker, K., Dietz, K., Dickhuth, H. H., & Ulrich, R. (2006). Anabolic ergogenic substance users in fitness sports: A distinct group supported by the health care system. *Drug and Alcohol Dependence, 81*(1), 11–19.

Sturmi, J. E., & Diorio, D. J. (1998). Anabolic agents. *Clinical Sports Medicine, 17*(2), 261–282.

Su, T. P., Pagliaro, M., Schmidt, P. J., Pickar, D., Wolkowitz, O., & Rubinow, D. R. (1993). Neuropsychiatric effects of anabolic steroids in male normal volunteers. *Journal of the American Medical Association, 269*(21), 2760–2764.

Tan, R. S., & Scally, M. C. (2009). Anabolic steroid-induced hypogonadism – Towards a unified hypothesis of anabolic steroid action. *Medical Hypotheses, 72*(6), 723–728.

Thevis, M., Schrader, Y., Thomas, A., Sigmund, G., Geyer, H., & Schanzer, W. (2008). Analysis of confiscated black market drugs using chromatographic and mass spectrometric approaches. *Journal of Analytical Toxicology, 32*(3), 232–240.

Thiblin, I., Lindquist, O., & Rajs, J. (2000). Cause and manner of death among users of anabolic androgenic steroids. *Journal of Forensic Sciences, 45*(1), 16–23.

Thiblin, I., & Parlklo, T. (2002). Anabolic androgenic steroids and violence. *Acta Psychiatrica Scandinavica Supplement, 412*, 125–128.

Thiblin, I., & Petersson, A. (2005). Pharmacoepidemiology of anabolic androgenic steroids: A review. *Fundamental & Clinical Pharmacology, 19*(1), 27–44.

van Amsterdam, J., Opperhuizen, A., & Hartgens, F. (2010). Adverse health effects of anabolic–androgenic steroids. *Regulatory Toxicology and Pharmacology, 57*(1), 117–123.

van Amsterdam, J., Opperhuizen, A., Koeter, M., & van den Brink, W. (2010). Ranking the harm of alcohol, tobacco and illicit drugs for the individual and the population. *European Addiction Research, 16*(4), 202–207.

Waddington, I. (2000). *Sport, health and drugs: A critical sociological perspective.* London: E & FN Spon, Taylor & Francis Group.

Wade, N. (1972). Anabolic steroids: Doctors denounce them, but athletes aren't listening. *Science, 176*(4042), 1399–1403.

Wagman, D., Curry, L., & Cook, D. (1995). An investigation into anabolic androgenic steroid use by elite US powerlifters. *Journal of Strength and Conditioning Research, 9*(3), 149–154.

Werner, F., & Berendonk, B. (1997). Hormonal doping and androgenization of athletes: A secret program of the German Democratic Republic government. *Clinical Chemistry, 43*, 1262–1279.

Wichstrom, L., & Pedersen, W. (2001). Use of anabolic–androgenic steroids in adolescence: Winning, looking good or being bad? *Journal of the Study of Alcohol, 62*(1), 5–13.

Wood, R. I. (2008). Anabolic–androgenic steroid dependence? Insights from animals and humans. *Frontiers in Neuroendocrinology, 29*(4), 490–506.

World Anti-Doping Agency. (2008). *Adverse analytical findings and atypical findings reported by accredited laboratories.* Retrieved from www.wada-ama.org/rtecontent/document/WADA_2008_LaboratoryStatisticsReport_Final.pdf

Wu, F. C., Farley, T. M., Peregoudov, A., & Waites, G. M. (1996). Effects of testosterone enanthate in normal men: Experience from a multicenter contraceptive efficacy study. World Health Organization task force on methods for the regulation of male fertility. *Fertility and Sterility, 65*(3), 626–636.

Yesalis, C. E., Courson, S. P., & Wright, J. (1993). History of anabolic steroid use in sport and exercise. In C. E. Yesalis (Ed.), *Anabolic steroids in sport and exercise.* Champaign, IL: Human Kinetics.

10

PROFESSIONAL DEVELOPMENT IN STRENGTH AND CONDITIONING COACHES

David Tod

ABERYSTWYTH UNIVERSITY, UK

David Lavallee

UNIVERSITY OF STIRLING, UK

As an applied science, strength and conditioning (S&C) has been influenced by two knowledge sources (Fry & Newton, 2002). First, the practical knowledge developed from the role of S&C in society. As far back as ancient Egypt, Ireland, China, Greece and Rome, records show that strength abilities were admired and celebrated (Fry & Newton, 2002). Many individuals since these times have engaged in conditioning regimes to develop their athletic abilities for entertainment, competitive, military, economic, health and display purposes. Throughout history, people have learned from their experiences and those of others about ways to develop physical attributes. Second, the influence science has had on the S&C field may be traced back to the renaissance, where knowledge about how the body worked began emerging (Fry & Newton, 2002). Understanding human physiology and anatomy has paved a way for learning how to train the body. More recently, sport and exercise science has influenced S&C knowledge.

As a profession, the modern S&C field has experienced tremendous growth over the later years of the twentieth and early years of the twenty-first centuries. One way to illustrate the growth is to chart the development of the National Strength and Conditioning Association (NSCA) from North America. The NSCA was formed in 1978, with a membership of 76, and its original name was the National Strength Coaches Association (NSCA, 2008). The organisation's purpose was to 'unify members and facilitate a professional exchange of ideas in strength development as it relates to the improvement of athletic performance and fitness'. By 1981, the organisation had over 2,250 members and had changed its name to the NSCA to reflect membership expertise. The NSCA membership had expanded beyond strength coaches to include various individuals contributing to the field. The discipline was no longer the sole providence of weightlifters, powerlifters and bodybuilders. S&C coaches were being recognised as having roles to play in other sports and for well-being purposes. There are now more than 30,000 members worldwide, and the NSCA has two recognised certification schemes, helping individuals demonstrate they have the knowledge and skills to work in the field.

Educating professionals, athletes and coaches is a major NSCA goal. The knowledge considered important for professionals is embodied in the organisation's flagship textbook *The Essentials of Strength Training and Conditioning* (Baechle & Earle, 2008), now into its third edition. Examining the table of contents reveals that S&C coaches draw on various disciplines such as physiology, biomechanics, psychology, nutrition and rehabilitation. Similar to other young professions that arose around the same time (e.g. sport psychology), the S&C field is technically oriented, focusing on the tests and interventions that may assist athletes in meeting their physical conditioning goals. Individuals, however, need more than technical knowledge to be effective. Helpful professionals have other attributes, such as interpersonal skills, allowing them to help clients. For example, experienced practitioners acknowledge that establishing positive working relationships with clients, in whatever way that is expressed, is fundamental to ensuring athletes follow their training programmes. It seems reasonable to suggest that theory and personality drive effective S&C interventions. The theory component represents knowledge about the best ways to measure and develop strength, power, endurance and other physical attributes. The personality component represents practitioners' abilities to get alongside their clients and inspire them to work towards their conditioning goals.

A review of S&C research reveals that, although the technical body of knowledge has advanced rapidly, there is less understanding of the practitioner. There has not been much research, for example, on topics such as the characteristics of effective versus ineffective professionals. Of the existing research, investigators have focused primarily on the typical profile of practitioners, along with certain career-related behaviours and beliefs, such as leadership style and job satisfaction (Duehring & Ebben, 2010; Magnusen, 2010; Martinez, 2004). Investigators have seldom examined how practitioners develop the skills to help athletes or the ways in which professionals change with experience. Research focused on these topics will provide information that practitioners may find beneficial. Practitioners might draw on professional development knowledge to help them plan their careers.

Despite limited literature on S&C coaches' professional development, there is a large body of knowledge in related disciplines, such as clinical, counselling and sport psychology (Rønnestad & Skovholt, 2003; Tod, Andersen, & Marchant, 2009, 2011). There are sufficient similarities between the roles of applied psychologist and S&C coach to allow informed hypotheses to be proposed that may guide research. Each individual, for example, is involved in a helping profession, albeit with a different focus. S&C coaches help athletes and exercisers achieve their physical development-related goals. Applied psychologists assist clients in resolving psychological issues so that they can lead happy, fulfilling lives.

It is possible that knowledge about how psychologists become competent may inform the understanding of how S&C coaches master their discipline. In this chapter, we briefly overview psychologist development theory that may contribute to knowledge in the S&C field. Then we illustrate the applicability of this knowledge with quotes from two highly experienced S&C coaches whom we interviewed about their careers, before identifying applied implications and research directions.

Psychologist development theory

A number of psychologist development theories, describing professional growth from trainee to senior practitioner, have been proposed (Hogan, 1964; Loganbill, Hardy, & Delworth, 1982; Stoltenberg & McNeill, 2009). The different models are somewhat analogous to fine New Zealand wines. Although they have different nuances, they are quite similar (Worthington, 1987). Initially, for example, trainee psychologists are dependent on the guidance of teachers, supervisors and readings because they lack sufficient experience to guide their client-related decision making. Experienced practitioners, however, draw on internalised knowledge gained from their service-delivery experience. Trainees often experience self-doubts and anxieties regarding their competence. Typically, beginning psychologists focus on learning specific intervention techniques that they implement in rigid ways, and they prefer to learn by imitating mentors. Seasoned practitioners are adaptable and flexible in using intervention techniques and adjust them to suit their clients' needs and circumstances. Research has indicated parallels between counselling and sport psychologist development (Tod et al., 2009, 2011; Tod & Bond, 2010). Given that sport psychologists work with athletes, there may be similarities with S&C coaches' professional development.

Professional development in S&C coaches

To explore possible developmental themes in S&C coaches and to identify applied implications and research directions, we interviewed two experienced practitioners, and in this section, we present the results.[1]

To maintain the two individuals' confidentialities, we have changed their names to Asterix and Obelix. We have also changed or deleted other details that might reveal their identities. Asterix is a 39-year-old man working as a full-time S&C coach in a national sports institute. He has been helping athletes for 16 years and is accredited with the NSCA. His clients have included athletes from various sports, ranging from recreational to elite, and exercise participants across the lifespan from children to the elderly. He has a PhD in S&C and has published widely in the area. Obelix is a 35-year-old man with 9 years of experience in helping athletes from many sports, mostly at the elite and professional levels. He is currently working in a university and is accredited with the NSCA, the United Kingdom Strength and Condition Association (UKSCA), the British Association of the Sport and Exercise

Sciences and the American College of Sports Medicine. Similar to Asterix, Obelix has a PhD in S&C and has published widely in the area.

Changes in role and style

Increased flexibility

The two practitioners gave several examples of how the ways they work with athletes had changed as they gained experience. Obelix stated:

> I tended to be very, very rigid in my programming and very prescriptive as well [when I first started], whereas that has definitely changed now to where I am a lot more flexible in terms of my approach and less prescriptive.

The following quote may help to explain why he was rigid and prescriptive: 'When you first start working with athletes you are very much ... led by textbooks ... whereas now I have very much moved onto now you have developed a bank of your own experiences.' As Obelix illustrates, often when practitioners first start working with clients, they rely on external knowledge sources, such as textbooks. Many times external sources of knowledge may contain the general principles associated with S&C work and may not provide the necessary guidance to help individuals apply that information to specific situations. With experience, however, practitioners develop an understanding of how to apply general principles to specific circumstances (a theme echoed in psychologist development).

Increased focus on key elements

Associated with being rigid and prescriptive, inexperienced professionals may also overwhelm athletes with technical information, as explained by Asterix:

> When I first started out I was a bit more technical and I think it's one of those things when you are in your twenties ... you think like you know everything, you think you have got a pretty good handle on what an athlete needs and what's required, so I probably tended to over-coach a bit more and try and impart too much information ... I think now I tend to be a bit more selective and not try and impart everything and try and keep it simple and focus on key things with the athlete.

Asterix indicated that over time he became increasingly client-led and, rather than giving them everything he knew about a topic, he began to focus on what athletes needed for their development. Asterix's following quote may signal one reason why he tended to impart too much information when first working with athletes: 'I would have told them everything, I think to the athlete and the coach as well, and baffle them with BS to make myself look impressive.' As explained below, research has shown that beginning applied psychologists, when first working with clients in the early phases of their careers, often experience anxiety and question whether they are competent (Rønnestad & Skovholt, 2003; Tod et al., 2009). One way to justify to themselves they are capable is to provide athletes with a lot of information.

More emphasis given to relationships

Both practitioners also discussed how they now spent more time getting to know athletes and building good working relationships with them. According to Asterix:

> I previously would have put more emphasis on the actual information and the knowledge base, but I think now … even more critical is the way you impart the information and the relationships you build with the athlete.

It appears that Asterix and Obelix focused on delivering knowledge and interventions early in their careers and over time became more aware of the role relationships play when working with athletes than they had initially. One reason for building good working relationships was to help individualise programmes to athletes' specific needs and situations, as illustrated by Obelix: 'I learned very, very quickly that the best way to adapt an exercise for an athlete is to let the athlete adapt it themselves … no one knows the athlete's body better than the athletes themselves.' Another reason for building relationships with athletes was to gain their trust, and according to Obelix 'you develop that trust on a number of levels'. He believed that S&C coaches could develop trust in a number of ways, such as if they (a) looked like they trained themselves, (b) had played the sport, (c) had worked with other athletes effectively, or (d) were assessing their programmes and then gave feedback to the athlete. He mentioned that it was possible to 'get the athlete to buy in on numerous levels'. Furthermore, Obelix believed that 'it's about targeting what, which one of those the athletes like, and making sure you emphasise your strengths in each one of those areas'. Although having played the athlete's sport may assist in building a working relationship, Obelix went on to say:

> It was a misconception I had a few years ago, that you had to have played the sport to get the athletes to respect you. No, I think you have to have a good knowledge of the sport. A good training ethic yourself, I always found from a personal perspective, helps you break down barriers with athletes, but also one of the main underlying factors is your knowledge in the area and the athletes trust what your are trying to programme and you are trying to develop.

Playing experience is not a necessity to working with athletes effectively, although it may assist in establishing a rapport. Also, practitioners with playing experience may have a good understanding of the sport and its demands. It is possible, however, to gain knowledge about a sport and its demands in a variety of ways, such as watching videos and speaking to athletes and coaches. Having played the sport may have some disadvantages. For example, practitioners may be tempted to overstep their professional boundaries and offer advice that belongs in the province of another professional, such as a technical skills coach or a sports medicine specialist. There is potential for conflict among support staff and athletes may be unsure who to trust.

As a third reason, Asterix mentioned that developing good relationships with athletes helped him 'present it [information] to them in such a way that it's really clear for them, that they can see [the point I am making]'. As an example, he discussed how he had found athletes and coaches responded positively to visual feedback after undertaking a needs assessment. A sport psychology colleague had shared with him a method for giving visual feedback to athletes using radar plots. Asterix had received positive feedback from athletes and coaches when he had given them radar plots modified to suit S&C contexts.

Broadened view of the S&C role and its place in athletic preparation

Asterix said:

> A view that I think a lot of people have is that a S&C person … as just personal trainers, or like gym instructors, or strength heads and they do the stuff in the gym, and that was my view I would think when I was first starting out … [whereas now] it's more about total athlete preparation, not just the physical side, so it's the recovery and it's the monitoring of them during their training and those sorts of things.

Asterix's view seems to parallel the NSCA's early development. By 1981, the organisation had changed its name to reflect that the services that S&C coaches could provide were connected to total athlete preparation and not just the development of strength. It is maybe understandable that Asterix's view broadened over time. Before becoming an S&C specialist, he had a strong background in competitive weightlifting where preparation is focused heavily on strength. As he became exposed to other sports and contexts, he realised that there were other roles for people with his expertise.

Alongside his broadened view, Asterix also said: 'I think that something else I have developed is an appreciation of other disciplines and what they can bring, and I think that's pretty critical for what we do as well, which is being able to integrate.' Obelix also discussed the place of the S&C coach within an athlete support team. He talked about how initially he was generous in his assessment of his contribution to athlete success:

> You probably feel that [anxiety] a little bit more when you first get into it [become a practitioner], because maybe you have overanalysed how important you are in the grand scale of things and then as you get more experienced, and you see a lot of other things going on, you realise that you do play a role, but it's probably quite a small role, it's all the small roles that go together that bring it together [success].

The discussion above echoes a developmental theme associated with psychologists. Over time psychologists gain greater insight into the complexity of psychotherapy and the role it can play in helping people resolve their issues (Rønnestad & Skovholt, 2003). At the same time practitioners also realise their influence over others is not as great as they initially thought when they were trainees.

Asterix's and Obelix's experiences with anxiety

Many applied psychologists experience anxiety throughout their careers regarding their professional competence (Rønnestad & Skovholt, 2003; Tod et al., 2011). Similarly, both Asterix and Obelix talked about times when they had doubted their abilities and had been anxious. Obelix said:

> No matter how much preparation you put in … you probably lack a little bit of confidence in what you have done, until you actually carry it out, and then once you have carried it out and you see that its beneficial you adapt. I have a lot more conviction in my approach now, I'm a lot more confident in what I'm doing.

In applied psychology, although students may feel high levels of anxiety regarding their initial client interactions, by the time they have become experienced practitioners their stress has decreased and they have become confident in their competence (Rønnestad & Skovholt, 2003). Obelix illustrates that changes in anxiety and confidence levels may also be observed in S&C coaches. One of the most potent sources of confidence is performance accomplishment (Bandura, 1997). As Obelix indicates, before practitioners have built a history of helping athletes develop their physical attributes, it is possible they will question whether they have the abilities to be effective. Practitioners' anxieties may be influenced by a number of factors. They might, for example, feel more anxious if they magnify the consequences of being ineffective. As another example, if practitioners are being evaluated by others, such as coaches, administrators, supervisors and mentors, then their desire not to appear incompetent in front of significant others might also increase their anxieties. Helping trainees learn to manage their anxieties may be one mentor and educator role.

In contrast to Obelix, Asterix indicated that he had not experienced anxiety when first working with clients. Early in his career, Asterix had worked a lot with sub-elite athletes before spending some time as an academic. He had then moved back into applied work:

> I think me moving from quite an academic role to a more applied role … probably initially there was some, there was a little bit more apprehension in that situation, I mean I knew I could do the job and I had done plenty of stuff with athletes, but I found moving into this [applied] environment that,

> what's the way to put it, you know the way people view academia in applied settings ... sometimes they don't really rate what we might have done if we have worked with athletes or worked on a training study and actually trained athletes.

Although over time applied psychologists' anxiety levels tend to decrease, there are periods when practitioners' worries and doubts increase, such as when they start working with new client groups, in different ways or in unfamiliar settings. It seems that Asterix also found his anxieties increased when he moved from academia to an applied setting because in the new environment he perceived that there were others who questioned his capabilities. Similarly, research has suggested that confidence levels may increase or decrease depending on the feedback others provide (Bandura, 1997).

Learning how to work with athletes

In addition to talking about the ways in which their service-delivery thoughts, emotions and behaviours had changed, both Asterix and Obelix described some of the processes and information sources they believed had underpinned their development. In this section, two sub-themes are discussed including the information sources (people, events and literature) from which Asterix and Obelix had learned about helping athletes, and the value of self-reflection in the learning process.

Sources of information contributing to professional development

The sources of information that applied psychologists consider contribute most to their growth as practitioners include client experience, assistance from mentors and being a therapy client (Tod et al., 2011). Asterix and Obelix discussed three sources that paralleled those indicated by psychologists: athlete experience, assistance from mentors and their own athletic background. When asked about the experiences and interactions that had taught him how to work with athletes, Asterix responded that the first key element had been

> going back to [my first job after university]. I think that was a great opportunity ... I think the ability just to be able to design programmes and work with athletes one on one, even though I didn't really know what I was doing, it was a great opportunity to cut your teeth with a cohort; there were still some pretty good athletes in that group.

The exercise physiology specificity principle may provide a useful analogy to interpret Asterix's quote. If athletes wish to improve their performance capabilities, they need to train the physiological demands associated with their sport. For S&C coaches, the most specific form of training they can undertake is working with athletes, and both Asterix and Obelix talked about how they had learned much from their interactions with clients. Athlete experience will help practitioners learn a great deal including how to adapt exercises and programmes to suit clients' needs and circumstances, the contexts in which training occurs, and the demands of the sports in which their clients participate.

Asterix followed up his quote above with:

> I think the next key thing for me [after my first job] would have been that opportunity to go to the States … and be able to rub shoulders with some of those academics and professionals that work over there, like [name of a well-known S&C specialist] … That one year that I spent with him was huge just in terms of being immersed in research, but really quite applied research, like day-to-day, running training studies and being in the lab and also having to work with kids and athletes and do monitoring and testing and all that sort of stuff.

Asterix's story reveals that mentors have an enormous influence on practitioners' development, and the same theme emerges from applied psychologist research (Rønnestad & Skovholt, 2003). For example, applied psychologists have discussed how when working with clients they may recall the guidance received from supervisors, even if they have not interacted with their mentors for many years. In many applied psychology training programmes, mentoring is formalised through the supervision process, and students are required to meet with supervisors on a regular basis to help them develop their competence and to ensure the services they provide clients are ethical, safe and effective. Asterix and Obelix believed that the formal supervision process could be given greater emphasis in the training of S&C coaches and by the organisations through which they gained their professional qualifications.

Related to having mentors, both Obelix and Asterix discussed how collegial interactions had helped their development. Obelix said: 'The other thing that has helped me has been to develop a really good network of colleagues who I trust, who I can feed ideas off, and they can feed ideas off me.' There may be other professional development benefits to interacting with colleagues in addition to sharing ideas. For example, interacting with colleagues in both professional and social settings may provide practitioners with opportunities to refine the interpersonal skills that help them form good client relationships.

In addition to athlete–client interactions and mentors, Asterix discussed how his own athletic training taught him much about S&C. Many practitioners have probably been either athletes themselves or recreational trainers who see becoming S&C coaches as a way to build a career in an area for which they have a passion. Asterix highlighted various benefits from having been an athlete for his development as an S&C practitioner, such as appreciating the demands of daily training, learning about the process from his coaches and fellow athletes and moulding his philosophical approach. There may well be other benefits such as becoming aware of (a) what it is like being an athlete striving for personal excellence, (b) the mistakes they make when training and (c) the obstacles they face. Another benefit may involve being the sports participant in the coach–athlete relationship. Being exposed to a range of coaches and S&C specialists may allow individuals to reflect on the types of coaching behaviours and attitudes that encourage suitable training behaviours in athletes.

Both individuals interviewed discussed how they learned much from the S&C research. Throughout their careers, they had tried to base their practice on scientific evidence where possible, as illustrated by Asterix:

> I really believe in when you do something there has got to be a reason for it and it's good to have evidence to back up what you are doing, and it doesn't have to be published research necessarily, but I mean just having that base of something that's systematic … [for example] if you are going to test then it's really important that you have a test that is reliable, because otherwise how do you know that what you're seeing in terms of a decrease or increase in that test is a result of your practice or is it just a result of the test and all that is associated with it?

Asterix's view reflects the core belief of S&C organisations, such as the UKSCA or NSCA, that sound knowledge and research underpins effective practice. Such a belief helps justify S&C as a profession. One feature of a profession is that practitioners have specialist knowledge that they offer for remuneration. To label themselves professionals, S&C coaches need to demonstrate they have specialist knowledge, and one way is to argue that their expertise is based on science.

In the following quote, Obelix discussed the relative importance of practical experience and research on his professional development:

> Initially very much coaches and athletes helped me a lot … whereas now I have a pretty good understanding of how coaches and athletes function and what they want from a practitioner, what they need, and now it's probably more research that dictates [my practice] and probably because of now the way I work, because I am very much programming, overseeing, and less implementing, it's probably more important that I'm more knowledgeable of the research now and it informs me more now, and the level of athlete, although I have always worked with a good standard of Olympic athlete, the level I'm working with now, [national sports team], [professional sports team], you need to be a lot more innovative and [know the] research, current research, a lot of it is not actually published and you actually have to start contacting people about what they are doing now instead of what they have actually published.

Obelix's views may reflect his developmental needs as he has gained experience. When first working with clients, Obelix was nervous and he questioned his competence: he was uncertain if he had the skills to help athletes. Specific doubts were similar to those issues mentioned above, such as understanding how athletes function, what they need and what they desire from an S&C coach. Actual service delivery allowed Obelix to find answers to those questions more readily than reading current research. As a seasoned practitioner, Obelix now has the contextual knowledge that informs his practice and understanding of his role as an S&C coach. His development needs have changed. Having mastered the ability to work with clients effectively, Obelix can now focus more of his attention than he was able to initially on being creative and helping his clients find competitive advantages over their opposition.

The value of self-reflection in the learning process

In the realm of psychologist growth, some researchers consider that self-reflection contributes a great deal to professional development (Cropley, Miles, Hanton, & Niven, 2007; Tod, 2007), a theme that Obelix echoed when he said:

> [One] main thing would be the re-evaluation of your programmes at all times … the best example I can give is that I look at the volume and some of the training volumes I had for my [early] athletes in the gym and, if I were to programme for the same athletes now, I would probably halve my programme, because although I knew what they were doing in the pool or on the track or on the pitch I still wanted to get in everything that I felt they needed as well, whereas I realise or I look at it now and go 'well they are doing that many sessions there so I would actually cut my volume quite a lot'. That is the only thing I would say is to continuously re-evaluate what you're doing and don't be scared to go away from the textbook because you have to put it into context of their complete programme; if not you are probably not going to enhance their performance that much, or you are going to predispose them to injury and everything else.

S&C service-delivery effectiveness may be influenced by several practitioner characteristics, including knowledge, expertise, contextual understanding and reflective abilities. Practitioners who can evaluate the ways they have assisted previous athletes may be able to identify how they can provide current and future clients with improved services, as evident in Obelix's quote above. By reviewing his early client experiences, he realised he was not considering athletes' overall training enough when developing their S&C component. He even implies that he might have hindered their training or predisposed them to injury.

On its own, self-reflection is unlikely to lead to improved service delivery (Kolb, Boyatzis, & Mainemelis, 2001). Instead, improved service delivery will probably occur when practitioners change the way they assist athletes based on their self-reflection, as implied by Obelix when he suggests that professionals should not be afraid to deviate from the textbook. A similar theme is present in the psychology literature where researchers propose that learning and improved performance (in this case S&C coaches' effectiveness) result from a combination of self-evaluation and active experimentation (Anderson, Knowles, & Gilbourne, 2004).

Applied implications

In their interviews, Asterix and Obelix discussed ways they had changed as practitioners and some of the processes underpinning their development. Understanding practitioner development may provide knowledge on which to suggest practical implications to assist educators, students and professionals towards becoming (or helping others become) effective service providers. The recommendations below are based on Asterix's and Obelix's interviews and applied psychologist development literature.

Matching teaching strategies with trainees' needs

Trainees will likely appreciate high levels of structure and guidance early in their development, because such assistance might help them cope with anxiety and provide them with direction for helping athletes. As trainees' competence and knowledge increases, they are able to take responsibility for their growth. Loganbill et al.'s (1982) instructional interventions for psychologist education will likely help S&C educators match teaching practices to trainees' needs. *Facilitative interventions* refer to attitudes and behaviours that encourage supportive environments in which trainees feel secure and safe. Ways to develop supportive environments include demonstrating warmth, respect, empathy and tolerance towards trainees, and placing the evaluation of their progress within the broader goal of their development. Supportive environments help lessen trainee anxiety and afford them opportunities to engage in self-reflection.

Conceptual interventions include efforts to help trainees use research and theory to guide their client interactions. Educators could, for example, ask trainees to explain how they used McGuigan's (this volume) chapter on resistance training monitoring to prepare for a client session. One way to match conceptual interventions to trainees' needs is to consider their preferred learning styles. People who pursue careers in the helping professions typically favour working with others, generating and exchanging new ideas, receiving personalised feedback and considering specific situations from multiple perspectives (Kolb et al., 2001); themes echoed in Asterix's and Obelix's interviews. Based on such research, trainee development might be enhanced via group supervision or classroom discussions in which specific situations are considered from different viewpoints; for example, discussing the relevant ethical principles to consider when S&C coaches no longer feel comfortable working with particular athletes. After completing formal training, practitioners could belong to informal groups that regularly (and confidentially) discuss clients and other athlete situations (e.g. those reported in the media).

When using *prescriptive interventions*, educators provide trainees with specific guidance for particular situations. Prescriptive interventions might include giving beginning students action plans for use with athletes or instructions to eliminate specific unhelpful behaviours from their service-delivery practices; a mentor might ask a trainee to follow Bird, Tarpenning, and Marino's (2005) programme design recommendations for use with healthy exercise participants. Such prescriptive interventions help trainees maintain client welfare, provide effective services to athletes and cope with anxiety. Although prescriptive interventions might help trainees during their early professional development, such instructional strategies might stifle advanced students' progress towards autonomy and independence.

Confrontive interventions refer to attempts by educators and supervisors to highlight discrepancies among trainees' behaviours, attitudes, feelings and external factors. For example, a mentor might identify a discrepancy between a trainee's verbal and non-verbal behaviours (e.g. the trainee might say they listen to athletes to find out their specific needs, but then prescribe generic programmes). Confrontive interventions might be perceived as negative evaluations of trainee abilities. Skilful mentors can diffuse the negative perceptions associated with confrontive interventions by emphasising the positive components of the discrepancies, such as highlighting unused strengths (the practitioner above might have a sound understanding of programme design principles). Effective mentors can also convey their acceptance of trainees and belief in their potential as practitioners. In addition, it might be beneficial to separate the specific behaviours, feelings or attitudes being examined from the trainee as an individual. Confrontive interventions may be suitable for advanced students and novice professionals, who typically have begun to consider the ways that they influence service delivery.

Catalytic interventions are designed to promote change through making unconscious abilities, thoughts, emotions and behaviours conscious (Loganbill et al., 1982). For example, questions from astute mentors might help male trainees become aware of the adoption of macho posturing towards female clients. With such insight, trainees might be able to understand how they influence client interactions, refrain from such stereotypical behaviour and improve service-delivery competence. Goal setting and self-reflection are useful catalytic interventions. In developing short-term goals, for instance, trainees and mentors could observe a video recording of the beginning practitioner collaborating with an athlete to identify unconscious strengths, such as behaviours or verbal statements that communicate engagement with the client. Trainees might then set goals and develop achievement strategies to help ensure that such strengths are repeated with other athletes (such as a reminder card that is reviewed before meeting with a client). Another catalytic intervention is to encourage practitioners to experiment with different coaching styles. Being able to adopt different coaching behaviours to suit athletes' needs and preferences likely contributes to consultant effectiveness. Role plays and supervised placements provide opportunities for practitioners to experiment with different coaching behaviours. Catalytic interventions might be most suitable for advanced students and practitioners to help expand their awareness of client variation, themselves and the service-delivery process.

Observed, simulated and real service-delivery experiences

Early in training, students can observe service delivery in action (e.g. watching recordings of practitioners working with clients), engage in simulated client interactions (e.g. role plays) or undertake supervised work experience. Typically, beginning students are trying to understand how S&C service delivery is conducted. Providing opportunities to observe experienced practitioners in action or engage in role plays help trainees develop knowledge to guide their initial service-delivery attempts. The focus of these opportunities may be on both the application of scientific knowledge and the development of coaching skills.

Modelling is an effective way to develop service-delivery competencies (Hill & Lent, 2006). The value of modelling might be enhanced if mentors encourage discussion, perhaps in group settings where several trainees can compare their perspectives. In addition, the individuals who are modelling service delivery are likely suitable for beginning students if their modelling displays helpful behaviours for the client, the models have high status among the trainees, and they are able to clearly demonstrate specific skills.

Role plays afford trainees opportunities to engage in or observe simulated service delivery (Tod, Marchant, & Andersen, 2007). Beginning and advanced students might find role plays uncomfortable, because typically they are in front of a perceived evaluative audience (e.g. teachers and classmates). There are ways, however, to ensure that role plays occur in safe and encouraging environments. For example, it might be helpful to avoid labelling trainees' behaviour as right or wrong. Instead, describing trainees' role-playing attempts as more or less helpful to clients might relieve students from feeling like they have to act in rigid, correct ways. Also, educators can explain to students that classrooms are safe places to make mistakes because the other people involved (teachers and classmates) understand the complexities associated with service delivery and so can empathise, be supportive and offer alternatives for improvement. In addition, mistakes in the classroom provide opportunities for everybody present to learn, not just the student in the role play. Reducing the number of people watching, or even eliminating the audience altogether, might also lessen evaluation anxiety. In a classroom situation, for example, separating students into small groups and running several role plays simultaneously might help them begin to gain some insights into service delivery and reduce large audience evaluation anxiety. Allowing trainees to stop role plays at any time lets them take breaks when they are uncomfortable or explore issues as they arise.

Most people training to become S&C practitioners likely have a training history themselves. Encouraging students to reflect on their training experiences might lead to substantial professional benefits. Having been an athlete can help trainees understand how other clients experience service delivery and the influence that practitioners have on athletes' physical development. Trainees can reflect on the different

S&C practitioners who have helped them and identify behaviours and attitudes that were associated with effectiveness.

Assisting trainees to manage anxiety and self-doubt

Awareness of the self-doubt and anxieties that beginning practitioners may experience can help mentors when interacting with trainees. The counselling psychology literature provides insights into some of the reactions anxious trainees might display (e.g. Rønnestad & Skovholt, 1993). When talking with mentors, for example, anxious trainees might want to only discuss athletes who are making progress or choose topics with which they feel comfortable. Mentors might provide support in various ways, such as encouraging self-awareness and emotional expression. For example, mentors might ask questions designed to help trainees explore their self-doubts and reactions. Reviewing trainees' case notes might help them recall their thoughts, feelings and reactions when working with athletes. Once anxiety sources have been identified, trainees might be in positions to make helpful changes to lessen anxiety. For example, trainees might become aware of communication skills that need developing. Mentors who communicate unconditional positive regard and acceptance might help relieve trainees of rigid imperatives that they must behave in particular ways. Stress-management techniques might help anxious trainees, such as deep breathing or goal setting, but they need to be used judiciously. Although unpleasant, anxieties could signal areas that beginning students would benefit from addressing. For example, trainees might be nervous about starting to work with highly trained athletes because they believe they will not be able to give the clients useful advice or write suitable programmes. The mentor might help the trainee adopt a client-led approach and begin by finding out what the clients are already doing and arranging a suitable testing battery. Along with stress-management techniques, assertiveness training could help trainees cope with some anxiety-provoking situations, such as communicating with difficult clients. Stress-management and assertiveness-training techniques might be taught to students as part of psychology classes or during supervision. Mentors might suggest trainees undertake continuing-education classes offered by universities or professional bodies.

Another way to help students cope with anxiety is to build their confidence that they can help athletes. Bandura's (1997) self-efficacy theory might help mentors identify confidence-building techniques. For example, short-term goal setting might assist trainees in obtaining positive service-delivery experiences, such as developing and administrating a test battery that provides information relevant to clients' needs.

Research directions

S&C knowledge has advanced tremendously, and researchers are able to furnish practitioners with guidelines about the types of programmes that help clients achieve training goals. As discussed above, however, researchers have not focused much attention on practitioner development. Based on Obelix's and Asterix's experiences, technical knowledge, on its own, is insufficient for ensuring practitioners are effective. Their stories indicate, for instance, that adapting services to athletes' needs and having relationship-building skills contributes towards intervention success. Their stories also reveal ways in which practitioners may evolve with experience and that these changes in behaviour and attitude may lead to increased effectiveness. Further research about practitioner competencies and the ways individuals develop their attributes will help the S&C field to become an applied science in the broadest, and not just in the technical, sense.

There are a number of research topics that could be explored. In one line of inquiry, investigators might examine relationships between markers of professional growth and service-delivery outcomes. For example, do athletes make greater training gains as practitioners gain more experience? Is effectiveness associated with education? Are individuals with PhDs more helpful than those with bachelors' or masters' degrees? As a second line of research, practitioners could be tracked over time to help document scientifically the changes that Asterix and Obelix observed in themselves and that occur in applied psychologists. As a third line of inquiry, recording eminent S&C coaches' stories would complement longitudinal studies. Related to the previous two suggestions, investigators could compare practitioners at different phases in their careers on a range of attributes believed to contribute to successful practice. For example, do individuals with 20 years' client experience write better training programmes than those people just starting out on their careers? As a fifth line of research, investigators could explore how practitioners' personal characteristics influence service delivery. For example, the reasons individuals decide to become practitioners likely varies, and knowledge about how these different motives influence service delivery may help individuals to assess and monitor their own motivations for being in the field. For instance, some practitioners might be failed athletes for whom being a practitioner allows them to remain in sport. The ways such individuals react to client failure (or success) may be different compared with folks who have become practitioners for other reasons.

The topics suggested above focus on the attributes of effective and ineffective practitioners and the ways they might change over time. Researchers could also examine the factors believed to influence professional growth. As one possibility, the influence that research and theory has on professional behaviour could be examined. Do practitioners stay up to date with current knowledge? If individuals do stay current, how do they make use of the literature and in what ways does it influence their practice? Given that Asterix and Obelix thought supervision and mentoring could be given more emphasis in training and continuing education, researchers who examine these topics might provide useful information for educators and professional organisations. Among the various options (e.g. literature, mentors, colleagues and athletes), what would individuals identify as the most influential sources of information about how to help athletes? Do the influential information sources change over time in their salience for practitioners? Perhaps, for example, client experience is more salient for students until they have developed a working knowledge about how to help people, after which they are better able to evaluate the research and apply it to their situations than they did when first starting their careers.

Conclusion

Working as an S&C practitioner may be enticing for a number of reasons, such as (a) working in an area about which individuals are passionate, (b) helping others pursue a goal, (c) working with elite athletes, (d) being labelled an expert in physical development or (e) the satisfaction of helping exercise participants improve the quality of their lives. As illustrated by Asterix and Obelix, individuals quickly learn that effective practitioners have a skill set that includes more than just a scientific understanding of S&C. In addition, practitioners find that professional development does not end with graduation, but is a career-long process that involves the continual reconfiguration and broadening of their knowledge and skills to meet the needs of the situations and client populations they encounter. Just as there are possibilities for practitioners to obtain satisfaction and joy from their work, they may also experience anxieties, self-doubts and insecurities that may hinder their growth as practitioners. Mentors, educators and supervisors are in positions similar to sport coaches; they help individuals develop their skills and manage their behaviours (e.g. performance), thoughts and emotions. Mentors, educators and supervisors also experience the joys and pains of observing their charges develop and perform in evaluative environments. The study of S&C professional development may provide glimpses into the processes that occur as beginning practitioners grow, develop and leave their university 'training grounds', enter the competitive work environment and forge careers in their chosen industry.

Discussion questions

1. Psychologists often suggest people influenced their development more than the professional literature; discuss whether this might be true for S&C coaches.
2. The characteristics of effective S&C coaches emerging in this chapter are common to most sport scientists and psychologists; evaluate your own level of proficiency in each.
3. Having rated yourself, identify ways you could develop your proficiency in each characteristic.
4. Identify an S&C coach, applied sport scientist or psychologist you respect and compare how they are different or similar to Asterix and Obelix.

Note

1 Asterix's and Obelix's quotes are from a larger project, accepted for publication: Tod, D., Bond, K., & Lavallee, D. Professional development themes in strength and conditioning coaches. *Journal of Strength and Conditioning Research*.

References

Anderson, A. G., Knowles, Z., & Gilbourne, D. (2004). Reflective practice for sport psychologists: Concepts, models, practical implications, and thoughts on dissemination. *The Sport Psychologist, 18*, 188–203.

Baechle, T. R., & Earle, R. W. (Eds.). (2008). *Essentials of strength training and conditioning* (3rd ed.). Champaign, IL: Human Kinetics.

Bandura, A. (1997). *Self-efficacy: The exercise of control.* New York: Freeman.

Bird, S. P., Tarpenning, K. M., & Marino, F. E. (2005). Designing resistance training programmes to enhance muscular fitness: A review of the acute programme variables. *Sports Medicine, 35,* 841–851.

Cropley, B., Miles, A., Hanton, S., & Niven, A. (2007). Improving the delivery of applied sport psychology support through reflective practice. *The Sport Psychologist, 21,* 475–494.

Duehring, M. D., & Ebben, W. P. (2010). Profile of high school strength and conditioning coaches. *The Journal of Strength and Conditioning Research, 24,* 538–547.

Fry, A. C., & Newton, R. U. (2002). A brief history of strength training and basic principles and concepts. In W. J. Kraemer, & K. Häkkinen (Eds.), *Strength training for sport* (pp. 1–19). Oxford: Blackwell Science.

Hill, C. E., & Lent, R. W. (2006). A narrative and meta-analytic review of helping skills training: Time to revive a dormant area of inquiry. *Psychotherapy: Theory, Research, Practice, Training, 43,* 154–172.

Hogan, R. A. (1964). Issues and approaches in supervision. *Psychotherapy: Theory, Research and Practice, 1,* 139–141.

Kolb, D. A., Boyatzis, R. E., & Mainemelis, C. (2001). Experiential learning theory: Previous research and new directions. In R. J. Sternberg, & L. F. Zhang (Eds.), *Perspectives on thinking, learning, and cognitive styles* (pp. 227–247). Mahwah, NJ: Erlbaum.

Loganbill, C., Hardy, E., & Delworth, U. (1982). Supervision: A conceptual model. *The Counseling Psychologist, 10,* 3–42.

Magnusen, M. J. (2010). Differences in strength and conditioning coach self-perception of leadership style behaviours at the National Basketball Association, division IA, and division II levels. *The Journal of Strength & Conditioning Research, 24,* 1440–1450.

Martinez, D. M. (2004). Study of the key determining factors for the NCAA Division I head strength and conditioning coach. *The Journal of Strength & Conditioning Research, 18,* 5–18.

National Strength and Conditioning Association. (2008). *The National Strength and Conditioning Association: A brief history.* Retrieved from www.nsca-lift.org/AboutNSCA/history.shtml

Rønnestad, M. H., & Skovholt, T. M. (1993). Supervision of beginning and advanced graduate students of counseling and psychotherapy. *Journal of Counseling & Development, 71,* 396–405.

Rønnestad, M. H., & Skovholt, T. M. (2003). The journey of the counselor and therapist: Research findings and perspectives on professional development. *Journal of Career Development, 30,* 5–44.

Stoltenberg, C. D., & McNeill, B. W. (2009). *IDM supervision: An integrative developmental model for supervising counselors and therapists* (3rd ed.). London: Routledge.

Tod, D. (2007). The long and winding road: Professional development in sport psychology. *The Sport Psychologist, 21,* 94–108.

Tod, D., Andersen, M. B., & Marchant, D. B. (2009). A longitudinal examination of neophyte applied sport psychologists' development. *Journal of Applied Sport Psychology, 21*(Supp. 1), S1–S16.

Tod, D., Andersen, M. B., & Marchant, D. B. (2011). 6 years up: Applied sport psychologists surviving (and thriving) after graduation. *Journal of Applied Sport Psychology, 23,* 93–109.

Tod, D., & Bond, K. (2010). A longitudinal examination of a British neophyte sport psychologist's development. *The Sport Psychologist, 24,* 35–51.

Tod, D., Marchant, D., & Andersen, M. B. (2007). Learning experiences contributing to service-delivery competence. *The Sport Psychologist, 21,* 317–334.

Worthington, E. L., Jr. (1987). Changes in supervision as counselors and supervisors gain experience: A review. *Professional Psychology: Research and Practice, 18,* 189–208.

INDEX